Fodor's 99
Chicago

D1268786

The complete guide, thoroughly up-to-date

Packed with details that will make your trip

The must-see sights, off and on the beaten path

What to see, what to skip

Vacation itineraries, walking tours, day trips

Smart lodging and dining options

Essential local dos and taboos

Transportation tips

Key contacts, savvy travel advice

When to go, what to pack

Clear, accurate, easy-to-use maps

Books to read, videos to watch, background essays

Fodor's Travel Publications, Inc.
New York • Toronto • London • Sydney • Auckland
www.fodors.com

Fodor's Chicago

EDITOR: Anastasia Redmond Mills

Editorial Contributors: Eve Becker, David Brown, Joanne Cleaver, Stuart Courtney, Mary Gillespie, Robin Kurzer, Lisbeth Levine, Helayne Schiff, M. T. Schwartzman (Gold Guide editor), Anne Taubeneck, Phil Vettel

Editorial Production: Stacey Kulig

Maps: David Lindroth, *cartographer*; Steven Amsterdam, *map editor*

Design: Fabrizio La Rocca, *creative director*; Guido Caroti, *associate art director*; Jolie Novak, *photo editor*

Production/Manufacturing: Robert B. Shields

Cover Photograph: Robert Holmes

Database Production: Phebe Brown, Janet Foley, Mark Laroche, Victoria Lu, Andrea Pariser, Priti Tambi, Julie Tomasz, Martin Walsh, Lucy Wu, Alexander Zlotnick

Copyright

Special Sales

Fodor's Travel Publications are available at special discounts for bulk purchases for sales promotions or premiums. Special editions, including personalized covers, excerpts of existing guides, and corporate imprints, can be created in large quantities for special needs. For more information, contact your local bookseller or write to Special Markets, Fodor's Travel Publications, 201 East 50th Street, New York, NY 10022. Inquiries from Canada should be directed to your local Canadian bookseller or sent to Random House of Canada, Ltd., Marketing Department, 2775 Matheson Boulevard East, Mississauga, Ontario L4W 4P7. Inquiries from the United Kingdom should be sent to Fodor's Travel Publications, 20 Vauxhall Bridge Road, London SW1V 2SA, England.

PRINTED IN THE UNITED STATES OF AMERICA

10 9 8 7 6 5 4 3 2 1

CONTENTS

ON THE ROAD WITH FODOR'S

WHEN I PLAN A VACATION, the first thing I do is cast around among my friends and colleagues to find someone who's just been where I'm going. That's because there's no substitute for a recommendation from a good friend who knows your tastes, your budget, and your circumstances, someone who's just been there. Unfortunately, such friends are few and far between. So it's nice to know that there's *Fodor's Chicago '99.*

In the first place, this book won't stay home when you hit the road. It will accompany you every step of the way, steering you away from wrong turns and wrong choices and never expecting a thing in return. It includes a wonderful, full-color map from Rand Mc-Nally, the world's largest commercial mapmaker. Most important of all, it's written and assiduously updated by the kind of people you *would* hit up for travel tips if you knew them. They're as choosy as your pickiest friend, except they've probably seen a lot more of Chicago. In these pages, they don't send you chasing down every town and sight in the Windy City but have instead selected the best ones, the ones that are worthy of your time and money. To make it easy for you to put it all together in the time you have, they've created itineraries and neighborhood walks that you can mix and match in a snap. Just tear out the map at the perforation, and join us on the road in Chicago.

About Our Writers

Our success in helping to make your trip the best of all possible vacations is a credit to the hard work of our extraordinary writers.

Phil Vettel has been covering the Chicago-area entertainment and dining scenes for 19 years, the last 9 of them as restaurant critic for the *Chicago Tribune.* His weekly reviews appear in the *Tribune*, America Online, and CLTV News. He lives with his wife, two sons, and a dog, some of whom accompany Phil on his restaurant visits.

Mary Gillespie, a Chicago-born journalist who spent 14 years covering the city and suburbs as a reporter for the *Chicago Sun-Times,* now covers the world for the *Sun-Times* and a variety of national magazines. Of all the cities she's explored, her hometown remains her favorite place to be a tourist. Mary updated the Exploring chapter and wrote its Close-Ups on Pullman, Bucktown and Wicker Park, and Devon Avenue.

Reared in a Loehmann's dressing room, **Lisbeth Levine** can outshop the best of 'em, as her Shopping chapter shows. Lisbeth, a Chicago-based freelancer, writes about fashion, style, and travel for national magazines, including *In Style,* and contributes regularly to newspapers, including the *Chicago Tribune.*

Eve Becker, who updated the Nightlife and the Arts chapter and wrote the Close-Ups on Chicago's connections to the blues and to gangsters, has lived in her adopted hometown of Chicago for nine years. During this time she has shuttled her out-of-town visitors across town to hit all the hot spots. Eve is an assistant editor for Tribune Media Services and is a stringer for *Glamour* magazine.

Stuart Courtney, assistant sports editor of the *Chicago Sun-Times,* has lived in the Chicago area for two decades and has spent many a summer afternoon enjoying baseball from the bleachers of the most beautiful ballpark in America— Wrigley Field.

Usually accompanied by a minivan load of young reviewers, **Joanne Y. Cleaver** has been exploring greater Chicago for 11 years, researching articles for national magazines and major newspapers. She is the author of *Somewhere over the Dan Ryan,* a day trip guide for Chicago-area families.

Chicago is the adopted hometown of **Robin Kurzer,** who updated the Lodging chapter. When she's not tapping the keyboard as a newspaper reporter, copywriter, or fiction writer, she revels in the peace of a good night's sleep in one of the city's fine hotels.

Connections

We're pleased that the American Society of Travel Agents continues to endorse Fodor's as its guidebook of choice. ASTA is the world's largest and most influential travel trade association, operating in more than 170 countries, with 27,000 members pledged to adhere to a strict code of ethics reflecting the Society's motto, "Integrity in Travel." ASTA shares Fodor's devotion to providing smart, honest travel information and advice to travelers, and we've long recommended that our readers—even those who have guidebooks and traveling friends—consult ASTA member agents for the experience and professionalism they bring to your vacation planning.

On Fodor's Web site (www.fodors.com), check out the new Resource Center, an online companion to the Gold Guide section of this book, complete with useful hot links to related sites. In our forums, you can also get lively advice from other travelers and more great tips from Fodor's experts worldwide.

How to Use This Book

Organization

Up front is the **Gold Guide,** an easy-to-use section arranged alphabetically by topic. Under each listing you'll find tips and information that will help you accomplish what you need to in Chicago. You'll also find addresses and telephone numbers of organizations and companies that offer destination-related services and detailed information and publications.

The first chapter in the guide, Destination: Chicago helps get you in the mood for your trip. New and Noteworthy cues you in on trends and happenings, What's Where gets you oriented, Pleasures and Pastimes describes the activities and sights that make Chicago unique, Great Itineraries lays out a selection of complete trips, Fodor's Choice showcases our top picks, and Festivals and Seasonal Events alerts you to special events you'll want to seek out.

The Exploring chapter is divided into neighborhood sections; each recommends a walking or driving tour and lists neighborhood sights alphabetically, including sights that are off the beaten path. The remaining chapters are arranged in alphabetical order by subject (dining, lodging, nightlife and the arts, outdoor activities and sports, shopping, and side trips).

At the end of the book you'll find Portraits, which has a wonderful essay about the city's world-renowned architecture, followed by suggestions for pretrip research, from recommended reading to movies on tape that use Chicago as a backdrop.

Icons and Symbols

★	Our special recommendations
✕	Restaurant
🏠	Lodging establishment
♺	Good for kids (rubber duck)
☞	Sends you to another section of the guide for more information
⊠	Address
☎	Telephone number
☉	Opening and closing times
💲	Admission prices (those we give apply to adults; substantially reduced fees are almost always available for children, students, and senior citizens)

Numbers in white and black circles ③ ❸ that appear on the maps, in the margins, and within the tours correspond to one another.

Credit Cards

The following abbreviations are used: **AE,** American Express; **D,** Discover; **DC,** Diners Club; **MC,** MasterCard; and **V,** Visa.

Don't Forget to Write

You can use this book in the confidence that all prices and opening times are based on information supplied to us at press time; Fodor's cannot accept responsibility for any errors. Time inevitably brings changes, so always confirm information when it matters—especially if you're making a detour to visit a specific place.

Were the restaurants we recommended as described? Did our hotel picks exceed your expectations? Did you find a museum we recommended a waste of time? Keeping a travel guide fresh and up-to-date is a big job, and we welcome your feedback, positive *and* negative. If you have complaints, we'll look into them and revise our entries when the facts warrant it. If you've discovered a special place that we haven't included, we'll pass the information along to our correspondents and have them check it out. So send us your thoughts via e-mail at editors@fodors.com (specifying the name of the book on the subject line) or on paper in care of the Chicago editor at Fodor's, 201 East 50th Street, New York, NY 10022. In the meantime, have a wonderful trip!

Karen Cure
Editorial Director

Chicago

Walton

Delaware Pl.

TO LINCOLN PARK, WRIGLEY FIELD

Hancock
Building

Chestnut

Water
er Place

Pearson

Museum of
Contemporary Art

Chicago Ave.

Superior

Huron

Erie

400E McClug Ct.

Lake Shore Dr.

Rush

Michigan Ave.

MAGNIFICENT MILE

St. Clair

Fairbanks Ct.

STREETERVILLE

North Pier

ve.

Illinois

Grand Ave.
Navy Pier

gley
ding

Tribune
Tower

Water

Streeter Dr.

E. Wacker Dr.

Chicago River

Lake
Michigan

ter

ke

Beaubien Ct.

Stetson Ave.

Randolph

Randolph

41

Chicago
Harbor

shall
's

M Randolph St.
Station

Chicago
Cultural
Center

Columbus Dr.

Michigan Ave.

ie

Monroe Dr.

Art Institute
of Chicago

Roosevelt
Rd.

Roosevelt/
Wabash

M

Columbus Dr.

Lake Shore Dr.

estra
Hall

Jackson Blvd.

14th St.

Arts
ding

M Van Buren
Station

Grant
Park

18th St.

M
18th

Michigan Ave.

Indiana Ave.

McCormick
Place

Auditorium
heatre

Congress
Plaza

Columbus Dr.

son

Buckingham
Fountain

Lake Shore Dr.

. Balbo Ave.

Balbo Dr.

23rd
St.

M
23rd

TO SHEDD AQUARIUM,
ADLER PLANETARIUM,
FIELD MUSEUM,
McCORMICK PLACE (SEE INSET),
KENWOOD,
HYDE PARK,
MUSEUM OF SCIENCE
AND INDUSTRY

h St.

Michigan Ave.

St.

St.

N

KEY	
——	Metra Lines
▬▬	CTA Lines

0   550 yards

0   500 meters

The Midwest and Great Lakes

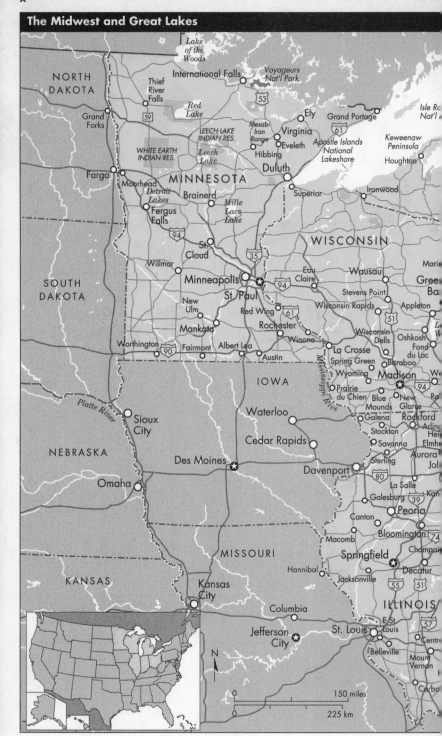

NORTH DAKOTA

Lake of the Woods

International Falls

Thief River Falls

Voyageurs Nat'l Park

53

Red Lake

Ely

Grand Portage

61

Isle Ro Nat'l

Grand Forks

59

Mesabi Iron Range

Virginia

Keweenaw Peninsula

LEECH LAKE INDIAN RES.

Eveleth

Apostle Islands National Lakeshore

Houghton

WHITE EARTH INDIAN RES.

Hibbing

Leech Lake

Duluth

Fargo

Moorhead

Detroit Lakes

Brainerd

Mille Lacs Lake

Superior

Ironwood

Fergus Falls

MINNESOTA

94

St. Cloud

WISCONSIN

SOUTH DAKOTA

Willmar

35

Minneapolis

Eau Claire

Wausau

Mari

Gree Ba

St. Paul

94

Stevens Point

New Ulm

Red Wing

61

Wisconsin Rapids

51

Appleton

Mankato

Rochester

Winona

La Crosse

Oshkosh

Fond du Lac

L W

Worthington

90

Fairmont

Albert Lea

Austin

Spring Green

Baraboo

Wisconsin Dells

IOWA

Wyoming

Madison

W

Platte River

Sioux City

Waterloo

Prairie du Chien

Blue Mounds

New Glarus

94

Ra

Galena

Rockford

Arling Hei

NEBRASKA

Cedar Rapids

Stockton

Savanna

Elmh

Aurora Jol

Des Moines

Davenport

Sterling

80

Omaha

La Salle

Galesburg

39

Kan

Canton

Peoria

Macomb

Bloomington

74

MISSOURI

Springfield

Champai

Hannibal

Jacksonville

Decatur

55

51

KANSAS

Kansas City

Columbia

ILLINOIS

Jefferson City

St. Louis

E. St. Louis

57

Belleville

Centr

Mount Vernon

Carbo

N

0

0

150 miles

225 km

SMART TRAVEL TIPS A TO Z

Basic Information on Traveling in Chicago, Savvy Tips to Make Your Trip a Breeze, and Companies and Organizations to Contact

ADDRESSES

When traveling in the city, **keep in mind that Chicago's streets follow a grid pattern.** Madison Street is the baseline for streets and avenues that run north–south; Michigan Avenue, for example, is called North Michigan Avenue above Madison Street and South Michigan Avenue below it. Street-address numbers start at the baseline and climb in each direction, generally by 100 a block, with eight blocks to a mile; thus the Fine Arts Building at 410 South Michigan Avenue is four blocks (½ mi) south of Madison Street. For streets that run east–west, State Street is the baseline; 18th Street, for example, is East 18th Street east of State Street and West 18th Street west of State Street.

"The Loop" denotes the section of downtown that is roughly circled by the famous El train's elevated tracks, although the Loop's actual boundaries—Michigan Avenue on the east, Wacker Drive on the north and west, and Congress on the south—enclose a larger area than the tracks. The area immediately north of the Loop, from Wacker Drive to North Avenue, is known as the Near North; included are the Magnificent Mile and such neighborhoods as Streeterville, River North, and the Gold Coast. Lincoln Park is the neighborhood stretching north from North Avenue to Diversey Parkway. The northern neighborhoods are bounded on the west by the north branch of the Chicago River. South of the Loop the city is less clearly defined. The South Side neighborhoods you'll hear about most often are Hyde Park and Kenwood, which comprise the area south from 41st Street to 63rd Street, bounded on the west by Martin Luther King Jr. Drive.

AIR TRAVEL

BOOKING YOUR FLIGHT

Price is just one factor to consider when booking a flight: frequency of service and even a carrier's safety record are often just as important. Major airlines offer the greatest number of departures. Smaller airlines—including regional and no-frills airlines—usually have a limited number of flights daily. On the other hand, so-called low-cost airlines usually are cheaper, and their fares impose fewer restrictions, such as advance-purchase requirements. Safety-wise, low-cost carriers as a group have a good history—about equal to that of major carriers.

When you book, **look for nonstop flights** and **remember that "direct" flights stop at least once.** Try to **avoid connecting flights,** which require a change of plane. Two airlines may jointly operate a connecting flight, so ask if your airline operates every segment—you may find that your preferred carrier flies you only part of the way.

Ask your airline if it offers electronic ticketing, which eliminates all paperwork. There's no ticket to pick up or misplace. You go directly to the gate and give the agent your confirmation number. There's no worry about waiting on line at the airport while precious minutes tick by.

CARRIERS

➤ MAJOR AIRLINES: **Air Canada** (☎ 800/776–3000). **American** (☎ 800/433–7300). **Continental** (☎ 800/525–0280). **Delta** (☎ 800/221–1212). **Northwest** (☎ 800/225–2525). **TWA** (☎ 800/221–2000). **United** (☎ 800/722–5243). **US Airways** (☎ 800/428–4322).

➤ SMALLER AIRLINES: **America Trans-Air** (☎ 800/225–2995). **America**

West (☎ 800/235–9292). Southwest Airlines (☎ 800/435–9792).

CHECK IN & BOARDING

Airlines routinely overbook planes, assuming that not everyone with a ticket will show up, but sometimes everyone does. When that happens, airlines ask for volunteers to give up their seats. In return these volunteers usually get a certificate for a free flight and are rebooked on the next flight out. If there are not enough volunteers, the airline must choose who will be denied boarding. The first to get bumped are passengers who checked in late and those flying on discounted tickets, so **get to the gate and check in as early as possible,** especially during peak periods.

Although the trend on international flights is to drop reconfirmation requirements, many airlines still ask you to reconfirm each leg of your international itinerary. Failure to do so may result in your reservation being canceled.

Always **bring a government-issued photo ID to the airport.** You may be asked to show it before you are allowed to check in.

CONSOLIDATORS

Consolidators buy tickets for scheduled international flights at reduced rates from the airlines, then sell them at prices that beat the best fare available directly from the airlines, usually without restrictions. Sometimes you can even get your money back if you need to return the ticket. Carefully read the fine print detailing penalties for changes and cancellations, and **confirm your consolidator reservation with the airline.**

➤ CONSOLIDATORS: **Cheap Tickets** (☎ 800/377–1000). **Discount Travel Network** (☎ 800/576–1600). **Uni-travel** (☎ 800/325–2222). **Up & Away Travel** (☎ 212/889–2345). **World Travel Network** (☎ 800/409–6753).

CUTTING COSTS

The least-expensive airfares to Chicago are priced for round-trip travel and usually must be purchased in advance. It's smart to **call a num-**ber of airlines, and when you are quoted a good price, book it on the spot**—the same fare may not be available the next day. Airlines generally allow you to change your return date for a fee. If you don't use your ticket, you can apply the cost toward the purchase of a new ticket, again for a small charge. However, most low-fare tickets are nonrefundable. To get the lowest airfare, **check different routings.** Compare prices of flights to and from different airports if your destination or home city has more than one gateway. Also price off-peak flights, which may be significantly less expensive.

When flying within the U.S., **plan to stay over a Saturday night** and **travel during the middle of the week** to get the lowest fare. These low fares are usually priced for round-trip travel and are nonrefundable. You can, however, change your return date for a fee ($75 on most major airlines).

Travel agents, especially those who specialize in finding the lowest fares (☞ Discounts & Deals, *below*), can be especially helpful when booking a plane ticket. When you're quoted a price, **ask your agent if the price is likely to get any lower.** Good agents know the seasonal fluctuations of airfares and can usually anticipate a sale or fare war. However, waiting can be risky: The fare could go *up* as seats become scarce, and you may wait so long that your preferred flight sells out. A wait-and-see strategy works best if your plans are flexible. If you must arrive and depart on certain dates, don't delay.

ENJOYING THE FLIGHT

For better service, **fly smaller or regional carriers,** which often have higher passenger-satisfaction ratings. Sometimes you'll find leather seats, more legroom, and better food.

For more legroom, **request an emergency-aisle seat.** Don't sit in the row in front of the emergency aisle or in front of a bulkhead, where seats may not recline.

If you don't like airline food, **ask for special meals when booking.** These can be vegetarian, low-cholesterol, or kosher, for example.

THE GOLD GUIDE / SMART TRAVEL TIPS

FLYING TIMES

Flying time is about two hours from New York and about four hours from Los Angeles.

HOW TO COMPLAIN

If your baggage goes astray or your flight goes awry, complain right away. Most carriers require that you **file a claim immediately.**

➤ AIRLINE COMPLAINTS: U.S. Department of Transportation **Aviation Consumer Protection Division** (✉ C-75, Room 4107, Washington, DC 20590, ☎ 202/366-2220). **Federal Aviation Administration Consumer Hotline** (☎ 800/322-7873).

AIRPORTS & TRANSFERS

AIRPORTS

The major gateway to Chicago is O'Hare International Airport. One of the world's busiest airports, it is 20 mi from downtown, in the far northwest corner of the city. Midway Airport, on Chicago's Southwest Side, about 7 mi from downtown, is smaller and relatively uncrowded. Meigs Field, just south of downtown, serves commuter airlines with flights to downstate Illinois.

➤ AIRPORT INFORMATION: **O'Hare International Airport** (☎ 773/686-2200). **Midway Airport** (☎ 773/767-0500). **Meigs Field** (☎ 312/922-5454).

BY BUS

When taking an airport shuttle bus to O'Hare to catch a departing flight, be sure to **allow at least 1½ hours.** If you're going from the South Side Midway, **call 24 hours in advance.**

Airport Express coaches provide service from both airports to major downtown and Near North hotels; call for reservations. The trip downtown from O'Hare takes an hour or longer, depending on traffic conditions and your destination; the fare is $15.50. The trip downtown from Midway takes about half an hour; the fare is $11.

CW Limo offers moderately priced express van service. Vans travel from O'Hare International Airport to Midway Airport, with departures every hour and a fare of $14. Travel time to Midway is roughly an hour. CW also departs from both airports to locations in Hyde Park and the South Side. The fare is $14 from O'Hare to Hyde Park and $11 from Midway to Hyde Park.

➤ AIRLINE BUS SHUTTLES: **Airport Express** (☎ 312/454-7800 or 800/654-7871). **CW Limo** (☎ 773/493-2700).

BY PUBLIC TRANSIT

For cheap and convenient transportation to the North Side or downtown, **take rapid transit to or from the airports.** Follow the "Trains to City" signs.

In O'Hare Airport the Chicago Transit Authority (CTA) Blue Line station is in the underground concourse between terminals. Travel time to the city is about 45 minutes. Get off at the station closest to your hotel, or from the first stop in the Loop (Washington and Dearborn streets) you can take a taxi to your hotel or change to other transit lines.

At Midway Airport the Orange Line El runs to the Loop. The stop at Adams Street and Wabash Avenue is the closest to the hotels on South Michigan Avenue; for others, the simplest strategy is to alight anywhere in the Loop and hail a cab to your final destination.

The fare is $1.50, which you will need in either dollar bills (turnstiles don't give change) and/or coins. A farecard is another option (☞ Public Transportation, *below*). Pick up brochures outside the entrances to the platforms that detail the stops of the train lines; the "Downtown Transit Sightseeing Guide" is also helpful.

➤ INFORMATION: **CTA** (☎ 312/836-7000).

BY RENTAL CAR

Leaving the airport, follow the signs to I-90 east (Kennedy Expressway) which merges with I-94 (Edens Expressway). Take the eastbound exit at Ohio Street for Near North locations, the Washington or Monroe Street exit for downtown. After you exit, continue east about a mile to get to Michigan Avenue.

THE GOLD GUIDE / SMART TRAVEL TIPS

BY TAXI

Metered taxicab service is available at both O'Hare and Midway airports. Trips to and from O'Hare incur a $1 surcharge. Expect to pay about $25–$30 plus tip from O'Hare to Near North and downtown locations, about $17–$22 plus tip from Midway. Some cabs participate in a share-a-ride program in which each cab carries two or three individuals going from the airport to downtown; the cost per person, $15, is substantially lower than the full rate.

BIKE TRAVEL

BIKES IN FLIGHT

Most airlines will accommodate bikes as luggage, provided they are dismantled and put into a box. Call to see if your airline sells bike boxes (about $5; bike bags are at least $100) although you can often pick them up free at bike shops. International travelers can sometimes substitute a bike for a piece of checked luggage for free; otherwise, it will cost about $100. Domestic and Canadian airlines charge a $25–$50 fee.

BUS TRAVEL

Greyhound has nationwide service to its main terminal in the Loop and to neighborhood stations, at the 95th Street and Dan Ryan Expressway CTA station and at the Cumberland CTA station, near O'Hare Airport. The Harrison Street terminal is far from most hotels, so plan on another bus or a cab to your hotel.

See Public Transportation, *below,* for information on CTA buses.

➤ INFORMATION: **Greyhound Lines** (✉ 630 W. Harrison St., ☎ 312/408–5970 or 800/231–2222).

BUSINESS SERVICES

➤ AUDIOVISUAL RENTALS: **AVS** (✉ 955 W. Washington Blvd., ☎ 312/733–3370). **Midwest Visual** (✉ 121 N. Jefferson St., ☎ 312/559–1060). **Video Replay** (✉ 118 W. Grand Ave., ☎ 312/822–0221).

➤ CATERERS: **The Bountiful Board** (✉ 2826 N. Lincoln Ave., ☎ 773/549–1999). **Corner Bakery Catering** (✉ 516 N. Clark St., ☎ 312/527–1956). **Lettuce Off-Premise Catering**

(✉ 440 S. LaSalle St., ☎ 312/663–8835). **Spoonful** (✉ 1045 W. Madison St., ☎ 312/421–8700).

➤ CHAMBER OF COMMERCE: **Chicagoland Chamber of Commerce** (✉ 330 N. Wabash Ave., Suite 2800, ☎ 312/494–6700).

➤ COMPUTER RENTALS: **GE Capital Computer Rental** (✉ 4000 Sussex Ave., Aurora, ☎ 630/585–4700). **Inacom Computer Rentals** (✉ 5535 Milton Pkwy., Rosemont, ☎ 847/678–0222).

➤ CONVENTION AND EXHIBITION CENTERS: **McCormick Place** (✉ 2300 S. Lake Shore Dr., ☎ 312/791–7000). **Navy Pier** (✉ 600 E. Grand Ave., ☎ 312/595–5100). **United Center** (✉ 1901 W. Madison St., ☎ 312/455–4500).

➤ FORMAL WEAR: **Gingiss Formal Wear** (✉ 151 S. Wabash Ave., ☎ 312/263–7071). **Seno Formal Wear** (✉ 6 E. Randolph St., ☎ 312/782–1115).

➤ LIMOUSINES: **American Limousine** (☎ 630/920–8888). **Chicago Limousine Service** (☎ 312/726–1035). **Presidential Limousine** (☎ 773/278–9900).

➤ MESSENGERS: **Arrow Messenger** (☎ 773/489–6688). **Cannonball** (☎ 312/829–1234).

➤ NOTARIES PUBLIC: **Chicago & LaSalle Currency Exchange** (✉ 777 N. LaSalle St., ☎ 312/642–0220).

➤ OVERNIGHT DELIVERY: **Federal Express** (☎ 800/463–3339). **UPS** (☎ 800/742–5877). **U.S. Postal Service Express Mail** (☎ 800/222–1811).

➤ PHOTOCOPYING: **Copies Now By Sir Speedy** (✉ 28 N. Clark St., ☎ 312/236–5587). **Kinko's** (✉ 6 W. Lake St., ☎ 312/251–0441; ✉ 444 N. Wells St., ☎ 312/670–4460; ✉ 29 S. LaSalle St., ☎ 312/578–8520).

➤ SECRETARIAL SERVICES: **A-EC Secretarial Services** (✉ 39 S. LaSalle St., ☎ 312/236–6847). **HQ Business Centers** (✉ 70 W. Madison St., Suite 1400, ☎ 312/214–3100). **Kinko's** (✉ 6 W. Lake St., ☎ 312/251–0441; ✉ 444 N. Wells St., ☎ 312/670–4460; ✉ 29 S. LaSalle St., ☎ 312/578–8520).

CAMERAS & COMPUTERS

EQUIPMENT PRECAUTIONS

Always **keep your film, tape, or computer disks out of the sun.** Carry an extra supply of batteries, and **be prepared to turn on your camera, camcorder, or laptop** to prove to security personnel that the device is real. Always **ask for hand inspection of film,** which becomes clouded after successive exposure to airport X-ray machines, and **keep videotapes and computer disks away from metal detectors.**

TRAVEL PHOTOGRAPHY

➤ PHOTO HELP: **Kodak Information Center** (☎ 800/242–2424). *Kodak Guide to Shooting Great Travel Pictures,* available in bookstores or from Fodor's Travel Publications (☎ 800/533–6478; $16.50 plus $4 shipping).

CAR RENTAL

Rates in Chicago begin at $46 a day and $170 a week for an economy car with air-conditioning, an automatic transmission, and unlimited mileage. This does not include tax on car rentals, which is 18%.

➤ MAJOR AGENCIES: **Alamo** (☎ 800/327–9633, 0800/272–2000 in the U.K.). **Avis** (☎ 800/331–1212, 800/879–2847 in Canada, 008/225–533 in Australia). **Budget** (☎ 800/527–0700, 0800/181181 in the U.K.). **Dollar** (☎ 800/800–4000; 0990/565656 in the U.K., where it is known as Eurodollar). **Hertz** (☎ 800/654–3131, 800/263–0600 in Canada, 0345/555888 in the U.K., 03/9222–2523 in Australia, 03/358–6777 in New Zealand). **National InterRent** (☎ 800/227–7368; 0345/222525 in the U.K., where it is known as Europcar InterRent).

CUTTING COSTS

To get the best deal, **book through a travel agent who is willing to shop around.** When pricing cars, **ask about the location of the rental lot.** Some off-airport locations offer lower rates, and their lots are only minutes from the terminal via complimentary shuttle. You also may want to **price local car-rental companies,** whose rates may be lower still, although

their service and maintenance may not be as good as those of a name-brand agency. Remember to ask about required deposits, cancellation penalties, and drop-off charges if you're planning to pick up the car in one city and leave it in another.

Also **ask your travel agent about a company's customer-service record.** How has the company responded to late plane arrivals and vehicle mishaps? Are there often lines at the rental counter? If you're traveling during a holiday period, does a confirmed reservation guarantee you a car?

Be sure to **look into wholesalers,** companies that do not own fleets but rent in bulk from those that do and often offer better rates than traditional car-rental operations. Prices are best during off-peak periods.

➤ RENTAL WHOLESALERS: **Auto Europe** (☎ 207/842–2000 or 800/223–5555, FAX 800–235–6321). **Kemwel Holiday Autos** (☎ 914/835–5555 or 800/678–0678, FAX 914/835–5126).

INSURANCE

When driving a rented car you are generally responsible for any damage to or loss of the vehicle. You also are liable for any property damage or personal injury that you may cause while driving. Before you rent, **see what coverage you already have** under the terms of your personal auto-insurance policy and credit cards.

For about $15 to $20 per day, rental companies sell protection, known as a collision- or loss-damage waiver (CDW or LDW), that eliminates your liability for damage to the car; it's always optional and should never be automatically added to your bill. In Illinois you pay only for the first $200 of damage to the rental car.

In most states you don't need a CDW if you have personal auto insurance or other liability insurance. However, **make sure you have enough coverage to pay for the car.** If you do not have auto insurance or an umbrella policy that covers damage to third parties, purchasing liability insurance and a CDW or LDW is highly recommended.

REQUIREMENTS

In Illinois you must be 21 to rent a car, and rates may be higher if you're under 25. You'll pay extra for child seats (about $3 per day), which are compulsory for children under five, and for additional drivers (about $2 per day). Non-U.S. residents will need a reservation voucher, a passport, a driver's license, and a travel policy that covers each driver, in order to pick up a car.

SURCHARGES

Before you pick up a car in one city and leave it in another, **ask about drop-off charges or one-way service fees,** which can be substantial. Note, too, that some rental agencies charge extra if you return the car before the time specified in your contract. To avoid a hefty refueling fee, **fill the tank just before you turn in the car,** but be aware that gas stations near the rental outlet may overcharge.

CAR TRAVEL

Chicago's network of buses and rapid transit rail is extensive, and taxis and limousines are readily available (the latter often priced competitively with metered cabs), so **rent a car only to visit the outlying suburbs that are not accessible by public transportation.** Chicago traffic is often heavy, on-street parking is nearly impossible to find, parking lots are expensive, congestion creates frustrating delays, and other drivers may be impatient with those who are unfamiliar with the city and its roads. **Expect snarled traffic during rush hours.** In these circumstances you may find a car to be a liability rather than an asset. The Illinois Department of Transportation gives information on expressway congestion travel times, and lane closures and directions on state roadways.

GETTING TO CHICAGO

Travelers coming from the east can take the Indiana Toll Road (I–80/90) westbound for about 30 mi to the Chicago Skyway (also a toll road), which runs into the Dan Ryan Expressway (I–90/94). Take the Dan Ryan north (westbound) just past the turnoff for I–290 to any of the eastbound downtown exits (Jackson, Monroe, Washington, Lake) and drive east about a mile to reach Michigan Avenue. If you are heading to the Near North, take the Ohio Street exit eastbound and continue straight for about a mile to reach Michigan Avenue. Travelers coming from the south should take I–57 northbound to the Dan Ryan Expressway.

From the west follow I–80 eastbound across Illinois to I–55, the major artery from the southwest. Continue east on I–55 to Lake Shore Drive. Those coming from areas due west of Chicago may prefer to pick up I–290 eastbound, which forks as it nears the city, heading to O'Hare in one direction (where it meets I–90) and to downtown Chicago in the other (where it ends).

From the north take I–90 eastbound, which merges with I–94 south (eastbound) to form the Kennedy Expressway (I–90/94) about 10 mi north of downtown. (I–90/94 is called the Kennedy Expressway north of I–290 and the Dan Ryan Expressway south of I–290.)

CHILDREN & TRAVEL

CHILDREN IN CHICAGO

Be sure to plan ahead and **involve your youngsters** as you outline your trip. When packing, include things to keep them busy en route. On sightseeing days try to schedule activities of special interest to your children. If you are renting a car don't forget to **arrange for a car seat,** if necessary, when you reserve. When you arrive, pick up a copy of *Chicago Parent*, a monthly publication with events and resource listings, available free at locations throughout the city.

➤ LOCAL INFORMATION: *Chicago Parent* (✉ 139 S. Oak Park Ave., Oak Park 60302, ✆ 708/386–5555).

FLYING

If your children are two or older, **ask about children's airfares.** As a general rule, infants under two not occupying a seat fly at greatly reduced fares or even for free.

In general the adult baggage allowance applies to children paying half or more of the adult fare.

THE GOLD GUIDE / SMART TRAVEL TIPS

Experts agree that it's a good idea to use safety seats aloft for children weighing less than 40 pounds. Airlines, however, can set their own policies: U.S. carriers allow FAA-approved models but usually require that you buy a ticket, even if your child would otherwise ride free, since the seats must be strapped into regular seats. Airline rules vary, so it's important to **check your airline's policy about using safety seats during takeoff and landing.** Safety seats cannot obstruct the movement of other passengers in the row, so get an appropriate seat assignment as early as possible.

When making your reservation, **request children's meals or a free-standing bassinet** if you need them; the latter are available only to those seated at the bulkhead, where there's enough legroom. Remember, however, that bulkhead seats may not have their own overhead bins, and there's no storage space in front of you—a major inconvenience.

GROUP TRAVEL

When planning to take your kids on a tour, look for companies that specialize in family travel.

➤ FAMILY-FRIENDLY TOUR OPERATORS: **Families Welcome!** (✉ 92 N. Main St., Ashland, OR 97520, ☎ 541/482–6121 or 800/326–0724, FAX 541/482–0660).

HOTELS

Most hotels in Chicago allow children under a certain age to stay in their parents' room at no extra charge, but others charge them as extra adults; be sure to **ask about the cutoff age for children's discounts.**

CONSUMER PROTECTION

Whenever possible, **pay with a major credit card** so you can cancel payment or get reimbursed if there's a problem, provided that you can provide documentation. This is the best way to pay, whether you're buying travel arrangements before your trip or shopping at your destination.

If you're doing business with a particular company for the first time, **contact your local Better Business Bureau and the attorney general's offices** in your state and the company's home state, as well. Have any complaints been filed?

Finally, if you're buying a package or tour, always **consider travel insurance** that includes default coverage (☞ Insurance, *below*).

➤ LOCAL BBBs: **Council of Better Business Bureaus** (✉ 4200 Wilson Blvd., Suite 800, Arlington, VA 22203, ☎ 703/276–0100, FAX 703/525–8277).

CUSTOMS & DUTIES

When shopping, **keep receipts** for all of your purchases. Upon reentering the country, **be ready to show customs officials what you've bought.** If you feel a duty is incorrect, appeal the assessment. If you object to the way your clearance was handled, get the inspector's badge number. In either case, first ask to see a supervisor, then write to the appropriate authorities, beginning with the port director at your point of entry.

IN AUSTRALIA

Australia residents who are 18 or older may bring back $A400 worth of souvenirs and gifts (including jewelry), 250 cigarettes or 250 grams of tobacco, and 1,125 ml of alcohol (including wine, beer, and spirits). Residents under 18 may bring back $A200 worth of goods.

➤ INFORMATION: **Australian Customs Service** (Regional Director, ✉ Box 8, Sydney, NSW 2001, ☎ 02/9213–2000, FAX 02/9213–4000).

IN CANADA

Canadian residents who have been out of Canada for at least seven days may bring in C$500 worth of goods duty-free. If you've been away less than seven days but more than 48 hours, the duty-free allowance drops to C$200; if your trip lasts 24–48 hours, the allowance is C$50. You may not pool allowances with family members. Goods claimed under the C$500 exemption may follow you by mail; those claimed under the lesser exemptions must accompany you. Alcohol and tobacco products may be included in the seven-day and 48-hour exemptions but not in the 24-hour exemption. If you meet the age requirements of the province or territory through which you reenter Canada, you may bring in, duty-free, 1.14 liters (40 imperial ounces) of wine or liquor *or* 24 12-ounce cans or bottles of beer or ale. If you are 16 or older you may bring in, duty-free, 200 cigarettes and 50 cigars.

You may send an unlimited number of gifts worth up to C$60 each duty-free to Canada. Label the package UNSOLICITED GIFT—VALUE UNDER $60. Alcohol and tobacco are excluded.

➤ INFORMATION: **Revenue Canada** (✉ 2265 St. Laurent Blvd. S, Ottawa, Ontario K1G 4K3, ☎ 613/993–0534, 800/461–9999 in Canada).

IN NEW ZEALAND

Although greeted with a "Haere Mai" ("Welcome to New Zealand"), homeward-bound residents with goods to declare must present themselves for inspection. If you're 17 or older, you may bring back $700 worth of souvenirs and gifts. Your duty-free allowance also includes 4.5 liters of wine or beer; one 1,125-ml bottle of spirits; and either 200 cigarettes, 250 grams of tobacco, 50 cigars, or a combo of all three up to 250 grams.

➤ INFORMATION: **New Zealand Customs** (✉ Custom House, ✉ 50 Anzac Ave., Box 29, Auckland, New Zealand, ☎ 09/359–6655, ☎ 09/309–2978).

IN THE U.K.

From countries outside the EU, including the United States, you may import, duty-free, 200 cigarettes or 50 cigars; 1 liter of spirits or 2 liters of fortified or sparkling wine or liqueurs; 2 liters of still table wine; 60 milliliters of perfume; 250 milliliters of toilet water; plus £136 worth of other goods, including gifts and souvenirs.

➤ INFORMATION: **HM Customs and Excise** (✉ Dorset House, ✉ Stamford St., London SE1 9NG, ☎ 0171/202–4227).

IN THE U.S.

Non-U.S. residents ages 21 and older may import into the United States 200 cigarettes or 50 cigars or 2 kilograms of tobacco, 1 liter of alcohol, and gifts worth $100. Prohibited items include meat products, seeds, plants, and fruits.

➤ INFORMATION: **U.S. Customs Service** (Inquiries, ✉ Box 7407, Washington, DC 20044, ☎ 202/927–6724; complaints, Office of Regulations and Rulings, ✉ 1301 Constitution Ave. NW, Washington, DC 20229; registration of equipment, Resource Management, ✉ 1301 Constitution Ave. NW, Washington DC 20229, ☎ 202/927–0540).

DISABILITIES & ACCESSIBILITY

ACCESS IN CHICAGO

At O'Hare Airport, American and United airlines have specially designated lounges to provide assistance to travelers with disabilities. If needed, **ask for a wheelchair escort,** available from all airlines at O'Hare. The CTA Blue Line train provides rapid transit service between O'Hare and downtown Chicago. The O'Hare station is equipped with an elevator; downtown stops with elevators are at Clark/Lake and Jackson Boulevard.

The Chicago Mayor's Office for People with Disabilities maintains an information and referral service for disability resources. The office publishes guides, including *Access Chicago,* which contains more than 200 pages of detailed information about Chicago's airports, accessible ground transportation, hotels, restaurants, sights, shopping, and resources regarding medical equipment and supplies.

The RTA Travel Information Center's Chicago Transit Map includes information on more than 70 lift-equipped bus routes and accessible subway and El stations. The Chicago Transit Authority offers a paratransit program with curb-to-curb service for those unable to use conventional mainline bus or rail services. To use this service, out-of-town visitors must make travel arrangements at least one week in advance.

➤ LOCAL RESOURCES: **Mayor's Office for People with Disabilities** (✉ 121 N. LaSalle St., Room 1104, ☎ 312/744–7050, TTY 312/744–4964). **RTA Travel Information Center** (☎ 312/836–7000, ☎ TTY 312/

836–4949). **Chicago Transit Authority paratransit program** (☎ 312/432–7025, TTY 312/432–7140).

MAKING RESERVATIONS

When discussing accessibility with an operator or reservations agent, **ask hard questions.** Are there any stairs, inside *or* out? Are there grab bars next to the toilet *and* in the shower/tub? How wide is the doorway to the room? To the bathroom? For the most extensive facilities meeting the latest legal specifications, **opt for newer accommodations,** which are more likely to have been designed with access in mind. Older buildings or ships may have more limited facilities. Be sure to **discuss your needs before booking.**

TRANSPORTATION

➤ COMPLAINTS: **Disability Rights Section** (✉ U.S. Department of Justice, Civil Rights Division, ✉ Box 66738, Washington, DC 20035–6738, ☎ 202/514–0301 or 800/514–0301, TTY 202/514–0383 or 800/514–0383, FAX 202/307–1198) for general complaints. **Aviation Consumer Protection Division** (☞ Air Travel, *above*) for airline-related problems. **Civil Rights Office** (✉ U.S. Department of Transportation, Departmental Office of Civil Rights, S-30, ✉ 400 7th St. SW, Room 10215, Washington, DC, 20590, ☎ 202/366–4648, FAX 202/366–9371) for problems with surface transportation.

TRAVEL AGENCIES & TOUR OPERATORS

As a whole, the travel industry has become more aware of the needs of travelers with disabilities. In the U.S., the Americans with Disabilities Act requires that travel firms serve the needs of all travelers. Note, though, that some agencies and operators specialize in making travel arrangements for individuals and groups with disabilities.

➤ TRAVELERS WITH MOBILITY PROBLEMS: **Access Adventures** (✉ 206 Chestnut Ridge Rd., Rochester, NY 14624, ☎ 716/889–9096), run by a former physical-rehabilitation counselor. **Flying Wheels Travel** (✉ 143 W. Bridge St., Box 382, Owatonna,

MN 55060, ☎ 507/451–5005 or 800/535–6790, FAX 507/451–1685), a travel agency specializing in customized tours and itineraries worldwide. **Hinsdale Travel Service** (✉ 201 E. Ogden Ave., Suite 100, Hinsdale, IL 60521, ☎ 630/325–1335), a travel agency that benefits from the advice of wheelchair traveler Janice Perkins.

➤ TRAVELERS WITH DEVELOPMENTAL DISABILITIES: **Sprout** (✉ 893 Amsterdam Ave., New York, NY 10025, ☎ 212/222–9575 or 888/222–9575, FAX 212/222–9768).

DISCOUNTS & DEALS

Be a smart shopper and **compare all your options** before making a choice. A plane ticket bought with a promotional coupon may not be cheaper than the least expensive fare from a discount ticket agency. For high-price travel purchases, such as packages or tours, keep in mind that what you get is just as important as what you save. Just because something is cheap doesn't mean it's a bargain.

CLUBS & COUPONS

Many companies sell discounts in the form of travel clubs and coupon books, but these cost money. You must use participating advertisers to get a deal, and only after you recoup the initial membership cost or book price do you begin to save. If you plan to use the club or coupons frequently, you may save considerably. Before signing up, find out what discounts you get for free.

➤ DISCOUNT CLUBS: **Entertainment Travel Editions** (✉ 2125 Butterfield Rd., Troy, MI 48084, ☎ 800/445–4137; $20–$51, depending on destination). **Great American Traveler** (✉ Box 27965, Salt Lake City, UT 84127, ☎ 801/974–3033 or 800/548–2812; $49.95 per year). **Moment's Notice Discount Travel Club** (✉ 7301 New Utrecht Ave., Brooklyn, NY 11204, ☎ 718/234–6295; $25 per year, single or family). **Privilege Card International** (✉ 237 E. Front St., Youngstown, OH 44503, ☎ 330/746–5211 or 800/236–9732; $74.95 per year). **Sears's Mature Outlook** (✉ Box 9390, Des Moines, IA 50306, ☎ 800/336–6330; $19.95

per year). **Travelers Advantage** (✉ CUC Travel Service, ✉ 3033 S. Parker Rd., Suite 1000, Aurora, CO 80014, ☎ 800/548–1116 or 800/648–4037; $59.95 per year, single or family). **Worldwide Discount Travel Club** (✉ 1674 Meridian Ave., Miami Beach, FL 33139, ☎ 305/534–2082; $50 per year family, $40 single).

CREDIT-CARD BENEFITS

When you use your credit card to make travel purchases you may get free travel-accident insurance, collision-damage insurance, and medical or legal assistance, depending on the card and the bank that issued it. American Express, MasterCard, and Visa provide one or more of these services, so **get a copy of your credit card's travel-benefits policy.** If you are a member of an auto club, always **ask hotel and car-rental reservations agents about auto-club discounts.** Some clubs offer additional discounts on tours, cruises, and admission to attractions.

DISCOUNT RESERVATIONS

To save money, **look into discount-reservations services** with toll-free numbers, which use their buying power to get a better price on hotels, airline tickets, even car rentals. When booking a room, always **call the hotel's local toll-free number** (if one is available) rather than the central reservations number—you'll often get a better price. Always ask about special packages or corporate rates.

➤ AIRLINE TICKETS: ☎ 800/FLY–4–LESS. ☎ 800/FLY–ASAP.

➤ HOTEL ROOMS: **Accommodations Express** (☎ 800/444–7666). **Hotel Reservations Network** (☎ 800/964–6835). **Quickbook** (☎ 800/789–9887). **Room Finders USA** (☎ 800/473–7829). **RMC Travel** (☎ 800/245–5738). **Steigenberger Reservation Service** (☎ 800/223–5652).

PACKAGE DEALS

Packages and guided tours can save you money, but don't confuse the two. When you buy a package, your travel remains independent, just as though you had planned and booked the trip yourself. Fly/drive packages, which combine airfare and car rental, are often a good deal. In cities, ask

the local visitor's bureau about hotel packages. These often include tickets to major museum exhibits and other special events.

EMERGENCIES

➤ EMERGENCIES: **Police, fire, and ambulance** (☎ 911).

MEDICAL EMERGENCIES

Northwestern Memorial Hospital is in the Near North area. Rush Presbyterian St. Luke's Medical Center is just west of the Loop. The Columbia Michael Reese Hospital is on the South Side. The Bernard Mitchell Hospital at the University of Chicago is in Hyde Park. Michael Reese and other hospitals sponsor storefront clinics for fast treatment of minor emergencies. Call the hospitals for information or check the Chicago Consumer Yellow Pages under "Clinics." Chicago Dental makes referrals at all hours.

➤ HOSPITALS: **Northwestern Memorial Hospital** (✉ 250 E. Superior St., at Fairbanks Ct., ☎ 312/908–2000). **Rush Presbyterian St. Luke's Medical Center** (✉ 1653 W. Congress Pkwy., ☎ 312/942–5000). **Columbia Michael Reese Hospital** (✉ 2929 S. Ellis Ave., ☎ 312/791–2000). **Bernard Mitchell Hospital at the University of Chicago** (✉ 5841 S. Maryland Ave., ☎ 773/702–1000).

➤ DENTISTS: **Chicago Dental** (☎ 312/726–4321).

➤ 24-HOUR PHARMACIES: **Osco** (☎ 800/654–6726 for nearest location). **Walgreens** (✉ 757 N. Michigan Ave., at Chicago Ave., ☎ 312/664–8686).

GAY & LESBIAN TRAVEL

➤ GAY- AND LESBIAN-FRIENDLY TRAVEL AGENCIES: **Corniche Travel** (✉ 8721 Sunset Blvd., Suite 200, West Hollywood, CA 90069, ☎ 310/854–6000 or 800/429–8747, FAX 310/659–7441). **Islanders Kennedy Travel** (✉ 183 W. 10th St., New York, NY 10014, ☎ 212/242–3222 or 800/988–1181, FAX 212/929–8530). **Now Voyager** (✉ 4406 18th St., San Francisco, CA 94114, ☎ 415/626–1169 or 800/255–6951, FAX 415/626–8626). **Yellowbrick Road** (✉ 1500 W. Balmoral Ave., Chicago, IL 60640, ☎ 773/561–1800 or 800/642–2488,

THE GOLD GUIDE / SMART TRAVEL TIPS

FAX 773/561–4497). **Skylink Travel and Tour** (⊠ 3577 Moorland Ave., Santa Rosa, CA 95407, ☎ 707/585–8355 or 800/225–5759, FAX 707/584–5637), serving lesbian travelers.

HEALTH

MEDICAL PLANS

No one plans to get sick while traveling, but it happens, so **consider signing up with a medical-assistance company.** Members get doctor referrals, emergency evacuation or repatriation, 24-hour telephone hot lines for medical consultation, cash for emergencies, and other personal and legal assistance. Coverage varies by plan, so **review the benefits of each carefully.**

➤ MEDICAL-ASSISTANCE COMPANIES: **International SOS Assistance** (⊠ 8 Neshaminy Interplex, Suite 207, Trevose, PA 19053, ☎ 215/245–4707 or 800/523–6586, FAX 215/244–9617; ⊠ 12 Chemin Riantbosson, 1217 Meyrin 1, Geneva, Switzerland, ☎ 4122/785–6464, FAX 4122/785–6424; ⊠ 10 Anson Rd., 14-07/08 International Plaza, Singapore, 079903, ☎ 65/226–3936, FAX 65/226–3937).

INSURANCE

Travel insurance is the best way to **protect yourself against financial loss.** The most useful plan is a comprehensive policy that includes coverage for trip cancellation and interruption, default, trip delay, and medical expenses (with a waiver for preexisting conditions).

Without insurance, you will lose all or most of your money if you cancel your trip, regardless of the reason. Default insurance covers you if your tour operator, airline, or cruise line goes out of business. Trip-delay covers unforeseen expenses that you may incur due to bad weather or mechanical delays. It's important to compare the fine print regarding trip-delay coverage when comparing policies.

For overseas travel, one of the most important components of travel insurance is its medical coverage. Supplemental health insurance will pick up the cost of your medical bills

should you get sick or injured while traveling. Residents of the United Kingdom can buy an annual travel-insurance policy valid for most vacations taken during the year in which the coverage is purchased. If you are pregnant or have a preexisting condition, make sure you're covered. British citizens should buy extra medical coverage when traveling overseas, according to the Association of British Insurers. Australian travelers should buy travel insurance, including extra medical coverage, whenever they go abroad, according to the Insurance Council of Australia.

Always **buy travel insurance directly from the insurance company**; if you buy it from a cruise line, airline, or tour operator that goes out of business you probably will not be covered for the agency or operator's default, a major risk. Before you make any purchase, **review your existing health and home-owner's policies** to find out whether they cover expenses incurred while traveling.

➤ TRAVEL INSURERS: In the U.S., **Access America** (⊠ 6600 W. Broad St., Richmond, VA 23230, ☎ 804/285–3300 or 800/284–8300). **Travel Guard International** (⊠ 1145 Clark St., Stevens Point, WI 54481, ☎ 715/345–0505 or 800/826–1300). In Canada, **Mutual of Omaha** (⊠ Travel Division, ⊠ 500 University Ave., Toronto, Ontario M5G 1V8, ☎ 416/598–4083, 800/268–8825 in Canada).

➤ INSURANCE INFORMATION: In the U.K., **Association of British Insurers** (⊠ 51 Gresham St., London EC2V 7HQ, ☎ 0171/600–3333). In Australia, the **Insurance Council of Australia** (☎ 613/9614–1077, FAX 613/9614–7924).

LODGING

APARTMENT & VILLA RENTALS

If you want a home base that's roomy enough for a family and comes with cooking facilities, **consider a furnished rental.** These can save you money, especially if you're traveling with a large group of people. Home-exchange directories list rentals (often second homes owned by prospective house swappers), and some services search for a house or apartment for you (even a castle if that's your fancy) and handle the paperwork. Some send an illustrated catalog; others send photographs only of specific properties, sometimes at a charge. Up-front registration fees may apply.

➤ RENTAL AGENTS: **Property Rentals International** (✉ 1008 Mansfield Crossing Rd., Richmond, VA 23236, ☎ 804/378–6054 or 800/220–3332, FAX 804/379–2073). **Rent-a-Home International** (✉ 7200 34th Ave. NW, Seattle, WA 98117, ☎ 206/789–9377 or 800/488–7368, FAX 206/789–9379). **Hideaways International** (✉ 767 Islington St., Portsmouth, NH 03801, ☎ 603/430–4433 or 800/843–4433, FAX 603/430–4444; membership $99) is a club for travelers who arrange rentals among themselves.

HOME EXCHANGES

If you would like to exchange your home for someone else's, **join a home-exchange organization,** which will send you its updated listings of available exchanges for a year and will include your own listing in at least one of them. It's up to you to make specific arrangements.

➤ EXCHANGE CLUBS: **HomeLink International** (✉ Box 650, Key West, FL 33041, ☎ 305/294–7766 or 800/638–3841, FAX 305/294–1148; $83 per year).

HOSTELS

No matter what your age, you can **save on lodging costs by staying at hostels.** In some 5,000 locations in more than 70 countries around the world, Hostelling International (HI), the umbrella group for a number of national youth hostel associations, offers single-sex, dorm-style beds and, at many hostels, "couples" rooms and family accommodations. Membership in any HI national hostel association, open to travelers of all ages, allows you to stay in HI-affiliated hostels at member rates (one-year membership is about $25 for adults; hostels run about $10–$25 per night). Members also have priority if the hostel is full; they're eligible for discounts around the world, even on rail and bus travel in some countries.

➤ HOSTEL ORGANIZATIONS: **Hostelling International—American Youth Hostels** (✉ 733 15th St. NW, Suite 840, Washington, DC 20005, ☎ 202/783–6161, FAX 202/783–6171). **Hostelling International—Canada** (✉ 400-205 Catherine St., Ottawa, Ontario K2P 1C3, ☎ 613/237–7884, FAX 613/237–7868). **Youth Hostel Association of England and Wales** (✉ Trevelyan House, ✉ 8 St. Stephen's Hill, St. Albans, Hertfordshire AL1 2DY, ☎ 01727/855215 or 01727/845047, FAX 01727/844126); membership in the U.S. $25, in Canada C$26.75, in the U.K. £9.30).

MONEY

CREDIT & DEBIT CARDS

Should you use a credit card or a debit card when traveling? Both have benefits. A credit card allows you to delay payment and gives you certain rights as a consumer (☞ Consumer Protection, *above*). A debit card, also known as a check card, deducts funds directly from your checking account and helps you stay within your budget. When you want to rent a car, though, you may still need an old-fashioned credit card. Although you can always *pay* for your car with a debit card, some agencies will not allow you to *reserve* a car with a debit card.

Otherwise, the two types of plastic are virtually the same. Both will get you cash advances at ATMs worldwide if your card is properly programmed with your personal identification number (PIN).

➤ ATM LOCATIONS: **Cirrus** (☎ 800/424–7787). **Plus** (☎ 800/843–7587) for locations in the U.S. and Canada, or visit your local bank. Note that in Chicago ATMs are called cash stations.

EXCHANGING MONEY

For the most favorable rates, **change money through banks.** Although fees charged for ATM transactions may be higher abroad than at home, Cirrus and Plus exchange rates are excellent, because they are based on wholesale rates offered only by major banks. You won't do as well at exchange booths in airports or rail and bus stations, in hotels, in restaurants, or in stores, although you may find their hours more convenient. To avoid lines at airport exchange booths, **get a bit of local currency before you leave home.**

➤ EXCHANGE SERVICES: **Chase *Currency To Go*** (☎ 800/935–9935; 935–9935 in NY, NJ, and CT). **International Currency Express** (☎ 888/842–0880 on the East Coast, 888/278–6628 on the West Coast). **Thomas Cook Currency Services** (☎ 800/287–7362 for telephone orders and retail locations).

TRAVELER'S CHECKS

Do you need traveler's checks? It depends on where you're headed. If you're going to rural areas and small towns, go with cash; traveler's checks are best used in cities. Lost or stolen checks can usually be replaced within 24 hours. To ensure a speedy refund, buy your own traveler's checks—don't let someone else pay for them: irregularities like this can cause delays. The person who bought the checks should make the call to request a refund.

PACKING

LUGGAGE

How many carry-on bags you can bring with you is up to the airline. Most allow two, but the limit is often reduced to one on certain flights. Gate agents will take excess baggage—including bags they deem oversize—from you as you board and add it to checked luggage. To avoid this situation, make sure that everything you carry aboard will fit under your seat. Also, get to the gate early, and request a seat at the back of the plane; you'll probably board first, while the overhead bins are still empty. Since big, bulky baggage attracts the attention of gate agents and flight attendants on a busy flight, make sure your carry-on is really a carry-on. Finally, a carry-on that's long and narrow is more likely to remain unnoticed than one that's wide and squarish.

If you are flying internationally, note that baggage allowances may be determined not by piece but by weight—generally 88 pounds (40 kilograms) in first class, 66 pounds

(30 kilograms) in business class, and 44 pounds (20 kilograms) in economy.

Airline liability for baggage is limited to $1,250 per person on flights within the United States. On international flights it amounts to $9.07 per pound or $20 per kilogram for checked baggage (roughly $640 per 70-pound bag) and $400 per passenger for unchecked baggage. You can buy additional coverage at check-in for about $10 per $1,000 of coverage, but it excludes a rather extensive list of items, shown on your airline ticket.

Before departure, **itemize your bags' contents** and their worth, and label the bags with your name, address, and phone number. (If you use your home address, cover it so that potential thieves can't see it readily.) Inside each bag, **pack a copy of your itinerary.** At check-in, **make sure that each bag is correctly tagged** with the destination airport's three-letter code. If your bags arrive damaged or fail to arrive at all, file a written report with the airline before leaving the airport.

PACKING LIST

Try to **pack light** because porters and luggage carts are hard to find. Be prepared for cold, snowy weather in the winter and hot, sticky weather in the summer. Jeans (shorts in summer) and T-shirts or sweaters and slacks are fine for sightseeing and informal dining. For many expensive restaurants, men will need jackets and ties, women dressy outfits. In winter pack boots or a sturdy pair of shoes with nonslip soles for icy sidewalks and a hat and scarf to protect your ears and neck from the numbing winds that buffet Michigan Avenue. In summer bring a swimsuit for Lake Michigan swimming or sunning.

In your carry-on luggage **bring an extra pair of eyeglasses or contact lenses** and **enough of any medication you take** to last the entire trip. You may also want your doctor to write a spare prescription using the drug's generic name, since brand names may vary from country to country. **Never put prescription drugs or valuables in luggage to be checked.** To avoid customs delays, carry medications in their original packaging. And don't forget to copy down and carry addresses of offices that handle refunds of lost traveler's checks.

PASSPORTS & VISAS

When traveling internationally, **carry a passport even if you don't need one** (it's always the best form of ID), and make **two photocopies of the data page** (one for someone at home and another for you, carried separately from your passport). If you lose your passport, promptly call the nearest embassy or consulate and the local police.

➤ U.K. CITIZENS: **U.S. Embassy Visa Information Line** (☎ 01891/200–290; calls cost 49p per minute, 39p per minute cheap rate), for U.S. visa information. **U.S. Embassy Visa Branch** (✉ 5 Upper Grosvenor St., London W1A 2JB), for U.S. visa information; send a self-addressed, stamped envelope. Write the **U.S. Consulate General** (✉ Queen's House, ✉ Queen St., Belfast BTI 6EO) if you live in Northern Ireland.

PASSPORT OFFICES

The best time to apply for a passport or to renew is during the fall and winter. Before any trip, be sure to check your passport's expiration date and, if necessary, renew it as soon as possible. (Some countries won't allow you to enter on a passport that's due to expire in six months or less.)

➤ AUSTRALIAN CITIZENS: **Australian Passport Office** (☎ 13/1232).

➤ NEW ZEALAND CITIZENS: **New Zealand Passport Office** (☎ 04/494–0700 for information on how to apply, 0800/727–776 for information on applications already submitted).

➤ U.K. CITIZENS: **London Passport Office** (☎ 0990/21010), for fees and documentation requirements and to request an emergency passport.

PUBLIC TRANSPORTATION

CTA BUSES & TRAINS

Chicago's extensive public transportation network includes buses and rapid transit trains, both subway and elevated (the latter known as the El).

Each of the seven CTA lines has a color name as well as a route name: Blue (O'Hare-Congress-Douglas),

Brown (Ravenswood), Green (Lake-Englewood-Jackson Park), Orange (Midway), Purple (Evanston), Red (Howard–Dan Ryan), Yellow (Skokie Swift). In general, the route names indicate the first and last stop on the train. Chicagoans refer to trains both by the color and the route name. Most, but not all, rapid transit lines operate 24 hours; some stations are closed at night. Pick up the brochure "Downtown Transit Sightseeing Guide" for hours, fares, and other pertinent information. In general, late-night CTA travel is not recommended. Of note is that the red and blue lines are subways; the rest are elevated. This means if you're heading to O'Hare and looking for the Blue Line, look for a stairway down, not up.

Exact fares must be paid in cash (dollar bills or coins; no change given by turnstiles on train platforms or fareboxes on buses) or by transit card. Transit cards are flimsy plastic and credit-card size and can be purchased from machines at CTA train stations as well as at Jewel and Dominicks grocery stores and currency exchanges. These easy-to-use cards are inserted into the turnstiles at CTA train stations and into machines as you board CTA buses; directions are clearly posted. Use them to transfer between CTA vehicles. To transfer between the Loop's elevated lines and the subway or between rapid transit trains and buses, you must either use a transit card with at least 30¢ stored on it, or, if you're not using a transit card, **buy a transfer when you board the first conveyance.** If two CTA train lines meet, you can **transfer for free.** You can also **obtain free train-to-train transfers** from specially marked turnstiles at the Washington/State subway station or the State/Lake El station, or ask for a transfer card, good on downtown trains, at the ticket booth.

Buses generally stop on every other corner northbound and southbound (on State Street they stop at every corner). Eastbound and westbound buses generally stop on every corner. Buses from the Loop generally run north–south. Principal transfer points are on Michigan Avenue at the north side of Randolph Street for north-bound buses, Adams Street and Wabash Avenue for westbound buses and the El, and State and Lake streets for those southbound.

Pace runs suburban buses in a six-county region; these connect with the CTA and use CTA transit cards, transfers, and passes.

The CTA fare structure is as follows: The basic fare for rapid transit trains and buses is $1.50, and transfers are 30¢. A transit card with $15 worth of rides can be purchased for $13.50. If you pay cash and do not use a transit card, you must buy a transfer when you first board the bus or train. Transfers can be used twice within a two-hour time period. Transfers between CTA train lines are free—no transfer card is needed. Transit cards may be shared.

Visitor passes are another option. For $5 a one-day pass offers 24 hours of unlimited CTA riding from the time you first use it. Passes are sold at hotels, museums, and other places visitors frequent. A two-day pass is $9, a three-day pass is $12, and a five-day pass is $18.

The CTA publishes an excellent map of the transit system, available at subway or El fare booths or on request from the CTA. The RTA Travel Information Center provides information on how to get around on city and suburban (including Metra and Pace) transit and bus lines. **Call for maps and timetables.**

➤ INFORMATION: **CTA** (✉ Merchandise Mart, 350 N. Wells St., 60654, ☎ 312/836–7000 or 888/968–7282 for advance sales of visitor passes). **RTA Travel Information Center** (☎ 312/836–7000).

COMMUTER TRAINS

Commuter trains serve the city and surrounding suburbs. The Metra Electric railroad (often referred to by its old name, the IC railroad), which has a line close to Lake Michigan, has a fare structure based on the distance you ride. Metra Electric trains stop in Hyde Park.

The Metra commuter rail system has 11 lines to suburbs and surrounding

cities including Aurora, Elgin, Joliet, and Waukegan; one line serves the North Shore suburbs, and another has a stop at McCormick Place. Trains leave from a number of down-town terminals, and fares vary with the distance traveled. A Metra week-end pass costs $5 and is valid for rides on any of the eight operating lines all day on weekends, except for the South Shore line.

➤ INFORMATION: **Metra information line** (☎ 312/322–6777).

MCCORMICK PLACE

Convention goers can **take advantage of several alternatives to cabs or shuttle buses.** CTA trains do not serve McCormick Place, but CTA Bus 3 (King Drive), Bus 4 (Cottage Grove), and Bus 21 (Cermak) stop at 23rd Street and Martin Luther King Drive and travel north to downtown Chicago. Another option is the Metra commuter train, which has a 23rd Street stop, accessible from the North Building, on the Metra Electric and South Shore lines. Visitors going downtown can get off at one of two stations: Van Buren Street or the northernmost and final stop, Randolph Street. On weekdays Metra trains run fairly often, but weekend service is less frequent.

RADIO STATIONS

Alternative Rock: Q101 101.1 FM, WXRT 93.1 FM. Classical: WFMT 98.7 FM, WNIB 97.1 FM. Country: WUSN 99.5 FM. Jazz: WNUA 95.5 FM. National Public Radio: WBEZ 91.5 FM. News Stations: WBBM 780 AM, WMAQ 670 AM. Rock: WCKG 105.9 FM, WLUP 97.9 FM. R&B: WGCI 107.5 FM. Talk Radio and Local Sports: WGN 720 AM. Top 40: B-96 96.3 FM.

SAFETY

The most common crimes in public places are pickpocketing, purse snatching, jewelry theft, and gambling scams. Men: keep your wallet in a front coat or pants pocket. Women: close your purse securely and hold it in front of you with both hands. Also **beware of someone jostling you and of loud arguments**; these could be ploys to distract your attention while another person grabs your wallet.

Leave unnecessary credit cards at home and hide valuables and jewelry from view.

Although crime on CTA buses and trains has declined, several precautions can reduce the chance of your becoming a victim: Look alert and purposeful; **know your route** ahead of time; have your fare ready before boarding; and **guard your purse or packages** during the ride.

"Trouble-Free Travel," from the AAA, is a booklet of tips to protect your and your belongings. Send a stamped, self-addressed legal-size envelope to **Trouble-Free Travel** (✉ Mail Stop 75, 1000 AAA Dr., Heathrow, FL 32746).

SENIOR-CITIZEN TRAVEL

To qualify for age-related discounts, **mention your senior-citizen status up front** when booking hotel reservations (not when checking out) and before you're seated in restaurants (not when paying the bill). Note that discounts may be limited to certain menus, days, or hours. When renting a car, **ask about promotional car-rental discounts,** which can be cheaper than senior-citizen rates.

The Chicago Department on Aging provides information and referrals to seniors 60 years of age and older. The department's Renaissance Court offers free programs for senior citizens every weekday, including exercise classes, arts and crafts, and games. Trips and tours are available at additional cost.

➤ LOCAL RESOURCES: **Chicago Department on Aging** (✉ 121 N. LaSalle St., ☎ 312/744–4016, TTY 312/744–6777). **Renaissance Court** (✉ 77 E. Randolph St., ☎ 312/744–4550).

➤ EDUCATIONAL PROGRAMS: **Elderhostel** (✉ 75 Federal St., 3rd floor, Boston, MA 02110, ☎ 617/426–8056).

SIGHTSEEING TOURS

BUS TOURS

American Sightseeing's North tour along State Street and North Michigan Avenue covers the Loop, State Street, Wacker Drive, the Magnificent Mile, and the lakefront, with a stop at the Lincoln Park Zoo and Conservatory. The South tour covers the financial district, Grant Park, the University of Chicago, the Museum of Science and Industry, and Jackson Park. Tours leave from the Palmer House Hilton, at 17 East Monroe Street, or you can be picked up at your hotel (downtown or Near North only). The cost is $15 for a two-hour tour; a combined four-hour tour of north and south costs $25.

The double-decker buses of Chicago Motor Coach Company take visitors on 90-minute narrated tours of downtown Chicago and the lakefront. Climb on at the Sears Tower (Jackson Boulevard and Franklin Street), the Field Museum (Lake Shore Drive at East Roosevelt Road), the Art Institute (Michigan Avenue at Adams Street), or the Water Tower (Michigan Avenue at Pearson Street). Tours cost $15.

Visitors to the city can get a glimpse of all the downtown highlights from the seat of an open-air trolley from Chicago Trolley Charters. Venture from the Sears Tower to the Water Tower, or board at Planet Hollywood for a trip to the Adler Planetarium. These trolleys also stop at the Art Institute, the Lincoln Park Zoo, and Navy Pier as well as other notable sights. Stop at any scheduled stop and board at another one along the 13-mi route. Tours vary in price, call for details.

➤ INFORMATION: **American Sightseeing** (☎ 312/251–3100). **Chicago Motor Coach Co.** (☎ 312/666–1000). **Chicago Trolley Charters.** (☎ 312/663–0260).

BOAT TOURS

Boat tour schedules vary by season; be sure to call for exact times and fares. The season usually runs from May 1 through October 1. Mercury Chicago Skyline Cruiseline has 90-minute river and lake cruises that leave from Wacker Drive at Michigan Avenue (the south side of the Michigan Avenue Bridge); the cost is $12.

Shoreline Marine runs half-hour boat trips on Lake Michigan: Narrated tours leave from the Shedd Aquarium

THE GOLD GUIDE / SMART TRAVEL TIPS

during the day and from Buckingham Fountain in the evening; the cost is $9. Tours also depart from Navy Pier every half hour from 10 AM to 11 PM (same price). The company's Shoreline Water Taxi takes you to Chicago's favorite destinations: Sears Tower, Navy Pier, and Shedd Aquarium. The fleet of taxis makes frequent departures from 10:30 until 6 daily from Memorial Day to Labor Day. The fare is $6.

From April to October, Wendella Sightseeing Boats has 90-minute guided tours that traverse the Chicago River to south of the Sears Tower and through the locks; on Lake Michigan, they travel between the Adler Planetarium on the south and Oak Street Beach on the north. The company also has evening tours. All tours leave from lower Michigan Avenue at the foot of the Wrigley Building on the north side of the river. The cost for 90-minute tours is $12; hour-long lake tours cost $10; two-hour evening tours are $14.

The Chicago Architecture Foundation River Cruise, aboard Chicago's *First Lady*, highlights more than 53 sights. The 90-minute tours depart from the southwest corner of Wacker Drive and Michigan Avenue from April to October. The cost is $18; reservations are recommended.

Get a blast from the past as you sail Lake Michigan on the *Windy*, a 148-ft ship modeled on old-time commercial vessels. Passengers may help the crew or take a turn at the wheel on the 90-minute, $25 cruise.

➤ INFORMATION: **Chicago Architecture Foundation River Cruise** (☎ 312/922–3432 for information, 312/902–1500 for tickets). **Mercury Chicago Skyline Cruiseline** (☎ 312/332–1353 for recorded information). **Shoreline Marine** (☎ 312/222–9328). **Wendella Sightseeing Boats** (✉ 400 N. Michigan Ave., ☎ 312/337–1446). **Windy of Chicago Ltd.** (☎ 312/595–5555).

SPECIAL-INTEREST TOURS

The Chicago Mercantile Exchange has two visitors' galleries with views of the often-frenetic trading floors. The eighth-floor gallery overlooking the currency pit is open weekdays from 7:15 until 2. The fourth-floor gallery, open weekdays from 8 until 3:15, overlooks agricultural and stock index products trading and features a presentation that explains the activity.

On Chicago Supernatural Ghost Tours, you can visit famous murder sites, local Native American burial grounds, allegedly haunted pubs, and the scenes of various gangster rubouts, such as the St. Valentine's Day Massacre. Two five-hour tours operate daily during October and November and weekends the rest of the year; the cost is $28 per person.

The *Chicago Tribune* offers free one-hour tours of its Freedom Center production facility, a short cab ride from the Loop. Make reservations in advance. Note that Freedom Center's address is 777 W. Chicago Avenue, not 435 N. Michigan Avenue, the site of the famous Tribune Tower.

The Chicago Office of Tourism runs Loop Tour Trains on Saturday afternoons from June through October. Tickets are free from the Visitor Information Center on the first floor of the Chicago Cultural Center (☞ Visitor Information, *below*).

A Day in Historic Beverly Hills/Morgan Park is a two-hour tour of two Southwest Side neighborhoods with fancy Victorians and Frank Lloyd Wright houses; the cost is $10. Untouchable Tours captures the excitement of Jazz Age Chicago at old hoodlum haunts, brothels, gambling dens, and sites of gangland shootouts. Get a glimpse into the lives of the gangsters that made Chicago famous with a tour of sites where such notables as Al Capone and John Dillinger made history. Tours last two hours and cost $20. Times vary depending on the season; make reservations in advance.

The Black Metropolis Convention and Tourism Council, the Chicago Office of Tourism, Black Coutours, and Willie Dixon's Blues Heaven all offer tours of historic Bronzeville, spotlighting the historic significance of this African-American neighborhood.

Non–English speaking visitors to Chicago will find it easy to follow the tours given by Chicago Tour Guides Institute, Inc. Tour guides fluent in French, Italian, English, German, Spanish, Italian, Hebrew, and Portuguese coordinate personal and group tours. Ask about other languages.

➤ INFORMATION: **Antique Coach and Carriage** (☎ 773/735–9400). **Black Coutours** (☎ 773/233–8907). **Black Metropolis Convention and Tourism Council** (☎ 773/548–2579). **Chicago by Air** (☎ 708/524–1172). **Chicago Horse & Carriage Ltd.** (☎ 773/944–6773). **Chicago Mercantile Exchange** (☎ 312/930–8249). **Chicago Supernatural Ghost Tours** (☎ 708/499–0300). **Chicago Tour Guides Institutes, Inc.** (☎ 773/276–3729). **Chicago Tribune** (☎ 312/222–2116). **A Day in Historic Beverly Hills/Morgan Park** (☎ 773/881–1831). **Noble Horse** (☎ 312/266–7878). **Tour Black Chicago** (☎ 312/332–2323). **Untouchable Tours** (☎ 773/881–1195). **Willie Dixon's Blues Heaven** (☎ 312/808–1286).

WALKING TOURS

The Chicago Office of Tourism offers Audio Architecture, a 90-minute taped, self-guided walking tour of historic buildings, skyscrapers, and sculptures in the Loop. The tour, developed by the Landmarks Preservation Council of Illinois, costs $5 (with a $50 returnable deposit for the tape player) and is available at the Shop at the Chicago Cultural Center Welcome Center (☞ Visitor Information, *below*).

The Chicago Architecture Foundation has a selection of more than 50 tours. The popular Loop walking tour, which departs from the South Michigan Avenue center, is given daily throughout the year. The North Michigan Avenue tour departs from the John Hancock Center. The Foundation also offers other tours—Graceland Cemetery, Frank Lloyd Wright's Oak Park buildings, and bicycle tours of Lincoln Park—on an occasional, seasonal, or prescheduled basis. Tours vary in price, from $3 to $35 per person.

Friends of the Chicago River has Saturday-morning walking tours along the river ($10), as well as boat cruises and canoe days from May to October. Times vary, so call for a schedule. The organization also has maps of the walking routes, available for a small donation.

➤ INFORMATION: **Chicago Architecture Foundation** (Tour Centers: ⊠ Santa Fe Building, 224 S. Michigan Ave.; ⊠ John Hancock Center, 875 N. Michigan Ave., ☎ 312/922–3432). **Friends of the Chicago River** (⊠ 407 S. Dearborn St., Suite 1580, ☎ 312/939–0490).

STUDENT TRAVEL

TRAVEL AGENCIES

To save money, **look into deals available through student-oriented travel agencies.** To qualify you'll need a bona fide student ID card. Members of international student groups are also eligible.

➤ STUDENT IDs & SERVICES: **Council on International Educational Exchange** (⊠ CIEE, ⊠ 205 E. 42nd St., 14th floor, New York, NY 10017, ☎ 212/822–2600 or 888/268–6245, FAX 212/822–2699), for mail orders only, in the United States. **Travel Cuts** (⊠ 187 College St., Toronto, Ontario M5T 1P7, ☎ 416/979–2406 or 800/667–2887) in Canada.

➤ STUDENT TOURS: **Contiki Holidays** (⊠ 300 Plaza Alicante, Suite 900, Garden Grove, CA 92840, ☎ 714/740–0808 or 800/266–8454, FAX 714/740–2034).

TAXIS

Chicago taxis are metered, with fares beginning at $1.60 upon entering the cab and $1.40 for each additional mile. A charge of 50¢ is made for each additional passenger between the ages of 12 and 65. There is no extra baggage charge. Taxi drivers expect a 15% tip.

➤ CAB COMPANIES: **American United Cab Co.** (☎ 773/248–7600). **Checker Taxi** (☎ 312/243–2537). **Flash Cab** (☎ 773/561–1444). **Yellow Cab Co.** (☎ 312/829–4222).

TELEPHONES

COUNTRY CODE

The country code for the United States is 1.

THE GOLD GUIDE / SMART TRAVEL TIPS

LONG-DISTANCE CALLS

Competitive long-distance carriers make calling within the United States relatively convenient and let you avoid hotel surcharges. By dialing an 800 number, you can get connected to the long-distance company of your choice.

➤ LONG-DISTANCE CARRIERS: **AT&T** (☎ 800/225–5288). **MCI** (☎ 800/888–8000). **Sprint** (☎ 800/366–2255).

TOUR OPERATORS

Buying a prepackaged tour or independent vacation can make your trip to Chicago less expensive and more hassle-free. Because everything is prearranged, you'll spend less time planning.

Operators that handle several hundred thousand travelers per year can use their purchasing power to give you a good price. Their high volume may also indicate financial stability. But some small companies provide more personalized service; because they tend to specialize, they may also be more knowledgeable about a given area.

BOOKING WITH AN AGENT

Travel agents are excellent resources. In fact, large operators accept bookings made only through travel agents. But it's a good idea to **collect brochures from several agencies,** because some agents' suggestions may be influenced by relationships with tour and package firms that reward them for volume sales. If you have a special interest, **find an agent with expertise in that area**; ASTA (☞ Travel Agencies, *below*) has a database of specialists worldwide.

Make sure your travel agent knows the accommodations and other services. Ask about the hotel's location, room size, beds, and whether it has a pool, room service, or programs for children, if you care about these. Has your agent been there in person or sent others you can contact?

Do some homework on your own, too: Local tourism boards can provide information about lesser-known and small-niche operators, some of which may sell only direct.

BUYER BEWARE

Each year consumers are stranded or lose their money when tour operators—even very large ones with excellent reputations—go out of business. So **check out the operator.** Find out how long the company has been in business, and ask several travel agents about its reputation. If the package or tour you are considering is priced lower than in your wildest dreams, **be skeptical.** Try to **book with a company that has a consumer-protection program.** If the operator has such a program, you'll find information about it in the company's brochure. If the operator you are considering does not offer some kind of consumer protection, then ask for references from satisfied customers.

In the U.S., members of the National Tour Association and United States Tour Operators Association are required to set aside funds to cover your payments and travel arrangements in case the company defaults. It's also a good idea to choose a company that participates in the American Society of Travel Agent's Tour Operator Program (TOP). This gives you a forum if there are any disputes between you and your tour operator; ASTA will act as mediator.

➤ TOUR-OPERATOR RECOMMENDATIONS: **American Society of Travel Agents** (☞ Travel Agencies, *below*). **National Tour Association** (✉ NTA, ✉ 546 E. Main St., Lexington, KY 40508, ☎ 606/226–4444 or 800/755–8687). **United States Tour Operators Association** (✉ USTOA, ✉ 342 Madison Ave., Suite 1522, New York, NY 10173, ☎ 212/599–6599 or 800/468–7862, FAX 212/599–6744).

COSTS

The more your package or tour includes, the better you can predict the ultimate cost of your vacation. Make sure you know exactly what is covered, and **beware of hidden costs.** Are taxes, tips, and service charges included? Transfers and baggage handling? Entertainment and excursions? These can add up.

Prices for packages and tours are usually quoted per person, based on two sharing a room. If traveling solo, you may be required to pay the full double-occupancy rate. Some operators eliminate this surcharge if you agree to be matched with a roommate of the same sex, even if one is not found by departure time.

GROUP TOURS

Among companies that sell tours to Chicago, the following are nationally known, have a proven reputation, and offer plenty of options. The key differences among companies are usually in accommodations, which run from budget to better, and better-yet to best.

➤ FIRST-CLASS: **Gadabout Tours** (✉ 700 E. Tahquitz Canyon Way, Palm Springs, CA 92262, ☎ 619/325–5556 or 800/952–5068).

PACKAGES

Like group tours, independent vacation packages are available from major tour operators and airlines. The companies listed below offer vacation packages in a broad price range.

➤ CUSTOM PACKAGES: **Amtrak Vacations** (☎ 800/321–8684).

THEME TRIPS

➤ ARCHITECTURE: **Smithsonian Study Tours and Seminars** (✉ 1100 Jefferson Dr. SW, Room 3045, MRC 702, Washington, DC 20560, ☎ 202/357–4700, FAX 202/633–9250).

➤ PERFORMING ARTS: **Dailey-Thorp Travel** (✉ 330 W. 58th St., #610, New York, NY 10019-1817, ☎ 212/307–1555 or 800/998–4677, FAX 212/974–1420).

TRAIN TRAVEL

Amtrak offers nationwide service to Chicago's Union Station, at 225 South Canal Street. Some trains travel overnight, and you can sleep in your seat or book a roomette at additional cost. Most trains have attractive diner cars with acceptable food, but you may prefer to bring your own.

➤ INFORMATION: **Amtrak** (☎ 800/872–7245).

TRAVEL AGENCIES

A good travel agent puts your needs first. Look for an agency that has been in business at least five years, emphasizes customer service, and has someone on staff who specializes in your destination. In addition, **make sure the agency belongs to a professional trade organization,** such as ASTA in the United States. If your travel agency is also acting as your tour operator, *see* Buyer Beware in Tour Operators, *above*.

➤ LOCAL AGENT REFERRALS: **American Society of Travel Agents** (ASTA, ☎ 800/965–2782 24-hr hot line, FAX 703/684–8319). **Association of British Travel Agents** (✉ 55–57 Newman St., London W1P 4AH, ☎ 0171/637–2444, FAX 0171/637–0713). **Association of Canadian Travel Agents** (✉ Suite 201, 1729 Bank St., Ottawa, Ontario K1V 7Z5, ☎ 613/521–0474, FAX 613/521–0805). **Australian Federation of Travel Agents** (☎ 02/9264–3299). **Travel Agents' Association of New Zealand** (☎ 04/499–0104).

TRAVEL GEAR

Travel catalogs specialize in useful items, such as compact alarm clocks and travel irons, that can **save space when packing.**

➤ CATALOGS: **Magellan's** (☎ 800/962–4943, FAX 805/568–5406). **Orvis Travel** (☎ 800/541–3541, FAX 540/343–7053). **TravelSmith** (☎ 800/950–1600, FAX 800/950–1656).

U.S. GOVERNMENT

Government agencies can be an excellent source of inexpensive travel information. When planning your trip, **find out what government materials are available.**

➤ PAMPHLETS: **Consumer Information Center** (✉ Consumer Information Catalogue, Pueblo, CO 81009, ☎ 719/948–3334 or 888/878–3256) for a free catalog that includes travel titles.

VISITOR INFORMATION

For general information and brochures, contact the city and state tourism offices below. When you arrive, visit one of Chicago's three Welcome centers for more city information.

➤ CITYWIDE INFORMATION: **Chicago Office of Tourism** (✉ 78 E. Washing-

THE GOLD GUIDE / SMART TRAVEL TIPS

ton St., 60602, ☎ 312/744–2400 or 800/226–6632 TTY 312/744–2947 or 800/406–6418). **Chicago Convention and Tourism Bureau** (✉ 2301 S. Lake Shore Dr., 60616, ☎ 312/567–8500 or 800/226–6632, FAX 312/567–8533; 312/567–8528 for automated Fax Back Information Service). **Mayor's Office of Special Events, General Information, and Activities** (✉ 121 N. LaSalle St., Room 703 60602, ☎ 312/744–3315, FAX 312/744–8523).

➤ WALK-IN WELCOME CENTERS: **Chicago Cultural Center Welcome Center** (✉ 77 E. Randolph St.). **Chicago Office of Tourism Welcome Center** (✉ 811 N. Michigan Ave.). **Navy Pier Welcome Center** (✉ 700 E. Grand Ave.).

➤ STATEWIDE INFORMATION: **Illinois Bureau of Tourism** (✉ 100 W. Randolph St., Suite 3-400 60601, ☎ 800/226–6632 for brochures).

WALKING

Chicago's Pedway, a system of skywalks and underground walkways, links more than 40 blocks in the central business district, connecting hotels, shops, office buildings, and apartments. Though it probably won't get you to everything you wish to visit, you may want to **use it for a respite from crowded streets and unpleasant weather.** Many entrances to the Pedway are marked, and maps are posted. You may also be able to **get a map** when you're in the Pedway.

WEB SITES

Do check out the World Wide Web when you're planning. You'll find everything from up-to-date weather forecasts to virtual tours of famous cities. Fodor's Web site, www.fodors.com, is a great place to start your on-line travels. For more information specifically on Chicago, visit: **www.ci.chi.il.us/tourism**

www.chicagonights.com/start.htm

www.internetuniv.com/yourhere/chicago.html

www.transitchicago.com

WHEN TO GO

Chicago has activities and attractions to keep visitors busy at any time of year. If your principal concern is comfortable weather for touring the city, **consider a visit in spring or fall,** when moderate temperatures make it a pleasure to be out and about. Late fall in Chicago sees lavish Christmas decorations in the stores of the Magnificent Mile and the State Street Mall.

Summertime brings many opportunities for outdoor recreation, although temperatures will climb into the 90s in hot spells, and the humidity can be uncomfortably high.

Winters can see very raw weather and the occasional news-making blizzard, and temperatures in the teens are to be expected; **come prepared for the cold.** Yet mild winters, with temperatures in the 30s, are common, too. There are January sales to reward those who venture out, and many indoor venues allow you to look out on the cold in warm comfort.

➤ FORECASTS: **Weather Channel Connection** (☎ 900/932–8437), 95¢ per minute from a Touch-Tone phone.

CLIMATE

The following are the average daily maximum and minimum temperatures for Chicago.

Jan.	32F	0C	May	65F	18C	Sept.	73F	23C
	18	– 8		50	10		58	14
Feb.	34F	1C	June	75F	24C	Oct.	61F	16C
	20	– 7		60	16		47	8
Mar.	43F	6C	July	81F	27C	Nov.	47F	8C
	29	– 2		66	19		34	1
Apr.	55F	13C	Aug.	79F	26C	Dec.	36F	2C
	40	4		65	18		23	– 5

1 Destination: Chicago

WINDY CITY, WARM HEART

NOT SO LONG AGO a Chicagoan traveling abroad could almost certainly expect an immediate response after mentioning his hometown: the shaky pantomime of machine-gun fire accompanied by a single word: "Capone."

Not so anymore. Say the word "Chicago" almost anywhere around the world and Al hardly gets a mention. Instead of talk about shooting guns, the subject quickly turns to shooting hoops—thanks to Chicago Bulls megastar Michael Jordan. The bootlegging, murderous mob has faded from memory, replaced by a shaved-head basketball icon who hangs not with gangsters but with Bugs Bunny.

Chicago's image has changed. Capone is kaput, and so is that tired old nickname, Second City. America's midwestern metropolis has acquired a first-class luster around the world, particularly when it comes to the arts. Carl Sandburg's City of the Big Shoulders is now also City of the Big Limos on opening nights.

Exhibitions at the Art Institute of Chicago have drawn worldwide acclaim. You could spend days there drinking in the Impressionist paintings alone, then be happily transported into the 20th century by eye-popping works at the bold Museum of Contemporary Art, which overlooks Lake Michigan.

Gutsy Steppenwolf Theater productions, from *True West* to *The Libertine,* have jolted critics on both coasts. The city's scores of other theaters, including the Victory Gardens, the Goodman, the Court, and the Shakespeare Repertory, regularly showcase the talents of awesome local actors who may turn out to be the next John Malkovich or Gary Sinise.

The Grammy-laden Chicago Symphony Orchestra wins standing ovations both at home and abroad. At the other end of the Loop, the Lyric Opera's lavish productions boast world-class singers and conductors. Chicago's staggeringly varied architecture is lauded (and occasionally lambasted) around the globe. And don't forget film criticism and TV talk. Undoubtedly, the most famous thumbs in the country belong to Roger Ebert and Gene Siskel. And who doesn't know our gal Oprah?

Happily, though, Chicago never takes itself too seriously. After all, this is the home of the seminal Second City, the improvisation and comedy club on North Wells Street whose talented performers have included the brilliantly funny Mike Nichols and Elaine May, Jim and the late John Belushi, Bill Murray, and George Wendt. And Chicagoans like to recall that one of Hollywood's nuttiest car chases took place in their city. In the *Blues Brothers,* John Belushi and Dan Aykroyd as Jake and Elwood Blues crash through the Daley Center, just missing the controversial Picasso sculpture in the plaza. Even city hall, headed by no-nonsense mayor Richard M. Daley, lightens up in March and dyes the Chicago River green in honor of St. Patrick.

Perhaps one reason Chicagoans have a sense of humor is the weather. As local film director Joel Sedelmaier contends, "Colder-than-hell winters saved this city." In an essay in the handsome book *Great Chicago Stories,* he wrote, "If Chicago had weather like Florida, we'd be L.A. and I wouldn't wish that on anybody." Though residents complain that the city's four seasons are "winter, winter, winter, and the Fourth of July," at least on a winter day, when the snow is blowing horizontally across the Michigan Avenue Bridge, Chicagoans can duck into popular clubs like Andy's, where there's hot jazz even at noon.

When I moved to the heart of the city in my twenties, after growing up close to cornfields in central Illinois, I wasn't sure I could adjust to my new neighborhood of skyscrapers. But I soon found Chicago to be an inviting urban paradox—a hulking giant of a city that still manages to offer the openness of the midwestern prairie. Whenever I need to escape the big city, I simply head east—to Lake Michigan—to watch the sun rising orangey-red and unobstructed over the water, to walk on the wide sandy beaches, to take in the huge expanse of sky.

TO GET A GRIP ON CHICAGO, a trip to the lakefront—smack against the city's jagged, jazzy skyline—is essential. Walk the shoreline or drive along Lake Shore Drive, one of the most seductive roadways in urban America. Zooming along the Drive, as Chicagoans call it, from as far north as Hollywood Avenue or as far south as Hyde Park, you'll watch downtown Chicago grow gradually larger and larger, rising like Oz in the distance. It's a sight that never fails to thrill me.

You'll also want to do a little Chicago-style time traveling to a period when horses clip-clopped downtown. You'll see firsthand that among America's big cities, Chicago is still remarkable for its downtown mélange of very new buildings and very old ones that are bustling, not boarded up. Walk down canyonlike LaSalle Street, Chicago's busy boulevard of high finance, to a rugged gem of a 19th-century building called the Rookery. Step inside the dazzling skylighted lobby, redesigned in 1905 by Frank Lloyd Wright. Climb the grand staircase with its white marble steps and lacy ironwork. The feeling of landing back in turn-of-the-century Chicago is palpable. Then travel a block south, two blocks west, and 100 years forward to the 110-story Sears Tower. Gawk upward (I always do, feeling happily like a visitor from Omaha), and then ride to the 103rd-floor Skydeck to see Chicago laid out like a tantalizing toy city.

Back down on the ground, a musical trip is also in order. The House of Blues, in the Marina City complex on Wacker Drive, has big-time acts and big-time prices. Visitors in search of the heart and soul of Chicago should not overlook smaller clubs such as Buddy Guy's Legends in the South Loop and Blue Chicago on North Clark Street. Sit at a table a few feet from some of the city's great bluesmen—perhaps Son Seals, Otis Rush, Buddy Guy, or movie-star-handsome harpist Billy Branch—and listen long into the night to the music labeled "the facts of life" by legendary Chicago blues bassist and songwriter Willie Dixon. Like the city itself, Chicago blues is gritty and aggressive, with edgy, eloquent electric-slide guitar and a rock-solid beat that will make you want to dance. And that's just the thing to do at a Chicago blues club, even if your only space is cramped between two tables.

At the Sears Tower and at blues clubs, you'll be bumping into other out-of-towners. So where can you go to encounter a richly diverse mix of Chicagoans? Stroll State Street ("that great street"), preferably at lunchtime on a weekday when the sidewalks are elbow to elbow with Loop secretaries and lawyers, shoppers and messengers, cops, street musicians, city sweepers, and the occasional ragtag urban philosopher orating noisily on a corner. Though Chicago remains woefully segregated in its neighborhoods, in the Loop everyone mingles easily, fostering hope that someday residential barriers may break down.

If you happen to be in the city on a steamy summer day, grab a ticket at ivy-webbed Wrigley Field—the National League's oldest ballpark. Sit with the "bleacher bums," ever loyal to their ever-losing Cubs. (The team last won a pennant in 1945.) You may catch a fly, you may catch a little sloshed beer, and you'll certainly catch a good glimpse of Chicago.

As actor William Petersen, co-founder of the city's innovative Remains Theater, has said, "Chicago is a place to take risks, a place to fail, a place to grow. It's a place where you're not judged as being unworthy."

In other words, a Cubs kind of town.

—Anne Taubeneck

NEW AND NOTEWORTHY

The **Nature Museum**, which is expected to open in Lincoln Park in the spring of 1999, is the first new museum to be built in Chicago's parks in more than six decades. Visitors will learn about creatures and the environment, and there will be a gallery for children. The **Field Museum** is proud of "Sue," the largest and most complete Tyrannosaurus rex ever found, which will go on display in the year 2000. Throughout 1999, visitors can watch museum scientists prepare her 65 million-year-old fossilized bones.

Reconstruction of **Michigan Avenue** was completed in 1998, restoring foot traffic to the **Magnificient Mile** after two years of construction. Michigan Avenue is successfully maintaining its shimmering status, even as the River North entertainment district threatens to encroach on its territory. At press time, a 39,000-square-ft Virgin Megastore was scheduled to open in late '98 or early '99 at the corner of Michigan Avenue and Ohio Street. Polo/Ralph Lauren was scheduled to open its largest U.S. store at 750 N. Michigan Avenue in late '98, fronted by a limestone facade. Other new additions to Michigan Avenue in '98 included Ermenegildo Zegna and Pottery Barn, along with expansions by Tiffany & Co. and Banana Republic. The year saw the closing of Henri Bendel and the expansion of Barneys New York. A major renovation of the Marriott hotel at 540 N. Michigan Avenue, long regarded as a 46-story eyesore, will bring more retail to street level. Coupled with the return of State Street to its intended use as a thoroughfare, the Loop is seeing a new life.

In dining, a lot of attention is being focused to the west—specifically to the so-called Market District, an area between the Loop and the United Center on the **Near West Side.** Marché, a pioneering restaurant that set up shop in this area five years ago, has been joined by an ever-growing number of competitors, and chefs with successful restaurants in other parts of the city are eyeing the Near West Side for possible expansion. The Loop itself has been making some dining noise of its own; the new Symphony Center, home to the Chicago Symphony Orchestra, is also home to **Rhapsody,** the most ambitious restaurant to open in the Loop in years.

The **Chicago Bulls** staked their claim as the National Basketball Association's team of the '90s by winning their third consecutive NBA championship and their sixth overall in eight years. The future of the Bulls is uncertain: At press time, Michael Jordan was considering retirement, Scottie Pippen and Dennis Rodman were going to be free agents, and coach Phil Jackson had spoken of leaving the team.

Move over, blues—**swing music** is capturing the hearts of Chicagoans, with more and more dance clubs tuning in to the days of the jumping jive. Having two left feet won't let you off the hook, since most clubs offer instruction to both the novice and the advanced hoofers in the crowd.

A new theater for the Shakespeare Repertory is being built, and several old theaters (Oriental, Shubert) have recently been renovated downtown. The lovely **Palace Theater,** next door to the fabulous new **Hotel Allegro Chicago** on Randolph Street in the Loop, is due to reopen, after major renovation, by summer 1999. The proposed 1,500-seat **Music and Dance Theatre Chicago** has been victim to delays, and no opening date is set yet, but the plan is for the building to go up at Cityfront Center, just west of Lake Shore Drive and a block north of the Chicago River. The five-story glass-curtain building, designed by Thomas Beeby (who also designed the Harold Washington Library Center in the South Loop), is the proposed site of performances by 11 companies, including Ballet Chicago, Hubbard Street Dance Chicago, Chicago Opera Theatre, and Music of the Baroque.

WHAT'S WHERE

The Chicago most visitors see first is the commercial and cultural heart of the city, the downtown and Near North areas that contain the world-famous architecture, impressive skyline, department stores, major hotels, and fine restaurants that together define a great American city. Yet there is another, equally interesting Chicago, vibrant with neighborhoods and their distinctive populations. Fodor's *Chicago '99,* through its walking tours and essays, examines the two Chicagos—the downtown and the neighborhoods—and tries to suggest the greater political and human entity that is the foremost city of the American Midwest.

The Loop

The heart of Chicago is the downtown area loosely bounded by elevated train lines, also known as the Loop. Constantly evolving, the area in and around the tracks is stacked with handsome old landmark buildings and shimmering new ones. These are the centers of business and the mainstays of culture; they also provide new residential areas and are the anchors of renewed older districts.

Downtown South

Just south of the Loop, old forms take on new functions that merge with the life of the central city. Once thriving, this area decayed as its core business—the printing industry—moved out. Since the 1980s, however, a gradual revival led by an aspiring restaurateur and ambitious investors has turned Downtown South into a thriving urban neighborhood enclave.

Hyde Park and Kenwood

Site of the World's Columbian Exposition of 1893 and today's Museum of Science and Industry, home of the University of Chicago, and locale of five houses designed by Frank Lloyd Wright, Hyde Park and the adjoining Kenwood are important historically, intellectually, and culturally. Turn-of-the-century mansions and working-class cottages are still there for the looking, along with museums, churches, and bookstores. All around are signs of the process of urban renewal and the changes it has wrought in this exceptionally stable, racially integrated neighborhood.

South Lake Shore Drive

The best way to get back to the Loop from Hyde Park and Kenwood, which are south of downtown, is via South Lake Shore Drive. Chicago's skyline unfolds around every turn, and you can pick out many individual skyscrapers from the panorama. On the north end of the drive, a dazzling trio of museums—the Shedd Aquarium, the Field Museum, and the Adler Planetarium—make the most of their dramatic location on the lakefront.

Near North

For many, Chicago high life is the Near North, just across the Chicago River from the Loop. Glitzy shops along both sides of Michigan Avenue compose what's known as the Magnificent Mile, and the side streets of Streeterville aren't lacking in riches either. To the east are the thriving Navy and North piers. In River North rehabilitation has transformed an area of factories and warehouses into a neighborhood of upscale shopping strips and more than 65 art galleries.

Lincoln Park

The campuses of the old McCormick Seminary and De Paul University, the historic Biograph Theatre, and shopping districts on Halsted Street and North Lincoln Avenue are all part of Lincoln Park, a neighborhood that shares its name and part of its boundaries with the oldest park in Chicago's "emerald necklace," itself encompassing many wonders. Old Town Triangle, another section of the neighborhood, contains some of the most historic and appealing streets in town.

Wicker Park and Bucktown

Two hot, hip adjoining neighborhoods are centered on the intersection of diagonal Milwaukee Avenue, Damen Avenue (2000 W.), and North Avenue (1600 N.), west of the south end of Lincoln Park. Wicker Park lies south of Milwaukee Avenue, Bucktown to the north. Musicians, artists, and aspiring yuppies have staked their claims in these working-class areas. Rents are rising, and there's a profusion of restaurants, coffee bars, rock clubs, galleries, and shops.

North Clark Street

A ride up Clark Street, particularly north of Lincoln Park, is an urban tour through time and the waves of ethnic migration. Like north Milwaukee Avenue, which has gone from Polish to Hispanic to Polish again as new immigrants have arrived, Clark Street is a microcosm of the city of Chicago and the continuing ebb and flow of its populations, including Scandinavian, Asian, and Middle Eastern.

Argyle Street and Uptown

A walk along Argyle Street (5000 N.) on the north side is a total immersion in the tastes and sounds of Southeast Asia. You'll see the classic immigrant pattern, the process of successful Americanization, and you'll appreciate the sometimes conflicting forces at work as cities decay, are restored, and grow again. Here immigrant Vietnamese have created an economic miracle in one of Chicago's most depressed neighborhoods.

Devon Avenue

Along Devon Avenue, on the city's far north side, immigrants from the Indian subcontinent live virtually side by side with Orthodox Jews newly arrived from Russia. Here you can witness different customs and cultures in juxtaposition and sample ethnic wares and cuisines.

Beyond the City

Among the highlights of the western suburbs are Oak Park, with its rich architectural legacy from Frank Lloyd Wright; the Brookfield Zoo in Brookfield; and Lisle's Morton Arboretum. A drive north along the manicured shores of Lake Michigan can take in a lighthouse in Evanston, the Baha'i House of Worship in Wilmette, and the Chicago Botanical Garden in Glencoe.

PLEASURES AND PASTIMES

Architecture

The destruction wrought by the Chicago Fire of 1871 cleared a path for architectural experimentation. Architects flocked to rebuild the city, using new technology to develop the foundations of modern architecture. Louis Sullivan, William Holabird, John Wellborn Root, Frank Lloyd Wright, and Daniel Burnham are among the builders whose creations influenced Chicago as well as cities around the world. They developed the skyscraper, and this type of structure fills the downtown skyline in hundreds of incarnations, from the crenellated Wrigley Building (Graham Anderson Probst and White) to the boxlike Federal Center and Plaza (Mies van der Rohe). Chicago and its environs also inspired Wright's low-lying Prairie School, exemplified in many Oak Park houses. The city still buzzes with new construction, though today's architects often favor the postmodern, as in Helmut Jahn's James R. Thompson Center and the Harold Washington Public Library.

Blues

In the years following World War II, Chicago-style blues grew into its own musical form, flourishing during the 1950s, then fading during the 1960s with the advent of rock and roll. Today Chicago blues is coming back, although more strongly on the trendy North Side than on the South Side, where it all began. Isaac Tigrett's palatial House of Blues in the Marina City complex downtown hosts both local and nationally known musicians, though smaller clubs such as B.L.U.E.S. and Buddy Guy's Legends are still the best places to hear real Chicago-style blues.

Eating

In Chicago immigrants and their traditions give the dining scene impressive variety and spice, and their influence is felt not just in ethnic storefront eateries but in bastions of haute cuisine. You can sample cuisine from all over the food universe—Polish sausage, Swedish pancakes, Thai curry, Greek *mezes,* and more. There are also plenty of temples to the all-American steak.

The Lake

Chicago wouldn't be the same without Lake Michigan. The lake forms the city's eastern boundary, providing residents with a constant source of conversation—the weather. It also provides much in the way of recreational opportunities, with more than 20 mi of trails (for walkers, skaters, and cyclists) and harbors and beaches. It's easy to appreciate the lake from nearby, but it's also a beautiful backdrop to the view from city skyscrapers.

Outdoor Sculpture

You don't have to go indoors to see some of Chicago's finest art. Strolling in the Loop, you'll encounter arresting pieces, such as Picasso's beady-eyed sculpture in the Daley Plaza, Alexander Calder's arching red Flamingo in the Federal Center Plaza, and Marc Chagall's monolithic mosaic *The Four Seasons* in the First National Bank Plaza. Wander on to Michigan Avenue to see Jerry Peart's wild and whimsical *Splash* at the Boulevard Towers Plaza or—for something entirely different—Edward Kemeys's magnificent bronze lions in front of the Art Institute. Kids have fun sliding down the base of the Picasso and petting the lions, who wear wreaths at holiday time.

Theater

In Chicago you can find lavishly staged musicals presented in such magnificent settings as Adler and Sullivan's Auditorium Theatre as well as taut little dramas in intimate settings with bare-bones scenery. Tickets can be outrageously expensive at downtown theaters, but beyond the Loop prices are lower. Not every small theater (and there are at least 75 around the city) may achieve the success of Steppenwolf—where John Malkovich, Gary Sinise, and Joan Allen got their start—but take a chance on a small production that sounds enticing. There's a wealth of talent here in the heartland.

GREAT ITINERARIES

You could easily spend two weeks exploring Chicago, but if you're here for just a short period, you need to plan carefully so you don't miss the must-see sights. Those who like to start with a guided overview should try a **double-deck bus tour** (☎ 312/666–1000) or a **Chicago Architecture Foundation river cruise** (☎ 312/922–3432) of the city's astonishing buildings. The following suggested itineraries will help you structure your visit efficiently; see the neighborhood exploring tours in Chapter 2 for more information about individual sights.

If You Have 1 Day

Start at the top. Hit the heights of the **John Hancock Center** or the **Sears Tower Skydeck** for a grand view of the city and the lake. Then walk to Michigan Avenue and Adams Street for a morning of culture at the **Art Institute.** Either grab a bite at one of the museum's eateries or stroll back west for lunch at the venerable **Berghoff Restaurant.** Then wander north to the Michigan Avenue Bridge, where you can pick up a boat tour of the Chicago River, or grab a cab to **Navy Pier** for a lake cruise. You can eat on the boat or at the pier, but why not sample the ethnic delights of Greektown or Chinatown? (Most cabbies love to give restaurant recommendations.)

If You Have 3 Days

Follow the one-day itinerary, above. On your second day, head for Chicago's museum campus for a full day of exploring land, sea, and sky. Start with the dinosaurs, ancient Egyptians, and other wonders at the **Field Museum.** Then stroll over to the **Shedd Aquarium and Oceanarium,** where you can see marine mammals and exotic water dwellers. Gaze at the lake while lunching at the Oceanarium's restaurant; then fix your eyes heavenward on the **Adler Planetarium**'s Sky Show. If the weather's nice, take time to stroll along the lakefront outside the Adler—it has one of the loveliest skyline views in the city. For dinner, head north to **Pizzeria Uno** or **Pizzeria Due** for authentic Chicago-style pizza. Then amble over to the **House of Blues** for some after-dinner entertainment.

On day three, begin with a long walk (or run) along the lakefront. Or rent a bike and watch the waves on wheels. Then catch an El train north to **Wrigley Field** for a little Cubs baseball; grab a dog at the seventh-inning stretch. Afterward, soak up a little beer and atmosphere at one of the local sports bars. Then head back to River North for dinner at one of the restaurants bearing the name of a past or present Chicago sports luminary: **Michael Jordan's, Harry Caray's,** or **Iron Mike's.**

If You Have 5 Days

Follow the three-day itinerary. On day four, do the zoo. Spend the morning at the free **Lincoln Park Zoo and Conservatory.** Eat lunch at Cafe Brauer, and then stroll through the park to the **Chicago Historical Society** for an intriguing look at Chicago's yesterdays. A cab will get you back to **Old Town** for dinner at O'Brien's or another local institution. Then head for **Second City,** home of the famous local improv troupe. If your funny bone still needs tickling afterward, walk over to nearby **Zanies** for some stand-up laughs.

Finally, on day five, grab your bankroll and stroll the **Mag Mile** in search of great buys and souvenirs of Chicago. Heading north from around the Michigan Avenue Bridge, window-shop your way along the many upscale stores. (Dedicated shoppers will want to detour to State Street for a walk through the landmark **Marshall Field's.**) If you need a culture buzz, check out the **Terra Museum of American Art** and the **Museum of Contemporary Art,** both in the neighborhood. At the retail mecca that is **Water Tower Place,** you'll find plenty of places to refuel. But save some room for tea or cocktails at the lush **Ritz-Carlton.** After making that tough last-night restaurant choice, consider heading back to the **Signature Room at the 95th** bar at the top of the John Hancock Center for a *digestif*—it's a heady place to kiss the city good-bye.

FODOR'S CHOICE

No two people will agree on what makes a perfect vacation, but it's fun and helpful to know what others think. We hope you'll have a chance to experience some of our picks yourself while visiting Chicago. For detailed information about each entry, refer to the appropriate chapters in this guidebook.

Activities

★ Join hundreds of other visitors and Chicagoans **strolling, biking, or in-line skating along the lakefront.**

★ Get into the spirit of the past **exploring the tomb of Unis-ankh** at the Field Museum's *Inside Ancient Egypt.*

★ Put your heart into **singing "Take Me Out to the Ball Game" during the seventh-inning stretch** at Wrigley Field, regardless of who's winning.

★ **Bust a gut** at the Second City comedy club, which has launched some of the funniest comedians around.

★ **Walk in Frank Lloyd Wright's footsteps** in his Oak Park neighborhood.

★ **Experience real roots music** at a crowded, smoky blues bar, even if it's full of other out-of-towners trying to get soulful.

Architecture

★ Hordes of commuters rush through the modern train station–office tower of **Citicorp Center** every day; be sure to appreciate it outside and in.

★ Love it or hate it, you're sure to find the red, white, and blue postmodern, wedge-shape structure called **James R. Thompson Center** intriguing.

★ Take one look at the thick base walls of the **Monadnock Building** to see why the steel frame was such an innovation.

★ A cantilevered roof, leaded-glass windows, and lack of a basement are typical of Frank Lloyd Wright's Prairie style—and all are exemplified beautifully at the striking **Robie House.**

★ The exterior of the **Rookery** is imposing, but inside is an airy marble and gold-leaf lobby remodeled by Frank Lloyd Wright in 1905.

★ The shimmering glass of **333 West Wacker Drive** curves along with the river, giving sense to the building's odd shape.

Special Moments

★ Between May 1 and October 1 you can catch one of the pleasures of Grant Park, **Buckingham Fountain's evening light show.**

★ For a glimpse of the city at work, **gaze down upon the frenetic activity on the trading floor** from the fourth-floor visitor gallery at the Chicago Mercantile Exchange.

★ Visitors gather for **feeding time at the coral reef of the John G. Shedd Aquarium,** when sharks, eels, turtles, and the like get their lunch.

★ **At the Art Institute relax in the sky-lighted sculpture court** with some of the best sculpture you'll see indoors in Chicago.

★ A visit to the **winter orchid show at the Chicago Botanic Garden** in Glencoe is sure to brighten a blustery day.

Views

★ **Get a good look at the Chicago River** from the Michigan Avenue Bridge, with the wedding-cake-like Wrigley Building on one side, the Loop on the other.

★ Drive north from Hyde Park to **take in the Chicago skyline from South Lake Shore Drive,** each curve providing a unique vista.

★ Go for a ride and **see the Chicago skyline from the top of Navy Pier's Ferris wheel**: It's a beautiful, breezy view from an open-air car 15 stories off the ground.

★ **Ride an elevator 94 stories up for a panorama of the city** from the top of the John Hancock Center.

Restaurants

★ **Charlie Trotter's** small dining room can barely accommodate all the people who'd like to try its experimental American cuisine. *$$$$*

★ Chef Jean Joho's brilliance ensures that dining at **Everest** is a peak experience for French food lovers. *$$$$*

★ **Gibsons** is arguably the convention crowd's favorite steak house. *$$$–$$$$*

☺ Luxury Italian dining and good views combine brilliantly at **Spiaggia,** on North Michigan Avenue. *$$$–$$$$*

★ At **Arun's,** delicious Thai food that goes far beyond the usual is matched with an upscale atmosphere. *$$–$$$*

☺ Judicious seasoning and sauces enhance classic American food at the **Hubbard Street Grill.** *$$–$$$*

Eye-catching decor and an interesting Italian menu that's strong on pastas draw crowds to **Vivere.** *$$–$$$*

★ A cheery ambience, a constantly changing but always innovative and delicious Mexican menu, and the right price make the **Frontera Grill** a winner. *$–$$$*

★ **Le Bouchon** is a Bucktown bistro with superb French comfort food. *$$*

Hotels

★ Occupying a prominent bend of Lake Michigan, the **Drake** has fabulous views and an Italian Renaissance splendor that have attracted generations of royalty. *$$$$*

★ Excellent service and an old-world ambience are hallmarks of the **Four Seasons.** *$$$$*

★ For a totally modern take on luxury, try the **Sutton Place**—a testament to class and sophistication. *$$$$*

★ Elegant, gracious, and charming, the **Omni Ambassador East** is also home to the Pump Room, restaurant of the rich and famous. *$$$–$$$$*

★ The **Raphael** is an intimate oasis near the John Hancock Building, with good-size rooms and pleasant service. *$$$–$$$$*

★ An Old Chicago feel and a peaceful location draw guests to the **Belden-Stratford,** in Lincoln Park. *$$–$$$*

★ The **River North Hotel** attracts hordes of families with its proximity to River North's entertainment scene, free parking, and indoor pool. *$$–$$$*

★ Visitors seeking cheap sleeps can't say enough good things about the **Cass Hotel,** which is a stone's throw from River North and Michigan Avenue. *$*

FESTIVALS AND SEASONAL EVENTS

Chicagoans love celebrations. Spring and summer are the festival seasons, while celebrations move indoors for the winter. The following is a sampling of the many cultural, ethnic, and recreational events in the city. To find out precise dates and details and to ask about any special interests, contact the **Chicago Office of Tourism** (☎ 312/744–2400 or 800/226–6632; ☞ Visitor Information *in* the Gold Guide) or consult one of Chicago's local events calendars in the *Reader* and *New City,* two free weekly newspapers distributed on Thursday in many stores in Hyde Park, the Loop, and the North Side; the **Friday** section of *Chicago Tribune*; and the **Weekend Plus** section of the Friday *Chicago Sun-Times.*

➤ EARLY–MID-JAN.: The **Chicago Boat, Sports, and RV Show** displays more than 900 boats and 300 recreational vehicles at McCormick Place (☒ 2300 S. Lake Shore Dr., ☎ 312/946–6262).

➤ FEB.: **African-American Heritage Month** celebrations at the Museum of Science and Industry (☒ 57th St. and Lake Shore Dr., ☎ 773/684–1414), the DuSable Museum (☒ 740 E. 56th Pl., ☎ 773/947–0600), the **South Shore Cultural**

Center (☒ 7059 S. Shore Dr., ☎ 312/747–2536), the **Chicago Cultural Center** (☒ 78 E. Washington St., ☎ 312/346–3278), the **Field Museum** (☒ Roosevelt Rd. at Lake Shore Dr., ☎ 312/922–9410), the **Art Institute of Chicago** (☒ Michigan Ave. at Adams St., ☎ 312/443–3600), and other Chicago cultural institutions include arts-and-crafts exhibitions and theater, music, and dance performances.

➤ EARLY FEB.: The **3 on 3 Basketball Tournament** is the largest indoor event of its kind (☒ Navy Pier, ☎ 773/404–0554).

➤ MID-FEB.: The **Chicago Auto Show** previews the coming year's domestic and imported models at McCormick Place (☒ 2301 S. Lake Shore Dr., ☎ 312/949–8800).

➤ MID-FEB.: The **Azalea and Camellia Show** at Lincoln Park Conservatory (☒ 2400 N. Stockton Dr., ☎ 312/742–7736) and Garfield Park Conservatory (☒ 300 N. Central Park Ave., ☎ 312/746–5100) provides a welcome early glimpse of spring.

➤ MID-FEB.: **Winterbreak Festival** (☎ 312/744–3315) is a series of concerts, skating exhibitions, and other entertainment events in various locations; discount packages are available at many hotels.

➤ MID-FEB.–EARLY MAR.: The **Medinah Shrine Circus** at Medinah Temple (☒ 600 N. Wabash Ave., ☎ 312/266–5050) delights kids of all ages each year.

➤ MAR. 13: The **St. Patrick's Day parade** (☎ 312/942–9188) turns the city on its head: The Chicago River is dyed green, shamrocks decorate the street, and the center stripe of Dearborn Street is painted the color of the Irish from Wacker Drive to Van Buren Street.

➤ LATE MAR.–EARLY APR.: The **Spring Flower Show** blooms at the Lincoln Park and Garfield Park conservatories.

➤ APRIL 9–20: Celebrate Latino culture during the **15th Annual Chicago Latino Film Festival** at various locations around the city (☎ 312/663–1600).

➤ MAY 1–OCT. 1: **Buckingham Fountain,** in Grant Park, flows day and night. Colored lights illuminate it nightly from 9 until 11.

➤ MID-MAY: The **Art 1998 Chicago** exhibition at the Navy Pier (☒ 600 E. Grand Ave., ☎ 312/587–3300) showcases modern and contemporary art with 200 international exhibitors.

➤ MAY 15: The **Wright Plus House Walk** (☎ 708/848–1976) gives you a look at masterpieces in suburban Oak Park by Frank Lloyd Wright and other Prairie School architects.

➤ LATE MAY–EARLY JUNE: The **Printer's Row Book Fair** (☒ Dearborn St.

between Congress Pkwy. and Polk St., ☎ 312/987–9896) is a two-day event in the historic Printer's Row district, with programs and displays on the printer's and binder's arts.

SUMMER

➤ EARLY JUNE: The **Chicago Blues Festival** (☎ 312/744–3315), in Grant Park, is a popular four-day, three-stage event starring blues greats from Chicago and around the country.

➤ JUNE 4–5: The **57th Street Art Fair,** in Hyde Park's Ray School yard (✉ 57th St. and Kimbark Ave., ☎ 773/493–3247), is the oldest juried art fair in the Midwest, with paintings, sculpture, jewelry, ceramics, clothing, and textiles.

➤ JUNE 12–13: The **Old Town Art Fair** (✉ Lincoln Park W and Orleans Sts., ☎ 312/337–1938), one of the top summer art fairs, draws people from around the region to historic Old Town.

➤ EARLY–MID-JUNE: The **Chicago Gospel Fest** (☎ 312/744–3315) brings its joyful sounds to Grant Park.

➤ MID-JUNE: The **Boulevard-Lakefront Bicycle Tour** (☎ 312/427–3325) brings 6,000 cyclists to the city's network of boulevards and parks for a 35-mi ride.

➤ MID-JUNE–MID-AUG.: The **Grant Park Symphony Orchestra and Chorus**

(☎ 312/742–7638) gives free concerts Wednesday–Sunday.

➤ MID-JUNE: Summer fun with a Swedish flair can be found at the **34th Annual Andersonville Midsommarfest** (☎ 773/348–6784).

➤ LATE JUNE–EARLY JULY: **Taste of Chicago** (✉ Grant Park, Columbus Dr. between Jackson and Randolph Sts., ☎ 312/744–3315) dishes out pizza, cheesecake, and other Chicago specialties to 3½ million people over a 10-day period that includes entertainment.

➤ LATE JUNE–LABOR DAY: The **Ravinia Festival** (☎ 847/266–5100), in Highland Park, hosts a variety of jazz, classical, and popular musical artists in a pastoral setting north of the city.

➤ ALL SUMMER: **Noontime music and dance performances** are held outdoors weekdays at the **Daley Center Plaza** (✉ Washington St. between Dearborn and Clark Sts.) and at the **First National Bank of Chicago Plaza** (✉ Dearborn St. at Madison St.).

➤ JULY 3: **Fireworks along the lakefront** draw a crowd at dusk; bring a blanket and a portable radio to listen to the *1812 Overture* from Grant Park (☎ 312/744–3315).

➤ MID-JULY: The **Chicago to Mackinac Island Boat Race** originates at Belmont Harbor (☎ 312/861–7777).

➤ JULY 16–17: The **World's Largest Block Party,** at Old St. Pat's Church (✉ Madison and Des Plaines Sts., ☎ 312/

648–1021), has nationally recognized bands, food, drinks, and swarms of people.

➤ LATE JULY: The **Newberry Library Book Fair** (✉ 60 W. Walton St., ☎ 312/255–3510) sells thousands of good used books at low prices; the park across the street holds the Bughouse Square Debates the same weekend.

➤ LATE JULY: **Venetian Night** (✉ Monroe St. Harbor, Grant Park, ☎ 312/744–3315) features fireworks and boats festooned with lights.

➤ LATE AUG.: The **Air and Water Show** (☎ 312/744–3315) along North Avenue Beach thrills viewers with precision flying teams and antique and high-tech aircraft going through their paces.

➤ LATE AUG.: **Chicago Triathlon** (☎ 773/404–2372) participants plunge in at Ohio Street on the lakefront for a 1-mi swim, followed by a 25-mi bike race on Lake Shore Drive, and a 10-km run in the world's largest triathlon.

➤ LATE AUG.: The **Chicago Jazz Festival** (☎ 312/744–3315) holds sway for four days during Labor Day weekend at the Petrillo Music Shell in Grant Park.

➤ LATE AUG.–EARLY SEPT.: You'll get more than food at **Taste of Polonia** (✉ Lawrence and Milwaukee Aves., ☎ 773/777–8898), which also features carnival games, polka bands, and Polish handicrafts.

AUTUMN

➤ EARLY SEPT.: The **Around the Coyote** (☎ 773/342–6777) festival in Wicker Park and Bucktown features theater performances, poetry and fiction readings, dance, film, and a gallery walk that begins at the intersection of Milwaukee, North, and Damen avenues.

➤ SEPT.: The **Dia de los Muertos** celebration at the Mexican Fine Arts Center Museum (✉ 1852 W. 19th St., ☎ 312/738–1503) displays the work of Mexican and Mexican-American artists.

➤ EARLY–MID-SEPT.: **Viva Chicago** (☎ 312/744–3315) is a festival of Latin music in Grant Park.

➤ MID-SEPT.–EARLY OCT.: **Oktoberfest** brings out the best in beer and German specialties at the Berghoff Restaurant (✉ 17 W. Adams St., ☎ 312/427–3170) and Chicago area pubs.

➤ OCT. 11: The **Chicago Marathon** (☎ 312/243–3274) starts in Grant Park at Columbus and Balbo streets and follows a course through the city.

➤ MID-OCT.: The **Columbus Day Parade** follows Dearborn Street from Wacker Drive to Congress Parkway.

➤ MID-OCT.: The **Chicago International Film Festival** (☎ 312/425–9400) brings new American and foreign films to various Chicago theaters.

➤ SAT. BEFORE THANKS-GIVING: The **Magnificent Mile Lights Festival** (☎ 312/642–3570) kicks off the holiday season with a block-by-block illumination of hundreds of thousands of tiny white lights along Michigan Avenue and Oak Street.

➤ THANKSGIVING WEEK-END: The **lighting of Chicago's Christmas tree** takes place on Friday in the Daley Center Plaza (✉ Washington St. between Dearborn and Clark Sts.); the **Christmas Parade,** with balloons, floats, and Santa, travels down Michigan Avenue on Saturday.

➤ MID-NOV.–DEC.: The **Goodman Theatre** (✉ 200 S. Columbus Dr., ☎ 312/443–3800) presents *A Christmas Carol,* and *The Nutcracker* is performed at the **Arie Crown Theatre at McCormick Place** (✉ 2301 S. Lake Shore Dr., ☎ 312/791–6190).

➤ LATE NOV.: The **Chrysanthemum Show** holds center stage at the Lincoln Park and Garfield Park conservatories.

➤ LATE NOV.–DEC.: The **Christmas Around the World** display at the Museum of Science and Industry (✉ 57th St. and Lake Shore Dr., ☎ 773/684–1414) brings together trees decorated in the traditional styles of more than 40 countries.

➤ LATE NOV.–MAR.: **Skate on State** (✉ State Street between Washington and Randolph Sts., ☎ 312/744–3315) is a free outdoor ice-skating rink in the heart of the Loop.

➤ NOV. 27–JAN. 1: **Zoo Lights Festival** at the Lincoln Park Zoo (✉ 2200 N. Cannon Dr., ☎ 312/742–2000) shows off zoo animals, dinosaurs, and holiday themes with more than 100,000 lights.

➤ MID- TO LATE DEC.: At the **South Shore Cultural Center** (✉ 7059 S. Shore Dr., ☎ 312/747–2536), the city's largest **Pre-Kwanzaa Celebration,** a two-day family-oriented event, with performances, workshops, crafts and food, is held in advance of the African-American cultural holiday Kwanzaa, which runs from December 26 to January 1; other Kwanzaa-related events are held at the **New Regal Theatre** (✉ 1645 E. 79th St., ☎ 773/721–9301), DuSable Museum of African-American History, Chicago Cultural Center, Art Institute of Chicago, and other cultural institutions in the city.

➤ LATE DEC.–EARLY JAN.: The **Winter Festival Flower Show** at the Lincoln Park and Garfield Park conservatories provides welcome color.

2 Exploring Chicago

Rising at the southern edge of Lake Michigan, Chicago is a powerfully beautiful city with a stunning skyline, world-famous museums, glorious houses of worship, and tempting galleries and shops. Its spacious parks stretch along the shores of a lake that rages in winter and seduces in summer. You might start exploring in the energetic Loop, then travel as far south as Hyde Park, home of the Nobel-studded University of Chicago, or as far north as Devon Avenue, where scents of exotic Indian spices waft into the street.

Updated by
Mary Gillespie

CHICAGO'S VARIETY IS DAZZLING. The canyons of the Loop bustle with bankers, lawyers, traders, brokers, politicians, and wheeler-dealers of all kinds transacting their business in buildings that make architecture buffs swoon. Equally busy but sunnier is the Near North (near the Loop, that is), where the smart shops of Michigan Avenue give way to the headquarters of myriad trade associations, advertising agencies, one of the nation's leading teaching hospitals, and cathedrals of the Roman Catholic and Episcopal churches.

The city's skyline is one of the most exciting in the world. In the last three decades the Sears Tower, the Amoco Building, the John Hancock Center, the Stone Container Building, NBC Tower, the James R. Thompson Center, 333 West Wacker, Lake Point Tower, and others have joined such legendary structures as the Chicago Board of Trade, the Rookery, and the Wrigley Building. Chicago is a virtual primer of modern architecture; for some background and a who's who, read Barbara Shortt's essay, "The Builders of Chicago," in Chapter 9 before you start exploring.

Leave downtown and the lakefront, however, and you soon encounter a city of neighborhoods made up mostly of bungalows, two-flats, three-flats, and six-flats (as two-, three-, and six-story apartment buildings are called here). Churches and shopping strips with signs in Polish, Spanish, Chinese, Arabic, Hebrew, or Korean stand as symbols of vibrant ethnic community life. Visitors rarely venture to these neighborhoods, yet it is here that you may encounter people enjoying great ethnic feasts for a pittance; and you can visit the museums and churches that house cultural artifacts reflecting the soul and spirit of their communities. The hardscrabble Chicago of immigrant enterprise may seem worlds away from Chicago the glitzy megalopolis, but for a real understanding of the city you should experience both.

THE LOOP

Downtown Chicago is full of treasures for city lovers. Known as the Loop since the cable cars of the 1880s—and, later, the elevated railway—looped around the central business district, downtown comprises the area south of the Chicago River, west of Lake Michigan, and north of the Congress Parkway–Eisenhower Expressway. Downtown Chicago's western boundary used to be the Chicago River, but the boundary continues to push westward. Handsome skyscrapers now line every foot of South Wacker Drive east of the river, and investors have sent construction crews across the bridges in search of more land to fuel the expansion.

The dynamic area known as the Loop is a living architectural museum, where you can stroll past shimmering modern towers side by side with painstakingly renovated 19th-century buildings that snap you back in time. There are striking sculptures by Picasso, Miró, Chagall, and others; wide plazas lively with music and other entertainment in summer; noisy, mesmerizing trading centers; gigantic department stores that amazingly have avoided death-by-mall; and globally known museums that soothe the senses. (For immediate stress reduction, check out the Impressionists at the Art Institute.) And, of course, there is the rattling overhead train Chicagoans call the El, which loops the Loop.

Numbers in the text correspond to numbers in the margin and on the Loop map.

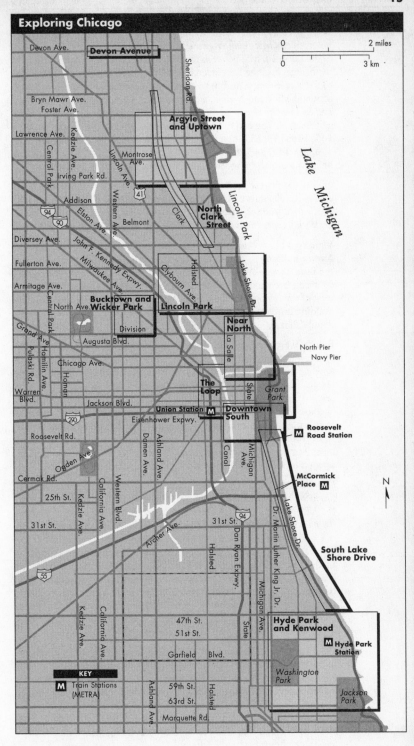

Exploring Chicago

Devon Ave.
Devon Avenue
Bryn Mawr Ave.
Foster Ave.
Lawrence Ave.
Central Park
Kedzie Ave.
Irving Park Rd.
Addison
Elston Ave.
Western Ave.
Lincoln Ave.
Montrose Ave.
Argyle Street and Uptown
Sheridan Rd.
Lake Michigan
North Clark Street
Belmont
Clark
Lincoln Park
Diversey Ave.
John F. Kennedy Expwy.
Fullerton Ave.
Milwaukee Ave.
Armitage Ave.
Central Park
North Ave.
Bucktown and Wicker Park
Clybourn Ave.
Halsted
Lincoln Park
Lake Shore Dr.
Grand Ave.
Augusta Blvd.
Division
Near North
North Pier
Navy Pier
Pulaski Rd.
Hamlin Ave.
Chicago Ave.
Holman
La Salle
Warren Blvd.
Jackson Blvd.
The Loop
State
Grant Park
Union Station
Eisenhower Expwy.
Downtown South
Roosevelt Rd.
Ogden Ave.
Damen Ave.
Ashland Ave.
Canal
Michigan Ave.
Roosevelt Road Station
Cermak Rd.
California Ave.
Western Blvd.
McCormick Place
25th St.
Kedzie Ave.
31st St.
Archer Ave.
31st St.
Don Ryan Expwy.
Dr. Martin Luther King Jr. Dr.
Lake Shore Dr.
South Lake Shore Drive
47th St.
Halsted
51st St.
Michigan Ave.
State
Garfield Blvd.
Hyde Park and Kenwood
Hyde Park Station
KEY
Train Stations (METRA)
California Ave.
59th St.
Washington Park
Jackson Park
Ashland Ave.
63rd St.
Halsted
Marquette Rd.

0   2 miles
0   3 km

N

A Good Walk

Begin your walk on North Michigan Avenue at South Water Street, not far from the Michigan Avenue Bridge. This is the far northeast corner of the Loop—a spot between the Magnificent Mile, running north from the bridge, and the long stretch of Michigan Avenue that slopes south to the Art Institute and beyond. The walk will take you a few blocks south on Michigan Avenue, across the north part of the Loop, then south and east into the heart of downtown before turning back toward Michigan Avenue. You can reach the starting point from the north via Bus 3, 145, 146, 147, 151, or 157. Coming from the south, you can take Bus 3, 6, 56, 145, 146, 147, 151, or 157; get off at Lake Street and head one block north to South Water Street. If you arrive by car, park it.

On the southwest corner of Michigan Avenue and South Water Street stands the elegant Art Deco **Carbide and Carbon Building** ①. Continue south to Randolph Street. On the northwest corner, the office building with the distinctively angled face is the **Stone Container Building** ②.

Walk two blocks east, with Grant Park on your right, to the 1,136-ft **Amoco Building** ③, the second-tallest building in Chicago. Just east is the Blue Cross–Blue Shield of Illinois Building, innovatively designed so it can eventually grow upward to a height of 54 stories. Directly west of the Amoco Building is the Prudential Building, Chicago's tallest building until the late '60s. Behind it rises the rocketship-like Two Prudential Plaza.

Return west on Randolph Street to Michigan Avenue, walk south a block, and turn right onto East Washington Street, to the **Chicago Cultural Center** ④, with a grand interior that houses an information center and the **Museum of Broadcast Communications.** Turn right after leaving the Cultural Center from the Washington Street side, walk across Wabash Avenue (crossing under the El tracks), and enter **Marshall Field's** ⑤, the landmark turn-of-the-century flagship of the department store. Exit Field's on **State Street** and head north along the Loop's most famous thoroughfare. State Street was reconstructed and reopened to traffic in 1996 after failing as a pedestrian mall.

If you're interested in architecture, cross Randolph Street. Half a block north on your right is the ornate, 1921 Beaux Arts Chicago Theatre (⊠ 175 N. State St.), a former movie palace that now hosts live performances. Next door, at 177 N. State, is the Page Brothers Building, one of only two buildings in Chicago known to have a cast-iron front. The handsome building directly across State Street, formerly the State-Lake Theatre, houses WLS-TV, Chicago's ABC affiliate. Turn back and head south along State Street. The vacant lot across from Marshall Field's is Block 37, a popular skating rink in winter and an outdoor art gallery in summer. On the southwest corner of State and Washington streets is the Reliance Building (⊠ 32 N. State St.), an important forerunner of the modern skyscraper that was completed in 1895.

Heading west on Washington Street, you come to the **Daley Center** ⑥. In the plaza is Picasso's controversial sculpture, known simply as "the Picasso." Directly opposite the Daley Center is the **Chicago Temple** ⑦, a Methodist church whose beautiful spire is so tall that it is best seen at some distance. Walk a half block west on Washington to Clark Street and turn right. Across from the Daley Center is the handsome, neoclassical **Chicago City Hall–Cook County Building** ⑧, where the city's legislators shout each other down.

Continue north on Clark for a block to reach the much-discussed **James R. Thompson Center** ⑨, a predominantly glass red, white, and blue government building that has been likened to a spaceship.

Walk one block west to Wells Street and three blocks south to Madison Street to see Louise Nevelson's sculpture **Dawn Shadows,** which is reflected in the high-rise behind it. Head west on Madison Street to Wacker Drive, where you'll see the pale grape–color twin towers of the **Chicago Mercantile Exchange** ⑩ to your left. Visitors can watch the frenetic action on the trading floors from two separate galleries. Upon exiting the Mercantile Exchange, cross Madison Street to view the Art Deco **Civic Opera House** ⑪, where Chicago's Lyric Opera gives its performances.

Turn back onto Madison Street and continue west, crossing the Chicago River to Canal Street and the smashing **Citicorp Center** ⑫, a busy commuter terminal. One block west is the chunky-looking **Social Security Building** ⑬, with Claes Oldenburg's jokey pop-art sculpture *Batcolumn* in its plaza. Directly across from the sculpture are the four buildings of the Presidential Towers residences, which house apartments, shops, and restaurants.

Retrace your steps, walking east on Madison Street. Turn right onto Canal Street and head south to check out the gargantuan skylighted waiting area of old **Union Station** ⑭, which serves both Amtrak and suburban trains. Just south of the station, turn left onto Jackson Boulevard. Cross the river and continue east to the hulking, 110-story **Sears Tower** ⑮, where the 103rd-floor Skydeck provides grand views. Across Jackson Boulevard from the Sears Tower is **311 S. Wacker Drive** ⑯. Its spectacular winter garden atrium is the perfect spot for lunch in the colder months.

Continue east on Jackson Boulevard and turn left onto cavernous LaSalle Street. On the east side of the street is the **Rookery** ⑰, an imposing red-stone building that is one of the city's 19th-century showpieces. Retrace your steps along LaSalle Street to Jackson Boulevard, where the street seems to disappear in front of the commanding **Chicago Board of Trade** ⑱, one of the few important Art Deco buildings in Chicago. Walk east on Jackson Boulevard a half block, where LaSalle Street continues. Turn right and head south, crossing Van Buren Street, to **One Financial Place** ⑲, where the Chicago Stock Exchange is located.

Walk back to Van Buren Street and turn right, heading east. Just past Clark Street, the odd, triangular poured-concrete building looming up on your right-hand side is the **Metropolitan Correctional Center** ⑳, a high-rise jail with a tree-filled plaza.

Walk four blocks farther east on Van Buren Street to State Street and turn right. Taking up an entire block between Van Buren Street and Congress Parkway is the **Harold Washington Library Center** ㉑, a postmodern homage to classical-style public buildings. Retrace your steps back to Van Buren Street, walking west. At 343 S. Dearborn is Daniel Burnham's beautifully ornamented Fisher Building, where carved cherubs frolic over the glassed-in Van Buren Street entrance. Across the street is the massive, darkly handsome **Monadnock Building** ㉒. Walk through the corridor, with its vintage light fixtures, to the north end.

Continue north on Dearborn, crossing Jackson Boulevard. On the left-hand side of the street is the 42-story Kluczynski Building; across Dearborn to the east is the similar 30-story Dirksen. Both are part of the **Federal Center and Plaza** ㉓, designed by Mies van der Rohe. Continue north on Dearborn Street to Adams Street and then jog a bit eastward to have a look at the rare cast-iron front of the westernmost building of the **Berghoff Restaurant** ㉔.

Walk back to Dearborn Street and turn right, heading north. The 1894 **Marquette Building** ㉕ features an exterior terra-cotta bas-relief and interior mosaics. Walk the rest of the block north to Monroe Street; on the southwest corner, the modern 55 West Monroe has an unusual wraparound aluminum-and-glass wall. Across Monroe Street is the bi-level **First National Bank Plaza** ㉖, running the length of the block from Dearborn to Clark Street.

From the Bank Plaza glance across Dearborn to the turquoise-tinted **Inland Steel Building** ㉗. Abutting the plaza that bears its name, at Dearborn and Madison streets, is the First National Bank of Chicago, the only building in the Loop that resembles a letter of the alphabet (view it from the side, and you'll guess which one).

Turning right onto Madison Street, walk one block to State Street and turn right again to see some classic older buildings. On the east side of the street is the department store **Carson Pirie Scott** ㉘, an outstanding example of Louis Sullivan's work. The **Palmer House** ㉙, one of Chicago's grand old hotels, is one block south of Carson's, between State and Wabash streets; enter from Monroe Street, about halfway down the block.

From the Palmer House, head east on Monroe Street and south on Michigan Avenue to Adams Street and the imposing entrance to the **Art Institute of Chicago** ㉚, one of the great art museums of the world. The grand-looking Orchestra Hall (⊠ 220 N. Michigan Ave.), opposite the Art Institute, is home to the internationally acclaimed Chicago Symphony Orchestra. Next door is the Railway Exchange Building, better known as the **Santa Fe Building** ㉛ because of the rooftop SANTA FE sign. From the corner of Michigan Avenue and Jackson Boulevard, peer west for a look at the **CNA Center** (⊠ 55 E. Jackson Blvd.), a rust-colored tower on the skyline.

Continuing south on Michigan Avenue, you'll reach the **Fine Arts Building** ㉜, an atmospheric edifice that has long housed artists and musicians. A bit farther south, on the corner of Michigan Avenue and Congress Parkway, is the massive granite-sheathed **Auditorium Theatre** ㉝.

Finally, head east on Congress Parkway to Columbus Drive and **Buckingham Fountain** ㉞, which is set in its own plaza on the lakefront. This romantic fountain's central jet shoots up to 135 ft and, blown by lake breezes, regularly cools off summertime visitors.

TIMING

You should allow two days for this walk to ensure time for leisurely visits to museums and sites. A good way to break up the tour is to walk as far as Union Station the first day, then resume at Sears Tower the next. Another option is to spend the first day traversing the whole tour and the second revisiting places that deserve more time: the Chicago Cultural Center, the Art Institute, the Sears Tower Skydeck, the Chicago Mercantile Exchange and the Board of Trade—and, for shoppers, Marshall Field's. If possible, do the walk on a weekday, when the Loop is bustling and the lobbies of office buildings are open.

Sights to See

❸ **Amoco Building.** This 80-story shaft was originally clad in marble from the same quarry Michelangelo used. Unfortunately, the thin slabs of marble, unable to withstand Chicago's harsh climate, began to warp and fall off soon after the building was completed. The marble was replaced with light-color granite. The building's massive presence is best viewed from a distance. It sits on a handsome (if rather sterile) plaza, and Harry Bertoia's wind-chime sculpture in the reflecting pool makes interesting sounds when the wind blows. ⊠ *200 E. Randolph St.*

★ ☙ ③ **Art Institute of Chicago.** Among the familiar and favorite paintings on exhibit at this world-famous museum are Grant Wood's *American Gothic,* Edward Hopper's *Nighthawks,* Pablo Picasso's *The Old Guitarist,* and George Seurat's *A Sunday on La Grande Jatte–1884.* The Art Institute is particularly renowned for its stunning collection of Impressionist and post-Impressionist paintings, with works by Monet, Renoir, Gaugin, and van Gogh, among others. The museum also has impressive collections of medieval, Renaissance, and modern art. Less well known are its fine holdings in Asian art and photography. Be sure to visit the Rubloff paperweight collection; a Chicago real-estate magnate donated these shimmering, multicolor objects. The Thorne Miniature Rooms show interior decoration in every historical style; they'll entrance anyone who's ever furnished a dollhouse or built a model. And don't miss the Stock Exchange Room, a splendid reconstruction of the trading floor of the old Chicago Stock Exchange, which was demolished in 1972. The Daniel F. and Ada L. Rice Building has three floors of exhibition galleries, a large space for temporary exhibitions, and a skylighted central court dotted with sculpture and plantings. The Galleries of Contemporary Art showcases post–WWII era paintings, sculptures and videos. The museum store has an outstanding collection of art books, calendars, and merchandise related to current exhibits, as well as gift items.

A map of the museum, available at the information desk, will help you find your way to the works or periods you want to visit. Especially helpful for first-time visitors is the 45-minute Introduction to the Collections tour, daily at 2. If you have a youngster with you, make an early stop at the **Kraft Education Center** downstairs. Your child can choose from an assortment of 25 or so Gallery Games, some of which come with picture postcards. The delightful and informative games will keep kids from becoming hopelessly bored as you tramp through the galleries. ⊠ *S. Michigan Ave. and Adams St.,* ☎ *312/443–3600.* ☞ *$7, free Tues.* ☽ *Mon. and Wed.–Fri. 10:30–4:30, Tues. 10:30–8, Sat. 10–5, Sun. noon–5.*

③ **Auditorium Theatre.** One of the city's architectural and cultural landmarks, this glorious Dankmar Adler and Louis Sullivan building from 1889 was restored by architect Harry Weese in 1967. The hall seats 4,000 people and has unobstructed sight lines and near-perfect acoustics. Though the theater is normally closed to the public unless there's a show or concert, you can call to arrange a 45-minute tour. The lobby facing Michigan Avenue has marble wainscoting and a truly grand staircase. The interior ornamentation, including arched rows of lights along the ceiling, is breathtaking. Another beautiful (though less well-known) space is the library on the 10th floor of the building. ⊠ *50 E. Congress Pkwy.,* ☎ *312/431–2331; 312/431–2354 for tour information.* ☞ *Tour $4.*

㉔ **Berghoff Restaurant.** There are only two known buildings in Chicago with cast-iron facades: this building, constructed in 1872, and the Page Brothers Building on State Street, built in the same year. The practice of using iron panels cast to imitate stone was common in the latter part of the 19th century. The restaurant itself is a longtime city favorite (☞ *Greater Downtown in* Chapter 3). ⊠ *17 W. Adams St.*

㉞ **Buckingham Fountain.** Given to Chicago by philanthropist Kate Sturges Buckingham in memory of her brother Clarence and dedicated in 1927, this decorative fountain was patterned on one at Versailles but is about twice as large as its model. See it in all its glory between May 1 and October 1, when it's elaborately illuminated at night. ⊠ *Grant Park, between Columbus and Lake Shore Drs. east of Congress Plaza.*

The Loop

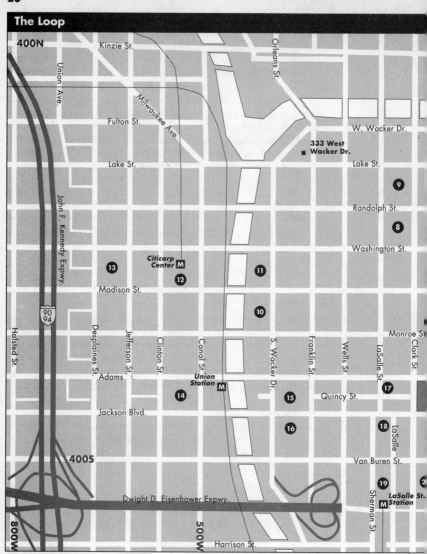

400N

Kinzie St.

Union Ave.

Milwaukee Ave.

Orleans St.

Fulton St.

W. Wacker Dr.

333 West
Wacker Dr.

Lake St.

Lake St.

⑨

John F. Kennedy Expwy.

Randolph St.

⑧

Washington St.

Citicorp
Center Ⓜ

⑬

⑫

⑪

90
94

Madison St.

⑩

Halsted St.

Desplaines St.

Jefferson St.

Clinton St.

Canal St.

S. Wacker Dr.

Franklin St.

Wells St.

LaSalle St.

Clark St.

Monroe St.

Adams St.

Union
Station Ⓜ

⑭

⑰

Quincy St.

⑮

Jackson Blvd.

⑯

⑱

LaSalle

400S

Van Buren St.

⑲

LaSalle
Station Ⓜ

St.

Dwight D. Eisenhower Expwy.

800W

500W

Sherman St.

Harrison St.

Amoco Building, **3**
Art Institute of Chicago, **30**
Auditorium Theatre, **33**
Berghoff Restaurant, **24**
Buckingham Fountain, **34**

Carbide and Carbon Building, **1**
Carson Pirie Scott, **28**
Chicago Board of Trade, **18**
Chicago City Hall–Cook County Building, **8**
Chicago Cultural Center, **4**

Chicago Mercantile Exchange, **10**
Chicago Temple, **7**
Citicorp Center, **12**
Civic Opera House, **11**
Daley Center, **6**
Federal Center and Plaza, **23**

Fine Arts Building, **32**
First National Bank Plaza, **26**
Harold Washington Library Center, **21**
Inland Steel Building, **27**
James R. Thompson Center, **9**

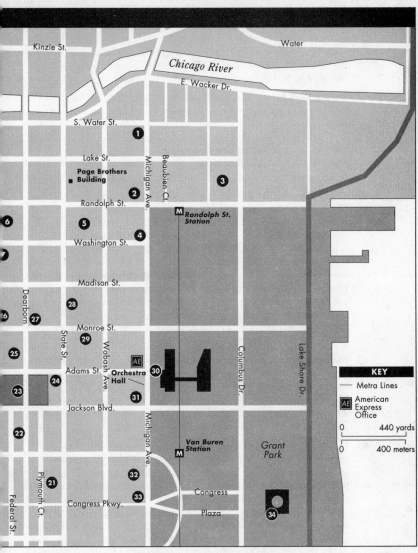

Marquette
Building, **25**

Marshall
Field's, **5**

Metropolitan
Correctional
Center, **20**

Monadnock
Building, **22**

One Financial
Place, **19**

Palmer House, **29**

The Rookery, **17**

Santa Fe
Building, **31**

Sears Tower, **15**

Social Security
Building, **13**

Stone Container
Building, **2**

311 South Wacker
Drive, **16**

Union Station, **14**

① **Carbide and Carbon Building.** A deep-green terra-cotta tower and a sleek gold-and-black exterior accented by curving, almost lacy brass work mark this significant Art Deco building, designed in 1929 by the Burnham Brothers, sons of city planner Daniel H. Burnham. Inside, the lobby is splendid, with more burnished brass, glass ornamentation, and marble. ✉ *230 N. Michigan Ave.*

★ **㉘** **Carson Pirie Scott.** Louis Sullivan, the architect of the original 1899 building and one of its later expansions, incorporated ornament even in his commercial work, as can be seen in the astonishingly rich flower and leaf designs on the main entrance. The building, housing one of the city's largest department stores, illustrates the windowpane developed by the so-called Chicago School of architects: a large fixed central pane with smaller movable windows on each side. ✉ *1 S. State St.*

★ **⑱** **Chicago Board of Trade.** Atop this Art Deco building at the foot of LaSalle Street is a gilded statue of Ceres, the Roman goddess of agriculture, an apt overseer of the frenetic commodities and financial trading that goes on within. Corn, wheat, soybeans, soybean meal and oil, government bonds, gold, and silver are what the traders are making deals for in the pits. The building was designed in 1930 by Holabird and Root and—along with the Civic Opera House and the Carbide and Carbon Building—is the city's most significant example of this style. The use of light and dark marbles and rectilinear designs makes a powerful statement. A 24-story glass-and-steel addition, facing south, was completed in 1980. ✉ *141 W. Jackson Blvd.,* ☏ *312/435–3590.* ☺ *Observation deck weekdays 8 AM–2 PM.*

⑧ **Chicago City Hall–Cook County Building.** The heavy Corinthian columns of this stately 1911 building stand in sharp contrast to the high-rising Daley Center across the street. Inside are spacious halls, plenty of marble, and lots of hot air, for this is where the Chicago City Council holds its infamous meetings. City council meetings are open to the public; call 312/744–3081 for times. ✉ *121 N. LaSalle St.*

④ **Chicago Cultural Center.** A grand Romanesque-style entrance with marble and mosaic decoration and a sweeping staircase are just a few of the elegant details in the former main building of the Chicago Public Library, built in 1897. Preston Bradley Hall, on the third floor, houses a splendid back-lighted Tiffany dome. Another Tiffany dome is on the second floor, and other parts of the building were modeled on Venetian and ancient Greek elements. The center has concerts and changing exhibitions, as well as **'Round & About the Loop,** an information center that shows a seven-minute video about Chicago's downtown. The **Museum of Broadcast Communications** (☞ *below*), also within the building, has exhibits about TV and radio and a large archive of programs and commercials. ✉ *78 E. Washington St.,* ☏ *312/346–3278.* ☺ *Mon.–Thurs. 10–7, Fri. 10–6, Sat. 10–5, Sun. noon–5.*

⑩ **Chicago Mercantile Exchange.** The traders you can watch from two different visitors' galleries exhibit an endless display of creative hand and body movements as they negotiate for the purchase and sale of billions in pork-belly futures (these have to do with the supermarket price of bacon), soybeans, currency rates, and other commodities on national and international markets. ✉ *10 and 30 S. Wacker Dr.,* ☏ *312/930–8249.* ☺ *Weekdays 7:30–3:15.*

NEED A   The **Wall Street Deli** (✉ 10 S. Wacker Dr., ☏ 312/993-3500), on the
BREAK?   first floor of the Chicago Mercantile Exchange, serves excellent soups (especially chicken gumbo), hot and cold sandwiches, and salads. If you really like your meal, you can purchase stock in the deli; it's publicly traded on the stock market.

❼ Chicago Temple. The Gothic-inspired headquarters of the First United Methodist Church of Chicago has a first-floor sanctuary, an eight-story spire (best viewed from the bridge across the Chicago River at Dearborn Street), and office space. Outside, along the building's east wall at ground level, several stained-glass windows relate the history of the church in Chicago. Joan Miró's sculpture *Chicago* (1981) is in the small plaza just east of the church. ⊠ *77 W. Washington St.*

⓬ Citicorp Center. The functions of commuter train station and office building unite in one stunning structure. The building combines a boxlike office tower with glass half cylinders piled one atop the other at the lower levels. Broad contrasting horizontal bands of mirrored and smoked glass alternate up the building for a ribbon effect that is reminiscent of a similar theme—by the same architects, Murphy/Jahn—at the James R. Thompson Center. Inside, the marble floors and exposed girders, painted a soft grayish blue, remind you of the grand old railroad stations in this country and in Europe. The gates to the tracks, elevated above street level to allow traffic to proceed east and west via underpasses, are reached by going up one level and heading to the north end of the building. Go up another flight for a view northward looking out over the tracks; at this level you'll also find the entrance to the building's office spaces. ⊠ *500 W. Madison St.*

⓫ Civic Opera House. The handsome Art Deco home of the Lyric Opera is grand indeed, with marble floors and pillars in the main hall, crystal chandeliers, and a sweeping staircase to the second floor. It was built by utilities magnate and manipulator Samuel Insull in 1929, shortly before his financial ruin, and is also an elegant older office building. Lyric Opera performances are oversubscribed (subscriptions are willed to succeeding generations), but the hopeful may be able to purchase turned-back tickets (☞ The Arts *in* Chapter 5). ⊠ *20 N. Wacker Dr.,* ☎ *312/332–2244.*

❻ Daley Center. Named for the late mayor Richard J. Daley, the father of the current holder of this office, this boldly plain high-rise is the headquarters of the Cook County court system, but it also draws visitors' attention because of what stands outside it. The building was constructed in 1965 of a steel known as Cor-Ten, which was developed as a medium that would weather naturally and attractively. In the plaza is a sculpture by Picasso made of the same material. Known simply as **"the Picasso,"** it provoked an outcry when it was installed in 1967. Speculation about what it is meant to represent (knowledgeable observers say it is the head of a woman; others have suggested it is an Afghan dog) has diminished but not ended. Still, the sculpture has become a recognized symbol of the city. In summer the plaza is the site of concerts, dance presentations, and a farmers' market, and in November, the city's official Christmas tree is erected here. ⊠ *Bounded by Washington, Randolph, Dearborn, and Clark Sts.*

㉓ Federal Center and Plaza. The Kluczynski and Dirksen federal buildings, both designed by Mies van der Rohe in 1964, are classic examples of his trademark glass-and-steel boxes. In the plaza you can't miss Alexander Calder's *Flamingo,* a colorfully contrasting, arching red stabile (a sculpture that looks like a mobile). It was dedicated on the same day in 1974 as Calder's *Universe* at the Sears Tower. It is said that Calder had a grand day, riding through Chicago in a brightly colored circus bandwagon accompanied by calliopes, as he headed from one dedication to the other. ⊠ *219 S. Dearborn St. (Dirksen), 230 S. Dearborn St. (Kluczynski).*

OFF THE
BEATEN PATH **FEDERAL RESERVE BANK** – Here, just south of the Rookery, you can learn how checks are processed and how money travels. A visitor center in the lobby has permanent exhibits of old bills, counterfeit money, and purportedly a million dollars in one-dollar bills. Call two weeks in advance for tour reservations. ⊠ *230 S. LaSalle St.,* ☎ *312/322–5111.* 🎦 *Free.* ☉ *Weekdays 9–5, 1-hr tour weekdays on the hr 9–1.*

㉜ Fine Arts Building. This fascinating, creaky old building was constructed in 1895 to house the showrooms of the Studebaker Company, then makers of carriages and later automobiles, and still evokes a time long past. Publishers, artists, and sculptors have used its spaces; today the principal tenants are professional musicians and those who cater to musicians' needs. Notice first the handsome exterior details; then step inside to see the marble and the woodwork in the lobby. The motto engraved in the marble as you enter says, ALL PASSES—ART ALONE ENDURES. The building has an interior courtyard, across which strains of piano music and soprano voices compete with tenors as they run through exercises and arias. The ground floor of the building was converted into a four-screen cinema in 1982 but still preserves much of the original ornamentation. The Fine Arts Theatre presents exceptional foreign films, art films, and movies by independent directors (☞ Nightlife *in* Chapter 5). ⊠ *410 S. Michigan Ave.*

㉖ First National Bank Plaza. Musicians and dancers perform here in summer, and picnickers and sunbathers hang out, too. Like the Daley Center and Federal Center plaza, this area fronts on Dearborn and gives the street a more open feeling than many urban canyons. In any season you can visit the 70-ft-long Chagall mosaic *The Four Seasons* (1974) at the northeast end of the plaza. It is said that when Chagall arrived in Chicago to install the mosaic, he found it a more vigorous city than he had remembered, and he immediately modified the work to reflect the stronger and more vital elements he found around him. ⊠ *Bounded by Dearborn, Clark, Monroe, and Madison Sts.*

㉑ Harold Washington Library Center. The country's largest municipal library, an imposing granite and brick structure built in 1991, has some of the most spectacular terra-cotta work seen in Chicago since the 19th century: Ears of corn, faces with puffed cheeks (representing the Windy City), and the logo of the Chicago Public Library are a few of the building's embellishments. In its final stages of construction, the library looked so much like the vintage skyscrapers around it that visitors mistook it for a renovation project. The center's holdings include the Chicago Blues Archives, the Jazz/Blues/Gospel Hall of Fame, and the Balaban and Katz Theater Orchestra Collection, all available for reference use. The excellent **children's library** on the second floor, an 18,000-square-ft haven, has a charming storytelling alcove with vibrant wall-mounted figures by Chicago imagist Karl Wirsum. Works by noted Chicago artists are displayed along a second-floor walkway above the main lobby. There is also an impressive Winter Garden on the ninth floor used for special events. Free programs and performances are offered regularly at the center. The library was named for the first African-American mayor of Chicago, and the primary architect was Thomas Beeby, of the Chicago firm Hammond Beeby Babka. ⊠ *400 S. State St.,* ☎ *312/747–4300.* ☉ *Mon. 9–7, Tues. and Thurs. 11–7, Wed. and Fri.–Sat. 9–5, Sun. 1–5. Tours Mon.–Sat. at noon and 2, Sun. at 2.*

OFF THE
BEATEN PATH **ILLINOIS INSTITUTE OF TECHNOLOGY** – Mies van der Rohe taught here and was the principal designer of the campus, with participation by the firms of Friedman, Alschuler, and Sincere; Holabird and Roche; and Pace Associates. Built between 1942 and 1958, the structures have the

characteristic box shape that is Mies's trademark. Unlike most of his other work, these are low-rise buildings. S. R. Crown Hall (⊠ 3360 S. State St.), made of black steel and clear glass, is the jewel of the collection; the other buildings have a certain sameness and sterility. Take I–94 (Dan Ryan Expressway) south from the Loop for the 15-minute drive to the 31st Street exit. ⊠ *S. State St. between 31st and 35th Sts.,* ☎ *312/ 567–3000.*

㉗ Inland Steel Building. Skidmore, Owings and Merrill designed this classic skyscraper in 1957. It was one of the first buildings to use supporting steel columns outside the glass-curtain wall, so office spaces are completely open. All the elevators, stairs, and service areas are in the taller structure behind the building proper. ⊠ *30 W. Monroe St.*

❾ James R. Thompson Center. People either intensely like or dislike the center: Former governor James Thompson, who selected the Helmut Jahn design for this state government building, hailed it in his dedication speech in 1985 as "the first building of the 21st century." Those who work here, and many other Chicagoans as well, have groaned in response, "I hope not!" The building's postmodern design presents multiple shapes and faces. Many features, such as the practically dissolving keystone structures around the exterior and the exposed escalator and elevator mechanics inside, were meant to break down barriers between the government and the people. Like all other good government buildings, it is capped by a dome. An enormous interior atrium is 17 stories high. The sculpture near the entrance is Jean Dubuffet's ***Monument to a Standing Beast.*** Its curved shapes, in white with black traceries, set against the curving red, white, and blue of the center, add to the visual variety. ⊠ *100 W. Randolph St.*

㉕ Marquette Building. Louis Sullivan's influence can be seen in the terracotta ornament on this 1894 Holabird and Roche-designed building, which was named for priest Jacques Marquette, an early explorer of the area. The lobby, an amazing little gem, has Tiffany glass mosaics depicting his adventures, and brass reliefs of explorers' and Native Americans' faces over the elevators. ⊠ *140 S. Dearborn St.*

❺ Marshall Field's. The original site of Chicago's best-known department store holds some 500 departments to please all shoppers (☞ Chapter 7). Designed by D. H. Burnham & Company and built between 1892 and 1907, the mammoth emporium has a spectacular Tiffany dome in the southwest corner, near State and Washington streets. A renovation in 1992 spruced up the entire store, though the synthetic look of the new atrium clashes drastically with the rest of the building's turn-of-the-century charm. Field's is a great place for a snack or a meal; for the former, try the Crystal Palace ice cream parlor; for the latter, check out the grand Walnut Room on the seventh floor or Hinky Dink Kenna's in the basement. Don't miss the landmark clock outside the entrance at State and Randolph streets. ⊠ *111 N. State St.*

⑳ Metropolitan Correctional Center. "Even a jail can be an architectural showstopper in Chicago," one writer noted. This triangular high-rise, erected in 1975, holds people awaiting trial as well as those convicted and awaiting transfer to penitentiaries. The building was designed by the same Harry Weese who saved the historic Auditorium Theatre; with its long slit windows (5 inches wide, so no bars are required), the jail looks like a postmodern reconstruction of a medieval fort. ⊠ *71 W. Van Buren St.*

㉒ Monadnock Building. This huge, imposing structure is the tallest building ever constructed with masonry-bearing walls. Burnham and Root built the northern section in 1891; the southern half, which has some vertical steel supports in the outer walls, was the work of Holabird and Roche in 1893. The problem with all-masonry buildings is that the higher they go, the thicker the base's walls must be to support the upper stories; the Monadnock's walls at the base are 6 ft thick. You can see why the introduction of the steel frame began a new era in construction. The building has been tastefully renovated inside (the original wrought-iron banisters, for example, have been retained) and cleaned outside. ⊠ *54 W. Van Buren St.*

NEED A BREAK? In the Monadnock Building, **Jacobs Bros. Bagels** (⊠ 53 W. Jackson St., ☎ 312/922–2245) is a great place to stop for deli sandwiches, homemade soups, delicious vegetarian-cashew chili, and, of course, bagels and cream cheese. The bagels are boiled and baked on the premises.

Museum of Broadcast Communications. A life-size cardboard cutout of Jack Benny greets you at the first-floor entrance to this radio and television museum, one of two in the country. In addition to seeing exhibits, you can select tapes from the second-floor archives of more than 70,000 television and radio programs and commercials. At a miniature TV studio, you can make a professional-quality videotape of yourself as a news anchor. The museum is housed in the Chicago Cultural Center (☞ *above*). ⊠ *78 E. Washington St.,* ☎ *312/629–6000.* ⊡ *Free.* ☉ *Mon.–Sat. 10–4:30, Sun. noon–5.*

OFF THE BEATEN PATH **MUSEUM OF HOLOGRAPHY** – Holograms are three-dimensional images produced by lasers. If you've never seen one, be sure to visit this museum, a short cab ride west of the Loop; the images seem to leap out at you from their frames. Exhibits of holographic art from around the world include computer-generated holograms, moving holograms, pulsed portraits of people, and color holograms. ⊠ *1134 W. Washington Blvd.,* ☎ *312/226–1007.* ⊡ *$2.50.* ☉ *Wed.–Sun. 12:30–5.*

OLD ST. PATRICK'S CHURCH – Chicago's oldest church, built from 1852 to 1856, withstood the great fire of 1871. Just west of Union Station and the Loop redevelopment area, the church towers, one Romanesque and one Byzantine, are symbolic of West and East. ⊠ *700 W. Adams St.,* ☎ *312/648–1021.*

⑲ One Financial Place. Rushing traffic on the Congress Parkway/Eisenhower Expressway flows right under an arched section of this 1985 building by Skidmore, Owings & Merrill. It houses the Chicago Stock Exchange, the superb Everest restaurant (☞ Greater Downtown *in* Chapter 3), and the LaSalle Club, which offers hotel accommodations to the public and health club and dining facilities for members. ⊠ *440 S. LaSalle St.,* ☎ *312/663–2980.* ☉ *Stock Exchange gallery weekdays 8:30–3:30.*

㉙ Palmer House. Patterned marble floors and antique lighting fixtures adorn the ground-floor level arcade of this bustling, beautiful old hotel, built in 1927 by Holabird and Roche. The firm also designed what is now the posh Chicago Hilton and Towers (☞ Downtown South, *below*). In the arcade are upscale shops, restaurants, and service establishments. However, it's the lobby—up one flight of stairs—that you must see: Richly carpeted, outfitted with fine furniture, and lavishly decorated (look at the ceiling murals), this room is one of the few remaining examples of the opulent elegance that was once de rigueur in Chicago's fine hotels. ⊠ *17 E. Monroe St.,* ☎ *312/726–7500.*

OFF THE
BEATEN PATH **PILSEN –** A formerly Bohemian neighborhood on the South Side is now home to many Mexican immigrants and a number of artists. Along 18th Street and elsewhere, murals show scenes from Mexican history, culture, and religion. The area is bordered by Halsted Street (800 W.) on the east and Damen Avenue (2000 W.) on the west and extends from 18th to 26th Street. The beautifully ornate **St. Michael's Italian Roman Catholic Church** (✉ 2325 W. 24th Pl., ☎ 773/847–2727) is a neighborhood institution. The **Mexican Fine Arts Center** (✉ 1852 W. 19th St., ☎ 312/738–1503) exhibits the work of contemporary Mexican artists Tuesday–Sunday 10–5. To get to Pilsen from the Loop, take I–290 south to Damen Avenue.

★ **⑰** **The Rookery.** Built partly of masonry and partly using the more modern steel-frame construction, this handsome building was designed by Burnham and Root in 1886 and restored in 1992. Its lobby, with a central court and surrounding office space off a second-floor walkway, was remodeled in 1905 by Frank Lloyd Wright. The 1992 renovation maintained his vision of airy marble and gold leaf, and the result is a marvelous lighthearted space that should not be missed. ✉ *209 S. LaSalle St.*

㉛ **Santa Fe Building.** Also known as the Railway Exchange Building, this structure was designed in 1904 by Daniel Burnham, who later had his office here. Its rooftop SANTA FE sign was put up early in the century by the Santa Fe Railroad, one of several railroads that had offices here when Chicago was the rail center of the country. The building was renovated in 1985, and the atrium lobby with its marble floor is glorious. The **Chicago Architecture Foundation (CAF) Shop,** on the ground floor, has an excellent selection of books on Chicago architecture as well as gifts. Tours of the Loop originate at the CAF Tour Center here. ✉ *224 S. Michigan Ave.,* ☎ *312/922–3432.*

★ **⑮** **Sears Tower.** The 110 stories of Skidmore, Owings & Merrill's bold design of 1974 gave Chicago the world's tallest building until the Petronas Towers in Kuala Lumpur, Malaysia, were completed in 1996. The steel frame is covered in black aluminum and bronze-tinted glass; the tower is built as nine framed tubes that narrow to just two. To take the ear-popping one-minute, 1,353-ft ride to the 103rd-floor **Skydeck,** enter on Jackson Boulevard. On a clear day you can see to Michigan, Wisconsin, and Indiana. (Check the visibility ratings at the security desk before you decide to ride up and take in the view.) Before you board the Skydeck elevator, enjoy the excellent photo exhibit on Chicago architecture. Back at ground level, don't miss the spiraling Calder mobile sculpture *The Universe* in the lobby on the Wacker Drive side. ✉ *233 S. Wacker Dr.,* ☎ *312/875–9696.* 🎫 *$8.* ☉ *Oct.–Feb., daily 9 AM–10 PM; Mar.–Sept., daily 9 AM–11 PM.*

⑬ **Social Security Building.** The Loop has pushed west of the Chicago River to the neighborhood surrounding this federal low-rise, one of several contemporary and renovated buildings in the area. Of particular interest in the building's plaza is Claes Oldenburg's pop-art sculpture **Batcolumn,** a gigantic baseball bat that failed to get critical acclaim when it was unveiled in 1977. Still, the 100-ft-high bat is an amusing sight. ✉ *600 W. Madison St.*

OFF THE
BEATEN PATH **ST. GABRIEL CHURCH –** Just south of the Irish Bridgeport neighborhood, St. Gabriel was designed more than 100 years ago by Daniel Burnham and John Root. The different elements form bold masses outside; the interior gives a feeling of breadth and spaciousness. Unlike many of Chicago's other neighborhoods, Bridgeport has remained the Irish com-

munity it was 100 years ago, despite expansionist pressures from Latin American Pilsen to the northwest and Chinatown to the northeast. The neighborhood has produced many of the city's mayors for decades, including the late Richard J. Daley and his son Richard M., the current mayor. Take I–94 south from the Loop (43rd St. exit). ✉ *4522 S. Wallace St.*, ☎ *773/268-9595.*

State Street. Known musically as "that great street," State Street wasn't so great after being turned into a pedestrian mall in 1979. City officials concluded the dreary mall failed principally because shoppers weren't able to drive there—though noisy buses lumbered through. As a result, by the end of 1996 the famous street was "de-malled," allowing auto traffic to return. Nine blocks, from Wacker Drive on the north to Congress Parkway on the south, were given a $24.5 million facelift that included widening the street and making sidewalks narrower, adding trees and shrubs, and installing old-fashioned streetlights with a 1920s look. The firm Skidmore, Owings & Merrill was in charge of the design.

❷ Stone Container Building. Some wags have said this shaft, with its diamond-shape sliced-off top, looks like a giant pencil sharpener. The painted aluminum sculpture in the plaza that looks like someone folded it is Yaacov Agam's *Communication X9.* ✉ *150 N. Michigan Ave.*

⑯ 311 S. Wacker Drive. The first of three towers intended for the site, this pale pink building was the work of Kohn Pedersen Fox, also designers of 333 West Wacker Drive. The 1991 building's most distinctive feature is its White Castle–type crown, blindingly lighted at night. During migration season so many birds crashed into the illuminated tower that the building management was forced to tone down the lighting. The building has an inviting atrium, with palm trees and a splashy, romantic fountain. Yvette Wintergarden, the restaurant just off the atrium, has live entertainment and dancing.

OFF THE
BEATEN PATH

333 W. Wacker Drive – For a look at a building roughly contemporary to the James R. Thompson Center (☞ *above*) that has had a much more positive public reception, head west on Randolph Street, turn right on LaSalle Street, left on Lake Street, and walk two blocks to Franklin Street to the green glass building at 333 West Wacker Drive. Walk through the building, exit at the north side, cross Wacker Drive, and look back to view its beautifully reflective curving exterior facing the river.

⑭ Union Station. A 10-story skylighted waiting room, Corinthian columns, and gilded statues grace a grand old station that was completed in 1925. Steep steps leading from Canal Street into the waiting area became the bumpy path for a baby carriage caught in a shootout in director Brian De Palma's 1987 film, *The Untouchables.* ✉ *210 S. Canal St.*

DOWNTOWN SOUTH

The Downtown South area, bounded by Congress Parkway–Eisenhower Expressway on the north, Michigan Avenue on the east, Roosevelt Road on the south, and the Chicago River on the west, presents a striking and often fascinating contrast to the Loop. Once a thriving commercial area and the center of the printing trades in Chicago, it fell into disrepair as the printing industry moved to other areas in the city because of changing needs for space. Sleazy bars, pawnbrokers, and pornographic shops filled the area behind what was then the Conrad Hilton Hotel, crowding each other on Wabash Avenue and State Street and on the side streets between.

HISTORIC PULLMAN

CONCEIVED AND CONSTRUCTED by railroad entrepreneur George Mortimer Pullman, a cabinetmaker who made a fortune developing the first modern railway sleeping and dining cars, the community that bore his name was the nation's first large-scale industrial town. Its founder clearly understood the idea of enlightened self-interest: Desirable surroundings, he believed, would attract the best workers; keeping them healthy and happy would mean higher productivity for his Pullman Palace Car Company.

Built between 1880 and 1885 on 3,000 acres surrounding the Illinois Central Railroad near Lake Calumet, Pullman thrived for 14 years as a company town. Home to about 12,000 at its peak, George Pullman's industrial utopia featured shops, parks, churches, its own hospital and bank, and many cultural and recreational facilities. His European-style retail arcade, a social as well as shopping center, was a model for the malls of the coming century.

Contained between 111th and 115th streets and Cottage Grove and Langley avenues, the tiny, tidy enclave (which once received a "World's Most Perfect Town" award) was designed to include architecturally varied rowhouses for workers, more spacious homes for middle managers, and individualized mansions for executives.

Nearly all the original buildings, now privately owned, remain. Many have been lovingly restored with accents in the "Pullman colors" of maroon and green. Its unique architectural continuity imbues this stately oasis with a haunting visual harmony in an undistinguished industrial desert. Present-day explorers can admire the carved wooden horse heads set into the facade of the Pullman stables (⊠ 11201 S. Cottage Grove), the serpentine-stone gargoyles of the Greenstone Church (⊠ 11211 S. St. Lawrence), and the 120-ft central clock tower (⊠ 11011 S. Cottage Grove) as they stroll back in time to the days when railroads ruled.

Pullman prospered until the depression of 1893–94, when financial pressures caused the boss to cut wages and hours but not rents. The result was the Pullman Strike, one of the most famous labor clashes in Chicago's history. It was a riotous, ultimately violent confrontation that left several strikers dead.

Pullman the man died in 1897. Soon after, the nonindustrial parts of his urban dream were sold off by court order. Pullman the town—which had been annexed to Chicago in 1890—became just another city neighborhood.

In 1960 loyal locals, many descended from the people who once worked at George Pullman's long-defunct factory, fought a plan to turn their Far South Side world-within-a-world into an industrial park. They succeeded instead in getting their unique hometown designated a city, state, and national historic landmark.

The Historic Pullman Foundation, headquartered at 11111 S. Forrestville Avenue, operates a visitor center and museum and sponsors year-round tours, events, and a lecture series. Special guided walking tours are available at 12:30 and 1:30 PM on the first Sunday of each month between May and October from 11141 S. Cottage Grove Avenue. For information, call 773/785–8181.

To get to Pullman, take I–94 south from the Loop to 111th Street, or the Metra train south from Randolph Street to the 11th Street stop.

Then, about two decades ago, investors became interested in renovating the run-down yet sturdy loft and office buildings in the old printing district. In 1981 Michael Foley, a young restaurateur from an old Chicago restaurant family, opened a restaurant on the edge of the redevelopment area. The innovative cuisine at Printer's Row (☞ Greater Downtown *in* Chapter 3) proved a success. Soon other restaurants, shops, and businesses moved in, and today the Printer's Row district is a thriving urban neighborhood enclave. In late May or early June the area attracts large crowds during the Printer's Row Book Fair (☞ Festivals and Seasonal Events *in* Chapter 1), a weekend event. Dealers sell books and prints, craftspeople give demonstrations of papermaking and bookbinding, and noted authors appear as guest speakers.

At about the time that the first renovations were being undertaken in Printer's Row, a consortium of investors, aided by preferential interest rates from downtown banks, obtained a large parcel of land in the old railroad yards to the south and put up an expansive new development. This was Dearborn Park, affordable housing targeted at young middle-class families.

To the west, the architect and developer Bertrand Goldberg (of Marina City fame) acquired a sizable tract of land between Wells Street and the Chicago River. Driven by a vision of an innovative, self-contained city within a city, Goldberg erected the futuristic River City, the massed, almost cloudlike complex that seems to rise from the river at Polk Street.

Spurred by signs of revitalization, the owners of the Conrad Hilton scrapped plans to abandon and even demolish the hotel and instead mounted a major renovation. Now one of the most beautifully appointed hotels in the city, the Chicago Hilton and Towers once again attracts the convention business it needs to fill its thousands of rooms.

There are still gritty, undeveloped areas in Downtown South. But the entire area near South Side, as far south as 26th Street, is attracting more and more residents who like its ethnic and racial mix, its proximity to the Loop and great museums (the Field Museum, Adler Planetarium, and Shedd Aquarium), and its growing community feeling.

Numbers in the text correspond to numbers in the margin and on the Downtown South map.

A Good Walk

Start at the corner of Balbo Drive and Michigan Avenue. You can drive to this point—traffic and parking conditions are far less congested in the Downtown South area than they are in the Loop—or you can take the Jeffery Express Bus 6 from the north (catch it at State and Lake streets) or from Hyde Park.

East of the intersection of Balbo Drive and Michigan Avenue is the heart of beautiful **Grant Park** ①, a lovely mix of gardens, tennis courts, and softball diamonds. From the park you can see what appears as a cliff of buildings, old and new, lining Michigan Avenue. The **Blackstone Hotel** ②, on the northwest corner of Michigan Avenue and Balbo Drive, is rich with nearly a century of history and atmosphere. Next door is the Merle Reskin Theatre, another vintage building, where Broadway-bound shows were once booked. The theater is now owned and run by DePaul University. Head north on Michigan Avenue to the small **Spertus Museum of Judaica** ③, with a permanent collection of Jewish art, a Holocaust memorial, themed temporary exhibits, and a hands-on children's museum.

Continue to the corner of Harrison Street, turn left, and walk four blocks to Dearborn Street. The pioneering Printer's Row restaurant (☞ Chapter 3), on the northwest corner of Dearborn and Harrison streets, is a wonderful place for an elegant (but not inexpensive) lunch during the week. North on Dearborn is the **Pontiac Building** ④, an early skyscraper from 1891. Just beyond, the **Hyatt on Printer's Row** ⑤ occupies a group of interconnected renovated buildings; on the corner is the excellent Prairie restaurant. Turn left and walk west to Federal Street and turn left again. To your right one block south is a massive, renovated, beige-gray brick apartment complex, **Printer's Square** ⑥.

Continue south, turn west on Polk, and walk four blocks to Wells Street. This area is quite desolate, so be cautious. Turn left at Wells Street and continue to the entrance to **River City** ⑦. Apartments, all with curving exterior walls (making it a bit difficult to place square or rectangular furniture), ring the circumference of the building.

Retrace your steps on Polk Street, heading east to Dearborn Street. You'll walk up the west side of this peaceful, tree-lined street to the end of the block and return on the east side. To see these century-old buildings, now with new uses, gives a comforting sense that the past can be creatively linked with the present. The first building on your left is the grand old **Franklin Building** ⑧, originally THE FRANKLIN CO.: DESIGNING, ENGRAVING, ELECTROTYPING, as its sign said, and now condominium apartments. Next door, **Sandmeyer's Bookstore** has a fine selection of books about Chicago.

Across the street is the rehabbed brick building **Grace Place** ⑨, creatively adapted for use by four religious congregations. The **Donohue Building** ⑩ down the block, another handsome commercial structure, now houses condominiums.

In the historic **Dearborn Station** ⑪, at the foot of Dearborn Street, shops, offices, and an airy galleria have replaced the waiting room. From the station walk east, turn right on Plymouth Court, and look south, where you can see **Dearborn Park** ⑫, a mix of high-rise, low-rise, and single-family units, some in redbrick and some in white.

Walk down Plymouth Court to 9th Street and turn left. Continue walking two blocks to Wabash Avenue and turn left again. At the corner of 8th Street and Wabash Avenue is the club of blues great Buddy Guy, the aptly named Buddy Guy's Legends; seven nights a week you can hear Chicago's signature sound (☞ Nightlife *in* Chapter 5). Walk east on 8th Street across Wabash Avenue to the **Chicago Hilton and Towers** ⑬, one of the city's grandest hotels. Enter by the revolving doors, head a bit to your right and then straight, and stroll through the opulent lobby, complete with gilded horses flanking the inner walls of the Michigan Avenue entrance.

TIMING

Allow about four hours to complete the walk. You could spend 45 minutes or more in the Spertus Museum, especially if you have children, who will love the ARTIFACT Center (open in the afternoon only). The area west of South Michigan Avenue tends to empty out on weekends and especially in the evenings, so it's best to visit during the daytime on weekdays. Be sure to exercise caution, as you would in any big city.

Sights to See

OFF THE BEATEN PATH **AMERICAN POLICE CENTER AND MUSEUM** – Exhibits about police work and relationships between the police and the public fill a small museum a few blocks south of Downtown South. Safety, crime and punishment, and drugs and alcohol are among the subjects; an electric chair and

32

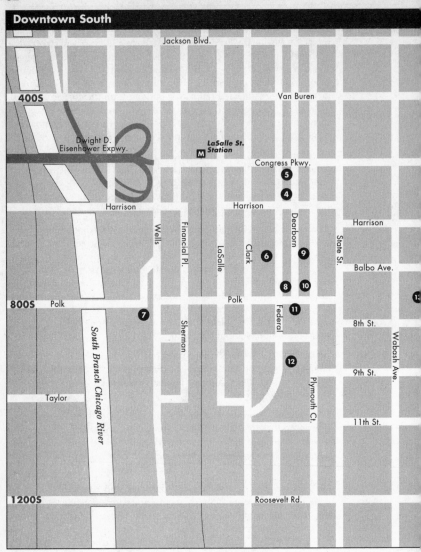

Blackstone Hotel, **2**
Chicago Hilton and Towers, **13**
Dearborn Park, **12**
Dearborn Station, **11**
Donohue Building, **10**
Franklin Building, **8**
Grace Place, **9**
Grant Park, **1**

Hyatt on Printer's Row, **5**
Pontiac Building, **4**
Printer's Square, **6**
River City, **7**
Spertus Museum of Judaica, **3**

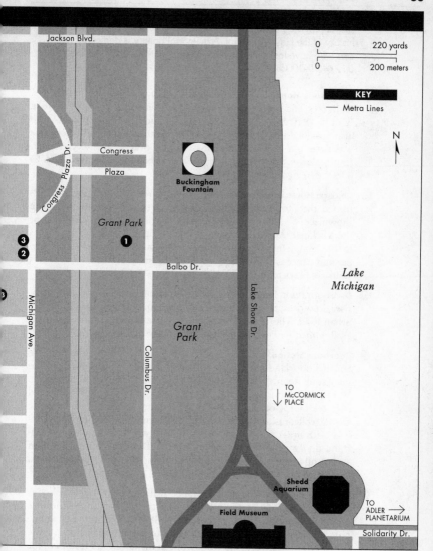

some crime photographs provide a few grisly touches. One exhibit shows how the police communication system works; another details the history of the Haymarket Riot. A memorial gallery is dedicated to officers who have lost their lives in the line of duty. ⊠ *1717 S. State St.,* ☎ *312/431-0005.* 🖂 *$4.* ☉ *Weekdays 9:30–4:30.*

② **Blackstone Hotel.** The intimate lobby still has impressive chandeliers, sculptures, and handsome woodwork that convey the feeling of the past. Built in 1910 and designed by Marshall and Fox, the architects who also designed the Drake Hotel on Michigan Avenue, the Blackstone was once one of Chicago's most elegant hotels. Teddy Roosevelt, Jimmy Carter, and a string of presidents in between all stayed here. ⊠ *636 S. Michigan Ave.*

⑬ **Chicago Hilton and Towers.** A $150 million renovation in the mid-'80s turned the 70-year-old Hilton, originally the Stevens Hotel, into a showplace. The Grand Ballroom, at the top of a sweeping stairway near the Michigan Avenue entrance, is one of the most spectacular rooms in the city. On opening night at the Lyric Opera, when a midnight supper and dance is held here, a brass quintet stationed at the top of this stairway plays fanfares as the guests arrive. ⊠ *720 S. Michigan Ave.*

⑫ **Dearborn Park.** Begun in the '70s, this planned neighborhood of high-rises, low-rises, town houses, and single-family homes has a tidy suburban look. The 1,800 housing units make it a key residential area. ⊠ *Bounded by Polk, 15th, State, and Clark Sts.*

⑪ **Dearborn Station.** Chicago's oldest standing passenger train station, a South Loop landmark, now serves as a galleria. Designed in Romanesque Revival style in 1885 by the New York architect Cyrus L. W. Eidlitz, it has a wonderful tall clock tower and a red-sandstone and redbrick facade ornamented with terra-cotta. Striking features inside are the white, rust, and jade marble floor, a handsome wraparound walkway with brass railings and attractive grillwork, and arching woodframe doorways. Since its opening in 1985, Dearborn Station has been successful in attracting office tenants but less so in attracting retailers. ⊠ *47 W. Polk St.* ☉ *Daily 7 AM–9 PM.*

⑩ **Donohue Building.** The main entrance is flanked by marble columns topped by ornately carved capitals, with tile work over the entrance set into a splendid granite arch. Built in 1883, the renovated Donohue now houses condominium lofts instead of a printing business. Note the beautiful ironwork and woodwork in the doors and frames of the first-floor retail establishments. ⊠ *711 S. Dearborn St.*

NEED A BREAK?   The **Moonraker Restaurant and Tavern** (⊠ 733 S. Dearborn St., ☎ 312/922-2019) offers outdoor seating, although its cool interior may be as welcome as a cool drink after a tramp through the city streets.

⑧ **Franklin Building.** Built in 1888 and initially the home of the Franklin Company, a printing concern, this condominium building has intricate decoration. The tile work on the facade leads up to *The First Impression*—a medieval scene illustrating the first application of the printer's craft. Above the entryway is a motto: THE EXCELLENCE OF EVERY ART MUST CONSIST IN THE COMPLETE ACCOMPLISHMENT OF ITS PURPOSE. ⊠ *720 S. Dearborn St.*

⑨ **Grace Place.** Grace Episcopal Church of Chicago, which owns this building, shares facilities with Christ the King Lutheran Church, a congregation of the Christian Reformed Church, and Makom Shalom/The Community. This former commercial building has a parish hall on the first floor and a modest sanctuary on the second. ⊠ *637 S. Dearborn St.*

★ ❶ Grant Park. Lake Michigan to the east and a spectacular skyline to the west create a uniquely lovely setting for this popular park. Here you'll find two of Chicago's greatest treasures—the Art Institute and Buckingham Fountain (☞ The Loop, *above*). This is also where the Chicago Bulls thanked fans during huge rallies after winning the NBA Championship six times—in 1991, 1992, 1993, 1996, 1997, and 1998. Grant Park is home to several blockbuster events: the Grant Park Society Concerts, held four times a week in the summer; notable blues, jazz, and gospel festivals; and the annual Taste of Chicago, a vast picnic featuring foods from more than 70 restaurants that precedes a fireworks show around the Fourth of July (☞ Festivals and Seasonal Events *in* Chapter 1). Outdoor concerts are held in a field surrounding the Petrillo Band Shell, at Columbus Drive and Monroe Street.

Grant Park has been the site of violence, too. On a hot summer night during the last week of August 1968, the park was filled with people protesting the Vietnam War and the Democratic presidential convention that was taking place at the Conrad Hilton Hotel down the street. Rioting broke out; heads were cracked, protesters were dragged away screaming, and Mayor Richard J. Daley gave police the order to "shoot to kill." Later investigations into the events of that evening determined that a "police riot"—not the misbehavior of the protesters, who had been noisy but not physically abusive—was responsible for the violence that erupted. Those who remember those rage-filled days cannot visit this idyllic spot without recalling that time. ✉ *Bounded by lakefront, Randolph St., Roosevelt Rd., and Michigan Ave.*

OFF THE BEATEN PATH **HULL HOUSE MUSEUM** – In redbrick, Victorian Hull House, Jane Addams and Ellen Gates Starr started the American settlement movement in 1889 and wrought social work miracles. The neighborhood was then a slum for new immigrants; the immediate area was demolished in 1963 to make way for the University of Illinois at Chicago. The house museum and residents' dining hall, now affiliated with the university's School of Social Work, have moving displays about the immigrant experience and the settlement's work. ✉ *800 S. Halsted St.,* ☎ *312/413-5353.* ✉ *Free.* ☉ *Weekdays 10–4, Sun. noon–5.*

❺ Hyatt on Printer's Row. This sleek hotel is housed in not one but three adjoining buildings, two of them built during the late 19th century. The hotel's entrance is in the 1896 Morton Building; north of that is the simpler redbrick Duplicator Building, which dates to 1886. The two are connected to a third and newer building, which also houses the Prairie restaurant (☞ Greater Downtown *in* Chapter 3). ✉ *500 S. Dearborn St.*

❹ Pontiac Building. An early Chicago School skyscraper, the 14-story Pontiac was designed by Holabird and Roche in 1891 and is their oldest existing building in Chicago. Booth/Hansen and Associates renovated it for office use in 1985. ✉ *542 S. Dearborn St.*

OFF THE BEATEN PATH **PRAIRIE AVENUE HISTORIC DISTRICT** – Several blocks south of Downtown South, two important historic homes and a beautiful church recall a vanished era. In the area around Prairie Avenue were the homes of many prominent merchants and manufacturers from the 1870s to the turn of the century. Later, houses of vice and the laying of train tracks led these residents to leave. The Greek Revival **Clarke House** (✉ 1800 S. Prairie Ave., ☎ 312/326–1480) dates from 1836, making it Chicago's oldest surviving building. Tours are conducted Wednesday through Sunday at noon, 1, and 2. Dating from 1886, the Romanesque Revival **Glessner House** (✉ 1800 S. Prairie Ave., ☎ 312/326–1480) is the only surviving building in Chicago by architect H. H. Richardson. Tours take place Wednesday through Sunday at 1, 2, and 3. Admission for each house is $5, or $8 for both. To get to the Prairie Avenue Historic District, drive south on Michigan Avenue or take Bus 1, 2, or 3. A block south and west of the Prairie Avenue Historic District is the handsome Victorian **Second Presbyterian Church** (⊠ 1936 S. Michigan Ave., ☎ 312/225–4951; 312/922–4533 for tours), originally designed by noted New York architect James Renwick. The 1874 church has seven Tiffany stained-glass windows. Services are held Sunday at 11.

❻ **Printer's Square.** Older manufacturing buildings designed in 1909, 1912, and 1928 were joined to create a huge apartment complex with 356 units. ⊠ 640–780 S. Federal St.

❼ **River City.** This curving complex of 446 apartments, built in 1986 by Marina City architect Bertrand Goldberg, has great views of beautiful boats from the expansive lobby. Interior spaces are used for shops, walkways, a health club, and tenant storage closets. The marina has 62 moorings; boats can remain year-round because the water is aerated to keep it from freezing. Tenants can walk to the Loop or take a shuttle and also enjoy a 1-acre rooftop park off the building's fifth floor. If you'd like to take a tour, ask the attendant at the front desk. ⊠ 800 S. Wells St.

Sandmeyer's Bookstore. This intimate store, with wooden floor and exposed brick walls, is a fine place to find books on Chicago history and architecture, travel books, and children's literature. The unusual iron stairway leading to the entrance is set with glass bricks. ⊠ 714 S. Dearborn St., ☎ 312/922–2104. ☉ Mon.–Wed. and Fri. 11–6:30, Thurs. 11–8, Sat. 11–5, Sun. noon–5.

🌡 ❽ **Spertus Museum of Judaica.** Of special interest in this museum, in the Spertus Institute of Jewish Studies, are many ritual objects from Jewish life and a poignant Holocaust memorial with many photos and a tattered concentration camp uniform. A hands-on children's museum called the **ARTIFACT Center** has a simulated archaeological dig. The museum mounts exhibitions on topics related to Judaism. ⊠ 618 S. Michigan Ave., ☎ 312/322–1747. ☒ $5, free Fri. ☉ Sun.–Thurs. 10–5, Fri. 10–3; children's museum Sun.–Thurs. 1–4:30.

OFF THE **UNIVERSITY OF ILLINOIS AT CHICAGO** – A few blocks west of Downtown
BEATEN PATH South's western edge is one of Chicago's major universities. Designed by Walter Netsch of Skidmore, Owings & Merrill beginning in 1965, the buildings seem to surge and weave toward one another. ⊠ 1200 W. Harrison St., ☎ 312/996–7000.

HYDE PARK AND KENWOOD

Although farmers and other settlers lived in Hyde Park in the early 1800s and Chicago's oldest Jewish congregation was founded here in 1847, the growth and development of this South Side neighborhood really got under way as a result of two events: the opening of the University of Chicago in 1892 and the World's Columbian Exposition of 1893. The Columbian Exposition, whose influence on American public architecture was far-reaching, brought about the creation of the Midway Plaisance and the construction of numerous classical-revival-style buildings, of which the Museum of Science and Industry is the most famous survivor. The Midway Plaisance, surrounding the heart of the 1893 fair, still runs along the southern edge of the University of Chicago's original campus. Another legacy from the exposition was the civic moniker "Windy City," used by *New York Sun* editor Charles Dana to ridicule Chicago's bid to host the exposition.

In the 1890s the university embarked on a program to build housing for its faculty members, and the mansions that line Woodlawn Avenue are the result. Then the neighborhood began to attract well-to-do private individuals who commissioned noted architects to construct homes suitable to persons of great wealth. Many of their houses still stand in Kenwood.

With the coming of the depression, followed by World War II, the neighborhood entered a period of decline. Grand homes fell into disrepair, and wartime housing shortages led to the conversion of stately houses into multifamily dwellings. Alarmed by the decline of the neighborhood, concerned citizens formed the Hyde Park–Kenwood Community Conference in 1949. Aided by $29 million from the University of Chicago, which was anxious that it might not be able to retain—never mind recruit—faculty members, this group set about restoring the neighborhood. Prizes were offered to those who would buy and "deconvert" rooming houses, and the city was pressured to enforce the zoning laws.

The effort that was to have the most lasting effect on the neighborhood was urban renewal; Hyde Park–Kenwood was the site of one of the first such undertakings in the nation. Beginning in the late 1950s, 55th Street from Lake Park Avenue to Cottage Grove Avenue was razed, with the backing and support of the University of Chicago. Most of the buildings on Lake Park Avenue and on many streets abutting 55th Street and Lake Park Avenue were torn down as well. With them went the workshops of painters and artisans; the quarters of "little magazines" (some 20 chapters of James Joyce's *Ulysses* were first published at one of them); the Compass Theatre, where Mike Nichols and Elaine May got their start; the Second City comedy club (since relocated to the Old Town area); and more than 40 bars where jazz and blues could be heard nightly. In their place came town houses designed by I. M. Pei and Harry Weese and a shopping mall designed by Keck and Keck. Cynics have described the process as one of "blacks and whites together, shoulder to shoulder—against the poor."

In the end, these efforts were successful beyond the wildest imaginings of their sponsors, though more than 20 years elapsed before the neighborhood regained its luster. But now Hyde Park and the south part of Kenwood are surrounded by areas that are much less prosperous and at times dangerous. Yet Hyde Park continues to be appealing to many because of the University of Chicago's presence, the diversity of its residents, and the proximity to Loop and lake, not to mention the beauty of its many tree-lined streets.

Numbers in the text correspond to numbers in the margin and on the Hyde Park and Kenwood map.

A Good Walk and Drive

This walk will take you from one of the city's greatest museums, on the lakefront, west and north into the main shopping area of Hyde Park, and then south to the heart of the University of Chicago's campus. If you're arriving by car, take Lake Shore Drive south to the 57th Street exit and turn left into the parking lot of the Museum of Science and Industry. You can also take the Illinois Central (IC) Railroad train from Randolph Street and Michigan Avenue; get off at the 55th Street stop and walk east through the underpass two blocks, then south two blocks. Either way, you are at the **Museum of Science and Industry** ①, a huge hands-on museum where adventures range from a visit to a U-505 submarine to a descent into a simulated coal mine.

Exiting the museum, cross 56th Street and head east to South Shore Drive to see some of the area's architectural history. Just north of 56th Street, on the west side of the street, are the **Promontory Apartments** ②, the first high-rise Mies van der Rohe built in Chicago. Backtrack to 56th Street and head west a few blocks to **Windermere House** ③, a huge apartment building that was originally an elegant hotel. Continuing west on 56th, go under the viaduct and then north on Lake Park Avenue. Halfway up the block, you'll pass the **Hyde Park Historical Society** ④, headquartered in a former cable-car terminus.

Walk north on Lake Park and west on 55th Street to one of the happier results of urban renewal, **1400–1451 E. 55th Street** ⑤, twin apartment buildings designed by I. M. Pei. Turn right and head up Blackstone Avenue, passing a variety of housing between 55th and 51st streets. These now-expensive houses were originally cottages for workers, conveniently located near the cable-car line that ran west on 55th Street. Continue north on Blackstone Avenue to 53rd Street, Hyde Park's main shopping strip. Across the street and a half block east is **Harper Court** ⑥, a small, inviting shopping center with some unique shops.

Leaving the north exit of Harper Court, on 52nd Street, go west four blocks (the street dead-ends, but there's a pedestrian walkway between Kimbark and Kenwood avenues to let you through) to Woodlawn Avenue and turn right. The yellow brick **Heller House** ⑦, No. 5132, was built by Frank Lloyd Wright in 1897. Proceed south on Woodlawn Avenue to 55th Street. Walk east, then north on Kimbark Avenue to the markedly untraditional **St. Thomas the Apostle Church** ⑧, designed by an apprentice of Wright's.

Go back to 55th Street, the northern edge of the University of Chicago campus, and continue west to University Avenue and the **Lutheran School of Theology** ⑨, a massive structure that seems almost to float from its foundation. Across the street at 5514 South University is Pierce Hall, a student dormitory designed by Harry Weese.

Head south on University Avenue and turn right onto 56th Street. Walk one block to Greenwood Avenue and the small but beautiful **David and Alfred Smart Museum of Art** ⑩, with an eclectic permanent collection ranging from classical Greek vases to contemporary paintings by Chicago imagist Roger Brown. Continue west on 56th Street to Ellis Avenue and the **Court Theatre** ⑪, home of a professional repertory company. A flag flies atop the theater when a show is on.

Walk south on Ellis Avenue about half a block beyond 56th Street; on your left is the Henry Moore sculpture **Nuclear Energy** ⑫, commemorating the first controlled nuclear chain reaction. Continue south on Ellis Avenue to 57th Street and walk three blocks west, crossing Cottage Grove Avenue, to the east side of Washington Park and the **DuSable Museum of African American History** ⑬, with its exhibits on history, art, and culture.

Backtrack on 57th Street to Ellis Avenue and turn right. Just across 57th Street, set into the small quadrangle on your right, is the **John Crerar Science Library** ⑭, with scientific and technical books. Farther down the block, the **University of Chicago Bookstore** ⑮ stocks everything from scholarly books to university souvenirs. On the plaza just south of the bookstore is *Grande Disco,* a bronze sculpture by Arnaldo Pomodoro that looks like a gigantic compact disc exploding at its center.

Directly across from the bookstore, on the east side of Ellis Avenue, is the University of Chicago Administration Building. Just south of it is **Cobb Hall** ⑯, the oldest building on campus and home of the Renaissance Society, an organization that celebrates modern art. Between the Administration Building and Cobb Hall, a small passageway leads to the quadrangle of the university—a classic college campus, green and grassy, with imposing neo-Gothic buildings. Tucked into the southwest corner between two other buildings is **Bond Chapel** ⑰.

From the chapel cross the quadrangle, heading to the circular drive, and then follow the path that leads north from the drive. You will pass a reflecting pool (Botany Pond) before you exit through Gothic Cobb Gate, elaborately decorated with grotesque figures that appear to be chasing each other up to the pinnacle. Directly ahead is the modern **Joseph Regenstein Library** ⑱, seemingly framed in the gate. The first floor of the "Reg" is open to the public during the day.

Head east on 57th Street to University Avenue. In the massive building on the southwest corner is **Mandel Hall** ⑲, a gem of a concert hall; peek in if you can. Before leaving, have a look at Hutchinson Commons, opposite the building's main entrance. The design of this lofty space—a university cafeteria with portraits of university presidents—was based on Oxford's Christ Church Hall.

Continue east on 57th Street one block to Woodlawn Avenue. On the northwest corner is the **First Unitarian Church** ⑳, whose graceful spire is visible throughout the area. Turn right on Woodlawn Avenue and head south, noting the stately brick mansions that line both sides of the street. To the north, the building at 5605 is on the National Register of Historic Places. Many of the buildings were erected by the University of Chicago in the 1890s to provide housing for professors. Professors continue to live in several of them; others have been repurchased by the university for institutional use. Continue south on Woodlawn Avenue to Frank Lloyd Wright's **Robie House** ㉑, considered one of the most striking domestic designs in the nation.

Cross Woodlawn Avenue and continue west one block to the **Chicago Theological Seminary** ㉒. Inside are two chapels and the broadly stocked Seminary Cooperative Bookstore. Across 58th Street, the **Oriental Institute** ㉓ has a museum focusing on the history, art, and archaeology of the ancient Near East. Go down University Avenue one block to 59th Street. To your left, set back handsomely on a grassy expanse, is **Rockefeller Memorial Chapel** ㉔, an accomplished example of the Gothic Revival style.

Continue south again, crossing 59th Street and entering the wide, grassy **Midway Plaisance** ㉕. At its west end, just beyond Cottage Grove Avenue, you can see Lorado Taft's masterful sculpture **Fountain of Time** ㉖; be sure to walk all around it. On Cottage Grove Avenue, head south to 60th Street and turn left, heading east. At 60th Street and Ingleside Avenue is **Midway Studios** ㉗, Taft's former workplace. One block east on 60th Street at No. 969 is the School of Social Service Administration, an undistinguished example of the work of Mies van der Rohe. On 60th Street between Ellis and University avenues is the Laird Bell Law Quadrangle. This attractive building, with fountains playing in front, is the work of Finnish architect Eero Saarinen. Two blocks farther east, between Kimbark and Kenwood avenues at No. 1307, is the New Graduate Residence Hall. This poured-concrete structure, elaborately ornamented, is reminiscent of the American embassy in New Delhi, India—architect Edward Durrell Stone designed both.

Hyde Park and Kenwood

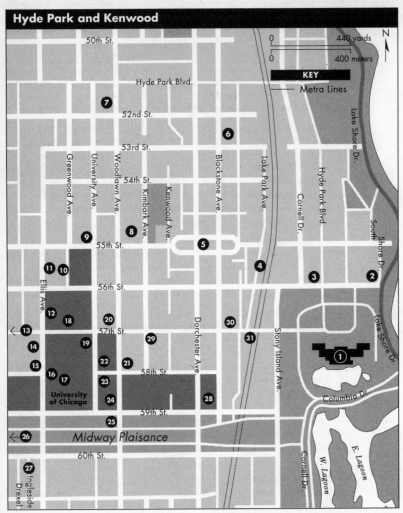

KEY

— Metra Lines

Bond Chapel, **17**

Chicago Theological Seminary, **22**

Cobb Hall, **16**

Court Theatre, **11**

David and Alfred Smart Museum of Art, **10**

DuSable Museum of African American History, **13**

57th Street Books, **29**

First Unitarian Church, **20**

Fountain of Time, **26**

1400–1451 East 55th Street, **5**

Harper Court, **6**

Heller House, **7**

Hyde Park Historical Society, **4**

International House, **28**

John Crerar Science Library, **14**

Joseph Regenstein Library, **18**

Lutheran School of Theology, **9**

Mandel Hall, **19**

Midway Plaisance, **25**

Midway Studios, **27**

Museum of Science and Industry, **1**

Nuclear Energy, **12**

O'Gara & Wilson Book Shop Ltd., **30**

Oriental Institute, **23**

Powell's Bookstore, **31**

Promontory Apartments, **2**

Robie House, **21**

Rockefeller Memorial Chapel, **24**

St. Thomas the Apostle Church, **8**

University of Chicago Bookstore, **15**

Windermere House, **3**

At Dorchester Avenue, cross the Midway again to 59th Street. On your right, just past Dorchester Avenue, is **International House** ㉘, where many foreign students live during their tenure at the university. Turn left on 59th Street and head west to Woodlawn Avenue, then north two blocks to 57th Street, where you can visit some of the area's fine bookstores. One block east is **57th Street Books** ㉙, which carries current books of general interest. On 57th Street, spanning the block between Kimbark and Kenwood avenues, is the Ray School complex. One of the best public elementary schools in the city, Ray hosts the annual Hyde Park Art Fair, one of the oldest (since 1947) annual outdoor art fairs in the country.

Continue east on 57th Street to Dorchester Avenue; on your right, at 5704 S. Dorchester Avenue, is an Italian-style villa constructed before the Chicago Fire of 1871. The two houses at 5642 and 5607 S. Dorchester Avenue also predate the fire.

Just past Blackstone Avenue, a block farther east, is **O'Gara & Wilson Book Shop Ltd.** ㉚, with used and out-of-print books. On the next corner as you go east, **Powell's Bookstore** ㉛ also has an exceptional selection of used books, with an emphasis on scholarly titles.

To get back to the museum and our starting point, continue east on 57th Street, go under the viaduct, and cross Stony Island Avenue. The museum will be in front of you, and to the right will be the lagoons of Jackson Park.

TIMING

You'll need to break your visit into parts. Distances between some sights are quite long, particularly around the Midway Plaisance. Consider doing the early part of the route by car, parking in the heart of the campus, and retrieving your car to see sights around the Midway. Remember to exercise big-city caution here.

Especially if you have children, you may want to spend at least a half day at the Museum of Science and Industry. Go during the week to avoid weekend crowds (Thursday is free, so it can be busy, too). A visit to the University of Chicago buildings is most rewarding on weekdays, when the campus is lively with student activity. However, the university offers an architectural walking tour on Saturday at 10; call 773/ 702–8374.

Sights to See

OFF THE
BEATEN PATH
BALZEKAS MUSEUM OF LITHUANIAN CULTURE – The small, little-known Balzekas Museum, a half-hour drive southwest of Hyde Park, will give you a taste of 1,000 years of Lithuanian history and culture on its three floors. There are exhibits on rural Lithuania; concentration camps; rare maps, stamps, and coins; textiles; and amber. The library can be used for research. ⊠ *6500 S. Pulaski Rd.,* ☎ *773/582–6500.* ☞ *$4, free Mon.* ☉ *Daily 10–4.*

⑰ **Bond Chapel.** The fanciful gargoyles outside this Gothic-style chapel belie the simple interior of dark wood, stained glass, and delicate ornamentation. The effect is one of intimacy and warmth. ⊠ *1025 E. 58th St.*

㉒ **Chicago Theological Seminary.** Of special interest for book lovers visiting this nondenominational seminary is the Seminary Cooperative Bookstore in the basement, so jam-packed with books (and, on the weekends, with people) that it's almost claustrophobic. On the second floor you can see the Reneker organ, a handcrafted replica of an 18th-century organ, in the Graham Taylor Chapel. Also worth visiting is the tiny Thorndike Hilton Memorial Chapel on the first floor. ⊠ *5757*

S. University Ave., ☏ *773/752–4381.* ⊙ *Bookstore weekdays 8:30 AM–9 PM, Sat. 10–6, Sun. noon–6; seminary grounds weekdays 8:30–4:30.*

⑯ Cobb Hall. The oldest structure (completed in 1892) on the University of Chicago campus houses classrooms, offices, and the Renaissance Society, which was founded in 1915 to identify living artists whose work would be of lasting significance and influence. It was among the first hosts of works by Matisse, Picasso, Braque, Brancusi, and Miró. Go to the Bergman Gallery on the fourth floor to see what the next generation of great art may look like. ⊠ *5811 S. Ellis Ave.,* ☏ *773/702–8670 for gallery.* 🎫 *Free.* ⊙ *Tues.–Fri. 10–5, weekends noon–5.*

⑪ Court Theatre. One of the city's finest professional theater companies is based here; the building was designed by Harry Weese and Associates in 1981. It's an intimate theater with unobstructed sight lines from every seat in the house. ⊠ *5535 S. Ellis Ave.,* ☏ *773/753–4472.*

⑩ David and Alfred Smart Museum of Art. Housing the fine-arts collection of the University of Chicago, the museum was founded in 1974 with a gift from the Smart Family Foundation, whose members David and Alfred founded *Esquire* magazine. The diverse 8,000-piece permanent collection includes works by old masters; photographs by Walker Evans; furniture by Frank Lloyd Wright; sculptures by Degas, Matisse, Rodin, and Henry Moore; ancient Chinese bronzes; and modern Japanese ceramics. There's also an adjacent sculpture garden. ⊠ *5550 S. Greenwood Ave.,* ☏ *773/702–0200.* 🎫 *Free.* ⊙ *Tues.–Wed. and Fri. 10–4, Thurs. 10–9, weekends noon–6.*

⑬ DuSable Museum of African American History. The DuSable opened in 1961 as a collection of art and objects relating to the black experience. It was named for trader Jean Baptiste Pointe du Sable, a black man who was Chicago's first permanent non–Native American resident. Among intriguing permanent exhibits is one on slavery; the poignant, disturbing artifacts include rusted shackles used on slave ships. Special exhibits change frequently; a recent one focused on the 50-year career of Duke Ellington. The museum also has a cinema series, jazz and blues concerts, lectures and symposiums, and children's programs. Its 1910 building, designed by Daniel Burnham and Company, has a lovely setting in Washington Park. ⊠ *740 E. 56th Pl.,* ☏ *773/947–0600.* 🎫 *$3, free Thurs.* ⊙ *Mon.–Sat. 10–4, Sun. noon–4.*

☕ ㉙ 57th Street Books. Copies of the *New York Times Book Review* and the *New York Review of Books* are always on a table toward the rear, next to the coffeepot, at this cooperatively owned general bookstore that is a Hyde Park institution. An extensive children's section has its own room, where reading aloud to youngsters is encouraged. On weekends and evenings the store has programs with authors. ⊠ *1301 E. 57th St.,* ☏ *773/684–1300.* ⊙ *Mon.–Sat. 10–10, Sun. 10–8.*

NEED A BREAK?	You'll find several spots on 57th Street where you can get a quick bite and rest your feet. **Medici Pan Pizza** (⊠ 1327 E. 57th St., ☏ 773/667-7394) has sandwiches and snacks as well as pizza. *Chicago* magazine voted **Edwardo's Natural Pizza** (⊠ 1321 E. 57th St., ☏ 773/241-7960) the best deep dish pie in the city in July 1998.

⑳ First Unitarian Church. The Gothic design of the church blends successfully with campus buildings. It was built in 1931 and contains the Hull Memorial Chapel. ⊠ *5650 S. Woodlawn Ave.,* ☏ *773/324–4100.*

㉖ Fountain of Time. A haunting sculpture created in 1922 by Lorado Taft (1830–1926) depicts the figure of Time observing humanity passing by. Taft was one of the most distinguished sculptors and teachers of his time; as such, he created pieces for the Columbian Exposition of 1893. One of these, the *Fountain of the Great Lakes*, is now at the Art Institute. Other works adorn Chicago's parks and public places, as well as those of other cities. ⊠ *West end of Midway Plaisance, west of Cottage Grove Ave.*

❺ 1400–1451 E. 55th Street. I. M. Pei, architect for the Louvre's controversial glass pyramids, designed the two 10-story university apartment buildings that sit on an island in the middle of the street. He also designed the town houses that border them on the north, between Blackstone and Dorchester avenues.

❻ Harper Court. A product of urban renewal, Harper Court was built to house craftspeople who were displaced from their workshops on Lake Park Avenue. Despite subsidized rents, it never caught on with the craftspeople, who moved elsewhere, while Harper Court evolved into a successful shopping center and community gathering place. ⊠ *Harper Ave. between 52nd and 53rd Sts.*

❼ Heller House. When he designed this house in 1897, Frank Lloyd Wright was still moving toward the mature Prairie style achieved in the Robie House (☞ *below*) 12 years later. Of special interest are the sculptured nymphs cavorting at the top. ⊠ *5132 S. Woodlawn Ave.*

❹ Hyde Park Historical Society. The restored redbrick building that serves as the society's headquarters was originally a cable-car station, built at the time of the 1893 Columbian Exposition. The group focuses on area history and sponsors lectures and tours. ⊠ *5529 S. Lake Park Ave.,* ☎ *773/493–1893.*

㉘ International House. Many foreign students and staff at the University of Chicago have passed through this modified Gothic limestone building designed in 1932 by the firm of Holabird and Root. ⊠ *1414 E. 59th St.*

OFF THE BEATEN PATH   **JACKSON PARK –** Frederick Law Olmsted designed this park for the World's Columbian Exposition of 1893. Just south of the Museum of Science and Industry, Jackson Park has lagoons, the Wooded Island, and a Japanese garden with authentic Japanese statuary. ⊠ *Bounded by E. 56th and 67th Sts., S. Stony Island Ave., and the lakefront.*

⑭ John Crerar Science Library. The library houses a large part of the University of Chicago's extensive biological, medical, and physical sciences collections and is open to the public. Chicago sculptor John David Mooney's work *Crystara,* made of Waterford crystal and aluminum, is suspended from the skylight in the library's three-story atrium. ⊠ *5730 S. Ellis Ave.,* ☎ *773/702–7715.*

⑱ Joseph Regenstein Library. The university's massive graduate research library has a distinctly modern look. Designed by Skidmore, Owings & Merrill and built in 1970, it has seven floors, two of them below ground. ⊠ *1100 E. 57th St.*

❾ Lutheran School of Theology. This striking structure, built in three sections, seems lightened by the transparency of its smoked-glass exteriors. It was constructed in 1968 by the firm of Perkins and Will. ⊠ *1100 E. 55th St.*

⑲ Mandel Hall. Professional musical organizations, including ensembles from the Chicago Symphony, perform in this beautifully restored 900-seat concert hall throughout the year. Gold leaf and soft greens contrast pleasantly with the dark wood of the theater. The building also houses the student union. ⊠ *1131 E. 57th St.,* ☎ *773/702–8068.*

㉕ **Midway Plaisance.** The broad, green, hollowed-out space at the southern edge of the University of Chicago campus, created for the World's Columbian Exposition of 1893, was intended to replicate a Venetian canal. But when the "canal" was filled with water, area houses were flooded as well, and the idea had to be abandoned. It was along the Midway that the world's first Ferris wheel, 250 ft in diameter, was erected and took passengers skyward during the exposition. Today students and neighborhood residents use this green refuge. ⊠ *Bounded by 59th and 60th Sts. and Jackson and Washington parks.*

㉗ **Midway Studios.** A National Historic Landmark since 1966, the former workplace of sculptor Lorado Taft now houses the University of Chicago's studio-art program and serves as an exhibit space for student works. ⊠ *6016 S. Ingleside Ave.,* ☎ *773/753–4821.* ☒ *Free.* ☉ *Weekdays 8:30–4.*

★ ☺ ❶ **Museum of Science and Industry.** More than 2,000 intriguing exhibits compete for visitors' attention at this sprawling landmark museum, Chicago's number one tourist attraction. You can walk through the middle of a 20-ft tall model of the human heart, explore a cantilevered Boeing 727 and a WWII German submarine, and make noises in the acoustically perfect Whispering Gallery. The museum also has the world's first permanent exhibit on HIV and AIDS. New exhibits include Lego MindStorms and the Idea Factory; Colleen Moore's Fairy Castle is a perennial favorite. Be sure to study the museum map to decide how you want to use your time.

Of special interest for families is the Imagination Station on the lower level, with hands-on activities for kids up to age 12. The Omnimax Theater shows science and space-related films on a giant five-story screen. The museum's classical revival building was designed in 1892 by D. H. Burnham & Company as a temporary structure to house the Palace of Fine Arts of the World's Columbian Exposition. It's the fair's only surviving building. ⊠ *5700 S. Lake Shore Dr.,* ☎ *773/684–1414.* ☒ *Museum $6, free Thurs.; combination museum and Omnimax $10.* ☉ *Memorial Day–Labor Day, daily 9:30–5:30; Labor Day–Memorial Day, weekdays 9:30–4, weekends 9:30–5:30.*

⑫ ***Nuclear Energy.*** Henry Moore's 12-ft-tall bronze sculpture marks the site where Enrico Fermi and other physicists set off the first controlled nuclear chain reaction on December 2, 1942. It occurred under the bleachers of what was then Stagg Field. The sculpture is said to represent both a human skull and an atomic mushroom cloud. ⊠ *East side of Ellis Ave. between 56th and 57th Sts.*

㉚ **O'Gara & Wilson Book Shop Ltd.** This bookstore, established in the mid-1930s, specializes in out-of-print and antiquarian titles and general used books and also sells interesting prints and maps. ⊠ *1448 E. 57th St.,* ☎ *773/363–0993.* ☉ *Mon.–Sat. 9 AM–10 PM, Sun. noon–10.*

NEED A
BREAK?

Caffé Florian (⊠ 1450 E. 57th St., ☎ 773/752–4100) serves pizza and Italian entrées as well as hearty sandwiches, homemade soups and salads, decadent desserts, and lots of java. (The backs of the restaurant's matches, in true U of C style, display the molecular structure of caffeine.)

㉓ **Oriental Institute.** The institute is full of fascinating art and artifacts from the ancient Near East, including statuary, small-scale amulets, mummies, limestone reliefs, gold jewelry, ivories, pottery, and bronzes from the 2nd millennium BC through the 13th century AD. One of the most intriguing items is a 40-ton sculpture of a winged bull from an Assyrian palace. ⊠ *1155 E. 58th St.,* ☎ *773/702–9520 or 773/702–9521.* ⬛ *Free.* ☉ *Call for current schedule.*

㉛ Powell's Bookstore. Outside, there is usually a box of free books; inside is a tremendous selection of used and remaindered titles, including books on philosophy, ancient history, anthropology, and social sciences, as well as art books, cookbooks, and mysteries. ⊠ *1501 E. 57th St.,* ☎ *773/955–7780.* ☉ *Daily 9 AM–11 PM.*

❷ Promontory Apartments. The building, designed by Mies van der Rohe in 1949, was named for nearby Promontory Point, which juts out into the lake. Mies's first Chicago high-rise exemplifies the postwar trend toward a clean, simple style. ⊠ *5530 South Shore Dr.*

★ ㉑ Robie House. Frank Lloyd Wright's Prairie-style masterpiece, built in 1909, is one of the most remarkable designs in modern American architecture. Study the exterior to see the horizontal lines, from the brickwork and the limestone sills to the sweeping roofs, which Wright felt reflected the prairies of the Midwest. The house sits on a pedestal; Wright abhorred basements, which he thought were unhealthy. A cantilevered roof provides privacy while allowing in light. You can tour Robie House and examine the interiors, including the great hearth, leaded-glass windows, built-in cupboards, and spacious kitchen. ⊠ *5757 S. Woodlawn Ave.,* ☎ *708/848–1976.* ⬛ *$3.* ☉ *Tours daily at 11, 1, and 3.*

★ ㉔ Rockefeller Memorial Chapel. An important example of the Gothic Revival style, this chapel, named for the University of Chicago's founder, was built in 1928 from plans by Bertram G. Goodhue. The imposing structure has a glorious vaulted ceiling, a beautiful hand-carved organ, and unusual stained glass in the north window above the altar. The window's five "petals" and center are composed of intensely colored glass; during the day the light pouring through it reflects strikingly on the chapel's ceiling. The chapel is elaborately decorated inside and out with carvings, sculpture, and inscriptions. Its 207-ft tower houses a carillon with 72 bells; a university carillonneur gives regular performances. ⊠ *5850 S. Woodlawn Ave.,* ☎ *773/702–2100; 773/702–8374 for tour.* ☉ *Daily 8–4; tour by appointment.*

❽ St. Thomas the Apostle Church. An open, modern look inside and terra-cotta ornamentation outside mark the design of Barry Byrne, who was once an apprentice of Frank Lloyd Wright. This Roman Catholic church built in 1922 also has impressive bronze bas-reliefs of the stations of the cross. ⊠ *5472 S. Kimbark Ave.,* ☎ *773/324–2626.*

University of Chicago. The University of Chicago was built through the largesse of John D. Rockefeller. Coeducational from the beginning, it was known for progressive education. The campus covers 184 acres, dominating the physical and cultural landscape of Hyde Park and South Kenwood. Much of the original campus was designed by Henry Ives Cobb, who was also responsible for the Newberry Library, at the corner of Dearborn and Walton streets on the Near North Side. The university's stately Gothic quadrangles recall the residential colleges in Cambridge and Oxford, England, and the Ivy League schools of the East Coast. But the material is Indiana limestone, and the U of C retains a uniquely midwestern quality.

The university boasts 68 Nobel laureates as faculty, researchers, or former students. Its schools of economics, law, business, and medicine are world famous, and the University of Chicago Hospitals are leading teaching institutions. Perhaps the most world-altering event to take place at U of C (or anywhere else, for that matter) was the first self-sustaining nuclear chain reaction, created here in 1942 by Enrico Fermi and his team of physicists under an unused football stadium. Although the stadium is gone, there's a plaque on the spot now, near the Crerar Science Library.

The University's Visitor Center, on the first floor of Ida Noyes Hall, provides maps, publications, and information on University events. Campus tours for prospective students are offered by appointment by the **Office of College Admissions** (☎ 773/702–8650). Campus tours, which leave from the Visitor Center, are given to the general public on Saturdays at 10. The Office of Special Events also offers guided tours of Robie House and Rockefeller Memorial Chapel (☞ *above*). A self-guided tour of campus architecture, *A Walking Guide to the Campus,* is available for purchase in the University of Chicago Bookstore (☞ *below*). ✉ *Visitor Center: Ida Noyes Hall, 1212 E. 59th St.* ☎ *773/ 702–9739.* ☉ *Weekdays 10–7.*

⓯ University of Chicago Bookstore. This carpeted campus store, now run by Barnes and Noble, has a broad selection of books and periodicals plus a café. It's also a good place to pick up university souvenirs, including T-shirts emblazoned with the names of the 68 Nobel laureates associated with the university. ✉ *970 E. 58th St.,* ☎ *773/702–8729.* ☉ *Weekdays 8:30–6:30, Sat. 8:30–5.*

❸ Windermere House. Originally one of the area's grandest hotels, Windermere House was designed in 1924 by Rapp and Rapp, known for their movie palaces. Among the hotel's guests were John D. Rockefeller, Babe Ruth, and Edna Ferber. The building now houses apartments. Notice the grand gatehouse in front of the sweeping semicircular carriage path at the entrance; notice also the heroic scale of the building, with its ornate carvings. ✉ *1642 E. 56th St.*

SOUTH LAKE SHORE DRIVE

If you've just visited Hyde Park and Kenwood and are returning north via car or bus, a ride along South Lake Shore Drive is especially worthwhile for its spectacular views of the downtown skyline and the lake. Those who have followed the Loop and the Near North walks in this chapter will get another perspective of the skyscrapers described in those tours—from a distance and in relation to the surrounding skyline. There are also some landmarks close to the road. In addition, the drive takes you to the museum campus that connects three of Chicago's most popular attractions: the Field Museum of Natural History, the Shedd Aquarium and Oceanarium, and the Adler Planetarium.

A Good Drive

You can drive your own car or take the Jeffery Express Bus 6 or (during the afternoon rush hour) the Hyde Park Express Bus 2. Enter Lake Shore Drive at 57th Street northbound, with the lake to your right. At 35th Street you will see, on your left, the **Stephen A. Douglas Tomb and Memorial,** honoring the U.S. senator who debated the merits of slavery with Abraham Lincoln. To get a close look, exit at Pershing-Oakwood Boulevard, go west a short distance to Lake Park Avenue, and continue north four blocks. This area is desolate, but outstanding views lie just ahead.

As you continue north on Lake Shore Drive, you will see the Sears Tower directly ahead in the distance. In case the perspective from here makes it appear unfamiliar, you can recognize it by the angular setbacks that narrow the building as it rises higher. To the left of the Sears Tower, note the White Castle top of 311 S. Wacker Drive, which is lighted at night. Ahead, on both sides of the drive, is the **McCormick Place complex,** the largest exhibition and meeting place in North America.

In the distance, the rust-color building to the east of the Sears Tower is the CNA Building. Farther north, the Stone Container Building is the structure with the more or less diamond-shape angled face at the top.

The tall white building to the right of the Stone Container Building is the Amoco Building, with its granite exterior. Just west of the Amoco Building is the severe gray Prudential Building, with its postmodern annex rising behind it.

The building with the twin antennae, to the right of the Amoco Building, is the 100-story John Hancock Center. Off to the right, seemingly out in the lake, are the sinuous curves of the Lake Point Tower condominiums. Ahead, the building with the massive columns reminiscent of ancient Greece is **Soldier Field,** home of the Chicago Bears.

Follow signs from Lake Shore Drive to the museum campus, where the Big Three—the **Field Museum of Natural History, the John G. Shedd Aquarium and Oceanarium,** and the **Adler Planetarium**—are united in one pedestrian-friendly, parklike setting. On the east side of the campus, at the far end of a peninsula that juts out into Lake Michigan (and provides wonderful views of Chicago's skyline), is the Adler Planetarium, with exhibits and a popular program of sky shows. The Shedd Aquarium, on the lakefront near the planetarium, has bizarre and fantastically beautiful fish and, in the dazzling new Oceanarium, several playful beluga whales and dolphins. Just west of the aquarium is the Field Museum, one of the country's great natural history museums.

After visiting the museums, retrieve your car and continue north. As you round the curve past the Shedd Aquarium, look to your right for a view of the Monroe Street harbor. Off to the left looms the handsome, massive complex of the Chicago Hilton and Towers, and soon thereafter Buckingham Fountain will appear immediately to your left. To the far right, at the north and east, you can just barely make out the ornate towers of the entertainment complex at Navy Pier. Having reached the north end of Grant Park, you've come to the end of this drive.

TIMING

The drive itself will take only 15 or 20 minutes, more in traffic. Try to avoid Lake Shore Drive during peak rush-hour traffic times: from 7 to 9 in the morning, from 4 to 6:30 in the afternoon. Plan on at least a day for a visit to the three museums (you could spend a day at the mammoth Field Museum alone). Allow extra time to enjoy the spectacular skyline and lake views from the new museum campus and to stroll along the harbor.

Sights to See

🅒 **Adler Planetarium.** Opened in 1930 as the first public planetarium in the western hemisphere, the Adler continues to unveil new and revamped exhibits and gallery space. Among recent additions are the high-tech StarRider Theater, the Atwood Sphere Planetarium, and exhibits on the solar system and the Milky Way galaxy. ⊠ *1300 S. Lake Shore Dr.,* ☎ *312/922–7827.* 🎫 *$3, Sky Show $2.* ☉ *Mon.–Thurs. 9–5, Fri. 9–9, weekends 9–6.*

....

OFF THE BEATEN PATH
BRONZEVILLE – A renaissance of restoration is under way in this historic community, originally settled by waves of African-Americans fleeing the South beginning after World War I. The most touching landmark may be the 15-ft statue at 26th Place and King Drive—the neighborhood's sym-

bolic entrance—that depicts a new arrival from the South bearing a suitcase held together with string. The neighborhood was dubbed Bronzeville after the *Chicago Bee,* a black newspaper of the time, held a contest in 1930 to elect a "Mayor of Bronzeville." The influential *Chicago Defender* newspaper, meanwhile, originally was based here and attracted talent that included Langston Hughes. Group tours are recommended for those unfamiliar with the area. The **Chicago Office of Tourism** (☏ 312/742–1190) offers a half-day bus tour; other tours are offered by the **Black Metropolis Convention and Tourism Council** (☏ 773/548–2579), **Tour Black Chicago** (☏ 312/332–2323) and **Black Coutours** (☏ 773/233–8907). ⊠ *Bounded roughly by 31st and 39th Sts. and by State St. and King Dr.*

★ ☾ **Field Museum.** More than 6 *acres* of exhibits fill this gigantic world-class natural history museum, which explores cultures and environments around the world. Originally funded by Chicago retailer Marshall Field, the museum was founded in 1893 to hold material gathered for the World's Columbian Exposition; its current classical-style home opened in 1921. Many exhibits have been redone thematically or in a more hands-on format. The remarkable Mastaba complex, part of Inside Ancient Egypt, includes a working canal, a living marsh where papyrus is grown, a shrine to the cat goddess Bastet, burial-ceremony artifacts, and 23 mummies. The reconstructed Pawnee earth lodge was completed with the assistance of the Pawnee tribe of Oklahoma; the museum's glittering gem room contains more than 500 gemstones and jewels. Don't miss the two-part permanent exhibit called Life over Time: DNA to Dinosaurs, which traces the evolution of life on earth from one-celled organisms to the great reptiles, and Teeth, Tusks, and Tar Pits, which moves from the dinosaurs' extinction to the evolution of humans. Throughout 1999, visitors can watch museum scientists prepare the 65-million-year-old fossilized bones of "Sue," the largest and most complete Tyrannosaurus rex ever found, which will go on display in the year 2000. At press time, volunteers were expected to be stationed outside the glass-enclosed lab to explain what the scientists are doing. There are more than 600 other fossils on exhibit, including gigantic posed dinosaur skeletons. The DinoStore sells a mind-boggling assortment of dinosaur-related merchandise.

People with children ages 4–10 should visit the Place for Wonder, a three-room exhibit that lets youngsters handle everything on display, including a ½-ton stuffed polar bear, shells, animal skins, clothing and toys from China, aromatic scent jars, and gourds. In addition to hosting special exhibits, the museum also schedules music, dance, theater, and film performances. Be sure to get a map and plan your time here. ⊠ *Lake Shore Dr. and E. Roosevelt Rd.,* ☏ *312/922–9410.* 🎟 *$7, free Wed.* ☾ *Daily 9–5.*

★ ☾ **John G. Shedd Aquarium.** The splashiest attraction at the world's largest indoor aquarium is the spectacular Oceanarium, with pools that seem to blend right into Lake Michigan, which is visible through the huge glass wall. In the Oceanarium you can have a stare-down with one of the knobby-headed beluga whales (they love to people-watch), observe Pacific white-sided dolphins at play, and explore the simulated Pacific Northwest nature trail, complete with tall pines, birdsongs, and tide pools. Be sure to check out the underwater viewing windows for the dolphins and whales and the information-packed, interactive, hands-on activities on the lower level. In the original aquarium facility, a highlight is the newly renovated Coral Reef Exhibit, where visitors can watch divers feed sharks and other denizens of the deep. Next year, the aquarium will open "River Journey" in Galleries 1 and 2, which will allow guests to take a trip through the seasons in an Amazon-flooded forest. Other exhibits have river otters, electric eels, piranhas, and hundreds of other aquatic animals. A special treat on Thursday evenings from mid-June to late August is live jazz on the Oceanarium's north terrace, with a great view of the lake and skyline. Buy timed entrance tickets for the Oceanarium at the box office, or, to avoid lines, buy them in advance from **Ticketmaster** (☎ 312/559–0200). ⊠ *1200 S. Lake Shore Dr.,* ☎ *312/939–2438 or 312/939–2426.* ⌘ *Aquarium and Oceanarium $10, Thurs. $6.* ☉ *Memorial Day–Labor Day, Fri.–Wed. 9– 6, Thurs. 9–9; Labor Day–Memorial Day, weekdays 9–5, weekends 9–6.*

McCormick Place Complex. Chicago's premier convention facility, Mc-Cormick Place comprises three buildings with 2.2 million square ft of exhibition space and a glass-enclosed pedestrian concourse with retail shops linking all three buildings. ⊠ *2301 S. Lake Shore Dr.,* ☎ *312/ 791–7000.*

Soldier Field. Home of the Chicago Bears since 1971, Soldier Field opened in 1924 and has been the site of many events besides football games, including a heavyweight-title boxing match in 1927 between Jack Dempsey and Gene Tunney, a visit in 1944 by President Franklin Roosevelt, and rock concerts by the Rolling Stones and other megabands. ⊠ *425 E. McFetridge Dr.*

Stephen A. Douglas Tomb and Memorial. A bronze sculpture of the "Little Giant," one of the greatest orators of his day, stands high on a pedestal in a small park just west of South Lake Shore Drive. A U.S. senator and Abraham Lincoln's political rival (their 1858 debates brought Lincoln national prominence), Douglas moved to Chicago in the late 1840s and owned property in this area; he died in 1861. ⊠ *636 E. 35th St.* ☉ *Daily 9–5.*

NEAR NORTH

Two outstanding art museums, dozens of art galleries, the entertainment-packed Navy Pier, and countless shops where you could spend anywhere from a few dollars to thousands: These are only some of the sights within short walks of the multitude of hotels on the Near North Side—north, that is, of the Chicago River. The walks in this section provide a feeling for the different history and character of the eastern and western parts of the area.

Magnificent Mile and Streeterville

The Magnificent Mile, a stretch of Michigan Avenue between the Chicago River and Oak Street, got its name because of the swanky shops that line both sides of the street—and from its once-elegant low-rise profile, which used to contrast sharply with the urban canyons of the Loop. The modest moniker was provided by developer Arthur Rubloff in 1947. Unfortunately, a parade of new high-rises with a combination of office, residential, and retail space is making the Mag Mile more canyonlike each year, as retail success fuels further development. Another trend on the avenue is the arrival of ubiquitous chain stores. Still, here and there you can see patches of what the entire street used to look like.

To the east of the Magnificent Mile is upscale Streeterville, which began as a disreputable landfill presided over by notorious lowlife Cap Streeter and his wife, Maria. The couple set out from Milwaukee in the 1880s on a small steamboat bound for Honduras. When their boat was stranded on a sandbar between Chicago Avenue and Oak Street,

BUCKTOWN AND WICKER PARK

CREATIVE TYPES CLUSTER in the hip, somewhat grungy enclaves called Bucktown and Wicker Park, centered on Milwaukee, Damen, and North avenues. Though both neighborhoods are still among Chicago's lesser-known destinations, they harbor an intriguing mix of nightclubs, cafés, theaters, coffeehouses, cutting-edge galleries, small businesses, and a bizarre bazaar of shops—plus an increasing parade of sightseers drawn by what is arguably the best people-watching in the city. Musicians, artists, and young professionals call this area home, and an abundance of Latin American–run shops and restaurants is evidence of the strong ethnic influences.

Bucktown—which is said to have taken its name from the goats kept by the area's original Polish and German immigrants—encompasses the neighborhood surrounding Milwaukee Avenue north of North Avenue. The area south of North Avenue is Wicker Park—named for Charles Wicker, who, with his brother Joel, established the community in the 1870s.

It you're driving, take the Kennedy Expressway to North Avenue, then go west on North Avenue until you reach the triangular intersection where it meets Milwaukee and Damen avenues. By El train, take the north-bound Blue line to the Damen/North Avenue stop. Head north on Damen to North Avenue, then briefly east to the **Flat Iron Building** (✉ 1579 N. Milwaukee Ave.), an 88,000-square-ft haven for artists and galleries, many of them open to the public.

From the Flat Iron Building you can make short forays to see some of Bucktown and Wicker Park's most colorful shops, theaters, and clubs. Among the quirky shops on Damen Avenue is the aptly named **Eclectic Junction** (✉ No. 1630). **Le Garage** (✉ No. 1649) specializes in secondhand jeans.

On North Avenue you can fuel up on caffeine at **Urbus Orbis** (✉ No. 1934), a must-see cornerstone of the Bucktown gestalt. On your way back toward the Flat Iron Building, look west for a great view of the remarkable triangular **Northwest Tower Building** (✉ 1600 N. Milwaukee Ave.), popularly known as the Coyote Building because of the Coyote Gallery that once stood in its place.

Milwaukee Avenue is lined with some of the area's best bars, cafés, and restaurants. The funky **Soul Kitchen** (✉ No. 1576); ☞ Lincoln Park and North *in* Chapter 3) serves creative regional American food. There are also offbeat furniture, clothing, and antiques stores here. **Green Acres** (✉ No. 1464; ☞ Antiques and Collectibles *in* Chapter 7) is a great antiques shop. **Modern Times** (✉ No. 1538) ☞ Antiques and Collectibles *in* Chapter 7) has furniture from the '40s, '50s, and '60s.

The most lively times to visit are late August, when Bucktown hosts its annual Arts Fest, and early September, during the Around the Coyote gallery walk (☞ Festivals and Seasonal Events *in* Chapter 1). Throughout the rest of the year, it's fun to visit the area in the evening—for dinner and nightlife. The **Rainbo Club** (✉ 1150 N. Damen Ave.) is a small bar with cheap beer and an art-school clientele. The **Double Door** (✉ 1572 N. Milwaukee Ave.) is a live-music venue. Or you can have a late breakfast on the weekend, followed by a long wander among the unique local businesses. The venerable **Busy Bee** (☞ Lincoln Park and North *in* Chapter 3) is a Polish joint. **The Bongo Room** (✉ 1470 N. Milwaukee Ave.) is a crowded, eclectic, hip cafe.

Streeter claimed the "land" as his own, seceding from both the city of Chicago and the state of Illinois. After building contractors were invited to dump their debris on his "property," the landfill soon mushroomed into 186 acres of saloons and shanties. Today this once-infamous area is filled with high-rise apartment buildings and a smattering of older structures and has attracted professionals who work nearby. Where Cap Streeter's own shanty once sat is the John Hancock Center.

West of Streeterville, from Michigan Avenue to Dearborn Street, is a stretch that mixes a few skyscrapers, lots of parking lots and garages, a sprinkling of shops and restaurants, and some isolated examples of the stone town houses that once filled the neighborhood. Despite its lack of cohesion, the area is the seat of various enclaves of power, containing two cathedrals and the headquarters of the American Medical Association, which is in a distinctive triangular high-rise at State Street and Grand Avenue. The building, by acclaimed Japanese architect Kenzo Tange, has an unusual four-story "opening" near its roof.

Numbers in the text correspond to numbers in the margin and on the Near North map.

A Good Walk

Begin your walk at the **Michigan Avenue Bridge** ①, which spans the Chicago River as a gateway to North Michigan Avenue. The low-rise building on the river, west of the bridge, is the headquarters of the *Chicago Sun-Times*, one of the city's two hotly competitive dailies. Just north of the bridge on the west side of Michigan Avenue is the **Wrigley Building** ②, corporate home of the Wrigley chewing gum empire. The stark white building's wedding-cake embellishments and clock tower make it a strikingly conspicuous sight.

Across Michigan Avenue rises the crenellated **Tribune Tower** ③, home of the *Chicago Tribune*. Walk across the plaza just east and north of Tribune Tower to Cityfront Plaza Drive and **NBC Tower** ④, which houses studios of the local NBC affiliate WMAQ-TV. The riverside glass-front building near NBC Tower is the University of Chicago's Graduate School of Business Downtown Center (⊠ 450 N. Cityfront Plaza Dr.). The university bookstore on the plaza has a selection of newspapers from around the world and, not surprisingly, many books on business and economics.

From Cityfront Plaza Drive, walk down the stairs to the river. Continue east along the riverbank, past the Sheraton Chicago Hotel and Towers, to the **Centennial Fountain and Arc** ⑤, where you can step inside the circular part of the fountain and stand next to a wall of water—a refreshing break on a hot summer day. (It's also possible to walk west to Michigan Avenue along the river—a delightful stroll in good weather, but not on blustery winter days.) From the fountain, head north on McClurg Court to Illinois Street and the shopping, office, and entertainment complex called **North Pier** ⑥. The walkway along Ogden Slip affords a fine view in summer of some of Chicago's fanciest speedboats.

Farther east on Illinois, under Lake Shore Drive and across a park, is the new-and-improved **Navy Pier** ⑦, a wonderful place to enjoy lake breezes, visit the **Chicago Children's Museum,** and sample various entertainments, including a ride on a giant Ferris wheel, a flashy addition that some condominium residents of Lake Point Tower, just east of the pier, find abominable.

Walking west from Navy Pier on either Illinois or Grand, you'll come back to McClurg Court. Walk north to Ontario Street; then turn left and walk west toward Michigan Avenue. If you see lots of people in white coats, don't be surprised: Stretching east of Michigan from Ontario Street to Chicago Avenue are various buildings belonging to one of the city's most prominent medical centers, Northwestern Memorial Hospital. The downtown campus of Evanston's Northwestern University, including the law school, is also in this area.

Cross Michigan Avenue, turn right, and walk a block and a half to see the 19th- and 20-century paintings and sculpture of the **Terra Museum of American Art** ⑧, a peaceful refuge on this shopping strip. Other sanctuaries in the area are of a different nature: Two blocks west of Michigan Avenue on Huron Street is **St. James Cathedral** ⑨, Chicago's oldest Episcopal church. Continue another block west to State Street and one block north to Superior Street, where **Holy Name Cathedral** ⑩, which has a grand interior, stands as a Catholic stronghold. Go east on Chicago Avenue to Rush Street and turn left (north). At Pearson and Rush streets is **Quigley Seminary** ⑪, with its beautiful chapel.

Continue east on Pearson Street to Water Tower Park, a Chicago icon. The **Water Tower** ⑫ and the matching **Pumping Station** ⑬ across the street are among the few buildings to survive the fire of 1871.

Head east one block to the imposing new quarters of the **Museum of Contemporary Art** ⑭. This museum concentrates on 20th-century art, principally works created after 1945.

Walk back to Michigan Avenue. Two blocks north on the west side is the elegant **Fourth Presbyterian Church** ⑮ and its peaceful courtyard. In contrast, across Michigan Avenue towers the tapering, 100-story **John Hancock Center** ⑯, the third-tallest building in Chicago, after the Sears Tower and the Amoco Building.

At the north end of the Magnificent Mile on Walton Place, past the grand Drake Hotel (☞ Gold Coast, *below*), you'll find one of Chicago's nicest walks: Cross Oak Street in front of the Drake and take the underground passage that leads to Oak Street Beach and the lakefront promenade (watch out for speeding bicyclists, skateboarders, and in-line skaters).

TIMING

Allow about four hours for the walk itself plus time to stop for a snack or drink. You can spend a good deal more time at a number of the attractions (or just shopping), depending on your interests. Add a couple of hours (especially if you have children) for Navy Pier, another hour if you stop at North Pier. At Navy Pier you could spend a few hours in the Chicago Children's Museum alone. Art lovers will want to set aside at least an hour to see the Terra Museum of American Art and one or two hours for the Museum of Contemporary Art. Note that these museums aren't open on Monday. On summer weekends, walking along the lakefront north of Oak Street is a special treat; Chicagoans throng to Oak Street Beach to soak up the sun and play beach volleyball in the shadows of skyscrapers.

Sights to See

❺ **Centennial Fountain and Arc.** This stepped fountain, which commemorates the beginning of providing clean water in and around the city, runs from May 1 to October 1 and shoots an awesome arc of water across the river for 10 minutes daily on the hour from 10 to 2 and from 5 to midnight. On a sunny afternoon you might see the hues of a rainbow in the arc. ✉ *300 E. McClurg Ct.*

☙ **Chicago Children's Museum.** This museum's 57,000 square ft contain many appealing and educational exhibits. Some favorites are an early childhood exhibit with a kid-size neighborhood complete with a bak-

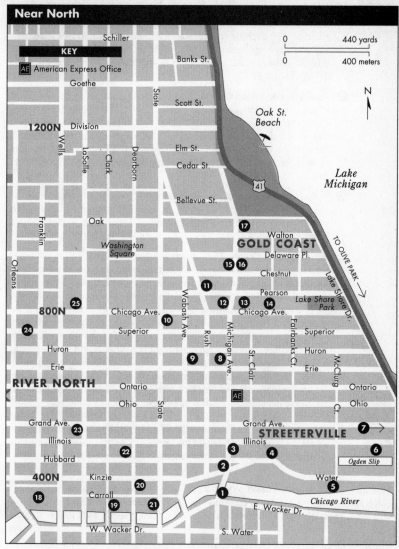

Near North

KEY

AE American Express Office

1200N

800N

400N

Schiller
Banks St.
Goethe
Scott St.
Division
Elm St.
Cedar St.
Bellevue St.
Oak St. Beach
Lake Michigan
GOLD COAST
Walton
Delaware Pl.
Chestnut
Pearson
Lake Shore Park
Chicago Ave.
Superior
Huron
Erie
Ontario
Ohio
Washington Square
Chicago Ave.
Superior
Huron
Erie
Ontario
Ohio
RIVER NORTH
Grand Ave.
Illinois
Hubbard
Kinzie
Carroll
Grand Ave.
Illinois
STREETERVILLE
Ogden Slip
Water
Chicago River
E. Wacker Dr.
W. Wacker Dr.
S. Water
TO OLIVE PARK

Schiller, State, Wells, LaSalle, Clark, Dearborn, Franklin, Oak, Orleans, Wabash Ave., Rush, Michigan Ave., St. Clair, Fairbanks Ct., McClurg Ct., Lake Shore Dr.

0 — 440 yards
0 — 400 meters

N

Anti-Cruelty Society Building, **23**
Centennial Fountain and Arc, **5**
Courthouse Place, **22**
Drake Hotel, **17**
Fourth Presbyterian Church, **15**
Holy Name Cathedral, **10**
John Hancock Center, **16**

Marina City, **21**
Merchandise Mart, **18**
Michigan Avenue Bridge, **1**
Moody Bible Institute, **25**
Museum of Contemporary Art, **14**
Navy Pier, **7**
NBC Tower, **4**

North Pier, **6**
Pumping Station, **13**
Quaker Oats Building, **19**
Quigley Seminary, **11**
River North Gallery District, **24**
St. James Cathedral, **9**
Terra Museum of American Art, **8**

33 West Kinzie Street, **20**
Tribune Tower, **3**
Water Tower, **12**
Wrigley Building, **2**

ery, service station, and construction site; a hands-on art studio; science exhibits on such subjects as recycling and inventing; and an activity-filled exhibit that provides children and adults with tools for addressing prejudice and discrimination. ⊠ *Navy Pier, 700 E. Grand Ave.,* ☎ *312/527–1000.* ☜ *$5, free Thurs. 5–8.* ☉ *Tues.–Wed. and Fri.–Sun. 10–5, Thurs. 10–8.*

⑮ Fourth Presbyterian Church. This granite church facing Michigan Avenue is a prime example of the Gothic Revival style popular at the turn of the century. The courtyard of the church, a grassy spot adorned with simple statuary and bounded by a covered walkway, has provided respite for many a weary shopper. Noontime organ concerts are given occasionally in the sanctuary; call for exact dates and times. ⊠ *126 E. Chestnut St.,* ☎ *312/787–4570.*

⑩ Holy Name Cathedral. A yellow-stone Victorian cathedral, built between 1874 and 1875, serves as the principal church of the archdiocese of Chicago. The interior is glorious; at the back of the church is a huge, beautiful organ. ⊠ *735 N. State St.,* ☎ *312/787–8040.*

⑯ John Hancock Center. The crisscross braces in this 1,107-ft-tall building help keep it from swaying in the high winds that come off the lake, although people in the apartments on the upper floors have learned not to keep anything fragile on a high shelf. Completed in 1969, Big John was the first building of such massive height on Michigan Avenue. The 94th floor has an observation deck; you can see the same view by having an exorbitantly priced drink in the bar that adjoins the Signature Room at the 95th restaurant (☞ Near North *in* Chapter 3). There are restaurants, shops, and a waterfall in the lower-level public plaza. The Chicago Architecture Foundation has a shop and tour center off the plaza. ⊠ *875 N. Michigan Ave.,* ☎ *312/751–3681.* ☜ *Observation deck $8.* ☉ *Daily 9 AM–midnight.*

NEED A BREAK?
For great fixings, try **L'Appetito** (⊠ 875 N. Michigan Ave., ☎ 312/ 337–0691), a take-out deli off the Hancock Center's lower-level plaza that has some of the best Italian sandwiches in Chicago.

OFF THE BEATEN PATH
LAKE SHORE DRIVE SYNAGOGUE – Ornate stained glass decorates the interior of what is arguably the city's most magnificent synagogue, a late-1800s structure a block north of Oak Street. ⊠ *70 E. Elm St.,* ☎ *312/337–6811.*

❶ Michigan Avenue Bridge. Completed in 1920, this bridge at the south end of the Magnificent Mile has impressive sculptures on its four pylons representing major Chicago events: its exploration by Marquette and Joliet, its settlement by trader Jean Baptiste Point du Sable, the Fort Dearborn Massacre of 1812, and the rebuilding of the city after the fire of 1871. The site of the fort, at the southeast end of the bridge, is marked by a commemorative plaque erected there by the city. The bridge has two decks for traffic and can be opened to allow tall-masted boats to pass. ⊠ *Chicago River at E. Wacker Dr.*

⑭ Museum of Contemporary Art. Founded in 1967 by a group of art patrons who felt the great Art Institute was unresponsive to modern work, the MCA reopened in June 1996 in dramatic new quarters designed by Berlin architect Josef Paul Kleihues. The new museum, in a park-like setting between the Water Tower and Lake Michigan, has nearly seven times the space of the old facility, yet it is still small in comparison to other city's modern art museums. Among its features are four barrel-vaulted galleries on the fourth floor and a terraced sculpture garden with outdoor café tables overlooking Lake Michigan. About half the museum is dedicated to temporary exhibitions; the other half show-cases objects from the MCA's growing 7,000-piece collection, which includes work by René Magritte, Alexander Calder, Bruce Nauman, Sol LeWitt, Franz Kline, and June Leaf. The museum hosts a party ($10) with live music and hors d'oeuvres from 6–10 PM on the first Friday of every month. ⊠ *220 E. Chicago Ave.,* ☎ *312/280–2660.* ☑ *$6.50, 1st Tues. of month free.* ☉ *Tues., Thurs., Fri. 11–6 (1st Fri. of month 11–10), Wed. 11–8, weekends 10–6.*

★ ☙ ❼ **Navy Pier.** Following a spectacular renovation completed in 1995, Navy Pier is now one of Chicago's busiest and most appealing entertainment destinations. Constructed in 1916 as a commercial-shipping pier, it was renamed in honor of the navy in 1927 (the army got Soldier Field). The once-deserted pier contains shopping promenades; an outdoor land-scaped area with a fountain, a carousel, a giant 15-story Ferris wheel, and an ice-skating rink, in addition to pretty gardens; the lakefront **Sky-line Stage** (☎ 312/595–7437), a 1,500-seat vaulted-roof theater; Crys-tal Gardens, one of the country's largest indoor botanical parks; an IMAX Theater; an outdoor beer garden; the **Chicago Children's Mu-seum** (☞ *above*); and myriad shops, restaurants, and bars. Navy Pier continues to serve as the home port for a number of tour and dinner cruises. Prices are premium for these cruises, and the food's better on land, but the voyage can be pleasant on a hot summer night. Dinner cruise operators include *Spirit of Chicago* (☎ 312/836–7899) and *Odyssey I* (☎ 630/990–0800); the *Cap Streeter* and the *Shoreline II* offer 30-minute shoreline cruises that don't require reservations (☎ 312/222–9328). **Riva** and **Joe's Be-Bop Cafe & Jazz Emporium** (☞ Near North *in* Chapter 3) are good restaurant choices. ⊠ *Grand Ave. at lakefront,* ☎ *312/595–7437.* ☉ *Daily 6 AM–11 PM.*

❹ **NBC Tower.** This 1989 limestone-and-granite edifice by Skidmore, Owings & Merrill looks suspiciously like a building from the 1930s-vintage Rockefeller Center complex in New York, another NBC home. ⊠ *455 N. Cityfront Plaza Dr.*

OFF THE BEATEN PATH **NEWBERRY LIBRARY** – This venerable research institution houses superb book and document collections in many areas and mounts exhibits in a small gallery space. ⊠ *60 W. Walton St.,* ☎ *312/943-9090.* ☑ *Free.* ☉ *Tues.–Thurs. 10–6, Fri.–Sat. 9–5.*

☙ ❻ **North Pier.** A former shipping terminal and pier was converted to a glitzy shopping mall and office space in the late '80s. You'll find a num-ber of interesting retail outlets, including the City of Chicago Store, which sells unique souvenirs; a food court; several bars and restaurants; and a host of recreational games, from miniature golf to traditional arcade games to high-tech interactive games. ⊠ *435 E. Illinois St.*

OFF THE BEATEN PATH **OLIVE PARK** – Just north of Navy Pier and Lake Point Tower (⊠ 505 N. Lake Shore Dr.), the green space of Olive Park juts out into Lake Michi-gan. It has no roads, just paved walkways and lots of benches, trees, shrubs, and grass. The marvelous views of the city skyline, in addition to the absence of vehicular traffic, make it seem as though you're miles from the city, not just blocks from the busy Near North Side. ⊠ *Grand Ave. at lakefront.*

⓭ **Pumping Station.** Water is still pumped to city residents at a rate of about 72 million gallons per day from this Gothic structure, which, along with the very similar Water Tower across the street, survived the Chicago Fire of 1871. The station is also a drop-in tourist informa-tion center. ⊠ *811 N. Michigan Ave.*

⓫ Quigley Seminary. The Catholic St. James Chapel in this 1918 Gothic-style building was modeled on the famous Sainte-Chapelle in Paris. It's a little jewel, with perfect acoustics and a splendid rose window. ✉ *Pearson and Rush Sts.,* ☎ *312/787–9343.* ☉ *Chapel tour Mon.–Tues., Thurs., and Sat. noon–2, or call for appointment.*

❾ St. James Cathedral. First built in 1856, the original St. James was largely destroyed by the Chicago Fire of 1871. The second structure, from 1875, is Chicago's oldest Episcopal church. The cathedral has a magnificent stenciled nave in the Arts and Crafts style. If the church doors are locked, ask at the church office (in building next door, east of the cathedral) for admission. ✉ *65 E. Huron St.,* ☎ *312/787–7360.*

★ **❽ Terra Museum of American Art.** Daniel Terra, ambassador-at-large for cultural affairs under Ronald Reagan, made his collection of American art available to Chicago in 1980; in 1987 it was moved here from Evanston. Subsequent acquisitions by the museum have added to the superb collections, which highlight American impressionists and folk art. Look for works by Whistler, Sargent, Winslow Homer, Cassatt, and three generations of Wyeths. ✉ *666 N. Michigan Ave.,* ☎ *312/664–3939.* ☞ *$5, free Tues.* ☉ *Tues. noon–8, Wed.–Sat. 10–5, Sun. noon–5.*

❸ Tribune Tower. In 1922 *Tribune* publisher Colonel Robert McCormick chose a Gothic design for the building that would house his paper, after rejecting a slew of functional modern designs. Embedded in the exterior wall of the tower are chunks of material taken from other famous buildings. Look for labeled blocks from Westminster Abbey, the Alamo, St. Peter's Basilica, the White House, and the Berlin Wall, among others; some of these bits and pieces were gifts to McCormick and others were "secured" by the *Trib*'s foreign correspondents. On the ground floor, behind plate-glass windows, are the studios of WGN radio, part of the *Tribune* empire, which also includes WGN-TV, cable-television stations, and the Chicago Cubs. (Modesty was not one of Colonel McCormick's prime traits: WGN stands for the *Tribune*'s self-bestowed nickname, World's Greatest Newspaper.) Call to schedule a free tour of the *Trib*'s production facility at the Freedom Center (✉ 777 W. Chicago, 312/222–2116); you will need to take a cab there. ✉ *435 N. Michigan Ave.,* ☎ *312/222–3232.*

⓬ Water Tower. This famous Michigan Avenue structure, completed in 1869, was originally built to house a 137-ft standpipe that equalized the pressure of the water pumped by the similar pumping station across the street. Oscar Wilde uncharitably called it "a castellated monstrosity with salt and pepper boxes stuck all over it." Nonetheless, it remains a Chicago landmark and a symbol of the city's survival spirit after the Great Fire of 1871. ✉ *835 N. Michigan Ave., at Pearson St.*

❷ Wrigley Building. Brightly illuminated at night, the landmark headquarters of the chewing gum company boldly marks the south end of the Magnificent Mile. It's sheathed in terra-cotta that's remained remarkably white thanks to diligent maintenance in the face of urban pollution. The tower was based on the Giralda Tower in Seville, Spain, and designed in the 1920s by the architectural firm Graham Anderson Probst and White, which also built the Merchandise Mart and Union Station. ✉ *400 N. Michigan Ave.*

....

NEED A   Behind and one level down from the Wrigley Building is the (in)famous
BREAK?   **Billy Goat Tavern** (✉ 430 N. Michigan Ave., ☎ 312/222–1525), the
                inspiration for *Saturday Night Live*'s classic "cheezborger, cheezborger"

skit and a longtime haunt of local journalists. Grab a greasy hamburger (or cheeseburger) at this very casual grill, or just have a beer and absorb the comic undertones.

Gold Coast

The name says it all: This posh pocket wears Chicago's greatest treasure—the Lake Michigan shoreline—like a gilded necklace. Made fashionable after the 1871 Great Chicago Fire by the social-climbing industrialists of the day, today's Gold Coast neighborhood is still a ritzy place to live, work, shop, and mingle.

The boundaries of this historic district are debated, thanks to gentrification that has expanded its borders; everyone wants to lay claim to a piece of Chicago's toniest turf. The generally agreed-upon limits are now the lake on the east, North Avenue on the north, Oak Street on the south, and LaSalle Street on the west.

Though the second half of this century has seen the destruction of some glorious old buildings (and the construction of some forgettable new ones), there is still plenty of period architecture to evoke a sense of the area's first wave of the wildly well-to-do. Entrepreneur Potter Palmer started it all in 1882 by abandoning the South Side to build a much-ballyhooed (and long since destroyed) mansion here. Following Palmer's lead, others among the already-monied and the nouveaux riches settled here, making the Gold Coast a center of wealth and power. Even the Roman Catholic Archdiocese of Chicago built its archbishop's residence here, where it remains.

A Good Walk

There's no place better to start an exploration of the Gold Coast than at the venerable **Drake Hotel** ⑰, at Oak Street and Michigan Avenue. (Near Division Street, look for the underground passageway to Oak Street Beach—a people-watching magnet in season, a pretty stroll anytime.) Cross Michigan westbound, and then walk north along Chicago's most famous thoroughfare, Lake Shore Drive.

On your left you'll see some of the city's most exclusive residences. Just north of Scott Street pause to admire two vintage beauties on your left: the 1891 Carol Constantine Heisen House (⊠ 1254 Lake Shore Dr.), designed by Frank Abbott, and its next-door neighbor, the Mason Bragman Starring House (⊠ 1250 Lake Shore Dr.), done in 1891 by Gustav Hallberg.

As you continue north across Goethe Street, make a mental note: If you're ever pressed for conversation in Chicago, just solicit opinions on how this street name should be pronounced. Then sit back and enjoy the fireworks.

The extremely eclectic mix of architecture along the Drive ranges from the ridiculous to the sublime. Some aristocratic examples can be found between Burton and North avenues: the seat of the Polish consulate (⊠ 1530 Lake Shore Dr.) and the adjoining International College of Surgeons and **International Museum of Surgical Science.**

At North Avenue turn left and proceed to the grande dame of Gold Coast promenades, Astor Street. (As you head south on Astor, don't forget to admire the archbishop's residence on the corner across the street.) On the northwest corner of Astor and Burton streets, you'll find the Georgian Patterson-McCormick Mansion, commissioned in 1891 by *Chicago Tribune* chief Joseph Medill as a wedding gift for his daughter Cissy and her husband, Robert Patterson. Where Astor Street jogs to meet Schiller Street stands the 1892 **Charnley House,** designed in part by Frank Lloyd Wright in a style that just slightly predates his Prairie homes.

At Division Street turn west to State Parkway. Those in need of refreshment can grab a bite at P. J. Clarke's (☒ 1204 N. State Pkwy.) or St. Germain (☒ 1210 N. State Pkwy.). Continue north to Goethe, where you'll come upon the Ambassador East Hotel—home of the famous Pump Room—and its across-the-street counterpart, the Ambassador West. Walk past the former Playboy Mansion (☒ 1340 N. State St.)— now a private residence—all the way to North Avenue for a splendid view of Lincoln Park.

Take North Avenue another block west to Dearborn Street; then head south again past the elite Latin School on the left and **St. Chrysostom's Episcopal Church** on the right. On your right you'll also see the Three Arts Club, a venerable residence for young women, and the Ruth Page Dance Foundation (☒ 1016 N. Dearborn St.).

Where Dearborn Street meets Oak Street—the Gold Coast's famous shopping district—turn right to go east. If your feet are weary, pay homage to the Dr. William Scholl College of Podiatric Medicine on your left—the college advertises a public exhibit called "Feet First: The Scholl Story." Then cross State Street, and you'll find yourself in the heart of the Oak Street shopping district, where storefronts touting Jil Sander, Versace, Sonia Rykiel, and other designers' wares compete to lure those with time and money to spend.

Where Oak Street ends, a quick crossing of Michigan Avenue puts you back at the Drake—just in time for tea or cocktails at the Coq d'Or.

TIMING

A stroll through the Gold Coast can be done in an hour, but what's the hurry? Make an afternoon of it. Especially pleasant are Saturday and Sunday afternoons in spring or fall or just before dusk any day in summer, when the neighborhood's leafy tranquillity and big-city energy converge.

Sights to See

Charnley House. This outwardly simple but splendid home at the corner of Astor and Schiller streets, finished in 1892 for lumberman James Charnley, gives visitors the chance to see the work of two renowned architects: Louis Sullivan and Frank Lloyd Wright, who was a young draftsman in Sullivan's office when the building was commissioned. Admission to the house is by tour (45 minutes) only. On Saturdays, an extended tour (90 minutes) visits the 1400 block of Astor Street and the Madlener House (☒ 4 Burton Pl.), a Prairie-style landmark. ☒ *1365 N. Astor St.,* ☎ *312/915–0105.* ☒ *$5 for Sat. tour; $9 for Sat. extended tour; Wed. tour free.* ☉ *Tours Wed. at noon, Sat. at 10 AM and 1 PM.*

⑰ Drake Hotel. Ever since it opened with a bang on New Year's Eve in 1920, the Drake has been a beloved Chicago landmark and gathering place. Built on landfill at the very end of North Michigan Avenue, this ornate north anchor of the Mag Mile was placed on the National Register of Historic Places in 1981. Cecil B. DeMille, Hillary Rodham Clinton, and Princess Diana have been guests. ☒ *140 E. Walton Pl.,* ☎ *312/787–2200.*

International Museum of Surgical Science. Filling four floors of a landmark Lake Shore Drive building patterned after a Louis XVI château, this unusual museum showcases 4,000-year-old skulls, amputation kits, an iron lung, and other intriguing (albeit slightly morbid) oddities. ⊠ *1524 Lake Shore Dr.,* ☎ *312/642–6502.* ⊠ *$3 suggested donation.* ⊙ *Tues.–Sat. 10–4.*

St. Chrysostom's Episcopal Church. The Gold Coast's earliest wealthy settlers worshiped in this 1895 English Gothic church, known for its 43-bell carillon imported from England. In 1926 it was awarded a gold medal by the American Institute of Architects for its outstanding design. ⊠ *1424 N. Dearborn St.,* ☎ *312/944–1083.*

| NEED A BREAK? | **3rd Coast,** a 24-hour, seven-day café, is a perfect place to recharge. Stop in for an elaborate breakfast, a sandwich, a stir-fry, or just a simple cappuccino. ⊠ *1260 N. Dearborn St.,* ☎ *312/649-0730.* |

River North

Bounded on the south and west by branches of the Chicago River, River North has eastern and northern boundaries that are harder to define than those of Streeterville and the Magnificent Mile. As in many other neighborhoods, the limits have expanded as the area has grown more attractive; today they extend roughly to Oak Street on the north and Clark Street on the east. Richly served by waterways and by railroad tracks that run along its western edge, the neighborhood was settled by Irish immigrants in the mid-19th century. As the 20th century approached and streetcar lines came to Clark, LaSalle, and Wells streets, the area developed into a vigorous commercial, industrial, and warehouse district.

As economic conditions changed and factories moved away, the neighborhood fell into disuse and disrepair. Despite its location less than a mile from Michigan Avenue and the bustling downtown area, River North became just another deteriorated urban area, a slide underscored by the depressed quality of life in the massive Cabrini Green public housing project, at the neighborhood's northern and western fringes.

Craftspeople moved into River North in the 1970s, attracted by low rents and the spacious abandoned storage areas and shop floors. Developers began buying up properties with an eye toward renovation. Today, scores of art galleries, dozens of restaurants, and numerous shops thrive here. The area's most charming feature is the almost complete absence of contemporary construction; the handsome buildings are virtually all renovations of properties nearly a century old. A typical River North building is a large, rectangular, solidly built structure made of Chicago redbrick, with high ceilings and hardwood floors. Even the buildings of the period that were intended to be strictly functional were often constructed with loving attention to the fine woodwork in doors and door frames, the decorative patterns set in the brickwork, the stone carvings and bas-reliefs, and the wrought-iron and handsome brass ornamentation.

A Good Walk

Begin your walk on the plaza of the massive **Merchandise Mart** ⑱, on the river between Orleans and Wells streets. The Mart has its own stop on the CTA Brown and Purple lines. Inside, along 7 mi of corridors, are showrooms, many of them containing home furnishings, as well as office space and retail shops. The nondescript building to the west is the Apparel Center, the Mart's equivalent for clothing.

From the plaza walk north on Wells Street to Kinzie Street. Turn east on Kinzie, cross Clark Street, and look to your right to see the handsome **Quaker Oats Building** ⑲, a glass-skin box that's the company's world headquarters. At Dearborn Street notice the splendid ornamental brickwork of **33 West Kinzie Street** ⑳, the home of the late Harry Caray's restaurant (☞ Near North *in* Chapter 3). Walk south on Dearborn Street to the bridge to see the distinctive twin corncobs of **Marina City** ㉑ and the bizarre structure that is the House of Blues club. Just to the east is Mies van der Rohe's austere 55-story, boxlike IBM Building, the last office building he designed (in 1971); there's a bust of the architect in the lobby.

Backtrack north on Dearborn Street two blocks to Hubbard Street, turn left, and pause at **Courthouse Place** ㉒, a splendid granite building that once housed the Cook County Criminal Courts. The restored lobby has black-and-white pictures of the original site and of Chicagoans associated with high-profile trials that took place here. Continue west on Hubbard Street, and then walk north on Clark Street, where you'll find two of Chicago's most popular Mexican restaurants, Frontera Grill and Topolobampo (☞ Near North *in* Chapter 3).

Go north on Clark Street one block to Grand Avenue. Turn left and continue one block west to LaSalle Street. The funny, charming edifice on the southwest corner is the **Anti-Cruelty Society Building** ㉓. Next door is Michael Jordan's Restaurant (⊠ 500 LaSalle St.), complete with an immense painting of the airborne one on its facade.

Walk north on LaSalle Street to Ontario Street and turn right. The Rock and Roll McDonald's (⊠ 201 Clark St.) has a standard Micky D's menu (with slightly higher prices), 24-hour service, and a profusion of rock-and-roll artifacts and '50s and '60s kitsch. This area has become a magnet for visitors enamored with the latest theme restaurants, with the Hard Rock Cafe (⊠ 63 W. Ontario St.) and Planet Hollywood (⊠ 633 N. Wells St.) vying with Michael Jordan's Restaurant and the Rainforest Cafe (⊠ 605 N. Clark St.) for business. Another popular spot for out-of-towners is Ed Debevic's (⊠ 640 N. Wells St.), a '50s-style diner. If you are more interested in food than kitsch, the Big Bowl Café (⊠ 159 W. Erie St.) is where you'll get the most for your money.

From McDonald's head west on Ontario Street. At Wells Street turn right and walk three blocks north to Superior Street and one block west to Franklin Street, the heart of the area known as the **River North Gallery District** ㉔. Virtually every building on Superior Street between Wells and Orleans streets houses at least one gallery. In the area bounded by Wells, Orleans, Chicago, and Erie streets are dozens of art galleries showing every kind of work imaginable. Galleries welcome visitors, so feel free to visit any that catch your eye.

For a look at a major institution in the area, go north on Franklin Street to Chicago Avenue. Two blocks east on Chicago Avenue is the large **Moody Bible Institute** ㉕. Other campus buildings spread out behind it to the north.

TIMING

You can do this walk in about two hours, but add another hour or more if you want to wander leisurely in and out of galleries on Superior Street and the nearby streets. Most galleries are closed Sunday and Monday. Friday evenings are when many galleries schedule openings of new shows.

Sights to See

➌ **Anti-Cruelty Society.** The original building dates to 1935; architect Stanley Tigerman's whimsical wood-and-glass addition was completed in 1982. ⊠ *157 W. Grand Ave.,* ☎ *312/644–8338.*

➋ **Courthouse Place.** The former Cook County Criminal Courts building, completed in 1892, was the setting for many sensational trials earlier this century, including the Leopold and Loeb murder trial, in which Clarence Darrow defended the two University of Chicago students who killed a 13-year-old boy just for a thrill. Journalists and *The Front Page* authors Ben Hecht and Charles MacArthur, as well as poet Carl Sandburg, all worked as newspaper reporters in the building's pressroom. It's now an office building; note the wonderful bas-reliefs over the arched, pillared doorway. ✉ *54 W. Hubbard St.*

㉑ Marina City. Bertrand Goldberg's twin corncob buildings on the river, completed in 1967, house condominium apartments (all pie-shape, with curving balconies). Goldberg also served as architect for a redevelopment project at Marina City. In addition to the apartments and marina, the complex now has four restaurants and a House of Blues (☞ Nightlife *in* Chapter 5) nightclub. ✉ *300 N. State St.*

⑱ Merchandise Mart. The Mart contains 4 million square ft—more than any other building in the country except the Pentagon. Built by the architectural firm Graham Anderson Probst and White in 1930, it's now owned by the Kennedys of political fame. Inside are more than 600 permanent wholesale showrooms for all sorts of merchandise, much of it related to interior decoration. You can view showrooms either accompanied by an interior designer or on one of the Mart's tours; the 13th-floor showrooms (kitchens and baths) are always open weekdays to the public. The first two floors of the Mart are a retail shopping mall, with stores from many national chains and a branch of the downtown department store Carson Pirie Scott. The somewhat macabre row of heads on the plaza is the Merchandise Mart Hall of Fame, installed at Joseph P. Kennedy's behest in 1953. The titans of retail portrayed here include Marshall Field, F. W. Woolworth, and Edward A. Filene. ✉ *300 N. Wells St.,* ☎ *312/527–7600 or 312/644–4664.* ⚑ *Tour $8.* ☉ *Weekdays 9–5, 1½-hr tour weekdays at noon.*

㉕ Moody Bible Institute. Here, in a massive contemporary brick structure, students of various conservative Christian denominations study and prepare for religious careers. ✉ *820 N. LaSalle St.,* ☎ *312/329–4000.*

OFF THE BEATEN PATH

POLISH MUSEUM OF AMERICA – Dedicated to gathering materials on the history of the Polish people in America, the Polish Museum has an eclectic collection that includes an art gallery, an exhibit on the Shakespearean actress Helena Modjeska, one on the American Revolutionary War hero Tadeusz Kosciuszko, and another on the pianist and composer Ignacy Paderewski. The stations of the cross from the first Polish church in America (which was in Texas) are on display; there's a library, too. The museum is in the East Village neighborhood, now mainly Hispanic, about a mile west of the Near North. It's worth noting that Chicago has the largest Polish population of any city outside Warsaw. ✉ *984 N. Milwaukee Ave.,* ☎ *773/384-3352.* ⚑ *$2.* ☉ *Daily 11–4.*

⑲ Quaker Oats Building. In case the name isn't clear enough, in the lobby there's an immense replica of the famous Quaker Oats box. Designed by Skidmore, Owings & Merrill and completed in 1987, this tall glass building on the river houses the headquarters of the famous maker of breakfast cereals. ✉ *321 N. Clark St.*

NEED A BREAK?

A riverside restaurant in the Quaker Oats Building's lower level, **Sorriso** (✉ 321 N. Clark St., ☎ 312/644-0283) has outdoor seating in summer with a great view of Wacker Drive's skyscrapers.

㉔ River North Gallery District. Don't be shy about walking in and browsing at one of the dozens of galleries in this area. On most Friday evenings many schedule openings of new shows and serve refreshments;

you can sip jug wine as you stroll through the newly hung exhibit. Although each gallery sets its own hours, most are open Tuesday through Saturday 10–5 or 11–5 and are closed Sunday and Monday. Take a look at Chapter 7 for a list of some galleries. For announcements of openings and other art-scene news, send away for the *Chicago Gallery News* (✉ Suite 308, 730 N. Franklin St., 60610) or pick up a copy at one of the visitor centers of the Chicago Office of Tourism. ✉ *Bounded by Wells, Orleans, and Erie Sts. and Chicago Ave.*

NEED A BREAK?	Nestled under the El tracks at Superior and Franklin streets is **Brett's Kitchen** (✉ 233 W. Superior St., ☎ 312/664–6354), an excellent spot for a sandwich or an omelet Monday through Saturday.

㉓ 33 West Kinzie Street. This Dutch Renaissance–style brick building looks as though it belongs in Amsterdam—except for the huge HOLY COW! banner that decorates it. That was the favorite expression of late Chicago Cubs announcer Harry Caray, who owned a restaurant here that's still popular (☞ Near North *in* Chapter 3).

OFF THE BEATEN PATH	**UKRAINIAN VILLAGE** – A number of sights are testimony to the ethnic roots of this neighborhood, currently 75% Ukrainian, which extends from Damen Avenue (2000 W.) on the east and Western Avenue (2400 W.) on the west, between Chicago Avenue (800 N.) and Division Street (1200 N.). **Holy Trinity Cathedral** (✉ 1121 N. Leavitt Ave., ☎ 773/486–6064) is a Russian Orthodox church in the heart of Ukrainian Village, designed by Louis Sullivan in 1903; it is said that Czar Nicholas of Russia contributed $4,000 to the construction. The Byzantine-style **St. Nicholas Ukrainian Catholic Cathedral** (✉ 2238 W. Rice St., ☎ 773/276–4537), with its 13 copper-clad domes, was built in 1914 and is similar to the Basilica of St. Sophia in Kiev. At the far western edge of Ukrainian Village, the **Ukrainian Institute of Modern Art** (✉ 2320 W. Chicago Ave., ☎ 773/227–5522) focuses on contemporary paintings and sculpture by artists of Ukrainian descent. It's open Wednesday through Sunday from noon to 4; admission is free.

LINCOLN PARK

In the early years of the 19th century, the area bounded by North Avenue (1600 N.) on the south, Diversey Parkway (2800 N.) on the north, the lake on the east, and the Chicago River on the west was a sparsely settled community of truck farms and orchards that grew produce for the city of Chicago, 3 mi to the south. The original city burial ground was on the lakefront at North Avenue. The park that today extends from North Avenue to Hollywood Avenue (5700 N.) was established in 1864, after the city transferred about 20,000 bodies to Graceland and Rosehill cemeteries, then far north of the city limits. Many of the dead were Confederate soldiers who perished at Camp Douglas, the Union's infamous prison camp on the lakefront several miles south. Called Lincoln Park after the then recently assassinated president, this swath of green became the city's first public playground. The neighborhood adjacent to the original park also became known as Lincoln Park (to the confusion of some visitors).

By the mid-1860s the area had become more populated. Germans predominated, and there were Irish and Scottish immigrants as well. The construction in 1860 of the Presbyterian Theological Seminary (later the McCormick Seminary, which moved to Hyde Park in 1977) brought modest residential construction. By the end of the century immigrants from Eastern Europe—Poles, Slovaks, Serbs, Hungarians, Romanians, and some Italians as well—had swelled the population, and much of the housing stock in the western part of the neighborhood dates from this period.

Between the world wars expensive new construction, particularly along the lakefront and the park, was undertaken in Lincoln Park. At the same time, however, the deteriorating, once elegant houses to the west were being subdivided into rooming houses—a process that was occurring at roughly the same period in Hyde Park, 10 mi to the south. Ethnic diversification and an increase in crime were also changing the face of the neighborhood, which was rocked by the St. Valentine's Day Massacre in 1929 and the FBI shooting of John Dillinger at the Biograph Theatre in 1934, both of which took place on North Lincoln Avenue.

Following World War II, the ethnic groups that had been first to arrive in Lincoln Park had achieved some affluence and began to leave for northern parts of the city and the suburbs. A new wave of aspiring immigrants moved to take their place. These new residents often lacked the resources to maintain their properties. By 1960 nearly a quarter of the housing stock in Lincoln Park was classified as substandard. As housing prices fell, artists and others who appreciated the aesthetic value of the decaying buildings and were willing to work to restore them moved to the southeastern part of the area. The newcomers joined established residents in forming the Old Town Triangle Association; residents to the north, who had successfully resisted subdivision, formed the Mid-North Association. In 1954 neighborhood institutions, including DePaul University, the McCormick Seminary, four hospitals, a bank, and others, dismayed by the decline of the area, formed the Lincoln Park Conservation Association. As the University of Chicago had done in Hyde Park, this association began exploring the possibilities of urban renewal as a means of rejuvenating the area.

Eventually, the original buildings along North Avenue were bulldozed and replaced with anonymous modern town-house developments, and many north–south streets were blocked off at North Avenue to create an enclosed community to the north. Since the 1960s the gentrification of Lincoln Park has moved steadily westward, spreading as far as Clybourn Avenue, formerly a light industrial strip. Today this lively neighborhood is home to countless thriving businesses: unique shops, hot restaurants, and clubs where lines form on weekends. It also has some of the loveliest residential streets in the city.

The walks in this section concentrate on the history and attractions of three distinct areas: the DePaul area and North Lincoln Avenue and Halsted Street; the Old Town Triangle; and the lakefront and Lincoln Park.

DePaul and North Lincoln Avenue

The serene setting of DePaul University, which rules the northern part of the neighborhood, makes a pleasant contrast to the busy shops and restaurants of two nearby upscale neighborhood arteries: North Lincoln Avenue—where the Biograph Theatre, site of John Dillinger's waterloo, still stands—and Halsted Street.

Numbers in the text correspond to numbers in the margin and on the Lincoln Park map.

A Good Walk

This walk starts at the Lincoln Park campus of DePaul University. The CTA is the best way to get here from the Loop or the Near North Side. Take the Howard (Red line) train or the Ravenswood (Brown line) train to Fullerton Avenue. Sheffield Avenue will be the nearest north–south street. If you're driving, take Lake Shore Drive to Fullerton Avenue and drive west on Fullerton Avenue to Sheffield Avenue. Parking is scarce, especially evenings and weekends, so public transit or a cab is recommended.

Begin a visit to **DePaul University** ①, one of the largest Catholic universities in the country, on its northern boundary—the southeast corner of Fullerton and Sheffield avenues. To the west across Sheffield Avenue, the massive brick complex extending halfway down the block is **Sanctuary Hall** ②, now a university residence hall.

For a look at the modern part of the campus, walk west on Fullerton Avenue one block to Kenmore Avenue and the **John T. Richardson Library** ③, where you should pop in to see the two-story reading room. Exit through the library's courtyard, where you can sit down next to a bronze sculpture of St. Vincent de Paul, the university's namesake, engaged in discussion with two college students. Continue west a short distance to what formerly was Seminary Avenue. In 1992 the street was closed off to create a grassy quadrangle for the campus.

Walk south down the quadrangle to Belden Avenue, then east to the portion of the campus between Sheffield Avenue and Halsted Street that was the former McCormick Theological Seminary grounds. Here antislavery groups met during the Civil War, and Chicagoans sought refuge from the Great Fire of 1871. The building on your right as you enter the campus from Belden Avenue, just past Dayton Avenue, was built as a chapel but is now the university's Concert Hall (⊠ 800 W. Belden Ave.). The small street inside the U on your left is **Chalmers Place** ④, a quiet cul-de-sac that may make you feel you've stepped into the 19th century. The large Queen Anne building on the north side has a great turret and decorative shingles.

Head to the west end of the street to Cortelyou Commons (⊠ 2324 N. Fremont Ave.), an imposing Gothic-style structure built in 1929 that is used for special events. Continue south past the Commons, east on Chalmers Place, and south again to exit the university grounds where you entered on Belden Avenue.

Continue east on Belden Avenue and turn left onto Halsted Street. Walk north to the three-way intersection of Fullerton Avenue, Halsted Street, and Lincoln Avenue. This section of Lincoln Avenue, which runs on a northwest–southeast diagonal, tells a good deal about the neighborhood. Upscale and trendy without being avant-garde, the strip caters to well-educated professionals, emphasizing recreation and leisure-time needs over more mundane requirements. In particular, there are a number of interesting shops catering to children. You'll be hard-pressed to find a drugstore or a shoe repair shop: those conveniences have moved to Clark Street, several blocks east, or to Sheffield Avenue.

On the southeast side of the intersection, where Halsted Street and Lincoln Avenue come together at a point, is the huge White Elephant Children's Memorial Resale Shop (⊠ 2380 N. Lincoln Ave.), which carries every kind of used merchandise imaginable. Earnings benefit Children's Memorial Hospital, just east and south of the shop. As you head southeast down the street, the building at **2312–2310 N. Lincoln Avenue** ⑤ was designed by Adler and Sullivan. At the corner of Lincoln and Belden avenues, cross the street. The **John Barleycorn Memorial Pub** ⑥ is one of Chicago's better-known pubs.

Head back up Lincoln Avenue, past the three-way intersection, to the **Biograph Theatre** ⑦, where gangster John Dillinger perished by FBI gunfire. The theater now shows current films—no Jimmy Cagney flicks. Across the street, the Threepenny Cinema shows a combination of art films and second-run features. Across Lincoln Avenue is the Red Lion (⊠ 2446 N. Lincoln Ave.), which advertises itself as "the only English pub in Chicago." Just south of the Red Lion is Lounge Ax (⊠ 2438 N. Lincoln Ave.), a great spot for rock (☞ Nightlife *in* Chapter 5).

Return now to the intersection where the White Elephant stands and head south on Halsted Street, one of the most vibrant, successful streets in Lincoln Park. Here you'll find a number of boutiques, trendy diners, and watering holes, plus such chain outposts as the Gap and Banana Republic.

Two blocks down, at Webster Avenue, walk east to **Oz Park** ⑧, a large green space named in honor of L. Frank Baum, author of the Oz storybooks, who lived and worked in Chicago. Back on Halsted, south of Webster, is Cafe Ba-Ba-Reeba! (⊠ 2024 N. Halsted St.), which serves great tapas and a notorious sangria (☞ Lincoln Park and North *in* Chapter 3).

Continue walking south one block to Armitage Avenue, then head west a few blocks to the **Old Town School of Folk Music** ⑨, a neighborhood institution housed in a turn-of-the-century building. A lively meeting place for lovers of folk music from around the world, the school has classes and concerts in an intimate setting.

To continue with an exploration of the Old Town Triangle, you'll want to either retrieve your car or jump on Bus 73, heading east on Armitage Avenue. Get off where Armitage dead-ends into Clark Street and Lincoln Park, a trip of just over a half mile.

TIMING

You could see the sights on this walk in an hour or two. If the weather is fine, you may want to allow an extra hour or two for exploring the beautiful residential streets just south of DePaul and for visiting the many shops along Halsted Street.

Sights to See

❼ **Biograph Theatre.** This theater is now on the National Register of Historic Places, since it was here that gangster John Dillinger met his end at the hands of the FBI in July 1934. The film playing was *Manhattan Melodrama.* Now a multiplex, the Biograph shows first-run movies. ⊠ 2433 N. Lincoln Ave., ☎ 773/348–4123.

❹ **Chalmers Place.** A pleasant cul-de-sac in the midst of DePaul University buildings is lined with private town houses, some of which are 100 years old and served as residences for McCormick Seminary faculty members. The homes have semicircular brickwork around the windows. ⊠ ½ block north of Belden Ave. between Fremont Ave. and Halsted St.

❶ **DePaul University.** Founded in 1898 by the Vincentian Fathers, DePaul is the largest Catholic university in the Midwest. It serves more than 17,000 students at its Lincoln Park location and four others in the Loop and suburbs. DePaul has a large continuing-education program, and thousands of Chicago adults attend the many evening and weekend classes. ⊠ *Bounded by Fullerton, Racine, and Belden Aves. and Halsted St.*

❻ **John Barleycorn Memorial Pub.** This popular pub in an 1890 building has a pleasant beer garden, a nautical theme, and plays classical music, not rock. Ship models adorn the walls, and the brass-plated door has not a window but a porthole. Some of the models date to the 1880s and were collected by a former owner during his travels to faraway

CHICAGO'S GANGSTER PAST

TIME HAS HELPED HEAL THE SCARS of Chicago's unsavory gangster past. Most of the gangster haunts have long since been razed, and city officials and residents have put the Prohibition-era crime and corruption well behind them. But Al Capone may still be the city's most famous citizen—a notoriety perhaps now shared by Chicago Bulls superstar Michael Jordan.

When Prohibition ended the legal sale of alcoholic beverages in 1920, a strong demand for illegal goods and services was created. Chicago fell into the hands of Al "Scarface" Capone, George "Bugs" Moran, Earl "Hymie" Weiss, "Bloody" Angelo Genna, and "Machine Gun" Jack McGurn, among others. The '20s were punctuated by gunfire, as wars erupted between the rivals.

Capone won control of Chicago's underworld on Feb. 14, 1929, during the bloody St. Valentine's Day Massacre. His henchmen, dressed as police offers, entered the S.M.C. Cartage garage at 2122 N. Clark Street, killing six of Bugsy Moran's men and a visitor. The seven men had been lined up against a wall and riddled with bullets; to this day, no one has been convicted of the murders. Seven bushes stand at the spot, which is now a grassy area next to a senior-citizens home.

Capone ran gambling, prostitution, and bootlegging rackets, with a fortune estimated at $60 million. Under the supervision of Elliot Ness, Prohibition agents dismantled Capone's bootlegging empire, while Internal Revenue Service agents convicted him of income tax evasion in 1931. Capone was sentenced to 11 years in prison, only to be released in 1939 to retire in Florida where he died from syphilis in 1947.

Deemed "public enemy number one," Indianapolis-born John Dillinger robbed a dozen banks over 13 months. After escaping jail in Crown Point, Indiana, he moved to Chicago in 1934. He was betrayed by the "lady in red," an acquaintance who told federal agents she would wear a red dress while accompanying him to the Biograph Theatre, a movie theater still in existence at 2433 N. Lincoln Avenue. Federal agents fatally shot Dillinger as he left the theater, although some historians maintain Dillinger was not the man killed there.

You can find pieces of gangster lore at spots sprinkled throughout the city. The **Green Mill** (☞ Nightlife *in* Chapter 5) became mobster territory when "Machine Gun" Jack McGurn gained a 25% ownership of the club, which still features a trapdoor from speakeasy days. The gangster alley at the **American Police Center and Museum** (⊠ 1717 S. State St., ☎ 312/431–0005) includes Dillinger's death mask, sawed off shotguns, and photos of gangsters felled by police; admission $4, open weekdays 9:30–4:30.

Untouchable Tours (☎ 773/881–1195, ⊜ $20) offers a two-hour bus tour of Prohibition-era gangster hot spots and hit spots. It's theater on wheels: the guides, dressed like wise guys and delivering wise cracks, retell gangland exploits, as well as relate other bits of Chicago history. Tours depart from in front of the Rock 'n' Roll McDonalds, at Clark and Ohio streets; advance reservations are required.

places, including Sri Lanka, Hong Kong, and Cambodia. ⊠ *658 W. Belden Ave.,* ☏ *773/348–8899.*

③ John T. Richardson Library. Built in 1992 and designed by Lohan Associates of Chicago, DePaul University's library has soaring ceilings, oak woodwork, stained-glass windows made by Tiffany Studios early in the century, and an impressive two-story reading room on the third floor. There's a statue of St. Vincent de Paul in the courtyard. ⊠ *2350 N. Kenmore Ave.*

⑨ Old Town School of Folk Music. Many notable musicians, including John Prine, the late Steve Goodman, Bonnie Koloc, Tom Chapin, Ella Jenkins, and Roger McGuinn of the Byrds, have either studied or performed at the Old Town School, which was founded in 1957. Far from being a hangout for '60s-style folkies, the school currently hosts eclectic concerts with live music from around the world, from Sardinian songs to African pop. The staff teaches some 2,500 students a week in a variety of classes. The school's store, A Different Strummer, has fine acoustical instruments, songbooks, world-music tape cassettes and compact discs, and music and instruments for children. ⊠ *909 W. Armitage Ave.,* ☏ *773/525–7793.*

⑧ Oz Park. The statue of the Tin Woodman and the yellow bricks in the northeast corner of this large grassy space give away the reason for its name. L. Frank Baum, who wrote the best-selling children's book *The Wizard of Oz* (the basis for the 1939 movie classic), once lived in this area. The park has endlessly intriguing wooden play equipment for kids.

NEED A BREAK?	**Nookies, too** (⊠ 2114 N. Halsted St., ☏ 773/327–1400), one of the better-known diners in this area, is a pleasant spot for an inexpensive snack or a meal of the burger or grilled-cheese variety. It has a casual counter area in front and is open 24 hours on both Friday and Saturday.

② Sanctuary Hall. Built in 1895 as the St. Augustine Home for the Aged, this huge building is now a DePaul University dormitory with apartments for students. ⊠ *2358 N. Sheffield Ave.*

OFF THE BEATEN PATH	**ST. ALPHONSUS REDEMPTORIST CHURCH** – Built between 1889 and 1897, the Gothic St. Alphonsus originally served a German neighborhood. The beautiful interior has a vaulted ceiling and stained glass. ⊠ *1429 W. Wellington Ave.,* ☏ *773/525–0709.*

St. Clement's Church. Combining both Romanesque and Byzantine elements in its design, St. Clement's has beautiful mosaics and lavish stained glass. ⊠ *642 W. Deming Pl.,* ☏ *773/281–0371.*

⑤ 2312–2310 N. Lincoln Avenue. In the 1880s Dankmar Adler and Louis Sullivan designed what was originally the Ferdinand Kaufman Store and Flat Building.

Old Town Triangle

What began in the 1850s as a modest neighborhood of working-class German families now accommodates a diverse population and has some of the oldest—and most expensive—streets in Chicago. Over the past three decades many houses in the Old Town historic district have been preserved. Besides its interesting architecture, Old Town is notable for being home to the comedy club Second City.

A Good Walk

To reach the Old Town Triangle, take Clark Street south to Wisconsin Avenue, go west on Wisconsin Avenue one short block, and turn

Lincoln Park

Abraham Lincoln statue, **21**

Biograph Theatre, **7**

Chalmers Place, **4**

Chess Pavilion, **27**

Chicago Historical Society, **20**

Crilly Court, **17**

DePaul University, **1**

1800 North Hudson Avenue, **15**

1800 North Sedgwick Street, **13**

1838 and 1836 North Lincoln Park West, **10**

John Barleycorn Memorial Pub, **6**

John T. Richardson Library, **3**

Lincoln Park Conservatory, **24**

Lincoln Park Zoo, **22**

Louis Sullivan row houses, **11**

Marge's Pub, **12**

Midwest Buddhist Temple, **14**

Moody Memorial Church, **19**

Nature Museum, **25**

North Avenue Beach, **26**

Old Town School of Folk Music, **9**

Oz Park, **8**

St. Michael's Church, **16**

Sanctuary Hall, **2**

Second City, **18**

Shakespeare Garden, **23**

2312–2310 North Lincoln Avenue, **5**

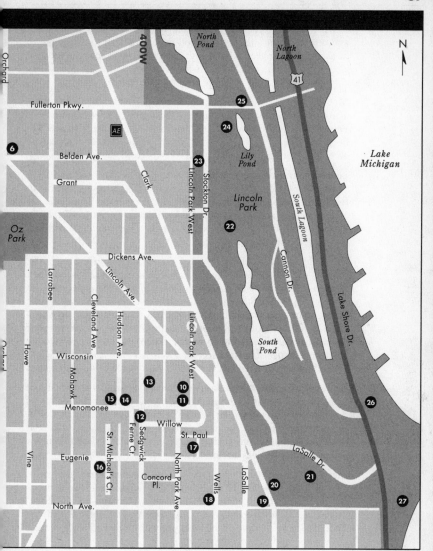

left onto Lincoln Park West. If you're on Lincoln Avenue, head south to where it intersects with Wisconsin Avenue and Lincoln Park West and turn right onto the latter. If you're driving to this starting point, be aware that the area is filled with courts and lanes that run for only a block or so; many have been made one-way.

The west side of Lincoln Park West between Wisconsin Avenue and Menomonee Street is a gold mine of historic residential architecture. The two marvelous frame houses at **1838 and 1836 N. Lincoln Park West** ⑩ were built in the early 1870s. Just past these are five **Louis Sullivan row houses** ⑪. The redbrick, Queen Anne–style homes provide an unusual glimpse of the architect's early work.

Before walking on, look across to the east side of the street and 1835 Lincoln Park West, a frame house built in 1874. Note the number in the stained glass above the door. That was the original house number when Lincoln Park West was called Franklin Street. At 1817 Lincoln Park West is a French Renaissance–style freestanding home with unusually elaborate carved wooden doors.

Continue south on Lincoln Park West to Menomonee Street. The brightly painted home on the northwest corner, at 1802 Lincoln Park West, was originally a farmhouse, built in 1874 for Henry Meyer. Turn east on Menomonee Street and walk a short distance to 216 Menomonee Street, a tiny cottage that dates to 1874. It was one of the first cottages to be built as temporary quarters after the Great Fire. Backtrack west on Menomonee Street, and go two blocks to Sedgwick Street. On the southwest corner of the intersection is **Marge's Pub** ⑫, the oldest commercial property in Lincoln Park and a good place to stop for a beer.

Turn right onto the **1800 N. Sedgwick Street** ⑬ block and proceed about halfway up. Each of the houses on the right, starting with 1811, was designed for its owner at an astronomical price by a different world-renowned architect. In the small park across the street, take a look at the two unusually shiny sculptures of horses by artist John Kearney. His medium: parts of car bumpers.

If you're on foot, retrace your steps to Menomonee Street, turn right, and walk one block to Hudson Avenue. The Japanese-style building where the street curves is the **Midwest Buddhist Temple** ⑭. In June, Old Town Triangle hosts the popular Old Town Art Fair, and the Midwest Buddhist Temple is one of the most popular food vendors at the fair (they serve food only during the fair).

Before continuing on Menomonee Street, notice the corner building, **1800 N. Hudson Avenue** ⑮, in a half-timber style that's unusual for Lincoln Park. Go west one block on Menomonee Street, then south on Cleveland Avenue to Eugenie Street and the ornate **St. Michael's Church** ⑯, constructed for the area's German community.

Walk east on Eugenie Street six blocks and turn left onto **Crilly Court** ⑰, one of the oldest and most charming streets in Chicago. The town houses and apartments here were built in the 1880s; it's easy to picture horse-drawn carriages in front of them. When you come to St. Paul Avenue at the street's north end, turn east, proceed to Wells Street, and turn right. **Second City** ⑱, the well-known comedy club (☞ Nightlife *in* Chapter 5), is 1½ blocks south, between Eugenie Street and North Avenue. This area on Wells Street is the main commercial strip in Old Town, with a number of good restaurants, clubs, and stylish shops.

If you want to continue on to Lincoln Park, go south on Wells Street to North Avenue, turn left, and walk east to Clark Street.

You can do this walk in one or two hours, or you can choose to explore Old Town's many intriguing side streets for up to half a day.

Sights to See

⑰ Crilly Court. This lovely tree-lined street was created in 1884 by South Side contractor Daniel Crilly, who built the row houses on the west side and the four-story apartment buildings on the east side. They were renovated about 50 years later by Edgar Crilly, one of his sons; their restoration was one of the first steps in the renewal and gentrification of the Old Town Triangle in particular and Lincoln Park in general. Above the doors of the east-side buildings are carved the names of Daniel Crilly's children: Isabelle, Oliver, Edgar, and Erminnie. ⊠ *Bounded by Eugenie and Wells Sts. and N. Park and St. Paul Aves.*

⑮ 1800 N. Hudson Avenue. A frame house built around the turn of the century has become a striking black-and-white half-timber building. In 1955 it was remodeled to look like a Bavarian dwelling after its owner, the late William Schmidt, returned from a trip to Germany, where he fell in love with this style of architecture.

⑬ 1800 N. Sedgwick Street. The materials used to build the houses numbered 1811–1847 begin with handsome contemporary redbrick and move on to poured concrete, oddly colored brick, and gray wood. All were custom designed by different architects in the late 1970s. Such were the egos involved that the architects could agree on nothing—not style, not materials, not lot size, not even the height of the buildings. Although some of the structures might look good on another site, here they look like transplanted misfits, jammed in together, out of character with the neighborhood and with each other. Despite their monetary value (some have been on the market recently for more than a million dollars), little about them is aesthetically pleasing.

⑩ 1838 and 1836 N. Lincoln Park West. Of these two frame buildings, the smaller, 1836, was built just after the fire of 1871; it has narrow clapboards, bay windows, leaded glass, and decorative iron grillwork around the miniature widow's walk above the front entrance. There are also decorative cutouts in the wood over the front door. The exterior painting has been done in contrasting brown, beige, and white to reveal the details of the woodwork. The larger house, painted gray and white, is a grand structure built to resemble a Swiss chalet. Both buildings were constructed for the Wacker family, prominent German brewers.

Frame houses are relatively uncommon in Lincoln Park, in part because of the restrictions on wood construction that went into effect following the Chicago Fire of 1871. (Some areas in southwestern Lincoln Park do have extensive frame construction; the regulations were not always strictly enforced.)

⑪ Louis Sullivan row houses. The love of geometric ornamentation that Sullivan eventually brought to such projects as the Carson Pirie Scott building is already visible in these row houses built in 1885. The terracotta cornices and decorative window tops are especially noteworthy. ⊠ *1826–1834 N. Lincoln Park W.*

⑫ Marge's Pub. A favorite watering hole in the neighborhood, Marge's was once a speakeasy. The building, with its redbrick construction and stone decoration around the windows, is in a style common among older Lincoln Park buildings. Inside, over the bar, are black-and-white drawings of famous Chicagoans, including the late mayor Richard J. "Boss" Daley and former Chicago Bears coach Mike Ditka. ⊠ *1758 N. Sedgwick St.,* ☎ *312/787–3900.*

⓮ **Midwest Buddhist Temple.** The temple's plain walls, landscaped gardens, and pagoda-like roof strike an unusual but harmonious note in a largely brick neighborhood. The congregation, about 80% Japanese-American, comes from all over the city and the suburbs. The temple was built in 1971 on an empty parcel of land purchased from the city in the 1960s. Call to arrange a tour. ⊠ *435 W. Menomonee St.,* ☎ *312/943–7801.*

⓰ **St. Michael's Church.** This massive brick Romanesque church, which dates to 1869, partially withstood the fire of 1871. German residents of the neighborhood restored the interior of the church after the fire. Their work is a legacy of exquisite craftsmanship. Inside are beautiful stained-glass windows and a stunning altar of carved wood. Outside are classical columns of different heights, elaborate capitals, many roofs with stonework at the top, and an elegant spire. The building stands on land that was donated in the 1850s by Michael Diversey (the early beer baron after whom Diversey Parkway is named) for the purpose of providing a church where the area's German community could worship. ⊠ *1633 N. Cleveland Ave.,* ☎ *312/642–2498.*

NEED A BREAK?   **Twin Anchors** (⊠ 1655 N. Sedgwick Ave., ☎ 312/266–1616), a popular Old Town restaurant and tavern for more than 60 years, is famous for its barbecued ribs.

⓲ **Second City.** Such talents as Elaine May, Mike Nichols, Alan Arkin, Joan Rivers, the late John Belushi, Bill Murray, Shelley Long, and Rick Moranis used this club, known for its improvisational comedy, as a training ground (☞ Nightlife *in* Chapter 5). It eventually inspired several branch theaters—Toronto's Second City, which produced Dan Aykroyd and the late John Candy and Gilda Radner, is probably the best known—as well as the hit TV show *SCTV.* ⊠ *1616 N. Wells St.,* ☎ *312/337–3992.*

NEED A BREAK?   **Topo Gigio** (⊠ 1516 N. Wells St., ☎ 312/266–9355) has a wide selection of wine and Italian cuisine; you can also order appetizers and salads for a snack. The *bruschetta*—grilled Italian bread brushed with garlic and olive oil and crowned with tomato—is particularly recommended. In the summertime a lovely garden is open for dining.

Lincoln Park

The city's oldest and most popular park is one of a number of lakefront greenbelts that Chicago wisely created as a refuge for city dwellers. Within and near Lincoln Park are a number of appealing attractions.

A Good Walk

You can reach Lincoln Park by taking the Sheridan Road Bus 151 north from North Michigan Avenue. Get off at North Avenue. If you're driving, take Lake Shore Drive to the LaSalle Street–North Avenue exit. Make a right turn onto Stockton Drive and look for metered parking. The area can be extremely congested, however, especially on weekends, so driving is not recommended.

The huge Romanesque structure on the west side of Clark Street is **Moody Memorial Church** ⑲, one of the largest Protestant churches in the nation. Across Clark is the southwest entrance to the park, but first stop in to see the exhibits at the **Chicago Historical Society** ⑳, at the northeast corner of North Avenue and Clark Street. The original Georgian structure was built in 1932; walk around to the east side (facing the lake) and see what it looked like at the time.

All of Chicago's parks, and Lincoln Park in particular, are dotted with sculptures—historical, literary, or just plain fanciful. East of the historical society is one of the most famous, the **Abraham Lincoln statue** ㉑. The figure is pensive—in marked contrast to the lively activities of the children who often play nearby.

Heading into the park and wandering north along the park's main north–south artery, Stockton Drive, will bring you to the **Lincoln Park Zoo** ㉒, one of the finest small urban zoos in the country. (Look for the red barn, home of Farm in the Zoo: The main entrance is just north of it.) The homely bronze figure just east of Stockton Drive and south of Dickens Street is Hans Christian Andersen, seated there since 1896. Beside him is the beautiful swan from his most famous story, "The Ugly Duckling."

Also near the zoo, at the western edge of the park opposite Belden Avenue, is the **Shakespeare Garden** ㉓, with a statue of the playwright. North of the zoo you can visit the **Lincoln Park Conservatory** ㉔, with its lush greenery. West of the conservatory, between Stockton Drive and Lincoln Park West, is Grandmother's Garden, a collection dating from 1893 of informal beds of perennials, including hibiscuses and chrysanthemums.

The conservatory garden, south of the building, has an uncommonly joyful fountain where bronze storks, fish, and small mer-boys cavort in the spraying water. The 1887 Bates Fountain was the collaborative effort of Augustus Saint-Gaudens and his assistant, Frederick MacMonnies.

Continue north to Fullerton Parkway, turn right, and proceed to Cannon Drive, site of the Chicago Academy of Science's **Nature Museum** ㉕, which is expected to open in spring of 1999. Coming out, stroll under Lake Shore Drive to the lakefront and **North Avenue Beach** ㉖. About a mile south of Fullerton, it is likely to be thronged on summer weekends but sparsely populated at other times. To stroll back to the Near North Side, about 2 mi from here, walk south past North Avenue Beach and follow the lakefront promenade. Notice the blue-and-white beach house, its portholes and "smokestacks" mimicking an old ocean liner. At the south end of the beach, stop by the 1950s vintage **Chess Pavilion** ㉗ to watch people of all ages engrossed in intellectual combat.

TIMING

You can visit the sights on this walk in three hours. That timing, however, does not allow for leisurely visits to Lincoln Park Zoo and the museums. You could easily spend two hours or more at each.

Sights to See

㉑ **Abraham Lincoln statue.** Known as the Standing Lincoln, this statue was completed in 1887 by the noted American sculptor Augustus Saint-Gaudens, whose portrayals of military heroes and presidents adorn almost every major city east of the Mississippi River. The sculptor used a mask of Lincoln's face and casts of his hands that were made before he became president. ⊠ *Lincoln Park, east of Chicago Historical Society.*

㉗ **Chess Pavilion.** The competition gets intense at this open-air structure on the lakefront. There are carved reliefs along its base, and statues of a king and queen flank it on either side. ⊠ *Lakefront at south end of Lincoln Park.*

★ ◔ ㉕ **Chicago Historical Society.** Chicago's oldest cultural institution (founded in 1856), the CHS is housed in a stately brick Georgian building dating to 1932 that was updated in 1971 with a striking addition facing

Clark Street. In the south end (the curved portion) is a terra-cotta arch designed by Daniel Burnham more than 100 years ago; it originally framed the doorway of the National Livestock Bank, near the now-closed Chicago stockyards. The historical society's permanent exhibits include the much-loved Diorama Room, which portrays scenes from Chicago's history and has been a part of the lives of generations of Chicago children. Other attractions are Chicago's first locomotive (which visitors may board), collections of costumes, and the popular Illinois Pioneer Life Gallery, where there are daily crafts demonstrations by costumed docents. ⊠ *1601 N. Clark St.,* ☎ *312/642–4600.* ☞ *$3, free Mon.* ☉ *Mon.–Sat. 9:30–4:30, Sun. noon–5.*

㉔ Lincoln Park Conservatory. The building, which dates to 1892, has a palm house, a fernery, a cactus house, and a show house in which displays are mounted: the Azalea Show in February, the Spring Show in March or April, the Chrysanthemum Show in November, and the Winter Festival Show in December. ⊠ *2400 N. Stockton Dr.,* ☎ *312/742–7736.* ☞ *Free.* ☉ *Daily 9–5.*

★ ☙ **㉒ Lincoln Park Zoo.** Begun in 1868 with a pair of swans donated by New York's Central Park, this very popular 35-acre urban zoo grew through donations of animals from wealthy Chicago residents and the purchase of a collection from the Barnum and Bailey Circus. Many of the big houses, such as the Lion House and the Elephant House, are built in the classical brick typical of 19th-century zoos. The older buildings are surrounded by newer outdoor habitats that try to re-create the animals' natural wild surroundings. Outside the Lion House there's a window that lets zoo visitors stand almost face to face with the animals (if the giant cats are in the mood).

Lincoln Park Zoo is particularly noted for its Great Ape House; the 24 gorillas are considered the finest collection in the world. Because the park participates in breeding programs, there are usually several babies about. It's fascinating to spend an hour watching the members of each community interact. The spectacular glass-domed Regenstein Small Mammal and Reptile House has simulated jungle, river, and forest environments for animal residents, including the much-loved koalas. In addition, the zoo has a large-mammal house (elephants, giraffes, black rhinos), primate house, a bird house complete with a lush free-flight area and a waterfall, a huge polar bear pool with two bears, plus several rare and endangered species, such as the spectacle bear (named for the eyeglasslike markings around its eyes). Youngsters will enjoy the children's zoo, the Farm in the Zoo (farm animals and a learning center with films and demonstrations), and the Conservation Station, with hands-on activities. ⊠ *2200 N. Cannon Dr.,* ☎ *312/742–2000.* ☞ *Free.* ☉ *Daily 9–5.*

| NEED A BREAK? | Just outside the park, the venerable R. J. Grunt's (⊠ 2056 N. Lincoln Park W, ☎ 773/929–5363) has fine burgers plus a variety of soups and a salad bar. |

⑲ Moody Memorial Church. This huge, nondenominational Protestant church, built in 1925, seats 4,000. It was named after 19th-century evangelist Dwight L. Moody and is affiliated with the nearby Moody Bible Institute (☞ River North, *above*). ⊠ *1609 N. LaSalle St.,* ☎ *312/943–0466.*

☙ **㉕ Nature Museum.** Expected to open in Lincoln Park in the spring of 1999, this creation of the Chicago Academy of Sciences is the first new museum to be built in Chicago's parks in more than six decades. Designed by Chicago architects Perkins and Will, the facility embraces the nat-

DEVON AVENUE: A BRILLIANT BAZAAR

FOR THE ULTIMATE TASTE of Chicago's vivid, vibrant ethnic scene, take a trip to Devon Avenue on the far North Side. To stroll between 2200 and 3000 west on Devon—a street that's never stopped metamorphosing since English settlers named it after Devonshire in the 1800s (although here it is pronounced deh-*von*)—is to inhale the heady scents of curry and smoked fish, to be dazzled by the sequined saris in store windows, and to become an eavesdropper on musical conversations in Hindi, Russian, and other tongues.

This area took its shape in the 1970s and '80s, when immigration laws relaxed and the number of immigrants settling in Chicago increased. The '70s saw new arrivals from the Indian subcontinent; in the '80s, Asians from Thailand, Korea, the Philippines, and Vietnam followed, as did significant numbers of Syrians, Lebanese, Turks, Palestinians, and Jewish "refuseniks."

Devon Avenue—about 7 mi from downtown—has become home to a spicy mix of these immigrants. In places its double street signs attest to its intriguing diversity: For a while it's Gandhi Marg, then Golda Meir Avenue. By any name, it's a sensory safari best undertaken on foot.

The neighborhood is reachable from downtown via the Howard Street El (exit at the Morse Avenue station), then the 155 (Devon Avenue) bus. By car take Lake Shore Drive north to Hollywood Avenue, and then turn west to Ridge Avenue. Turn right on Ridge Avenue and head north about a mile to Devon Avenue; turn left, drive west to Oakley Street, and park.

As you survey the multicultural bazaar west of Oakley—including video stores specializing in Indian and Pakistani films—you will likely begin to hear the music and vernacular of those countries from car radios and shop entrances; you'll also smell incense and all kinds of foods sizzling in restaurants and local groceries, which often double as fast-food havens.

The splendid clothing and jewelry shops in the 2500 and 2600 blocks are guaranteed to catch your eye. Go ahead—try on a sari or slip into a Western-cut dress beautifully embroidered and embellished in the Indian fashion. If the price isn't quite right, shop owners have been known to bargain a bit.

West of Talman Avenue you'll find kosher bakeries and butchers, and Cyrillic shop signs and windows decorated with Russian newspapers and handmade *matrioshkas* (nesting dolls)—all evidence of this section's concentration of Russian Jews. At **Three Sisters Delicatessen** (⊠ No. 2909), you can pick up an imported teapot or a doll with your Russian rye. Look for unusual cookbooks at **Rosenblum's Hebrew Bookstore** (⊠ No. 2906). Political dolls stare from behind glass at **Ilya Rudiak's Russian Books** (⊠ No. 2764).

When planning your visit, bear in mind that the Jewish businesses usually close early on Friday and stay closed on Saturday, making Devon Avenue a feast for the senses best enjoyed on a Sunday or a weekday summer evening.

ural landscape of park and pond. Extensive glass and multilevel open-air terraces enable visitors to connect with nature outside as they view exhibits inside. Visitors will walk among hundreds of Midwest species of butterflies in Butterfly Haven, meet the tiny creatures that inhabit every city home in City Science, explore environmental forces in a Wilderness Walk, and learn about the impact of rivers and lakes on daily life in Water Works. This new 73,000-sq-ft building will feature a Children's Gallery designed to teach three- to eight-year-olds about the environment. Admission prices and opening hours were not available at press time, so call ahead. ⊠ *Fullerton Pkwy. and Cannon Dr.,* ☎ *312/ 871–2668.*

㉖ **North Avenue Beach.** One of the city's most popular warm-weather destinations, North Avenue Beach is packed with volleyball players and sunbathers on summer weekends. ⊠ *Lakefront at North Ave.*

㉓ **Shakespeare Garden.** Flowers and plants mentioned in the Bard's works are cultivated here. The bronze statue of the great playwright was cast by William Ordway Partridge in 1894, after he had exhibited a plaster model of the work at the Columbian Exposition. ⊠ *East of intersection of Belden Ave. and Lincoln Park W.*

OFF THE
BEATEN PATH

TROMPE L'OEIL BUILDING – Although this building is on the northeast corner of LaSalle and Division streets, you should study its appearance from a block east, at Clark and Division streets, or approach it from the south for the full effect of its rose window, ornate arched doorway, stone steps, columns, and sculptures. As you move closer to the building, you'll discover that an ordinary high-rise has been elaborately painted to make it look like an entirely different work of architecture. ⊠ *1207 W. Division St.*

NORTH CLARK STREET

A car or bus ride up North Clark Street north of Lincoln Park provides an interesting view of how cities and their ethnic populations grow and change. Before the late 1960s the Clark Street area was solidly white and middle class. Andersonville, the Swedish community centered on Foster Avenue (5200 N.) and Clark Street, extended north half a mile and included residential buildings to the east and west as well as a vital shopping strip on Clark. Then, in the early 1970s, immigrants from Asia began to arrive. Chicago's first Thai restaurant opened at 5000 N. Clark Street. (The Thai population has since become dispersed throughout the city without establishing a significant concentration here.) The Japanese community, which had shops and restaurants in the upper North 3000s of Clark Street, became more firmly entrenched, joined by a substantial Korean population. Korean settlement has since grown to the north and west, along North Lincoln Avenue. As the 1970s ended, the Asian immigrants were being joined by newcomers from the Middle East. Currently, the surrounding neighborhood is a gentrifying mix of young professionals, gays, and Asian-American, African-American, and Middle Eastern families, and a few Swedish residents who all enjoy the neighborhood's convenient shopping and its proximity to the beach and to Lake Shore Drive.

A Good Drive and Walk

You can board the northbound Clark Street Bus 22 on Dearborn Street in the Loop or on Clark Street north of Walton Street. Or you can drive to Clark Street and North Avenue, where this ride begins. North Avenue (1600 N.) is the southern boundary of the Lincoln Park neighborhood, which extends north to Diversey Parkway (2800 N.). The ride through Lincoln Park affords views of handsome renovated housing as well as housing in the process of being restored and upscale shops.

As you cross Belmont Avenue (3200 N.), you'll notice an increasing number of ethnic restaurants and shops. You can get all of the ingredients for sushi at Star Market (No. 3349), Chicago's largest Japanese grocery. Check out the intriguing condiments, unusual greens, and the exquisitely fresh (and astronomically expensive) fish to be used raw and thinly sliced for sashimi. If you prefer to have your sushi prepared for you, try highly rated Matsuya (No. 3469; ☞ Lincoln Park and North *in* Chapter 3). For excellent Japanese noodle dishes, visit Nagano (No. 3475).

Continuing north to the intersection with Addison Street, you'll find an abundance of bars and restaurants with the word *sport* somewhere in their names, all because of nearby **Wrigley Field,** home of the Chicago Cubs and, to many, the ultimate classic baseball stadium. At Clark Street and Irving Park Road (4000 N.) is **Graceland Cemetery,** the fascinating final resting place of many 19th-century millionaires and other local luminaries.

Foster Avenue is the old southern boundary of Andersonville. At this point, park your car and take a walk up and down a two-block area of Clark Street, where there is a lively mix of restaurants, bakeries, delicatessens, and other shops. Although new immigrants have changed the face of the neighborhood, the 5200 block still shows many signs of the earlier wave of Swedish settlers.

Just west of Clark, on Foster Avenue, is the Middle Eastern Bakery and Grocery (✉ 1512 W. Foster Ave.). Here are falafel, meat pies, spinach pies, *baba ghannouj* (eggplant puree dip), oil-cured olives, grains, pita bread, and a seductive array of Middle Eastern sweets. On Clark north of Foster, the Kan Zaman Restaurant (No. 5204) serves some of the same foods. Just north, the Byblos I Bakery and Deli (No. 5212) has Middle Eastern bread and groceries. If you arrive at the right time, you'll see the window filled with fresh-baked pita breads still puffed.

Across the street, Cousins (No. 5203) serves Middle Eastern dishes accompanied by Middle Eastern music. Farther up the street, at Reza's Restaurant (No. 5255), you can dine on such outstanding Persian cuisine as kebabs, *must* and *khiyar* (yogurt and cucumber), pomegranate juice, and charbroiled ground beef with Persian rice.

Just north of Cousins, among the Scandinavian establishments on the block, is the Ann Sather restaurant (No. 5207; ☞ Lincoln Park and North *in* Chapter 3), which carries what may be the world's most tender, delicious cinnamon buns (you can buy some to carry out).

Up the street, the **Swedish-American Museum Center** has an interesting mix of exhibits—and a wonderful walk-in log cabin for the kids—as well as a gift shop packed with Scandinavian items. Farther north, Wikstrom's Gourmet Foods (No. 5247) stocks Swedish meatballs, lingonberries, and imported cheeses, and has a few small tables where you can sip a drink or enjoy homemade soup.

Across the street, the cozy Svea Restaurant (No. 5236) has mouthwatering breakfasts. Erickson's Delicatessen (No. 5250) has glogg mix in bottles as well as crispbreads, homemade spiced herring, and imported cheese. In the storefront windows adjacent to Erickson's, the Andersonville Artists Original Arts and Crafts Display features handpainted china, small sculptures, and paintings, all by local artisans.

If you have a sweet tooth, head north to the Swedish Bakery (No. 5348). Among its delicious baked goods are Swedish limpa and Jutland bread, *pepparkakor* cookies, and flaky strudels and turnovers.

TIMING

Any day would be fine for this trip, although weekends, when more people might be out shopping, are particularly interesting. Unless you choose to make the Clark Street drive at rush hour (which would not be a good idea), you can see all the sights by car in less than an hour. Add another two hours to park and stroll in Graceland Cemetery and in Andersonville. You may also want to allow time for lunch before or after your walk. If you're using the bus, remember that you have to pay $1.50 each time you get on.

Sights to See

OFF THE
BEATEN PATH

ALTA VISTA TERRACE – Lining a narrow block of Alta Vista Terrace are 40 town houses completed in 1904 as one architectural development. The facades show the influence of a number of styles; the harmonious overall effect is one you'd expect in Boston or London. ⊠ *3800 block of N. Alta Vista Terr., between Grace St. and Sheridan Rd., 2 blocks east of Clark St.*

ARGYLE STREET – If you've never been to Southeast Asia, a walk down Argyle Street between Sheridan Road and Broadway on the North Side may be the next best thing. Vietnamese, Cambodian, Laotian, Thai, and other immigrants have transformed this stretch into a bustling shopping and dining district where English is the second language. Visitors should exercise big-city caution in this uptown neighborhood. Weekends are the best time to stop by for a bit of thousand-year-old-egg cake at **Chiu Quon Bakery** (⊠ 1127 W. Argyle) or some fine Asian cuisine at **Pho Xe Lua** (⊠ 1021 W. Argyle St.), **Mekong** (⊠ 4953 N. Broadway), and countless other eateries. If you're interested in Vietnam War history, call the nearby **Vietnam War Museum** (⊠ 954 Carmen St., ☎ 773/728–6111) for the latest exhibits and hours of operation.

Graceland Cemetery. Among those interred at this cemetery, which stretches east over more than 100 landscaped acres from Clark Street, are many famous entrepreneurs, including Marshall Field, George Pullman, and Potter Palmer. Also here are some greats of architecture: Louis Sullivan, John Wellborn Root, Daniel Burnham, and Ludwig Mies van der Rohe. The Getty Tomb, designed in 1890 by Louis Sullivan, may be the most exquisite of the astonishingly varied monuments. You can pick up a map at the entrance and explore on your own. ⊠ *4001 N. Clark St.,* ☎ *773/525–1105.* ☉ *Daily 8–4:30.*

OFF THE
BEATEN PATH

MONTROSE HARBOR – A treeless hill near this harbor off Lincoln Park draws kite-flying enthusiasts of all ages on sunny weekends. Windsurfers often practice at nearby Montrose Beach. ⊠ *4400 N. block of Montrose Ave. at lakefront.*

OUR LADY OF MT. CARMEL CHURCH – Two blocks east of Clark Street on Belmont Avenue is this mother church for the North Side Catholic parishes, a serene oasis in the midst of urban cacophony. It was built in 1913 for what was then a predominantly Irish and German neighborhood. ⊠ *690 W. Belmont Ave.,* ☎ *773/525–0453.*

Swedish-American Museum Center. Tiny and welcoming, this museum has changing exhibits that focus on the art and culture of Sweden. On permanent display are items immigrants brought with them to Chicago, such as trunks, and clothes. A gift shop sells Swedish books, greeting cards, place mats, craft items, tablecloths, and candelabra. ✉ *5211 N. Clark St.,* ☎ *773/728–8111.* ⚐ *$4.* ☉ *Tues.–Fri. 10–4, weekends 10–3.*

NEED A   Take your time over a cappuccino and a pastry while you peruse
BREAK?   shelves full of travel books at the **Kopi Cafe** (✉ 5317 N. Clark St., ☎
                773/989–5674), a travel-themed place with a miniboutique in back.

Wrigley Field. The grass is real, the walls are covered with ivy, and the bleachers are always packed at the Chicago Cubs' beloved ballpark, which looms up right next to Clark Street. The team has been playing games at Wrigley Field, also known as "the friendly confines," since 1916. Although area residents and baseball purists lost their fight in 1988 against the installation of lights for night games, many Cubs games are still played in the afternoon. Just don't expect to see the home team win—the Cubs last appeared in the World Series in 1945, and it was 1908 when they last won. ✉ *1060 W. Addison St.,* ☎ *773/404–2827.*

3 Dining

Whether you want deep-dish pizza on the North Side or crunchy fried catfish on the South, Chicago's dining choices are as wide ranging as the city itself. In elegant establishments diners can scale culinary heights with exquisitely creative French or regional midwestern cuisine. Equally exciting are the superb ethnic eateries that fill neighborhoods as diverse as the food: Italian, Greek, Mexican, German, Swedish, Thai, and more. And although Chicago has far surpassed its meat-and-potatoes image, its fine steak houses still thrive.

By Phil Vettel

HOWEVER YOU JUDGE a city's restaurant scene—by ethnic diversity, breadth and depth of high-quality establishments, or nationally prominent chefs—Chicago ranks as one of the nation's finest restaurant towns. Here you'll find innovative hot spots, lovingly maintained traditional establishments, and everything in between. Chicago's more than 7,000 restaurants range from those ranked among the best in the country—and priced accordingly—to simple storefront ethnic places and old-fashioned, unpretentious pubs serving good food at modest prices.

The River North neighborhood, north of the Chicago River and roughly west of Michigan Avenue, continues to be hot; it's home to such tourist magnets as Michael Jordan's Restaurant, Planet Hollywood, and Hard Rock Cafe, as well as Spago and significant newcomers Harvest on Huron and Trattoria Parma. But the West Loop area is sizzling as well; beautiful people flock to established spots such as Marché and Vivo, and new hot spots Blackbird, Toque, and one sixtyblue (partly owned by Michael Jordan).

Chicago is not a particularly trend-sensitive town, and several trends begun a year or more ago are still coasting along. The renewed interest in French cooking lives on, as seen in the continuing successes of Brasserie Jo and Bistrot Zinc and the emergence of Voilà! and Toque. Martinis and cigars continue to be the rage among trendoids, a sure sign that the economy is going strong. The city's appetite for steak continues to grow; more steak houses have sprung up, including Capital Grille in the Streeterville area and the New York import Smith & Wollensky in the Marina City complex. And while some nervously feared that large-scale restaurants would crowd out more intimate operations, particularly in River North, the success of places such as Crofton on Wells seems to assure us that high-quality, intensely personal restaurants can still find an appreciative audience.

This chapter divides the restaurants of Chicago into four areas, each with its own dining map that locates the restaurants: (1) Greater Downtown, (2) South, (3) Near North, and (4) Lincoln Park and North. Several noteworthy suburban restaurants appear at the end, with no map; other good places to eat outside the city are listed in Chapter 8, Side Trips. Within each area the restaurants are grouped first by type of cuisine and then by price range.

Reservations

Reservations are always a good idea; the reviews here note only when they're essential or when they are not accepted. In Chicago reservations can often be made a day or two in advance or even on the same afternoon, but securing a table at the more popular restaurants may take planning, especially on weekends. Some trendy restaurants don't accept reservations; at such places a wait of an hour or more on weekends is common. A popular strategy among Chicago restaurants is the limited-reservations policy, in which about half a restaurant's available space is reserved, while the rest is left open on a first-come, first-served basis. Unless mentioned otherwise, restaurants serve lunch and dinner daily.

Tipping

As a rule, you should tip 15% in restaurants in the $ and $$ price categories. You can double the 8.5% meal tax (fractionally higher in some parts of town, thanks to special taxing initiatives) when you feel generous. More expensive ($$$ and $$$$) establishments have more service personnel per table, who must divide the tip, so it's appropri-

Dining

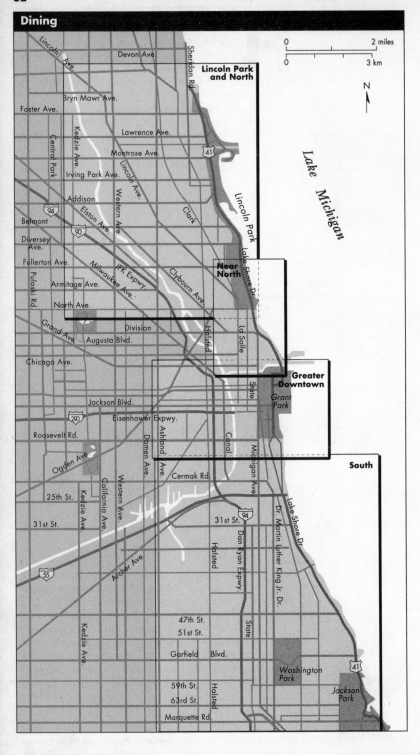

Lincoln Ave.

Devon Ave.

Sheridan Rd.

Lincoln Park and North

0 — 2 miles
0 — 3 km

N

Bryn Mawr Ave.

Foster Ave.

Lawrence Ave.

Kedzie Ave.

Central Park

Montrose Ave.

41

Irving Park Ave.

Lincoln Ave.

Addison

Western Ave.

Elston Ave.

Clark

94

Belmont

90

Diversey Ave.

Fullerton Ave.

Lincoln Park

Pulaski Rd.

JFK Expwy.

Milwaukee Ave.

Armitage Ave.

Clybourn Ave.

Lake Shore Dr.

Near North

North Ave.

Grand Ave.

Division

La Salle

Augusta Blvd.

Halsted

Chicago Ave.

State

Greater Downtown

Jackson Blvd.

Grant Park

290

Eisenhower Expwy.

Roosevelt Rd.

Damen Ave.

Ashland Ave.

Canal

Michigan Ave.

Ogden Ave.

Cermak Rd.

South

California Ave.

Western Ave.

25th St.

Kedzie Ave.

31st St.

31st St.

94

55

Halsted

Dan Ryan Expwy.

Archer Ave.

Dr. Martin Luther King Jr. Dr.

Lake Shore Dr.

Kedzie Ave.

47th St.

51st St.

State

Garfield Blvd.

Washington Park

41

59th St.

63rd St.

Halsted

Jackson Park

Marquette Rd.

Lake Michigan

ate to leave 20%, depending on the service. An especially helpful wine steward should be acknowledged with $2 or $3.

What to Wear

Chicago is largely an informal dining town, and neat, casual attire is acceptable dress in most places. Jackets, however, are appropriate in many formal hotel dining rooms. In our reviews dress is mentioned only when men are required to wear a jacket or jacket and tie.

Prices

Restaurant price categories are based on the average cost of a dinner that includes appetizer, entrée, and dessert.

CATEGORY	COST*
$$$$	over $45
$$$	$30–$45
$$	$18–$30
$	under $18

per person, excluding drinks, service, and sales tax (8.5%)

Greater Downtown

Contemporary

$$–$$$$ ✕ **Printer's Row.** Owner Michael Foley opened this stylish restaurant
★ when the historic, then-dilapidated Printer's Row district was just beginning to show signs of a renaissance. His is now the established institution in what has become an attractive neighborhood of renovated loft buildings and gracious older apartment houses—though prices remain remarkably low. The fresh American regional menu is especially noteworthy for its game meats and seafood: You might try seared scallops with truffle oil, grilled venison with dried cherries and wild rice cake, or grilled peppered duck breast with almond-raisin couscous. A well-chosen, fairly priced wine list is a plus. ⊠ *550 S. Dearborn St.,* ☎ *312/461–0780. AE, D, DC, MC, V. Closed Sun. No lunch Sat.*

$$–$$$ ✕ **Blackbird.** Though cramped, this west-of-the-Loop hot spot draws a well-dressed, trendy clientele that crowds in for artfully presented renditions of contemporary American food, such as duck confit with sweetbreads and celery root puree, and roasted sea bass with clams and roasted garlic broth. Decor is minimalist, even stark in its unbroken expanse of white walls, but this goes well with all the black most of the customers are wearing. Reservations aren't required, but weekends typically are booked solid. ⊠ *619 W. Randolph St.,* ☎ *312/715–0708. AE, D, DC, MC, V. No lunch weekends.*

$$–$$$ ✕ **one sixtyblue.** It's not the odd name that's gotten this West Side newcomer so much attention, nor its contemporary American cooking (though it's quite good), nor its arty, Adam Tihany design. No, the buzz is all about the restaurant's silent partner, Michael Jordan—even though, owing to legal issues, Jordan's name and likeness are nowhere to be found. But this stylish dining room is not likely to make points with the sports-bar crowd, anyway. Far from burgers and fries, the menu includes snapper and shrimp ceviche, presented in a jicama tepee and grilled salmon leaf (thin-sliced salmon) over a relish of crunchy cucumbers and sweet dates. ⊠ *160 N. Loomis St.,* ☎ *312/850–0303. AE, DC, MC, V. No lunch.*

$$–$$$ ✕ **Prairie.** The interior is inspired by the work of Frank Lloyd Wright and the food by the flavors of the midwestern states; the result is a thoroughly well-conceived American regional restaurant. Homey corn chowder and roasted buffalo with shallot sauce have strong Midwestern accents, as do such fish specialties as coho salmon and the acclaimed Lake Superior whitefish. ⊠ *500 S. Dearborn St.,* ☎ *312/663–1143. AE, D, DC, MC, V.*

Greater Downtown Dining

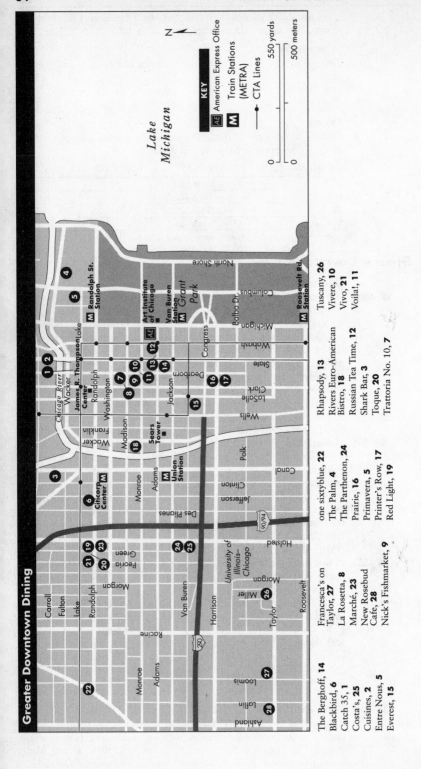

Lake Michigan

KEY

AE American Express Office

M Train Stations (METRA)

CTA Lines

The Berghoff, **14**
Blackbird, **6**
Catch 35, **1**
Costa's, **25**
Cuisines, **2**
Entre Nous, **5**
Everest, **15**

Francesca's on Taylor, **27**
La Rosetta, **8**
Marché, **23**
New Rosebud Cafe, **28**
Nick's Fishmarket, **9**

one sixtyblue, **22**
The Palm, **4**
The Parthenon, **24**
Prairie, **16**
Primavera, **5**
Printer's Row, **17**
Red Light, **19**

Rhapsody, **13**
Rivers Euro-American Bistro, **18**
Russian Tea Time, **12**
Shark Bar, **3**
Toque, **20**
Trattoria No. 10, **7**

Tuscany, **26**
Vivere, **10**
Vivo, **21**
Voilà!, **11**

$$–$$$ ✕ **Rhapsody.** Attached to the splendid new Symphony Center, home of the Chicago Symphony, Rhapsody is more than a handy spot for a pre-concert dinner or post-performance libation. This restaurant has serious fine-dining ambitions, and given that the chef and partner is culinary whiz Steven Chiappetti (he also owns Mango, in the River North neighborhood; ☞ Near North, *below*), it's already on its way to achieving them. Onion-crusted sturgeon is a splendid dish, and even such rustic-sounding creations as turkey pot pie (coddled in a sage cream sauce) are distinctly above the norm. If you're in the mood for something lighter, you can get sandwiches and salads in the bar area. ✉ 65 E. Adams St., ☎ 312/786–9911. AE, D, DC, MC, V.

$$–$$$ ✕ **Rivers Euro-American Bistro.** On the first floor of the Chicago Mercantile Exchange, this sophisticated mahogany-and-marble dining room serves breakfast to hungry traders and lunch and dinner to office workers and tourists. The menu is French- and Italian-inflected American: You might find grouper with grapefruit beurre blanc, barbecued shrimp and scallops, and crawfish ravioli. An outdoor dining area overlooks the Chicago River. Its proximity to the Civic Opera House and Loop theaters makes Rivers a handy pre-event destination. ✉ 30 S. Wacker Dr., ☎ 312/559–1515. AE, D, DC, MC, V. Closed Sun. No breakfast or lunch Sat.

$$–$$$ ✕ **Shark Bar.** An offshoot of the original Shark Bar in New York City, this sequel offers big portions of down-home southern cooking, though with enough modern twists that labels like "soul food" don't quite fit. For instance, appetizers include a tortilla wrap filled with cooked vegetables, rice, and greens. Among entrées, blackened tilapia and jerk Cornish hen are hits. The restaurant draws a well-dressed crowd, and in summer the rooftop deck, with one of the prettiest views in the city, is a popular evening hangout. ✉ 212 N. Canal St., ☎ 312/559–9057. AE, MC, V. No lunch Sat.

$$–$$$ ✕ **Toque.** Despite its French name and its French-influenced cooking, this west-of-the-Loop newcomer is an American restaurant, with dishes such as venison grilled over wood, served with pumpkin-sage spaëtzle, and a corn-crusted vegetable potpie. The stylish interior has sponge-painted walls, hardwood floors, and a display kitchen. It's a popular pre-event destination for those headed for the nearby United Center. ✉ 816 W. Randolph St., ☎ 312/666–1100. AE, D, DC, MC, V. No lunch weekends.

French

$$$$ ✕ **Everest.** As its name suggests, this restaurant reaches extraordinary
★ heights—and not only because it's 40 stories above the ground, with a sweeping view of the city's West Side. Pricewise, the dinner check can be formidable (for most people, this is a major-event destination). Cuisinewise, Everest hits highs that most restaurants can't begin to approach. The creative chef, Jean Joho, takes often-ignored, humble ingredients (particularly favoring foods from his native Alsace) and transforms them into regal, memorable dishes such as risotto with black trumpet mushrooms and quail or pheasant wrapped in savoy cabbage. The dining room is pleasingly neutral, focusing attention on the kitchen's exquisitely arranged plates; oversize tables provide plenty of room, and service is discreet and professional. The wine list has tremendous depth, particularly in its representation of Alsatian vintages. ✉ 440 S. LaSalle St., ☎ 312/663–8920. Reservations essential. Jacket required. AE, D, DC, MC, V. Closed Sun.–Mon.

$$–$$$$ ✕ **Marché.** This popular restaurant west of the Loop draws a see-and-be-seen crowd that includes many celebs; its cachet among the who's who almost overshadows the thoughtfulness of the bistro food. Soups are hearty and satisfying; such classics as duck confit are executed with

precision. What is undoubtedly Chicago's largest dessert menu entices with perfect examples of crème brûlée and coconut Bavarian cream. The open kitchen lets you see it all happen—if you can take your eyes off the clientele. ⊠ *833 W. Randolph St.,* ☎ *312/226–8399. AE, DC, MC, V. No lunch weekends.*

$$–$$$ ✕ **Entre Nous.** One of the highest-quality hotel dining rooms in the city
★ (inside the Fairmont hotel), Entre Nous has an understated elegance that's ideal for romantic dining or just a quiet, top-notch business meal. The menu is deceptively simple looking, filled with well-executed classics such as Maine lobster bisque and rack of lamb. The tiered dessert cart is impossible to resist, and the very thorough wine list is reasonably priced, as hotel restaurants go. ⊠ *The Fairmont, 200 N. Columbus Dr.,* ☎ *312/565–7997. AE, D, DC, MC, V. Closed Sun. No lunch.*

$$–$$$ ✕ **Voilà!** In the heart of the Loop, this bustling brasserie is perfectly situated for shoppers, office workers, and pretheater diners (the Shubert Theatre is across the street). Brasserie classics such as oven-roasted chicken, French onion soup, and various quiches are augmented by "les burgers" (served on brioche buns) and pizzas. There are plenty of salads and sandwiches for those looking for a lighter meal. ⊠ *33 W. Monroe St.,* ☎ *312/580–9500. AE, D, DC, MC, V.*

German

$–$$ ✕ **The Berghoff.** This Chicago institution has been serving its signature beer since the end of Prohibition; in fact, the Berghoff holds city liquor license No. 1. The handsome oak-panel interiors evoke an authentic Old Chicago feel. You can expect to wait for a table, but your meal will proceed rapidly—too rapidly, for some—once you're seated. (For even quicker service, grab a sandwich, a snort, and some elbow room among the businesspeople at the standing-only bar.) A menu of German classics (Wiener schnitzel, sauerbraten) is augmented by American favorites and, in keeping with the times, lighter dishes and even salads. ⊠ *17 W. Adams St.,* ☎ *312/427–3170. AE, MC, V. Closed Sun.*

Greek

$$–$$$ ✕ **Costa's.** One of the prettiest restaurants in Greektown, Costa's has a colorful, multilevel interior with terra-cotta tilework and rough-textured white walls and archways. It's an inviting atmosphere, though noisy; some of that noise, however, is due to the live nightly piano music. Sample from among a nice assortment of *mezés* (tapaslike Greek appetizers), and then move on to fresh fish or one of the many classic Greek dishes. ⊠ *340 S. Halsted St.,* ☎ *312/263–9700. AE, D, DC, MC, V.*

$–$$$ ✕ **The Parthenon.** *Saganaki,* the flaming Greek cheese dish, was invented here more than three decades ago. The Parthenon also claims to be the first restaurant in America to serve gyros, which are still available here. Besides having an abundance of history, this restaurant is notable for its festive atmosphere, happy customers, and hearty, inexpensive food. The dining room has high ceilings and art on the walls; a pass-through with plants separates the two dining areas. ⊠ *314 S. Halsted St.,* ☎ *312/726–2407. AE, D, DC, MC, V.*

Italian

$$–$$$ ✕ **La Rosetta.** A link in the Rosebud Restaurants chain (which also includes sister properties New Rosebud Cafe and Centro; ☞ *below*), La Rosetta sits in the heart of the Loop in the 3 First National Plaza Building. The menu includes enormous pasta portions, excellent chicken Vesuvio, and a handful of veal dishes. Lunch and early dinner are the busiest times, especially if there's a game at the nearby United Center; arrive after 7:30 PM for a more leisurely meal. ⊠ *70 W. Madison St.,* ☎ *312/332–9500. AE, D, DC, MC, V. Closed Sun.*

$$–$$$ ✕ **New Rosebud Cafe.** This extremely busy restaurant specializes in good old-fashioned southern Italian cuisine. One of the best red sauces in town can be found here, and the roasted peppers, homemade sausage, and exquisitely prepared pastas are not to be missed. The wait for a table can stretch to an hour or more, despite confirmed reservations, but those with patience—and tolerance for the extreme noise level— will find that the meal more than compensates. ⊠ *1500 W. Taylor St.,* ☏ *312/942–1117. AE, DC, MC, V. Closed Sun. No lunch Sat.*

$$–$$$ ✕ **Primavera.** Known best for its singing waiters (very talented, trained professionals—they get time off for touring), who do a great "Happy Birthday" chorus, this hotel restaurant can hit some culinary high notes, too. The menu sticks to straightforward, classic cuisine, in- cluding grilled seafood (the grilled tuna *caprese* is a good bet) and var- ious pastas. The restaurant also pours the best (and largest) cappuccino in town. ⊠ *The Fairmont, 200 N. Columbus Dr.,* ☏ *312/565–6655. AE, D, DC, MC, V.*

$$–$$$ ✕ **Trattoria No. 10.** Quarry-tile floors, theatrical lighting, and a burnt- orange, red, and ocher color scheme give this below-street-level din- ing room the charm and warmth of an outdoor café. Intriguing antipasti items include sea scallops with orange-fennel relish and *rotolo di moz- zarella* (homemade mozzarella cheese rolled around layers of pesto and prosciutto). Ravioli filled with lobster or mushrooms is a signature dish, and all the pastas are fresh. For dessert try the tiramisu or the triple- chocolate cannoli. ⊠ *10 N. Dearborn St.,* ☏ *312/984–1718. AE, D, DC, MC, V. Closed Sun. No lunch Sat.*

$$–$$$ ✕ **Tuscany.** As the name suggests, this restaurant focuses on the hearty, rustic flavors of the Tuscan countryside. The rotisserie-grilled chicken is especially good, as are the thin-crust pizzas and, for splurgers, the rack of lamb Vesuvio. The Taylor Street neighborhood, just southwest of the Loop, is a popular destination at lunchtime. ⊠ *1014 W. Taylor St.,* ☏ *312/829–1990. AE, D, DC, MC, V. No lunch weekends.*

$$–$$$ ✕ **Vivere.** This eye-catching dining room is worth a visit for looks alone: ★ A mesmerizing array of cones and bright colors guarantees an inter- esting view from every seat. The menu ranges from the traditional (flaw- less veal tenderloin with porcini-pancetta cream sauce) to the nouvelle (eggplant-and-chocolate dessert), and nearly everything works beau- tifully. The restaurant also has one of the city's—make that one of the country's—great Italian wine lists. ⊠ *71 W. Monroe St.,* ☏ *312/332– 7005. AE, D, DC, MC, V. Closed Sun. No lunch Sat.*

$$–$$$ ✕ **Vivo.** Well off the beaten path but still a leading see-and-be-seen restau- rant, Vivo is the darling of the high-fashion set. The people-watching is fascinating. Striking visuals, including dark walls, black ceiling, and open wine racks, and attentive service (the waiters themselves are stylishly turned out) are more memorable than the rather unadventurous contemporary Italian menu. But the antipasti assortment is a fine starter, and the kitchen does a good job with grilled Portobello mush- rooms and the thin-sliced veal chop. ⊠ *838 W. Randolph St.,* ☏ *312/ 733–3379. AE, D, DC, MC, V. No lunch weekends.*

$–$$$ ✕ **Francesca's on Taylor.** The newest Italian restaurant on Taylor Street, a stretch dominated by this cuisine, is run by a French-trained chef and his Irish-American wife. The food is nevertheless authentic: You might find ravioli stuffed with a spinach and artichoke mix or blue marlin with sea scallops and roasted peppers. There's not a lot of red meat on the menu—just the occasional veal dish—but that helps keep prices down, too. Folks heading to the United Center for a Bulls game, Blackhawks game, or special event make this a popular early dining spot. ⊠ *1400 W. Taylor St.,* ☏ *312/829–2828. AE, MC, V. No lunch weekends.*

Mediterranean

$$–$$$$ ✕ **Cuisines.** Chicago's first upscale Mediterranean restaurant success-
fully weds informal cuisine to formal standards. The café by the main
entrance has tapas-style dining for those in a hurry; in the dining
room, a particularly good paella highlights the main menu, along with
such sophisticated dishes as crabmeat and shiitake mushrooms wrapped
in phyllo dough. Just steps from the Chicago Theater, the restaurant
is a handy pre- and post-theater destination. ⊠ *Renaissance Chicago
Hotel, 1 W. Wacker Dr.,* ☎ *312/372–7200. AE, D, DC, MC, V. No
lunch weekends.*

Pan-Asian

$$–$$$ ✕ **Red Light.** The appropriately named British Occupation martini
makes a good accompaniment to the pan-Asian cuisine here, includ-
ing Chinese, Thai, Vietnamese, and Indonesian dishes. Standout menu
choices are tea-smoked squab, Thai-style mussels soup, and spicy
peanut noodles. An assortment of condiments at each table lets din-
ers adjust the heat level. Desserts, which come from the kitchen of sis-
ter property Marché (☞ *above*), are very western—and very good. ⊠
820 W. Randolph St., ☎ *312/733–8880. AE, DC, MC, V. No lunch
weekends.*

Russian

$$–$$$$ ✕ **Russian Tea Time.** In the heart of the Loop, steps from the Art Institute and Orchestra Hall, sits this delightful, dramatic gem. Ma-
hogany trim, samovars, and balalaika music create the perfect backdrop
for a wide-ranging menu of authentic dishes from Russia and neighboring republics (the owners hail from Uzbekistan). Highlights are
Ukrainian borscht, blinis (small, savory pancakes) with caviar and
salmon, *shashlik* (lamb kebabs), and *golubtes* (stuffed cabbage with
chicken and rice). Among 22 desserts are homemade strudel and
farmer's cheese blintzes. ⊠ *77 E. Adams St.,* ☎ *312/360–0000. Reservations essential for pre-event dining. AE, D, DC, MC, V.*

Seafood

$$$–$$$$ ✕ **Catch 35.** This restaurant at street level in the Leo Burnett Building
specializes in Pacific fish such as ahi tuna and mahimahi, often pre-
pared with an Asian flair; Thai curries and ginger make frequent ap-
pearances. The handsome multilevel dining room is wood-paneled
and designed to afford a measure of privacy. An "ad wall" displays
advertising-art photographs. ⊠ *35 W. Wacker Dr.,* ☎ *312/346–3500.
AE, D, DC, MC, V. No lunch weekends.*

$$$–$$$$ ✕ **Nick's Fishmarket.** Nick's is a two-tiered restaurant with a moder-
ately priced bar and grill in front and a main dining room that caters
to the high-powered business set, romantic couples, and indeed any-
one who appreciates overwhelmingly attentive service and is willing
to pay accordingly. Tuxedoed waiters greet you like a valued regular
even if it's your first visit. Nick's is best known for its wide assortment
of fresh seafood, particularly for Pacific catches such as mahimahi and
abalone; the menu also includes some Italian specialties and lighter
seafood-pasta pairings. Massive steaks are available, too. Nick's Fish-
market in Rosemont (⊠ *10275 W. Higgins Rd.,* ☎ *847/298–8200*),
near O'Hare Airport, is a virtual carbon copy of the downtown loca-
tion. ⊠ *1 First National Plaza,* ☎ *312/621–0200. Reservations essential.
AE, D, DC, MC, V. Closed Sun. No lunch Sat.*

Steak Houses

$$–$$$$ ✕ **The Palm.** Spacious, custom-built digs on the first floor of Swissôtel
Chicago make up the home for this handsome link in the Palm steak-
house chain. There's even an outdoor patio with a view of Navy Pier.
Inside, walls are covered with caricatures of local celebrities and reg-

ular customers. The latter group comes in droves (reservations are a must), drawn by big steaks and bigger lobsters. Even the occasional finned option, such as grilled tuna, is treated well here—and dessert is a must. ✉ *Swissôtel, 323 E. Wacker Dr.,* ☎ *312/616–1000. Reservations essential. AE, DC, MC, V.*

South

American

$–$$$ ✕ **Army & Lou's.** First-rate home-cooked soul food has earned a stellar reputation for this South Side institution. The fried chicken is arguably the city's best; barbecued ribs, roast turkey, collard and mustard greens, and crunchy fried catfish are other standouts. There's even a brief wine list. The setting is surprisingly genteel for such down-home fare: Waiters glide about in tuxedo shirts and bow ties, tables have starched white cloths, and African and Haitian art graces the walls. ✉ *420 E. 75th St.,* ☎ *773/483–3100. AE, DC, MC, V. Closed Tues.*

$$ ✕ **The Retreat.** Occupying a 200-year-old mansion in the South Pullman district, this gracious restaurant has soaring 14-ft ceilings and such lovely period touches as chandeliers, brass wall sconces, and carved wood trim. The cuisine, however, is a bit more modern: generally southern, with mustard-fried catfish leading the way. Dinner is served Friday and Saturday nights only; there's an extremely popular buffet brunch on Sundays. ✉ *605 E. 111th St.,* ☎ *773/568–6000. Reservations accepted for parties of 5 or more. MC, V. Closed Mon. No dinner Sun.–Thurs., no lunch Sat.*

$ ✕ **Soul Queen.** Come to Soul Queen for the food, not the ambience. Plentiful quantities of southern-style entrées and down-home specials are available on a large buffet. Best bets are channel catfish steaks served with Mississippi hush puppies, ham hocks with candied yams and fresh greens or peas, and stewed chicken with homemade dumplings, greens, and deep-dish apple pie. Prices are lowest before 5 PM Monday through Thursday. ✉ *9031 S. Stony Island Ave.,* ☎ *773/731–3366. Reservations not accepted. No credit cards.*

Chinese

$–$$$ ✕ **Emperor's Choice.** This sophisticated but comfortable restaurant sets out to demonstrate that Chinese seafood specialties can go well beyond deep-fried prawns. It succeeds admirably; seafood dishes like steamed oysters and Peking-style lobster are fresh and expertly prepared. A separate menu offers such "delicacies" as rattlesnake soup and pork bellies. Seating is a bit cramped, but the food is worth it. There's free parking (with validation) in the Cermak/Wentworth lot. ✉ *2238 S. Wentworth Ave.,* ☎ *312/225–8800. AE, D, DC, MC, V.*

$–$$$ ✕ **House of Fortune.** Elegant and spotless, this restaurant has a particularly large menu, with more than 150 entrées, including relatively uncommon items such as tripe and sea cucumber. Not to worry—there are plenty of more familiar dishes as well. ✉ *2407 S. Wentworth Ave.,* ☎ *312/225–0880. AE, D, DC, MC, V.*

$–$$$ ✕ **Phoenix.** A pretty-as-a-picture restaurant with a second-floor view of the Loop skyline, Phoenix has established itself as one of the area's best—thanks to lovely white-tablecloth surroundings, good cooking, and a wide-ranging menu. Rolling carts dispense dim sum daily from 8 to 3. Weekend dim sum crowds are substantial; arrive early or be prepared to wait. ✉ *2131 S. Archer Ave.,* ☎ *312/328–0848. AE, D, MC, V.*

$–$$ ✕ **Hong Min.** This no-frills Chinatown mainstay succeeds by virtue of its low prices and well-prepared food. The menu embraces everything from chop suey to stir-fried lobster; insiders tout the fresh oysters. And though decor is virtually nonexistent, the twin dining rooms, one of

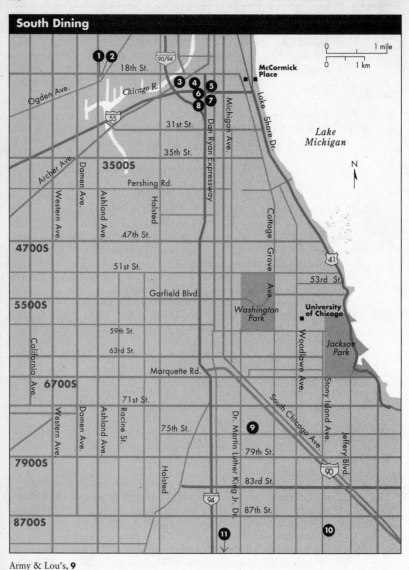

Army & Lou's, **9**
August Moon, **8**
Emperor's Choice, **5**
House of Fortune, **7**
Hong Min, **4**
Nuevo Leon, **1**
Phoenix, **3**
Playa Azul, **2**
The Retreat, **11**
Soul Queen, **10**
Three Happiness, **6**

which is for nonsmokers, are at least comfortable. Bring your own beer and wine. ⊠ *221 W. Cermak Rd.,* ☎ *312/842–5026. Reservations accepted for parties of 6 or more. MC, V. BYOB.*

$ ✕ **Three Happiness.** Lunch and dinner are served at Three Happiness, but folks in the know go for the dim sum, available daily from 10 to 2 (until 3 on weekends). On Sunday, in fact, the crowd begins to form at 9:30, and both floors of the spacious restaurant are full within minutes of opening. Try for a table near the door; that's closest to where the servers and their wheeled carts emerge from the kitchen. Each cart is loaded with six or so varieties of dim sum; servers tally your purchases on a "scorecard" at your table. You probably won't be able to keep track of what you've ordered or what it should cost, but don't worry: The per-person bill rarely exceeds $15. ⊠ *2130 S. Wentworth Ave.,* ☎ *312/791–1229. AE, D, DC, MC, V.*

Indonesian

$–$$$ ✕ **August Moon.** Although half the menu at this Chinatown restaurant is indeed Chinese, the Indonesian dishes are what set the place apart. The *rijsttafel* (Dutch for "rice table") dinner, an 18-course banquet ($35 per person; minimum four people; one-day advance notice requested) provides you with the widest possible variety of meat, fish, and vegetable dishes—and quite a full stomach. If you're not in so expansive a mood, it's quite all right to sample just a dish or two (the shrimp in spicy gravy is a good choice). The kitchen is conservative on the heat, so speak up if you like things spicy. ⊠ *225 W. 26th St.,* ☎ *312/842–2951. Reservations essential. MC, V. BYOB. Closed Mon.*

Mexican

$–$$ ✕ **Nuevo Leon.** A simple storefront houses this restaurant, a pleasant atmosphere for enjoying familiar or less familiar dishes, all of which leave you satisfied. In addition to a large selection of enchiladas, tacos, tostadas, and tamales, you'll find a rich and flavorful *menudo* (tripe soup), several beef soups, pork stew, chicken in mole sauce, tongue in sauce, and chopped steak simmered with tomatoes, jalapeño peppers, and onions (a house specialty). Not all servers are fluent in English, but cheerful goodwill prevails. ⊠ *1515 W. 18th St.,* ☎ *312/421–1517. Reservations not accepted. No credit cards.*

$–$$ ✕ **Playa Azul.** You will find wonderful fresh oysters at both the original 18th Street location and the sister house at Broadway and Irving Park Road, along with a full selection of fish and seafood soups, salads, and entrées, including abalone, octopus, shrimp, crab, clams, and lobster. Red snapper *Veracruzaná* (deep-fried) and *al mojo de ajo* (in garlic sauce) are house specialties, both delectable. Grilled meat dishes and chiles *rellenos* (stuffed with cheese and fried) round out the menu, and there are Mexican beers. ⊠ *1514 W. 18th St.,* ☎ *312/421–2552;* ⊠ *2005 N. Broadway,* ☎ *773/472–8924. Reservations not accepted. MC, V.*

Near North

American/Casual

$ ✕ **Billy Goat Tavern.** A favorite hangout for reporters, this counter-service bar and grill sits midway between the *Tribune* and the *Sun-Times.* Griddle-fried "cheeseborgers" are the featured chow, but frankly, if you're not interested in a glimpse of Fourth Estate history, don't bother. ⊠ *430 N. Michigan Ave., lower level,* ☎ *312/222–1525. Reservations not accepted. No credit cards.*

$ ✕ **Ed Debevic's.** This tongue-in-cheek re-creation 1950s diner is busy from morning till midnight. Gum-snapping waitresses in garish costumes trade quips and snide remarks with customers, but it's all in good humor. The menu lists eight different hamburgers, a large sandwich

Near North Dining

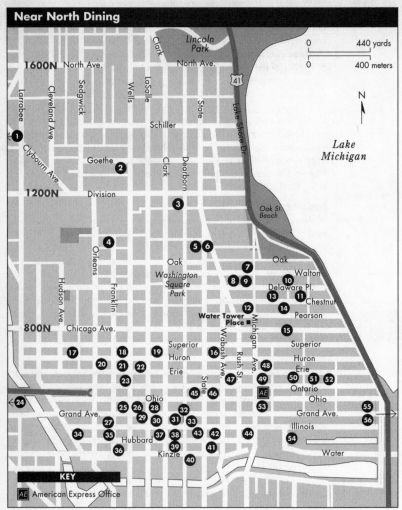

KEY

AE American Express Office

Avanzare, **48**

Ben Pao, **32**

Billy Goat Tavern, **44**

Bistro 110, **12**

Blackhawk Lodge, **16**

Brasserie Jo, **39**

Capital Grille, **51**

Centro, **18**

Coco Pazzo, **35**

Crofton on Wells, **26**

Cyrano's Bistrot & Wine Bar, **25**

The Dining Room, **14**

Ed Debevic's, **23**

Eli's the Place for Steak, **15**

Frontera Grill, **38**

Gene & Georgetti, **27**

Gibsons, **6**

Gordon, **30**

Harry Caray's, **40**

Harvest on Huron, **21**

Hat Dance, **20**

Hatsuhana, **49**

Havana, **36**

House of Hunan, **53**

Hubbard Street Grill, **34**

Iron Mike's Grille, **8**

Joe's BeBop Cafe & Jazz Emporium, **55**

Kiki's Bistro, **4**

Les Nomades, **50**

Maggiano's Little Italy, **28**

Mango, **19**

Mantuano Mediterranean Table, **54**

Michael Jordan's Restaurant, **29**

Morton's of Chicago, **5**

Mrs. Park's Tavern, **10**

Papagus, **45**

Park Avenue Cafe, **10**

Pizzeria Due, **47**

Pizzeria Uno, **46**

Restaurant Okno, **1**

Riva, **56**

Ruth's Chris Steak House, **33**

The Saloon, **11**

Salpicon, **2**

Savannah's, **24**

Scoozi!, **17**

Seasons, **9**

Shaw's Crab House and Blue Crab Lounge, **41**

Signature Room at the 95th, **13**

Spago, **43**

Spiaggia, **7**

Spruce, **52**

Topolobampo, **38**

Trattoria Parma, **37**

Tsunami, **3**

Wildfire, **22**

Woo Lae Oak, **42**

Zinfandel, **31**

selection, four chili preparations, five hot dogs, and a variety of such "deluxe plates" as meat loaf, pot roast, and chicken potpie. Unlike a real 1950s diner, Ed's has a selection of cocktails and wines, plus Ed Debevic's Beer. ⊠ *640 N. Wells St., ☎ 312/664–1707. Reservations not accepted. No credit cards.*

Barbecue

$–$$$ ✕ **Joe's Be-Bop Cafe & Jazz Emporium.** Live jazz is featured nightly at this casual barbecue restaurant, whose ribs are proving as popular as some of Chicago's finest. Or is it the delightful Navy Pier lake views? There's a kids' menu, so bring the whole family. ⊠ *Navy Pier, 600 E. Grand Ave., ☎ 312/595–5299. Reservations not accepted. AE, D, DC, MC, V.*

Chinese

$–$$$ ✕ **House of Hunan.** The original Magnificent Mile Chinese restaurant, House of Hunan continues to please. Porcelain and carvings decorate the large, elegant dining area. Spicy hot dishes are plentiful on the enormous menu, but so are mild ones. Pot stickers, scallop rolls, stuffed crab claws, drunken chicken, and jellyfish are highlights, along with shellfish, pork, duck, and *moo shu* (pancake-wrapped) specialties. ⊠ *535 N. Michigan Ave., ☎ 312/329–9494. AE, D, DC, MC, V.*

$–$$ ✕ **Ben Pao.** The hippest-looking Chinese restaurant in town has minimalist decor in black and shades of gray with soothing touches, such as two water walls; pinpoint halogen spotlights illuminate an otherwise dark room. Well-prepared selections include chicken *soong,* cooked chicken presented with soft lettuce leaves for wrapping. There's also a spicy eggplant dish that's not to be missed, and featured fish entrées are always a good bet. The waitstaff helps with explanations. ⊠ *52 W. Illinois St., ☎ 312/222–1888. AE, D, DC, MC, V. No lunch.*

Contemporary

$$$–$$$$ ✕ **Gordon.** Since 1976 this has been one of the most innovative restaurants in Chicago, from its nouvelle-cuisine past to its light, contemporary-American present. You'll find stellar efforts such as lamb loin with zucchini-eggplant tian, and irresistible desserts such as the signature flourless chocolate cake. All entrées come in petite portions, which allow you to experience a broader range of the kitchen's talents (full-size entrées are also available). The five-course prix-fixe dinner is a very good value. The restaurant's look is both sophisticated and whimsical: swag curtains held by tiebacks of plaster hands and subdued Asian touches giving way to a mural of Rubenesque cavorters. On weekends there's dancing to a jazz trio. ⊠ *500 N. Clark St., ☎ 312/467–9780. Reservations essential. Jacket required. AE, DC, MC, V.*

$$$–$$$$ ✕ **Park Avenue Cafe.** A re-creation of Manhattan's famed Park Avenue Café, Chicago's version serves imaginative American food, artistically presented and remarkable for its complexity and quality. Salmon cured pastrami style and a swordfish chop (a unique cut of the fish) are two signature dishes. There's even a prix-fixe brunch of American appetizers served tableside in the style of Chinese dim sum. ⊠ *198 E. Delaware Pl., ☎ 312/944–4414. AE, D, DC, MC, V. No lunch.*

$$$–$$$$ ✕ **Seasons.** This hotel restaurant has become a stop on the gourmet circuit, thanks to the creativity of executive chef Mark Baker. New England and Asian influences crop up everywhere on the menu: In addition to *bento* box appetizers (an assortment of Japanese goodies served in a box) and traditional Japanese breakfasts, you might find grilled Maine lobster, corn chowder, and pesto-crusted rack of lamb. The opulent dining room is uncommonly comfortable and roomy. Seasons also produces Chicago's best (and most expensive) Sunday brunch. ⊠ *Four Seasons Hotel, 120 E. Delaware Pl., ☎ 312/280–8800. Brunch reservations essential. AE, D, DC, MC, V.*

$$$–$$$$ ✗ **Signature Room at the 95th.** One of the best deals in town is the $8.95 lunch buffet served here weekdays: Choose from roasts, prepared entrées, vegetable sides, a soup of the day, and a full salad bar. Dinner is a very formal affair, highlighted by superb service. The Sunday brunch is splendid (and quite expensive) and one of the best in the city. Whether you visit for brunch, lunch, or dinner, the view from the 95th floor is always breathtaking. ⊠ *John Hancock Center, 875 N. Michigan Ave.,* ☎ *312/787–9596. Brunch reservations essential. AE, D, DC, V.*

$$–$$$$ ✗ **Iron Mike's Grille.** "Da Coach," as Mike Ditka is known affectionately (if not reverentially) by longtime fans, is behind this restaurant. Despite a strong emphasis on steaks and items such as the "Fridge burger" (named after William "the Refrigerator" Perry), the menu is more sophisticated than one expects: Witness the venison chops with sour-cherry sauce or the pulled-chicken, shiitake mushroom, and black olive fettuccine. The masculine dining room is dotted with Ditka and Bears memorabilia, and the restaurant is so successful that sequel editions— beginning with an Iron Mike's in New Orleans, where Ditka now coaches the Saints—are in the works. ⊠ *Tremont Hotel, 100 E. Chestnut St.,* ☎ *312/587–8989. D, DC, MC, V.*

$$–$$$$ ✗ **Michael Jordan's Restaurant.** His Airness has a private dining room (glass-enclosed, with wooden blinds) for his rather frequent appearances here. This typical sports-theme restaurant with adequate food succeeds because anything Michael Jordan touches, particularly in Chicago, turns to gold. You can spend a little or a lot, depending on how appealing you find the high-quality but pricey steaks. The all-American menu also includes burgers, fresh fish, and Juanita Jordan's macaroni and cheese. A massive bar area doubles as a memorabilia-laden shrine to pro sports—complete with a 25-ft video wall that makes MJ's one of *the* places to view a big game. Naturally, there's a large souvenir shop by the front door. ⊠ *500 LaSalle St.,* ☎ *312/644–3865. Reservations not accepted for dinner. AE, D, DC, MC, V.*

$$$ ✗ **Spago.** Wolfgang Puck's celebrated California concept has gone over
★ well with Chicagoans, who attend in such numbers that Saturday reservations take at least a month to secure (the noise level is correspondingly high). There are two dining options: the casual grill, open for lunch and dinner daily, featuring such Puck signature dishes as his outstanding meat loaf and gourmet pizzas; and the main dining room, where the menu is more refined—you might find herb-stuffed bass with basil-mashed potatoes or grilled quail over chanterelle risotto. ⊠ *520 N. Dearborn St.,* ☎ *312/527–3700. Reservations essential. AE, D, DC, MC, V. No lunch weekends.*

$$$ ✗ **Spruce.** One of the most ambitious restaurants to open in Chicago
★ in years, this contemporary American spot specializes in imaginative combinations and beautiful presentation. Sea bass fillets are draped over vivid red beet risotto; monkfish cassoulet is heady with truffle oil. The thoughtfully chosen wine list abounds in lesser-known offerings. The dining room is low on flash, making the occasional bursts of floral arrangements and serious art all the more dramatic. Tables are nicely spaced, making this a good option for an intimate meal. ⊠ *238 E. Ontario St.,* ☎ *312/642–3757. Reservations essential. AE, MC, V. Closed Sun. No lunch Sat.*

$$–$$$ ✗ **Blackhawk Lodge.** Rustic vacation-lodge furnishings give this Amer-
★ ican regional restaurant a distinct mood. Hickory-smoked cuisine is a specialty, so the aromas coming from the kitchen are irresistible. The bacon, salmon, smoky corn chowder, and ribs are particularly good. The regional emphasis varies; southwestern influences may prevail in summer, but the kitchen may prepare more New England dishes in fall— or vice versa. ⊠ *41 E. Superior St.,* ☎ *312/280–4080. AE, D, DC, MC, V.*

$$–$$$ ✕ **Crofton on Wells.** Chef and owner Suzy Crofton breaks a few contemporary-dining rules with her first solo venture. She doesn't pack tables too closely together (the 64-seat dining room, while small, is surprisingly comfortable), she keeps the noise level down, and there's no sponge painting on the walls. Her food is similarly short on clichés but gratifyingly long on flavor. Dig into gutsy Cajun barbecued shrimp over sweet-potato hay, or indulge in the luxury of grilled foie gras with chanterelles and red pearl onions. And save room for dessert. ✉ *535 N. Wells St.,* ☎ *312/755–1790, AE, DC, MC, V. No lunch weekends.*

$$–$$$ ✕ **Harvest on Huron.** One of the young stars of the River North neighborhood, Harvest on Huron combines colorful, arty decor; superior service; and outstanding contemporary American food by Alan Sternweiler (for years the chef at renowned Printer's Row; ☞ Greater Downtown, *above*). There are always one or two vegetarian entrées, such as acorn squash filled with mushroom risotto, along with dishes such as roast rabbit rolled around rabbit sausage and ancho-chile glazed pork tenderloin. Lovers of fine spirits will wax rhapsodic over the massive collection, available in half-pours for financially prudent experimentation. ✉ *217 W. Huron St.,* ☎ *312/587–9600. AE, D, DC, MC, V. No lunch weekends.*

$$–$$$ ✕ **Hubbard Street Grill.** David Schy shows a deft hand with season-
★ ings and a fine respect for classic American food at this well-conceived restaurant, where grilled meats and fish are enlivened by various spicy or sweet sauces, chutneys, and relishes. The ahi tuna burger justifies a visit in itself. The interior is contemporary, comfortable, casual, and free of trendy sensibilities. ✉ *351 W. Hubbard St.,* ☎ *312/222–0770. AE, D, DC, MC, V. No lunch weekends.*

$$–$$$ ✕ **Mango.** This 75-seat restaurant is a bit noisy, but it's easy to un-
★ derstand why. Creative, well-executed American entrées at prices that rarely top $16 are a powerful draw. Don't-miss dishes including pork chops in a hearty mustard sauce, molasses-glazed lamb shank, and Mediterranean fish soup. The restaurant's namesake pops up in a duck prosciutto salad and an apple-mango tart. ✉ *712 N. Clark St.,* ☎ *312/337–5440. Weekend reservations essential. AE, D, DC, MC, V. No lunch weekends.*

$$–$$$ ✕ **Mrs. Park's Tavern.** At street level in the DoubleTree Guest Suites
★ is this handy café, a cousin to the Park Avenue Cafe upstairs. The small-ish menu nevertheless includes some dandy offerings, often packaged intriguingly, such as the oyster assortment delivered in a wooden wine box. Chili-rubbed chicken comes with garlic mashed potatoes. The kitchen is open from 7 AM to 2 AM, a rarity in this posh neighborhood. ✉ *198 E. Delaware Pl.,* ☎ *312/280–8882. AE, D, DC, MC, V.*

$$–$$$ ✕ **Restaurant Okno.** This is a young person's hangout—if the blaring techno-industrial music isn't enough of a clue—complete with oddly shaped tables, funkily attired clientele, and a quirky menu that includes Chinese vegetarian dishes, chicken with quinoa waffles and garlic sauce, and beef fillet with horseradish mashed potatoes. Even the beverage list is wacky, tucked in accordion folds inside a CD case and heavy on whimsical martini creations. ✉ *1332 N. Milwaukee Ave.,* ☎ *773/395–1313. Reservations not accepted. AE, MC, V. No lunch.*

$$–$$$ ✕ **Savannah's.** This is Chicago's sole proponent of Low Country cuisine, the West African–influenced cooking of the Carolina coastal plain—food that resembles Creole cooking in some respects, though with a greatly diminished spice level. Of course, if you like it spicy, there are plenty of bottled hot sauces. Offbeat choices are smoked oyster sausage with horseradish cream; hopping John, a traditional dish of black beans and rice; and excellent crab cakes. Beige walls, oak floors, and brown butcher paper on the tables strike a simple, cheerful note, and the back room is a designated cigar-friendly area. ⊠ *1156 W. Grand Ave.,* ☎ *312/666–9944. AE, D, DC, MC, V. No lunch Sept.–May*

$$–$$$ ✕ **Wildfire.** The name wasn't chosen capriciously; everything in this wide-open restaurant is cooked over an open flame. Indeed, a triple hearth of roaring fires is a focal point of the room. No culinary innovations here, but you'll find exceptional aged prime rib, barbecued ribs, and roasted fish, along with wood-fired pizzas and skillet-roasted mussels. ⊠ *159 W. Erie St.,* ☎ *312/787–9000. AE, D, DC, MC, V.*

$$–$$$ ✕ **Zinfandel.** Classic regional American recipes are given a touch of '90s cooking sensibility at this ambitious restaurant. Burgoos (thick meat-and-vegetable stews popular in the South), New England clambakes, and Pacific seafood all share space on the sea-to-shining-sea menu. Warm southwestern colors are enhanced by eclectic American folk art; that and the aromas from the kitchen create a homey atmosphere. ⊠ *59 W. Grand Ave.,* ☎ *312/527–1818. AE, D, MC, V. Closed Sun.–Mon.*

Cuban

$$–$$$ ✕ **Havana.** A little taste of pre-Castro Cuba is on display in this River North spot, across the street from the Merchandise Mart. Tropical plants, ceiling fans, and louvered windows set the mood, while Cuban and Caribbean dishes sate the appetite. Duck-filled croquettes with sweet-and-sour cabbage make a good beginning, as do coconut-crusted shrimp with a spicy jam for dipping. Entrées include grilled salmon over black beans with papaya-mango salsa and chipotle-spiced flank steak; lighter appetites can settle for any of several sandwiches, including a *hamburguesa.* ⊠ *230 W. Kinzie St.,* ☎ *312/595–0101. AE, DC, MC, V. No lunch weekends.*

French

$$$–$$$$ ✕ **The Dining Room.** Gracious service and fine food in a beautiful set-
★   ting make this Ritz-Carlton restaurant a classic. Walnut paneling, tapestry carpeting, and crystal chandeliers grace the room in classic French style. Chef Sarah Stegner's kitchen turns out exemplary French cuisine with nouvelle accents, such as squab breast with roasted garlic sauce and turbot in shellfish broth. Daily specials complement the seasonal menu selections. ⊠ *Ritz-Carlton, 160 E. Pearson St.,* ☎ *312/ 266–1000. Reservations essential. Jacket and tie. AE, D, DC, MC, V. No lunch.*

$$$ ✕ **Les Nomades.** A very formal restaurant, Les Nomades has the same
★   owners as the acclaimed Le Français (☞ Worth a Trip, *below*). Plan on two to three hours of dining, but you're likely to agree that the carefully prepared classic French food, from almond-crusted foie gras to roasted monkfish, is worth the wait—and the significant expense. ⊠ *222 E. Ontario St.,* ☎ *312/649–9010. Dinner reservations essential. Jacket and tie. AE, MC, V. Closed Sun.–Mon. No lunch.*

$$–$$$ ✕ **Bistro 110.** Like any other good bistro, this place can be noisy and chaotic at times, but consider that a testimony to its popularity. Besides the lively bar scene and Water Tower views, the real draw is the food from the wood-burning oven; the kitchen consistently offers excellent renditions of French classics. The Sunday jazz brunch is a standout. ⊠ *110 E. Pearson St.,* ☎ *312/266–3110. AE, D, DC, MC, V.*

$$–$$$ ✕ **Brasserie Jo.** When Jean Joho, chef-proprietor of the acclaimed
★   Everest (☞ Greater Downtown, *above*), opened this authentic brasserie in late 1995, it became an overnight hot spot for discerning diners eager to sample Joho's food at relatively moderate prices. Don't miss the *choucroute,* a crockful of pork cuts with Alsatian sauerkraut; shrimp in a phyllo-dough bag; or classic coq au vin. Have the profiteroles for dessert and watch as a waiter decants chocolate syrup over the ice-cream-filled puff pastries. ⊠ *59 W. Hubbard St.,* ☎ *312/595–0800. AE, D, DC, MC, V. No lunch weekends.*

In case you want to see the world.

At American Express, we're here to make your journey a smooth one. So we have over 1,700 travel service locations in over 120 countries ready to help. What else would you expect from the world's largest travel agency?

do more

http://www.americanexpress.com/travel

Travel

In case you want to be welcomed there.

We're here to see that you're always welcomed at establishments everywhere. That's why millions of people carry the American Express® Card – for peace of mind, confidence, and security, around the world or just around the corner.

do more

Cards

And just in case.

We're here with American Express® Travelers Cheques and Cheques *for Two*.® They're the safest way to carry money on your vacation and the surest way to get a refund, practically anywhere, anytime.

Another way we help you...

do more

Travelers Cheques

$$–$$$ ✕ **Kiki's Bistro.** Country French decor meets urban contemporary
★ cooking in this modern bistro. The kitchen seasons dishes aggressively
and likes to experiment, but the food generally stays true to its roots.
Grilled rabbit sausage with garlic and rosemary is a fine starter; for an
entrée try grouper with an herb-scented fish bouillon and vegetable med-
ley. Classics, such as steak *frites,* are always reliable. ⊠ *900 N. Franklin
St.,* ☎ *312/335–5454. AE, D, DC, MC, V. Closed Sun. No lunch Sat.*

$$ ✕ **Cyrano's Bistrot & Wine Bar.** Chef and owner Didier Durand pre-
sents the food of his birthplace, Bergerac (hence the restaurant's name),
in this accomplished restaurant. Traditional dishes such as onion tart
and bouillabaisse are handled deftly; the restaurant also specializes in
rotisserie chicken, rabbit, and duck. The wine list is especially inter-
esting, with many vintages from lesser-known producers in southern
France. For lunch, the Grand Lunch Express presents four courses si-
multaneously on a large platter—ideal for time-constrained diners. The
dining room is done in bright blue and yellow, the walls hung with large
mirrors in ornate frames. ⊠ *546 N. Wells St.,* ☎ *312/467–0546. AE,
D, DC, MC, V. No lunch weekends.*

Greek

$$–$$$ ✕ **Papagus.** Chicago's best Greek restaurant is bright and cheerful but
★ also rustic and comfortable. The menu focuses on *mezes,* literally
"small plates," appetizers resembling Spanish tapas. Servers proffer an
assortment; you point to what you want and start grazing. There are
additional appetizers on the menu, as well as substantial salads and
fairly traditional entrées. Fine choices are *tirosalata* (feta-cheese spread),
sensational grilled octopus, and lamb chops. Desserts, so often a throw-
away on Greek menus, are remarkably good, especially the unusual
dried-cherry-filled baklava. The all-Greek wine list has some wonder-
ful inexpensive bottles; trust your waiter's recommendation. ⊠ *Em-
bassy Suites, 620 N. State St.,* ☎ *312/642–8450. AE, D, DC, MC, V.*

Italian

$$$–$$$$ ✕ **Spiaggia.** Here you'll find luxury-level Italian dining that is unsur-
★ passed in the city. Marble-clad columns, stylish table appointments,
and shades of pink and teal add up to modern elegance; a three-story
bank of windows overlooks Michigan Avenue and Lake Michigan. The
food, as opulent and complex as its surroundings, includes a veal chop
coddled in a luscious vodka-cream sauce and several elaborate filled-
pasta dishes. The scholarly wine list is no place for bargain hunters,
but there are some remarkable bottles. You can sample Spiaggia's
wonders next door at Cafe Spiaggia, a lower-priced, casual sidekick.
⊠ *980 N. Michigan Ave.,* ☎ *312/280–2750. Reservations essential.
Jacket required. AE, D, DC, MC, V.*

$$$ ✕ **Coco Pazzo.** The Chicago branch of a very successful Manhattan
★ restaurant, Coco Pazzo shines with solid, mature, and professional ser-
vice and a kitchen that focuses on Tuscan cuisine—lusty, aggressively
seasoned fare. Grilled game is a particular strength, as are the risotto
dishes. ⊠ *300 W. Hubbard St.,* ☎ *312/836–0900. AE, DC, MC, V.
No lunch weekends.*

$$–$$$ ✕ **Avanzare.** Sleek and urban looking, Avanzare has long been a fa-
vorite of business travelers and those looking for sophisticated Italian
food. The menu has a wide range of pastas, unusual salads, and entrées; try an appetizer of tuna carpaccio with avocado and sweet
onions. The dozen regularly appearing pastas such as chicken tortellini
are carefully prepared, but the best pasta offerings come from the list
of daily specials. A sidewalk café is set up in summer. ⊠ *161 E. Huron
St.,* ☎ *312/337–8056. AE, D, DC, MC, V. No lunch weekends.*

$$–$$$ ✕ **Centro.** Reservations are tough to come by at this ultrapopular
restaurant, which draws trendies like moths to a flame. Even with a

reservation, expect a wait to be seated: VIPs arrive on a regular basis and force ordinary folk farther down the waiting list. Those who stick it out are rewarded with stupendously portioned pastas and a smattering of other traditional Italian dishes, such as grilled pork chops with fennel and garlic. Prices are reasonable—until you get to the prime cuts. ⊠ *710 N. Wells St.,* ☎ *312/988–7775. AE, D, DC, MC, V. No lunch Sun.*

$$–$$$ ✕ **Harry Caray's.** Famed Cubs announcer Harry Caray passed away in 1998, but his legend lives on, and fans continue to pour into his namesake restaurant (where Harry frequently held court). Though the Italian-American menu holds no surprises, the pastas, fine chicken Vesuvio, and hefty steaks and chops make this a good spot for baseball fans who like to eat and who don't take the dining experience too seriously. Thanks for the memories, Harry. Holy cow! ⊠ *33 W. Kinzie St.,* ☎ *312/465–9269. AE, D, DC, MC, V.*

$$–$$$ ✕ **Maggiano's Little Italy.** Enormous portions of red-sauce Italian food star in a cleverly realized Little Italy setting. Order two entrées for every three diners in your party, and you'll be as happy as the other cheerfully loud patrons in the wide-open dining room. This is the kind of Italian food we grew up with: brick-size lasagna, chicken Vesuvio, veal scallopini. The cuisine is hearty rather than inspiring, but maybe it'll bring back a memory or two. Lunchtime sandwiches are especially good. ⊠ *516 N. Clark St.,* ☎ *312/644–7700. AE, D, DC, MC, V. No lunch Sun.*

$$–$$$ ✕ **Scoozi!** You'll recognize Scoozi! by the gigantic tomato over the front door. A huge, noisy, trendy place, it draws the young professional crowd. Booths flank the walls of a multilevel dining room, and wooden beams and ceiling decorations complement the country Italian food. Choose from a large selection of antipasti, pizzas, and pasta or a smaller number of entrées. Steamed clams in garlic and white wine, steamed mussels in tomato sauce, and osso buco appear on a generally attractive menu that invites grazing. Many offerings are available in small or large portions. ⊠ *410 W. Huron St.,* ☎ *312/943–5900. AE, D, DC, MC, V. No lunch weekends.*

$$–$$$ ✕ **Trattoria Parma.** This rustic Italian trattoria has faux-aged walls and chandeliers resembling grapevines. The food exudes country charm as well: hearty *tagliatelle Bolognese,* stuffed artichokes, and, of course, an antipasto dish featuring prosciutto di Parma. Several more refined dishes, including Tuscan fish stew, are also options. ⊠ *400 N. Clark St.,* ☎ *312/245–9933. AE, DC, MC, V. No lunch weekends.*

$–$$ ✕ **Pizzeria Uno/Pizzeria Due.** Chicago deep-dish pizza got its start here in 1943. Uno has been remodeled to resemble its franchised cousins in other cities, but its pizzas retain their light crust and distinctive taste. Those not accustomed to pizza on a Chicago scale may want to skip the salad to save room. Pizzeria Due, a block away, has the same ownership and menu. Some say Uno's pizza is better, but the product at both establishments is among the best in town. ⊠ *Uno, 29 E. Ohio St.,* ☎ *312/321–1000;* ⊠ *Due, 619 N. Wabash Ave.,* ☎ *312/943–2400. Reservations not accepted. AE, D, DC, MC, V.*

Japanese

$$–$$$$ ✕ **Tsunami.** This Gold Coast spot looks more like a nightclub than a Japanese restaurant, thanks to faux-finished walls and moody lighting. Still, it's a respectable option for sushi, sashimi, and traditional options such as teriyaki dishes (shrimp, steak, or salmon), hibachi-grilled seafood, and the occasional noodle dish. ⊠ *1160 N. Dearborn Ave.,* ☎ *312/642–9911. AE, D, DC, MC, V. No lunch.*

$$–$$$ ✕ **Hatsuhana.** A long, angled sushi bar and wooden tables, white stucco walls, Japanese lanterns, and natural wood trim set the tone at what some consider Chicago's best sushi and sashimi restaurant. The printed menu lists numerous appetizers—broiled spinach in sesame-soy sauce, fried bean curd with sauce, steamed egg custard with shrimp, fish, and vegetables—and only a few entrées. Most diners come for the vinegared rice and raw fish delicacies. ⊠ *160 E. Ontario St.,* ☎ *312/ 280–8808. AE, D, DC, MC, V. Closed Sun. No lunch Sat.*

Korean

$–$$ ✕ **Woo Lae Oak.** Part of a Seoul-based chain, this nicely appointed restaurant is a good choice if you're looking for an accessible, unintimidating Korean dining experience. All tables have built-in cooktops, perfect for such communal dishes as *bul go ki* (thin sliced beef) and *dak gui* (boneless chicken). But the food is sophisticated enough to please experienced palates. Servers are eager to guide you through the menu and willingly demonstrate preparation procedures for first-timers. ⊠ *30 W. Hubbard St.,* ☎ *312/645–0051. AE, MC, V.*

Mediterranean

$$–$$$ ✕ **Mantuano Mediterranean Table.** Well-regarded chef Tony Mantu-
★ ano is behind this large restaurant in the NBC Tower. Dishes from throughout the Mediterranean include a few showstoppers such as roast salmon with pomegranate molasses, flaming ouzo-soaked shrimp, and a variety of thin-crust pizzas produced by an enormous brick oven. ⊠ *455 Cityfront Plaza, between Michigan Ave. and Columbus Dr.,* ☎ *312/832–2600. AE, D, DC, MC, V. No lunch weekends.*

Mexican

$$–$$$ ✕ **Hat Dance.** The colorful sombreros hanging over the bar tell you that you've come to the right place. The dazzling setting uses a dozen or more shades of white, and the effect is almost palatial. The Mexican and southwestern fare can be rather awe-inspiring, too: Try duck fajitas with pineapple-cantaloupe salad or pumpkinseed-crusted sea bass. One dessert option is the white-chocolate taco, consisting of a cookie shell with ice cream and fresh fruit sauce. ⊠ *325 W. Huron St.,* ☎ *312/ 649–0066. AE, D, DC, MC, V. No lunch Sun.*

$$–$$$ ✕ **Salpicon.** The dozen tables at this cozy, colorful restaurant are usu-
★ ally filled with folks eagerly devouring the authentic cooking. Chef Priscilla Satkoff's upbringing in Mexico City is reflected in such boldly seasoned dishes as an incendiary *pollo Yucateca* (chicken Yucatán style) with a hot-pepper salsa. Those lacking asbestos tongues will find plenty of tamer options, however. The Mexican-style Sunday brunch, with egg dishes and items such as grilled quail, is one of the city's best. ⊠ *1252 N. Wells St.,* ☎ *312/988–7811. AE, D, DC, MC, V. Closed Tues. No lunch.*

$$–$$$ ✕ **Topolobampo.** Located alongside Frontera Grill (☞ *below*), Topo-
★ lobampo shares Frontera's kitchen, address, and phone number—and its dedication to quality. Topolobampo is the more expensive room; it has a more stately atmosphere, accepts reservations and, most important, affords the chef the opportunity to experiment with more expensive ingredients. The ever-changing menu showcases game, seasonal fruits and vegetables, and exotic preparations: Homemade tortillas with pumpkinseed sauce and pheasant roasted in banana leaves are two examples. Good service and an interesting wine add to the appeal. ⊠ *445 N. Clark St.,* ☎ *312/661–1434. Reservations essential. AE, D, DC, MC, V. Closed Sun.–Mon. No lunch Sat.*

$–$$$ ✕ **Frontera Grill.** Chef-owner Rick Bayless and his wife, Deann, liter-
★ ally wrote the book (*Authentic Mexican*) on Mexican cuisine—and that's what you'll find at this casual café, along with a tile floor, bright colors, and Mexican folk art. The Baylesses learned about regional Mexican cuisine by tramping across Mexico, and they return once a year (with their entire staff) to further their research. The results are uncommonly delicious: Try charbroiled catfish Yucatán style (with pick-

led red onions and jicama salad) or garlicky skewered tenderloin, Aguascalientes style (with poblano peppers, red onion, and bacon). The menu changes frequently, and weekly specials are often the most tempting dishes. Frontera shares its address and kitchen with the more formal Topolobampo (☞ *above*). ⊠ *445 N. Clark St.,* ☎ *312/661–1434. AE, D, DC, MC, V. Closed Sun.–Mon.*

Seafood

$$$–$$$$ ⨯ **Shaw's Crab House and Blue Crab Lounge.** This East Coast–style
★ restaurant has an oyster bar, in exposed brick and wood, and a wood-paneled, softly lighted main dining room with loft ceilings. Though dressy in style, it's also fairly noisy, but the fresh seafood is worth the din. Preparations tend toward the simple and the classic; try the fried calamari, steamed blue mussels, and Maryland crab cakes for appetizers. Crab, lobster, and shrimp are menu standards, along with a half dozen varieties of fresh oysters. Softshell crabs, stone crab claws, and king salmon appear among the seasonal specialties. ⊠ *21 E. Hubbard St.,* ☎ *312/527–2722. AE, D, DC, MC, V. No lunch weekends.*

$$–$$$ ⨯ **Riva.** In the middle of Navy Pier, its windows gazing southward over Lake Michigan and the lakefront skyline, Riva gives diners unparalleled views—and charges for the privilege. Grilled fish and shellfish are distinctly pricey, though the hordes who crowd into the place, especially in summer, don't seem to mind (the good service helps). Simpler preparations—grilled salmon or the pastas, for example—are better bets than the menu's more overambitious efforts. The spacious dining room has rosewood trim and a colorful sea mural. ⊠ *Navy Pier, 700 E. Grand Ave.,* ☎ *312/644–7482. AE, DC, MC, V. No lunch Sun.*

Steak Houses

$$$–$$$$ ⨯ **Gibsons.** On the site once occupied by the famous Mister Kelly's
★ nightclub is now what is perhaps the convention crowd's favorite steak house. The reasons? Plenty of room, attractive decor with lots of dark wood trim, huge portions, and good service. You don't see chopped liver on many appetizer lists these days, but the version here is good. ⊠ *1028 N. Rush St.,* ☎ *312/266–8999. Reservations essential. AE, D, DC, MC, V. No lunch.*

$$$–$$$$ ⨯ **Morton's of Chicago.** This is Chicago's best steak house—and that's
★ no idle statement. Excellent service and a very good wine list add to the principal attraction: beautiful, hefty steaks cooked to perfection. White tablecloths, chandeliers, and off-white walls create a classy ambience. It's no place for the budget conscious, but for steak lovers, it's a 16-ounce (or more) taste of heaven. ⊠ *1050 N. State St.,* ☎ *312/ 266–4820. Reservations essential. AE, D, DC, MC, V. No lunch.*

$$–$$$$ ⨯ **Capital Grille.** The Chicago outpost of this steak-house chain can hold its own with the city's big boys. Prime steaks are dry-aged on the premises in a glassed-in room. The decor, while masculine, avoids at least some of the steak-house clichés, and the award-winning wine list includes a gratifying number of half bottles. ⊠ *633 N. St. Clair St.,* ☎ *312/337–9400. AE, D, DC, MC, V. No lunch weekends.*

$$–$$$$ ⨯ **Eli's the Place for Steak.** Clubby and inviting in leather and warm wood, Eli's developed its outstanding reputation through an unflagging commitment to top-quality ingredients prepared precisely to customers' tastes. Prime aged steaks are the specialty here; indeed, they're among the best in Chicago. You'll also find superb, thickly cut veal chops and excellent calves' liver. For dessert order Eli's renowned cheesecake, now sold nationally in countless varieties. ⊠ *215 E. Chicago Ave.,* ☎ *312/642–1393. AE, D, DC, MC, V. No lunch weekends.*

$$–$$$$ ⨯ **Gene & Georgetti.** A real guys' steak house, Gene & Georgetti is as far from trendy as you could get, and decor is nothing special—though

a remodeling has greatly improved the upstairs dining rooms. But for massive steaks, good chops, and the famed "garbage salad"—a kitchen-sink creation of greens with vegetables and meats—you simply can't go wrong. If you like rubbing elbows with the well connected, you can do that, too, though service may be brusque if you're not connected yourself. ⊠ *500 N. Franklin St.,* ☎ *312/527–3718. Reservations essential. AE, DC, MC, V. Closed Sun.*

$$–$$$$ ✕ **Ruth's Chris Steak House.** The country's largest fine-dining steakhouse chain established this Chicago outpost in 1992. With excellent steaks and outstanding service, Ruth's Chris quickly demonstrated that it could compete with the best in this definitive steak town. The lobster is good, although expensive—largely because the smallest lobster in the tank is about 3 pounds—and there are more appetizer and side-dish options than at most other steak houses. ⊠ *431 N. Dearborn St.,* ☎ *312/321–2725. AE, D, DC, MC, V. Closed Sun. No lunch Sat.*

$$–$$$ ✕ **The Saloon.** This self-proclaimed "steak house for the '90s" is notable for its wide-ranging selection of seafood and nonsteak options. But when there's a convention in town the restaurant is generally packed, and beef is king. The Kansas City strip (like the New York, only with the bone left in) and the massive porterhouse are the Saloon's best steaks, and the double pork chop is the city's finest. The bright and cheery interior defies steak-house tradition, but nobody complains. ⊠ *200 E. Chestnut St.,* ☎ *312/280–5454. Reservations essential. AE, D, DC, MC, V.*

Lincoln Park and North

Brazilian

$$–$$$ ✕ **Rhumba.** In a nightclub atmosphere (the joint actually converts to a nightclub during the wee weekend hours) on the North Side, you'll find Chicago's only Brazilian restaurant. Amid the Carnavale footage playing on the TVs (in the bar and both rest rooms) and the Carmen Miranda impersonator sashaying about, you can dine well on *churrascaria* (skewered and grilled meats, vegetables, or fish), barbecued ribs with a tasty orange-cumin sauce, and grilled salmon with mango salsa. The wine list sticks to light-bodied bottlings (to better match the spicy, but not too hot, food), and the bar churns out killer cocktails, including the Brazilian signature drink *caipirinhas,* made with a distilled sugar-cane liquor. ⊠ *3631 N. Halsted St.,* ☎ *773/975–2345. AE, DC, MC, V. No lunch.*

Chinese

$$ ✕ **Dee's.** Servers at this yuppie-friendly Chinese restaurant in Lincoln Park are excellent and articulate—and, wonder of wonders, very knowledgeable about the ambitious wine list. The menu is a cut above those of most other Chinese restaurants, with such treats as drunken chicken, eggplant in garlic sauce, and a good variety of noodle dishes. However, even the Szechuan dishes are tame with spices; if you like your food hot, be sure to speak up when you order. ⊠ *1114 W. Armitage Ave.,* ☎ *773/477–1500. AE, MC, V. No lunch.*

Contemporary

$$$$ ✕ **Charlie Trotter's.** This tastefully renovated town house has only 20
★ closely spaced tables, far too few for the people who would like to eat here. The owner and chef, Charlie Trotter, enjoys an international reputation for his light, experimental dishes. Menus change daily, but past triumphs have included such appetizers as antelope strudel with wild mushrooms and foie-gras ravioli with mango and lemongrass sauce. Dishes are presented in a multicourse, degustation format; choose

from the $75 all-vegetable degustation or grand degustations at $90 or more. Naturally, there's an expansive (and expensive) wine list to match the elegant cuisine, but prices are surprisingly fair. The smoke-free dining room is elegant in its simplicity, the better to focus the diner's attention on the world-renowned food. Make reservations at least a month in advance. ⊠ *816 W. Armitage Ave.,* ☎ *773/248–6228. Reservations essential. Jacket required. AE, DC, MC, V. Closed Sun.–Mon. No lunch.*

$$$ ✕ **Green Dolphin Street.** In an industrial area just north of Bucktown, this sprawling complex encompasses a cool green dining room, a stylish jazz club (no cover for dinner guests), a cigar-friendly bar, and an outdoor patio overlooking an unspoiled stretch of the Chicago River. The emphasis on good looks extends to the menu; dishes are picture-perfect when they reach the table. Globally influenced American dishes include blueberry-stuffed foie gras, grilled salmon over firm polenta cake, and mushroom-coated halibut. Valet parking is complimentary. ⊠ *2200 N. Ashland Ave.,* ☎ *312/395–0066. AE, DC, MC, V. No lunch.*

$$–$$$ ✕ **Brett's.** This charmer in a gentrifying neighborhood has soft lighting, classical music, and a mellow smoke-free environment. The menu, which changes monthly, is full of creative surprises: potato tacos with poblano chili sauce, Thai-style salmon, jerk pork chops. Soups are a particular strength, and desserts are heavenly. Don't miss the homemade bread. ⊠ *2011 W. Roscoe St.,* ☎ *773/248–0999. AE, DC, MC, V. Closed Mon.–Tues. No lunch.*

$$–$$$ ✕ **Café Absinthe.** A funky, theatrical spot in the oh-so-fashionable Bucktown neighborhood, Café Absinthe is a trend seeker's haven: It's noisy and full of stylishly dressed folks, and the menu is distinctly untraditional—from scallops in fennel bouillon to octopus with watercress-jicama salad. ⊠ *1954 W. North Ave.,* ☎ *773/278–4488. AE, D, DC, MC, V. No lunch.*

$$–$$$ ✕ **Confusion.** The name evokes images of unpredictability, and with a
   ★ menu that changes daily, there is an element of surprise to this eclectic Bucktown restaurant. But chef Kevin Shikami's cooking, which blends French technique and Asian influences, isn't out to shock anybody. Even among his offbeat-sounding creations, such as duck breast with apple-parsnip pot stickers and garlic black pepper sauce, the flavors blend seamlessly. And simpler dishes, such as grilled beef tenderloin with hoisin glaze and potato pancake, are impressive for the quality of their components. A not-the-usual-suspects wine list (the attitude-free sommelier is a reliable adviser) and solicitous service complete the impressive picture. ⊠ *1616 N. Damen Ave.,* ☎ *773/772–7100. AE, D, DC, MC, V. No lunch.*

$$–$$$ ✕ **Erwin.** This appealing spot brims with the sunny personalities of owners Erwin and Cathy Drechsler. You'll always find a chicken dish, a
   ★ vegetable tart, and a steak or chop on the menu, which changes monthly. Sunday brunch is popular with locals. Service is friendly and capable, and the wine list has some surprising inclusions. ⊠ *2925 N. Halsted St.,* ☎ *773/528–7200. AE, D, DC, MC, V. Closed Mon. No lunch.*

$$–$$$ ✕ **Meritage.** Like the style of wine it's named for, this Bucktown restaurant is tricky to categorize. The chef takes his inspiration from the flavors of the Pacific Northwest, which translates into a fair amount of fish (striped bass with dauphinoise potatoes and red-wine sauce) and a lot of Asian influence (duck spring rolls with pickled ginger and Vietnamese fish sauce). Lighting is subdued and romantic—that flickering votive at your table will come in handy while reading the menu. ⊠ *2118 N. Damen Ave.,* ☎ *773/235–6434, AE, DC, MC, V. No lunch.*

Lincoln Park and North Dining

Ambria, **29**
Ann Sather, **5, 21**
Arun's, **9**
Bando, **8**
Bistrot Zinc, **11**
Blue Mesa, **35**
Brett's, **14**
Busy Bee, **45**
Café Absinthe, **43**
Cafe Ba–Ba–Reeba!, **32**
Charlie Trotter's, **27**
Clark Street Bistro, **26**

Confusion, **42**
Dee's, **33**
Don Juan's, **1**
Erwin, **24**
Flat Top Grill, **37**
Golden Ox, **38**
Green Dolphin Street, **39**
Jezebel, **17**
Julie Mai's Le Bistro, **7**
La Donna, **6**
Le Bouchon, **41**
Luna Blu, **47**

Lutnia, **13**
Mama Desta's Red Sea, **15**
Matsuya, **16**
Meritage, **40**
Mia Francesca, **19**
Pasteur, **3**
Raj Darbar, **25**
Relish, **31**
Rhumba, **18**
Schulien's, **9**
Soul Kitchen, **46**
Starfish, **44**
Strega Nona, **12**

Thai Classic, **22**
Tomboy, **4**
Toulouse on the Park, **28**
Un DiAmo, **36**
Un Grand Cafe, **29**
Via Emilia, **30**
Via Veneto, **2**
Vinci, **34**
Yoshi's Cafe, **20**
Zum Deutschen Eck, **23**

$$ ✕ **Relish.** The important thing to remember here is to save room for
★ dessert. It's wonderful, even if you find it awkward to order something
called Very Chocolate Orgasm (stick to the free-form ice cream sand-
wich if you're feeling bashful). The wide-ranging menu, strewn with
international influences, includes such choices as lobster-mango que-
sadillas and savory bread pudding with ham and onions. ✉ *2044 N.
Halsted St.,* ☎ *773/868–9034. AE, DC, MC, V. Closed Mon. No lunch.*

$$ ✕ **Soul Kitchen.** Though the name implies soul food, that's not really
what you find here, despite such occasional offerings as pecan-breaded
catfish with mustard greens. The real thrust is creative regional American food, in decidedly funky surroundings. Once you get past the animal-
print tablecloths and loud music, you'll find quite a serious kitchen at
work. ✉ *1576 N. Damen Ave.,* ☎ *773/342–9742. Reservations not
accepted. AE, DC, MC, V. No lunch.*

$$ ✕ **Tomboy.** A funky place in Chicago's Andersonville neighborhood,
Tomboy draws an eclectic crowd that makes for great people-watching.
The food is visually interesting as well, from a fanciful "porcupine"
shrimp, coated with splayed-out spikes of phyllo dough, to crème brûlée
served in a cookie cone inside a martini glass. Desserts are about all
that come in martini glasses, by the way: There's no liquor license, but
there's plenty of stemware for whatever you bring, and no corkage fee.
✉ *5402 N. Clark St.,* ☎ *773/907–0636. AE, DC, MC, V. BYOB. Closed
Mon. No lunch.*

$ ✕ **Flat Top Grill.** This crowded, narrow spot is one of of the city's best
do-your-own stir-fry places. Patrons fill their bowls from an assortment
of fresh vegetables, meat, and fish; ladle on the sauce of their choice;
and watch a chef stir-fry it on a hot griddle. A handy sign gives de-
tailed advice for neophytes. ✉ *319 W. North Ave.,* ☎ *312/787–7676.
Reservations not accepted. DC, MC, V. No lunch Mon.–Thurs.*

Ethiopian

$ ✕ **Mama Desta's Red Sea.** Dramatically different from European cook-
ing, the stewlike dishes at Mama Desta's intriguingly combine herbs
and spices with complex aromas and interesting textures. Food such
as spicy chicken, lamb stew, and pureed lentils is flavorful, earthy, and
simple. Instead of relying on silverware, diners use spongy, slightly sour
flat bread to scoop up the chef's creations. ✉ *3216 N. Clark St.,* ☎
773/935–7561. AE, DC, MC, V. No lunch Mon.–Thurs.

French

$$$–$$$$ ✕ **Ambria.** In a spacious art nouveau atmosphere, Ambria combines
★ a classic haute-cuisine style and atmosphere with contemporary French
food—all without flash or bombast. The modestly understated menu
dazzles with blackberry-sauced venison, lobster gazpacho, and rosemary-
infused lamb loin. The assortment of cheeses, sherbets, fruits, and pas-
tries is upstaged by the sensational dessert soufflé. Sommelier Bob
Bansberg is a treasure. ✉ *2300 N. Lincoln Park W,* ☎ *773/472–5959.
Reservations essential. AE, D, DC, MC, V. Closed Sun. No lunch.*

$$$ ✕ **Toulouse on the Park.** An opulent red-and-gold dining room, with
a jazz cabaret next door (no cover charge for dinner guests) that at-
tracts top-notch talent, Toulouse is a level or two above bistro in its
ambitions. The surroundings are certainly more in keeping with fine
dining, but the prices are considerably more modest. Good desserts make
Toulouse an appealing nighttime stop. ✉ *2140 N. Lincoln Park W,* ☎
773/665–9071. AE, DC, MC, V. Closed Sun. No lunch.

$$–$$$ ✕ **Bistrot Zinc.** An authentic bistro, down to the vintage zinc-topped
★ bar imported from Paris, Bistrot Zinc has caught on big in the gentrified Southport Avenue corridor. Classics such as steak *frites,* bouill-
abaisse, and *poulet grandmére* (roasted chicken with bacon and garlic)
can't miss, and there are one or two modern interpretations as well—

a *brandade* made with monkfish and crawfish rather than salt cod, for instance. Cafe Zinc, to the left of the entryway, is a self-service counter with quick nibbles (crepes, quiche of the day, assorted patés) for eat-in or carryout; unlike the restaurant, it's open for lunch, but weekends only. ✉ *3443 N. Southport Ave.,* ☎ *773/281–3443. AE, DC, MC, V. No lunch at restaurant.*

$$–$$$ ✕ **Un Grand Cafe.** This attractive bistro with black-and-white tile floors, dark wood trim, and brass accents is the casual companion to the elegant Ambria (☞ *above*), at the same address. Steak *frites,* cassoulet, and roast chicken are specialties on a menu that also includes a substantial selection of fish. Though the ambience is relaxed, standards are consistently high. ✉ *2300 N. Lincoln Park W,* ☎ *773/348–8886. AE, D, DC, MC, V. No lunch.*

$–$$$ ✕ **Yoshi's Cafe.** Once a pricey fine-dining restaurant of considerable
★ renown, Yoshi's recast itself as an informal French-Asian cafe with much lower prices and a jeans-casual atmosphere; there's even a kids' menu. Still evident is Yoshi Katsumura's exceptional cooking, as seen in his grilled mahimahi with carrot juice and lobster essence or crab wontons with a gingered apricot sweet-and-sour sauce. The dining room is a slightly crowded sea of white-tablecloth tables, bentwood chairs, and beige walls with blond-wood trim. ✉ *3257 N. Halsted St.,* ☎ *773/248–6160. No lunch.*

$$ ✕ **Le Bouchon.** The French comfort food at this charming 40-seat
★ bistro in Bucktown is in a league of its own. Onion tart has been a signature dish of owner Jean-Claude Poilevey for years; other not-to-be-missed delights are hunter-style rabbit and *salade Lyonnaise* (mixed greens topped with a creamy vinaigrette and a poached egg). Don't miss the fruit tarts. ✉ *1958 N. Damen Ave.,* ☎ *773/862–6600. AE, D, DC, MC, V. Closed Sun. No lunch.*

German

$$–$$$ ✕ **Golden Ox.** Dark wood, stained-glass windows, murals depicting scenes from German mythology, a hand-carved bar of golden oak, and cheerful waitresses in traditional costume give this restaurant, which opened in 1920 in what was once a German neighborhood, authentic ethnic flavor. Among the two dozen specialties are four veal preparations, smoked pork loin, and *hasenpfeffer* (rabbit stew with red wine sauce)—but there are also steaks and a 16-ounce lobster tail. The hearty fare can leave diners with a contented glow—and a disinclination to move. ✉ *1578 N. Clybourn Ave.,* ☎ *312/664–0780. AE, D, DC, MC, V. Closed Mon. No lunch Sun.*

$$ ✕ **Schulien's.** Arguably more a German-American restaurant than a German one—decent steaks and terrific broiled whitefish are served alongside Wiener schnitzel—this venerable tavern celebrated its 110th anniversary in 1997. The draws: hearty, reasonably priced dishes; friendly, efficient service; and a festive atmosphere. Schulien's famed magicians will, on request, perform table-side magic after the meal (a $5–$10 tip is standard). ✉ *2100 W. Irving Park Rd.,* ☎ *773/478–2100. AE, D, DC, MC, V. Closed Mon. No lunch weekends.*

$$ ✕ **Zum Deutschen Eck.** In this warm, comfortable eatery, waitresses wear costumes and stained glass complements dark wood. The fare includes the typically German homemade *suelze* (headcheese), herring salad, potato pancakes, *Koenigsberger klops* (German meatballs), and schnitzel *à la jaeger* (veal cutlet sautéed in red wine with green peppers, onions, fresh mushrooms, and red pepper sauce). Old favorites are sauerbraten, half roast duckling, and Wiener schnitzel. Most entrées are accompanied by whipped potatoes and sauerkraut; a few come with buttered noodles or spaëtzle. ✉ *2924 N. Southport Ave.,* ☎ *773/525–8390. AE, D, DC, MC, V.*

Indian

$–$$ ✕ **Raj Darbar.** Raj occupies an important niche in Chicago's Indian dining scene: It is, perhaps, the ideal spot for novices. The menu covers the basics, and the knowledgeable, unintimidating, and mostly American waitstaff serves above-average food. Begin with a traditional sampling of Indian appetizers; then move on to the fine curried entrées; also sample the soft, delicious Indian breads, such as *paratha* and nan. Though some dishes are spicy, none are particularly hot. Wine and a wide selection of beers, including three from India, are reasonably priced. ✉ *2660 N. Halsted St.,* ☎ *773/348–1010. AE, D, DC, MC, V.*

Italian

$$–$$$ ✕ **La Donna.** Run by the sister of the Via Veneto owner (☞ *below*), La Donna has excellent pastas—try the pumpkin ravioli in creamy balsamic sauce or the fine penne *arrabiata* (spicy tomato sauce)—and good, cracker-crust pizzas. Like Via Veneto, it has a generally crowded dining room that makes customers feel like part of a very large party. The wine list is well chosen and fairly priced, and there's a bargain-price Sunday brunch. ✉ *5146 N. Clark St.,* ☎ *773/561–9400. AE, D, DC, MC, V.*

$$–$$$ ✕ **Mia Francesca.** Why is this tiny restaurant so insanely popular? Principally because of chef-owner Scott Harris's very good authentic Italian cooking. Its moderate prices and its pleasant and unpretentious atmosphere certainly don't hurt, either. Try the classic *bruschetta, quattro formaggi* (four cheese) pizza, or the full-flavored pasta and chicken dishes. While you wait for one of the small, tightly spaced tables in the single dining room—and you will wait—you can have a drink at the bar. ✉ *3311 N. Clark St.,* ☎ *773/281–3310. Reservations not accepted. MC, V. No lunch.*

$$–$$$ ✕ **Un DiAmo.** A tiny storefront eatery that seats 55 in tight proximity, Un DiAmo works because of its communal atmosphere (cross-table conversations among complete strangers are common), its clever decor (cherubic angels smile down on guests from various vantage points), and its imaginative cooking. It also helps that Second City (☞ Chapter 5), the popular comedy revue, is right across the street. The restaurant's signature dish is apple-filled ravioli with smoked chicken and a light cream sauce; another winner is blackened salmon over saffron risotto with mango salsa. ✉ *1617 N. Wells St.,* ☎ *312/337–8881. AE, DC, MC, V. Closed Mon. No lunch.*

$$–$$$ ✕ **Via Emilia.** Everything from the complimentary breads to the lovely desserts is made in the kitchen of this 50-seat Bolognese restaurant in the toniest section of Lincoln Park. The earthy, rustic menu includes veal slices with a coarse tuna puree, pasta with a meat-filled Bolognese sauce, and grilled fresh fish with chopped vegetables. Decor is simple but pretty, with an open kitchen at the far end of the narrow dining room—and, happily, it isn't too noisy. ✉ *2119 N. Clark St.,* ☎ *773/ 248–6283. AE, DC, MC, V. No lunch weekends.*

$$–$$$ ✕ **Vinci.** Paul LoDuca, who also owns the Near North restaurant Mare, created this very impressive, stylishly casual restaurant whose dining room is all faux finishes and rustic touches. The menu focuses on such robust regional dishes as grilled pork chops with fennel and garlic. Pizzas are creative; one combines fontina cheese, roasted garlic, bitter greens, and tomato. The restaurant is a particular hit among the pretheater crowd. ✉ *1732 N. Halsted St.,* ☎ *312/266–1199. Reservations essential for pretheater dining. AE, DC, MC, V. Closed Mon. No lunch.*

$$ ✕ **Luna Blu.** You'll find traditional Sicilian cooking in a friendly neighborhood atmosphere at this restaurant in Wicker Park. Pay attention to the daily specials; the best bets are often found there, including the day's featured fish (red snapper with white wine and Roma tomatoes, for instance) and pasta specials. Tiramisu is the only homemade dessert on the menu (a few other choices come from a local baker). ⊠ *1554 N. Milwaukee Ave.,* ☎ *773/862–2600. AE, DC, MC, V. No lunch.*

$$ ✕ **Strega Nona.** A fun, casual spot that takes its name from the eponymous children's stories, Strega Nona is large, loud, and lively. Pasta is king, as a glance at the menu will tell you: Traditional pastas come with roasted chicken in fontina cream sauce; global pastas include green tea noodles with shrimp in ginger-soy sauce. Another signature touch is the *bruschettone,* oversize slices of oil-glossed grilled bread topped with various ingredients. ⊠ *3747 N. Southport Ave.,* ☎ *773/244–0990. AE, D, DC, MC, V. No lunch.*

$$ ✕ **Via Veneto.** This family-run restaurant has simple decor and sophisticated food. Pastas are excellent, particularly the daily specials. Grilled veal with Chianti sauce and tuna carpaccio with bitter greens and mustard vinaigrette show the kitchen's range. On Saturday night the crowds are impossible; Friday is a better bet, midweek even better. There's a small parking lot in back, but street parking is never a problem in this extremely safe residential neighborhood. ⊠ *3449 W. Peterson Ave.,* ☎ *773/267–0888. AE, D, DC, MC, V.*

Japanese

$$ ✕ **Matsuya.** This small storefront restaurant has a sushi bar, wood paneling, a brown tile floor, and a floor-to-ceiling wood screen in front of the kitchen. Sushi and an extensive choice of appetizers dominate the menu: Deep-fried spicy chicken wings, steamed spinach with sesame, whitefish with white smelt roe, seafood and vegetables on skewers, and dumplings with sauce are just a few. Tempura, fish, and meat teriyaki round out the menu. ⊠ *3469 N. Clark St.,* ☎ *773/248–2677. MC, V. No lunch weekdays.*

Korean

$$ ✕ **Bando.** For a city with an abundance of Asian (especially Thai) restau-
★ rants, Chicago cannot claim many Korean establishments. Bando, however, goes a long way toward compensating for this inequity, thanks to its consistently excellent food. First-timers will like the *pajun,* a pancake made with oysters and scallions, and *bul-go-ki* (barbecued beef); the more experienced can attempt the *jun-gol,* a spicy seafood stew. Helpful waiters are reliable guides through the exotic menu. ⊠ *2200 W. Lawrence Ave.,* ☎ *773/728–7400. AE, MC, V.*

Mediterranean

$$–$$$ ✕ **Clark Street Bistro.** This neighborhood charmer has comfortable surroundings and more than fair prices. As a bonus, dishes are pretty as a picture, whether you've ordered a complex bouillabaisse or a simple saffron couscous with cilantro and cumin. ⊠ *2600 N Clark St.,* ☎ *773/525–9992. AE, D, DC, MC, V.*

$$–$$$ ✕ **Jezebel.** Just steps from the always-packed Mia Francesca (☞ *above*) is this quiet, solid restaurant that's rarely crowded yet certainly deserves to be. Faux-finish aged walls and eggshell-color table linen give the room a warm feeling. The food is simple—occasionally too simple—but there are treats for the adventurous. Baked shrimp in phyllo dough and sizzling calamari are highlights. Service is very attentive, probably because the owner is rarely out of the dining room. ⊠ *3517 N. Clark St.,* ☎ *773/929–4000. AE, D, DC, MC, V. No lunch.*

Mexican

$$–$$$ ✕ **Don Juan's.** This northwest-side Mexican spot is really two restaurants in one. The main menu has all the standards—tacos, enchiladas, and the like (albeit especially well done here)—but the daily specials are where chef Patrick Concannon displays his creativity and culinary

training. You might find six-chili Amish chicken with sweet potato–*chipotle* gratin or pepper-crusted filet mignon with blue cheese ravioli. The wine list has a sophistication to match the cuisine, including a large selection of fine tequilas for sipping. ⊠ *6730 N. Northwest Hwy.,* ☎ *773/775–6438. AE, D, DC, MC, V.*

Polish

$$–$$$ ✕ **Lutnia.** The menu here is Polish-Continental, but stick to the hearty, straightforward Polish creations unless you're dying for steak Diane or other similarly unremarkably prepared Continental dishes. Start with an assortment of pierogi, and perhaps some hunter's stew; then try the terrific stuffed quail. Decor is upscale, and a pianist performs most nights. ⊠ *5532 W. Belmont Ave.,* ☎ *773/282–5335. AE, D, MC, V. Closed Mon. No lunch.*

$ ✕ **Busy Bee.** This is among the best of the many unpretentious Polish restaurants throughout Chicago, with pleasing stick-to-your-ribs food at very low prices. Pierogi (stuffed with meat, potato, cheese, or potato and sauerkraut) are served with sour cream or applesauce. Homemade mushroom soup, *bigos* (hunter's stew), Polish sausages, boiled beef brisket, and roast duck are among the entrées. Standard American dishes are also available. The double storefront space includes a large U-shape counter and booths, as well as a carpeted area with cloth-covered tables. Service can be slow. ⊠ *1546 N. Damen Ave.,* ☎ *773/772–4433. D, MC, V.*

Seafood

$$–$$$ ✕ **Starfish.** A smoothly running operation in the burgeoning Bucktown neighborhood, Starfish emphasizes southern and Caribbean influences, as in cornmeal-breaded fried catfish and grilled escolar with a banana–pineapple reduction sauce. Start your meal with some fresh oysters from the pristine raw bar. Glazed off-white walls, arty chandeliers, and ceilings fans set a contemporary, casual mood. ⊠ *1856 W. North Ave.,* ☎ *773/395–3474. AE, DC, MC, V. No lunch.*

Southwestern

$$ ✕ **Blue Mesa.** Although this casual, festive restaurant is a noisy, popular neighborhood joint, the food is taken quite seriously. In fact, the kitchen is downright sophisticated in its use of hot chilies. Cases in point are jalapeño grilled shrimp, blackened tuna with a sesame-*pasilla* (smoked pepper) beurre blanc, and sizzling apple fritters. The brunch menu is full of eye-opening, spicy selections. ⊠ *1729 N. Halsted St.,* ☎ *312/944–5990. AE, D, DC, MC, V. No lunch Sat.*

Spanish

$$ ✕ **Cafe Ba-Ba-Reeba!** Chicago's best-known purveyor of tapas is usually crowded with upscale young people having a very good time. Choose from among a large selection of cold and warm tapas, ranging from cannelloni stuffed with tuna, asparagus, and basil, served with tomato-basil sauce and white wine vinaigrette, to veal with mushrooms, eggplant, tomato, and sherry sauce. A few soups and salads are available, as is an entrée menu that includes nearly a dozen paellas, baked salmon, and even venison. ⊠ *2024 N. Halsted St.,* ☎ *773/935–5000. AE, D, DC, MC, V.*

Swedish

$ ✕ **Ann Sather.** The two branches of this large, light, airy Swedish restaurant, a favorite for weekend breakfast, emphasize home-style food and service. The homemade cinnamon rolls are a local institution; potato sausage and chicken croquettes are also specialties; and there's even a full sandwich menu. A Swedish sampler lets you try duck breast with lingonberry glaze, a Swedish meatball, a potato sausage, a dumpling, and sauerkraut. Very reasonable entrée prices include an appetizer (Swedish fruit soup and pickled herring are among them), two side dishes (choose from Swedish brown beans, mashed or boiled potatoes, pickled beets, and more), and dessert. ⊠ *5207 N. Clark St.*, ☎ *773/271–6677;* ⊠ *929 W. Belmont Ave.*, ☎ *773/348–2378. Reservations not accepted at Clark St. location. AE, MC, V. No dinner at Clark St. location.*

Thai

$$–$$$ ✕ **Arun's.** This is the finest Thai restaurant in Chicago, and some
★ devotees say it's the finest in the country. Certainly the beauty of presentation and freshness of ingredients are far beyond what storefront Thai restaurants usually attempt. Prices are much higher, as a consequence, but worth every penny. Highlights include intricate golden pastry baskets filled with diced shrimp, corn, and shiitake mushrooms; medallions of veal with ginger-lemongrass sauce; and a delicious hot-and-sour soup. But your best bet is to ask for a degustation dinner and let Arun himself select the dishes. The two-level dining room has lots of natural wood, complemented by Thai art and a small art gallery. ⊠ *4156 N. Kedzie Ave.*, ☎ *773/539–1909. Reservations essential. AE, D, DC, MC, V. Closed Mon. No lunch.*

$–$$ ✕ **Thai Classic.** This attractive, spotless restaurant just a few blocks south of Wrigley Field stands out with its good service and meticulously prepared dishes. The charming, contemporary decor is better than average as well. It can be very difficult to park here (though the restaurant has a few free spaces in back) any day the Cubs are playing, so plan accordingly. ⊠ *3332 N. Clark St.*, ☎ *773/404–2000. AE, MC, V. No lunch Mon.*

Vietnamese

$$–$$$ ✕ **Julie Mai's Le Bistro.** Only in America would you find a Vietnamese restaurant with a partly French menu occupying a former Italian restaurant in an old Scandinavian neighborhood. The unchanged decor lets diners sit in secluded stucco alcoves while deciding among such choices as lemon-beef salad, Vietnamese fisherman's soup, or shrimp le Bistro (fried jumbo shrimp with hollandaise sauce). A serious wine list and very helpful servers make decisions—and the whole experience—a pleasure. ⊠ *5025 N. Clark St.*, ☎ *773/784–6000. AE, D, DC, MC, V. No lunch.*

$$–$$$ ✕ **Pasteur.** Ease back into the rattan-covered chairs, amid tropical plants and lazily spinning ceiling fans, and prepare to be impressed by the superb Vietnamese food that emerges from Pasteur's kitchen. The cuisine is exotic enough to most visitors that the menu sticks to the staples of Vietnamese cooking, including minced shrimp with sugarcane, spicy beef salad, crisply fried whole fish, and fragrant soups. Waiters are knowledgeable and communicative. Be a polite guest and don't steal the adorable fu-dog chopstick rests; Lord knows the locals do that often enough. ⊠ *5525 N. Broadway*, ☎ *773/878–1061. AE, D, DC, MC, V.*

Worth a Special Trip

Contemporary

$$$–$$$$ ✕ **Trio.** Wildly creative and visually stunning dishes are borne to the
★ table on anything from a slab of granite to a glass block. Recent standouts include "wild-mushroom cappuccino" with a Parmesan *tuile* (crisp wafer), apple-smoked beef fillet with wasabi mashed potatoes, and tea-smoked lobster with lemongrass. The decor is eclectic, with a faux-stone wall here, some stain-washed paneling there, and fabric-draped ceilings. ⊠ *1625 Hinman Ave., Evanston (14 mi north of downtown Chicago)*, ☎ *847/733–8746. Reservations essential. Jacket required. AE, D, DC, MC, V. Closed Mon. No lunch.*

French

$$$$ ✕ **Le Français.** The husband-wife team of Roland and Mary Beth Lic-
★   cioni has Le Français—to many, Chicago's finest restaurant—running
beautifully. Roland rules the kitchen, turning out contemporary French
creations. His plates are visual masterpieces, and portions are substantial
for cuisine this fine. Mary Beth is arguably the city's best pastry chef;
her desserts are unparalleled, and her chocolates—now available on a
retail basis—are equally superb. A veteran waitstaff inspires confidence
and imparts conviviality; intimidation isn't part of the experience.
Lunch at Le Français is one of Chicago's great gastronomic events and
substantially less expensive than dinner. The country French setting is
accented with paintings of the French countryside and antique copper
pots and pans hanging here and there. Wheeling is about 30 mi northwest of downtown Chicago. ⊠ *269 S. Milwaukee Ave., Wheeling,* ☎
*847/541–7470. Reservations essential. Jacket required. AE, D, MC,
V. Closed Sun. No lunch Sat. and Mon.*

$$$–$$$$ ✕ **Carlos.** This restaurant continues to challenge Le Français for the
★   title of best French restaurant in the area. Service is particularly good—
owner Carlos Nieto (himself a Le Français graduate) gets involved in
the front-room operations—but even the lowest-ranking assistant has
a firm grasp of the menu. Dishes are mainly contemporary French: You
might find squab ravioli with garlic sauce or rabbit tournedos with
creamed leeks and truffles. Desserts are heavenly. The substantial wine
list includes some magnificent vintages, although at eye-popping prices.
The main dining room is dark and woody; mismatched antique china
plates lend character. ⊠ *429 Temple Ave., Highland Park (26 mi north
of downtown Chicago),* ☎ *847/432–0770. Reservations essential.
Jacket required. AE, D, DC, MC, V. Closed Tues. No lunch.*

4 Lodging

*From the Loop to Lincoln Park,
Chicago's accommodations can satisfy
a yearning for old-world elegance
or high-tech sophistication. Not
surprisingly, the city has a number of
architectural showstoppers, along with
plenty of giant convention hotels and
several quiet hideaways a few steps
from the action on North Michigan
Avenue. Rates tend to be high in this
business-oriented city, but if you're
looking for good value, you'll find
options from historic charmers to
modern suite hotels scattered around.*

Revised by
Robin Kurzer

THEY DON'T CALL CHICAGO "the city that works" for nothing. Work is what brings most visitors to the city, and convention goers are the lifeblood of many hotels. Mammoth high-rises with thousands of square feet of meeting space serve this segment, but visitors desiring a more personal experience can also find smaller, European-style hostelries. Choices range from basic chain fare to unique establishments in convenient areas along the lakefront, whether downtown or in Lincoln Park to the north. As an added treat, many hotels have panoramic views of Lake Michigan or of the architecturally spectacular high-rises lining the Chicago River.

As one of the nation's most popular convention and trade show destinations, Chicago can be a challenging place to find a room. Advance reservations are essential, except perhaps in the dead of winter. When there's not a major show in town, though, most hotels do something to woo customers, whether it's corporate rates, shopping or theater packages, senior citizen savings, honeymoon deals, or discounts to the clergy and military personnel. If you plan to spend a lot of time in museums and stores and aren't averse to cold weather, visit in January or February, when hotel rates drop to their lowest prices. Weekend deals can pack in appealing extras at a purse-satisfying price. Always be sure to ask whether you're eligible for a discount.

Choosing a Neighborhood

Hotels are clustered primarily in three locations: the Loop, the Near North Side, and the airport area. They're listed in this chapter by location and then by price category within each location.

Business travelers may prefer Loop hotels because they're within walking distance of the financial district and government offices. Major cultural institutions are nearby as well: the Art Institute, Orchestra Hall, the Civic Opera House, and the Goodman Theatre. The Field Museum, Shedd Aquarium, and Adler Planetarium are just a short bus or cab ride away, and the skyscrapers that put Chicago on the architectural map of the world are all around. Loop hotels tend to be older and somewhat less expensive than those in Near North. The main drawback to staying here is how deserted, even a little spooky, the area becomes at night and on weekends. People traveling alone may prefer the brighter lights of North Michigan Avenue.

Dining and shopping are the big draws north of the river, where hotels line both sides of Michigan Avenue as well as area side streets. Association headquarters, art galleries, advertising agencies, and media companies are here. Hotels range from high-tech to homey. A bit north of Michigan Avenue and close to Lincoln Park and the lakefront is the Gold Coast, a stately residential neighborhood where the hotels are quiet and dignified. Farther up, around Diversey Parkway, less expensive properties occupy Lincoln Park and Lakeview—both lively, youthful neighborhoods with the Midwest's most eclectic array of clothing, book, and record stores.

A meeting or convention in Rosemont or a flight-related reason should be the only times to consider an airport hotel. Even though prices are slightly lower at airport hotels, the area around O'Hare is drab, depressing, and far from downtown. The 15-mi trip into the city can take an hour during rush hour, bad weather, or periods of heavy construction on the Kennedy Expressway, all of which are likely at any given time.

Booking Your Room

When you make your reservation, be sure to get a reservation number and keep it with you for reference. Notify the hotel if you anticipate arriving later than 5 PM; many hotels will guarantee your reservation with your credit card and have a room waiting for you no matter how late you arrive. Inquire about the hotel's cancellation policy at the time of booking to avoid paying for a room you didn't occupy. Should you need to cancel your reservation, notify the hotel as soon as possible— and be sure to get a cancellation number. Otherwise, you may be responsible for at least one night's charge.

One alternative to reserving a room through a hotel is to contact a booking service. These agencies book excess rooms at major hotels, often at a significant discount. A no-fee discount hotel-reservation service that specializes in Chicago is **Hot Rooms** (☎ 773/468–7666 or 800/468–3500).

Facilities

This guide lists the facilities that are available but doesn't specify whether they cost extra: When pricing accommodations, always ask what's included. Most of the upscale hotels have business centers or at least the capability to assist with faxing, copying, and word processing; many also have meeting rooms of different sizes. Most offer room service, as well as laundry and dry cleaning. Cable TV is the standard in Chicago hotels and often comes with free or pay-per-view movie channels. Some hotels charge for using on-site health facilities. Guests at hotels that don't have their own health club may be allowed to use one nearby, usually for a daily fee ranging from $7 to $12. Ask for specifics if a particular facility is important to you.

Many hotels in the Chicago area have adapted some accommodations for people using wheelchairs or for guests with vision or hearing impairments. If you have a special need, call the hotel for specific information.

Meal Plans

Assume that hotels operate on the **European Plan** (EP, with no meals) unless we specify that they use the **Continental Plan** (CP, with a Continental breakfast daily), **Breakfast Plan** (BP, with a full breakfast daily), **Modified American Plan** (MAP, with breakfast and dinner daily), or the **Full American Plan** (FAP, with all meals).

Bed-and-Breakfasts

Staying in a person's home lends a personal touch to your visit and is a good way to see residential neighborhoods. You may also save some money. **Bed & Breakfast/Chicago** (✉ Box 14088, 60614, ☎ 312/951–0085 or 800/375–7084, FAX 312/649–9243) is a clearinghouse for more than 70 options, from a guest room in a Victorian home to a furnished high-rise apartment. Accommodations range from $85 to $185 and are mostly in the Near North and Lincoln Park neighborhoods. Some are in Hyde Park, a good option for visitors who wish to stay close to the University of Chicago. Reservations can be made by phone (weekdays 9–5) or by mail. The office will mail or fax sample listings and a reservation form.

When Not to Go

Although Chicago's frigid winters should be a consideration when planning your trip, also be aware of the more than 1,000 conventions and trade shows scheduled in the area every year. During the National Restaurant Association show in May, the hardware show in August, and the manufacturing technology show in September, not only are rooms nonexistent, but so are tables at the city's popular restaurants. You can check your travel dates with the **Chicago Office of Tourism** (☎ 312/744–2400), or go on-line to www.chicago.il.org, the Web site of the **Chicago Convention and Tourism Bureau.**

Prices

Hotel price categories in this chapter are based on the standard weekday rate for one room, double occupancy. These are the rack rates—the highest price at which the rooms are rented. As noted above, discounts are often available. However, although standard rates are quoted *per room*, package rates are often quoted *per person, double occupancy.* Be warned that many Chicago hotels quote rates based on single occupancy, with a second person adding $10–$20 to the nightly rate.

CATEGORY	COST*
$$$$	over $200
$$$	$150–$200
$$	$100–$149
$	under $100

All prices are for a standard double room, excluding service charges and Chicago's unpleasantly high 14.9% room tax. The tax is slightly lower at suburban hotels.

Downtown

$$$$ 🏨 **Fairmont.** Just blocks from the Loop, this 45-story pink granite tower
★ is a true standout. The grand rooms are filled with marble-top dark-wood furniture and plants; marble bathrooms have mini-TVs next to the sink and separate shower stalls. Singing waiters at Primavera, the hotel's Italian restaurant, create a festive atmosphere. ⊠ *200 N. Columbus Dr., 60601,* ☎ *312/565–8000 or 800/527–4727,* ℻ *312/856–1032. 626 rooms, 66 suites. 2 restaurants, 3 bars, lobby lounge, in-room modem lines, minibars, no-smoking rooms, room service, golf privileges, cabaret, laundry service and dry cleaning, concierge, business services, meeting rooms, parking (fee). AE, D, DC, MC, V.*

$$$$ 🏨 **Hyatt on Printer's Row.** As close to a boutique hotel as Hyatt gets, this 161-room property near McCormick Place housed printing presses in its former life. The lobby and public areas show a distinctive Frank Lloyd Wright inspiration, with sober colors, dark woods, and Tiffany-style lamps. Black lacquer furniture lends an art deco look to the rooms, which all have a soothingly muted color scheme. The restaurant, Prairie, serves creative American cuisine (☞ *Greater Downtown in* Chapter 3). ⊠ *500 S. Dearborn St., 60605,* ☎ *312/986–1234 or 800/233–1234,* ℻ *312/939–2468. 157 rooms, 4 suites. Restaurant, bar, in-room modem lines, minibars, no-smoking rooms, room service, exercise room, laundry service and dry cleaning, meeting rooms, parking (fee). AE, D, DC, MC, V.*

$$$$ 🏨 **Renaissance Chicago Hotel.** Behind the modern stone-and-glass ex-
★ terior on the south bank of the Chicago River is a tidy '90s interpretation of turn-of-the-century splendor. Lavish floral carpets, tapestry upholstery, crystal-beaded chandeliers, and French Provincial furniture create rich-looking public areas. Rooms have sitting areas and rounded windows with spectacular river views. ⊠ *1 W. Wacker Dr., 60601,* ☎ *312/372–7200 or 800/468–3571,* ℻ *312/372–0093. 513 rooms, 40 suites. 2 restaurants, café, lobby lounge, in-room modem lines, minibars, no-smoking floor, room service, indoor pool, beauty salon, hot tub, sauna, exercise room, laundry service and dry cleaning, concierge, concierge floor, business services, meeting rooms. AE, D, DC, MC, V.*

$$$$ 🏨 **Swissôtel.** The Swissôtel's triangular Harry Weese design ensures panoramic lake and river vistas. The comfortable, contemporary-style guest rooms have two-line phones and marble bathrooms. Even those

Downtown Lodging

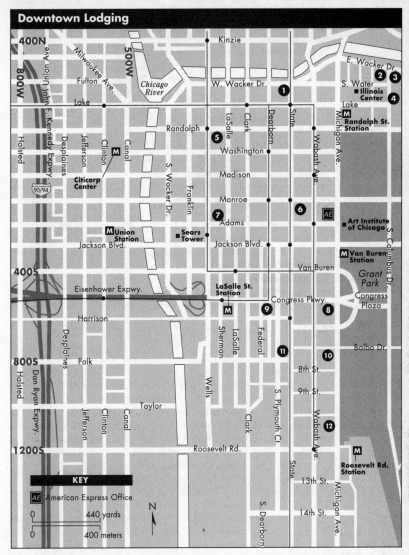

KEY

AE American Express Office

0 — 440 yards
0 — 400 meters

N

Best Western
Grant Park Hotel, **12**

Chicago Hilton and
Towers, **10**

Fairmont, **4**

Hostelling
International—
Chicago Summer
Hostel, **11**

Hotel Allegro
Chicago, **5**

Hyatt on Printer's
Row, **9**

Hyatt Regency, **2**

Midland Hotel, **7**

Palmer House
Hilton, **6**

Ramada Congress, **8**

Renaissance Chicago
Hotel, **1**

Swissôtel, **3**

who hate to sweat may be inspired by the stunning 42nd-floor fitness center, pool, and spa with its remarkable views. The hotel houses the Palm restaurant, a cousin of the New York steak house. ⊠ *323 E. Wacker Dr., 60601,* ☎ *312/565–0565 or 800/654–7262,* 𝔽𝔸𝕏 *312/565–0540. 595 rooms, 35 suites. Restaurant, 2 bars, café, patisserie, minibars, no-smoking floor, room service, indoor pool, hot tub, massage, sauna, spa, steam room, golf privileges, exercise room, laundry service and dry cleaning, concierge, business services, meeting rooms. AE, D, DC, MC, V.*

$$$–$$$$ 🏨 **Chicago Hilton and Towers.** On a busy day the lobby of this Hilton might be mistaken for a terminal at O'Hare Airport: It's a bustling convention hotel but one that retains its '20s heritage in its Renaissance-inspired entrance hall and its Grand Ballroom, a gold-and-gilt extravaganza. The 28,000-square-ft health club includes an indoor track and swimming pool. The location is convenient to McCormick Place and museums but can be isolated at night. ⊠ *720 S. Michigan Ave., 60605,* ☎ *312/922–4400 or 800/445–8667,* 𝔽𝔸𝕏 *312/922–5240. 1,476 rooms, 67 suites. 2 restaurants, 2 bars, deli, pub, in-room modem lines, minibars, no-smoking floors, room service, indoor pool, beauty salon, hot tub, massage, sauna, health club, laundry service and dry cleaning, concierge, concierge floor, business services. AE, D, DC, MC, V.*

$$$–$$$$ 🏨 **Hyatt Regency.** Ficus trees, palms, and gushing fountains fill the two-story greenhouse lobby, but it's hardly an oasis of tranquillity. Illuminated signs guide guests through the labyrinth of halls and escalators that snake through the two towers. In the comfortably sized guest rooms, large black-and-white photographs of Chicago landmarks add to the contemporary hotel decor. ⊠ *151 E. Wacker Dr., 60601,* ☎ *312/ 565–1234 or 800/233–1234,* 𝔽𝔸𝕏 *312/565–2966. 2,019 rooms, 175 suites. 4 restaurants, bar, breakfast room, café, deli, sports bar, in-room modem lines, minibars, no-smoking rooms, room service, beauty salon, massage, laundry service and dry cleaning, concierge, concierge floor, business services, convention center. AE, D, DC, MC, V.*

$$$–$$$$ 🏨 **Midland Hotel.** The Midland offers a lot of character for a business-oriented hotel, with an Italianate lobby that's grand but not intimidating. Rooms are scrupulously clean, and rates include a full breakfast and a newspaper. An attractive weekend package includes breakfast and makes it a good option for visitors heading to the nearby Art Institute or Lyric Opera. ⊠ *172 W. Adams St., 60603,* ☎ *312/332–1200 or 800/621–2360,* 𝔽𝔸𝕏 *312/332–5909. 253 rooms, 4 suites. Restaurant, bar, café, in-room modem lines, no-smoking floor, room service, exercise room, laundry service and dry cleaning, concierge, business services, meeting rooms. AE, D, DC, MC, V.*

$$$–$$$$ 🏨 **Palmer House Hilton.** This second-generation landmark hotel in the
★   heart of the Loop is the very essence of grand style. Ornate and elegant public areas include the opulent lobby, with its ceiling murals. Rooms are less spectacular, with reproduction antique furniture. Like many other big-meeting hotels, the Palmer House can get hectic, and service can be brusque. ⊠ *17 E. Monroe St., 60603,* ☎ *312/726–7500 or 800/445–8667,* 𝔽𝔸𝕏 *312/263–2556. 1,551 rooms, 88 suites. 3 restaurants, bar, coffee shop, in-room modem lines, minibars, no-smoking floor, room service, indoor pool, barbershop, hot tub, massage, sauna, steam room, exercise room, laundry service and dry cleaning, concierge, concierge floor, business services. AE, D, DC, MC, V.*

$$$–$$$$ 🏨 **Ramada Congress.** The original building opened in 1893, and its public areas still retain touches of period splendor. However, age hasn't treated the place well, and the corridors and some rooms look rather worn. Unless the city is entirely booked for a convention, try other options first. ⊠ *520 S. Michigan Ave., 60605,* ☎ *312/427–3800 or 800/ 635–1666,* 𝔽𝔸𝕏 *312/427–4280. 790 rooms, 50 suites. Restaurant, bar, no-smoking floor, room service, barbershop, exercise room, video*

games, coin laundry, laundry service and dry cleaning, meeting rooms, parking (fee). AE, D, DC, MC, V.

$$$ ⊞ **Hotel Allegro Chicago.** The former Bismarck Hotel has been transformed into a haven for the hip that is, however, not imposing. Throughout the Art Deco structure are bold patterns and splashes of color—rooms are a riot of coral, Tuscan yellow, and sea-foam green; and window treatments resemble the entrance to a sheik's tent. Each room has an iron and ironing board, hair dryer, and fax; suites have whirlpool tubs, CD players, VCRs, and robes. There's a wine reception every evening in the lobby. Reopening next door mid-1999 is the beautiful Palace Theater, an appropriate neighbor for this music-themed hotel: witness clefs on the shower curtains, piano in the music room off the lobby, *High Society*esque watercolor mural at the stairs at the entrance, a constant soundtrack at the hotel's entrance and in the elevators, and stereos in all rooms. ⊠ *171 W. Randolph St., 60601,* ☎ *312/236–0123 or 800/ 643–1500,* ℻ *312/236–3177. 452 rooms, 31 suites. Restaurant, bar, in-room modem lines, minibars, no-smoking floor, room service, massage, exercise room, shop, laundry service and dry cleaning, concierge, business services, meeting rooms, parking (fee). AE, D, DC, MC, V.*

$$ ⊞ **Best Western Grant Park Hotel.** By mid-1999, this hotel's massive renovation should bring some sorely needed life to its worn but cozy guest rooms. The South Loop location is isolated at night but near the cluster of museums at the south end of Grant Park. ⊠ *1100 S. Michigan Ave., 60605,* ☎ *312/922–2900 or 800/528–1234,* ℻ *312/922– 8812. 159 rooms, 13 suites. Restaurant, bar, in-room modem lines, no-smoking floor, room service, pool, sauna, exercise room, laundry service and dry cleaning, meeting room, parking (fee). AE, D, DC, MC, V.*

$ ⊞ **Hostelling International–Chicago Summer Hostel.** From early June to early September a dorm for Columbia College students is converted into a hostel. In Printer's Row, a loft-filled neighborhood just south of the Loop, the hostel has 24-hour access and security, linen rental, a kitchen, a TV lounge, and free walking tours. ⊠ *731 S. Plymouth Ct., 60605,* ☎ *773/327–5350,* ℻ *773/327–4287.* ⊠ *Mailing address for reservations: 2232 W. Roscoe St., 60618. 209 dorm beds, 8 private rooms. Exercise room, recreation room, coin laundry. MC, V.*

Near North

$$$$ ⊞ **Chicago Marriott Downtown.** This 46-story tower of white concrete stands as a city unto itself, with its own Kinko's business center, retail stores, and gourmet coffee counter in the lobby. Rooms are basic but full of amenities such as two-line phones, coffeemakers, irons, and hair dryers. ⊠ *540 N. Michigan Ave., 60611,* ☎ *312/836–0100 or 800/ 228–9290,* ℻ *312/836–6139. 1,147 rooms, 25 suites. 2 restaurants, bar, lobby lounge, sports bar, in-room modem lines, no-smoking floors, room service, indoor lap pool, beauty salon, hot tub, massage, sauna, steam room, basketball, exercise room, pro shop, video games, laundry service and dry cleaning. AE, D, DC, MC, V.*

$$$$ ⊞ **DoubleTree Guest Suites.** There are plenty of reasons to love this place, from the homemade chocolate chip cookies guests receive at check-in to the always-fresh flowers in the lobby. The striking postmodern lobby owes its character to Prairie School architecture. The hotel's location off Michigan Avenue is well suited to families or business travelers. The 30th-floor indoor pool and fitness room have incredible views of Lake Michigan. ⊠ *198 E. Delaware Pl., 60611,* ☎ *312/664–1100 or 800/222–8733,* ℻ *312/664–9881. 345 suites. 2 restaurants, 2 bars, in-room modem lines, minibars, no-smoking floors, room service, indoor lap pool, hot tub, sauna, exercise room, video games, coin laundry, laundry service and dry cleaning, concierge, business services, meeting rooms, parking (fee). AE, D, DC, MC, V.*

Near North Lodging

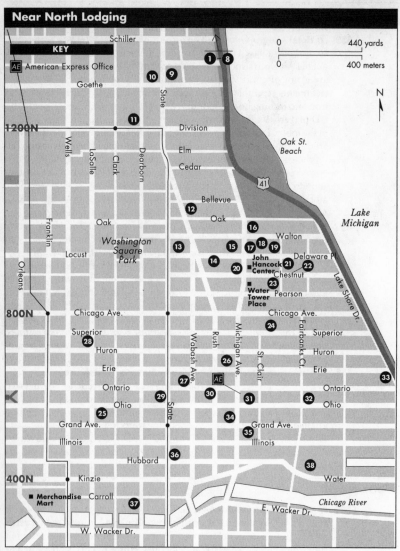

$$$$ ☆ **The Drake.** All hail to the grand dame of Chicago hotels—the Drake.
★ Built in 1920, the Drake presides over the northernmost end of Michigan Avenue. The lobby, inspired by an Italian Renaissance palace, envelops guests in its deep red walls and glimmering crystal. The sounds of a fountain and harpist beckon guests to the Palm Court, a lovely setting for afternoon tea. Local legend Buddy Charles tickles the ivories in the Palm d'Or most nights. ⊠ *140 E. Walton Pl., 60611,* ☎ *312/787–2200 or 800/553–7253,* ℻ *312/787–1431. 485 rooms, 50 suites. 3 restaurants, 2 bars, piano bar, lobby lounge, in-room modem lines, minibars, no-smoking floors, room service, barbershop, exercise room, laundry service and dry cleaning, concierge, concierge floor, business services, meeting rooms, parking (fee). AE, D, DC, MC, V.*

$$$$ ☆ **Embassy Suites.** Built primarily for business travelers, these fully equipped suites contain a microwave oven, mini-refrigerator, coffeemaker, and sleeper sofa. They're arranged around an 11-story plant-filled atrium lobby where fountains and birds add to the constant din. Here guests are served a complimentary full breakfast each morning and cocktails each evening. ⊠ *600 N. State St., 60610,* ☎ *312/943–3800 or 800/362–2779,* ℻ *312/943–7629. 358 suites. Restaurant, bar, in-room modem lines, kitchenettes, minibars, no-smoking rooms, room service, indoor lap pool, hot tub, sauna, exercise room, coin laundry, laundry service and dry cleaning, concierge, concierge floor, business services, meeting rooms. BP. AE, D, DC, MC, V.*

$$$$ ☆ **Four Seasons.** Visiting celebrities stay here for one reason: the pampering. The Four Seasons places a premium on service. The hotel sits
★ atop the 900 North Michigan Shops and delivers panoramic views, but it feels more like a grand English manor house than an urban skyscraper. The old-world feeling continues in the guest rooms, which are decorated with Italian marble, handcrafted woodwork, and botanical prints. ⊠ *120 E. Delaware Pl., 60611,* ☎ *312/280–8800 or 800/332–3442,* ℻ *312/280–1748. 190 rooms, 153 suites. 2 restaurants, bar, lobby lounge, in-room modem lines, in-room safes, minibars, no-smoking floors, room service, indoor pool, hot tub, massage, sauna, steam room, exercise room, laundry service and dry cleaning, concierge, business services, meeting rooms. AE, D, DC, MC, V.*

$$$$ ☆ **Hotel Inter-Continental Chicago.** The junior Olympic-size pool surrounded by majolica tile walls and tucked away on the 11th floor speaks to the hotel's first incarnation as the Medinah Athletic Club. The intriguing architecture throughout the public areas earned the 1929 building a spot of the National Register of Historic Places. An overall face-lift to the hotel's north tower in 1998 should bring those rooms up to the standards of the luxurious south tower. ⊠ *505 N. Michigan Ave., 60611,* ☎ *312/944–4100 or 800/628–2112,* ℻ *312/944–3050. 819 rooms, 25 suites. 2 restaurants, bar, lobby lounge, in-room modem lines, minibars, no-smoking floors, room service, indoor pool, massage, sauna, exercise room, laundry service and dry cleaning, concierge, business services, meeting rooms, parking (fee). AE, D, DC, MC, V.*

$$$$ ☆ **Omni Chicago Hotel.** A parade of celebrities passes through here,
★ thanks to the Omni's tie-in with *The Oprah Winfrey Show.* But this well-located Michigan Avenue all-suite hotel is also a favorite with business travelers who appreciate having their own faxes and printers, and separate living rooms. Throw pillows, Ralph Lauren bedding, and stocked bookshelves make the bedrooms cozier than most. ⊠ *676 N. Michigan Ave., 60611,* ☎ *312/944–6664 or 800/843–6664,* ℻ *312/266–3015. 347 suites. Restaurant-bar, in-room modem lines, in-room safes, minibars, no-smoking floors, room service, indoor lap pool, hot tub, sauna, exercise room, laundry service and dry cleaning, concierge, business services, meeting rooms, parking (fee). AE, D, DC, MC, V.*

$$$$ 🏨 **Ritz-Carlton.** The Ritz-Carlton, run by Four Seasons Hotels and Re-
★   sorts and not the Ritz-Carlton chain, is perched above Water Tower
      Place, Michigan Avenue's best-known vertical shopping mall. Mag-
      nificent flower arrangements adorn the public areas. The two-story green-
      house lobby serves afternoon tea, and the Dining Room's chef, Sarah
      Stegner, has earned a formidable reputation. The spacious rooms are
      a tasteful blend of European styles. ⊠ *160 E. Pearson St., 60611,* ☎
      312/266–1000 or 800/691–6906, F𝖆X *312/266–1194. 342 rooms, 85
      suites. 3 restaurants, bar, lobby lounge, in-room modem lines, in-room
      safes, minibars, no-smoking floor, room service, indoor lap pool, spa,
      health club, laundry service and dry cleaning, concierge, business ser-
      vices, meeting rooms, parking (fee), kennel. AE, D, DC, MC, V.*

$$$$ 🏨 **Sutton Place Hotel.** Formerly Le Meridien, this high-rise near Rush
      Street nightlife is a homage to modern art with its high-style black, gray,
      and white rooms, complete with black leather headboards and taste-
      ful Robert Mapplethorpe photos. There are CD players in all the rooms;
      the luxurious bathrooms have a separate shower stall, soaking tub, terry-
      cloth robes, and hair dryers. ⊠ *21 E. Bellevue Pl., 60611,* ☎ *312/266–
      2100 or 800/606–8188,* F𝖆X *312/266–2141. 206 rooms, 40 suites.
      Restaurant, bar, outdoor café, in-room modem lines, minibars, no-
      smoking floor, room service, in-room VCRs, exercise room, laundry
      service and dry cleaning, concierge, business services, meeting rooms,
      parking (fee). AE, D, DC, MC, V.*

$$$$ 🏨 **Talbott.** There's a special satisfaction to finding a small, comfort-
★   able hotel just off the Magnificent Mile where the clerk is reading
      Nietzsche. Thirty-five percent of the rooms and all of the suites have
      a kitchen and dining area—a legacy from the vintage structure's ear-
      lier life as an apartment building. The hunt-club atmosphere in the lobby's
      twin parlors is unusually personal and genuine. Discounts often make
      the prices a bargain for the neighborhood. ⊠ *20 E. Delaware Pl., 60611,*
      ☎ *312/944–4970 or 800/621–8506,* F𝖆X *312/944–7241. 113 rooms,
      32 suites. Bar, in-room modem lines, in-room safes, minibars, no-
      smoking floor, room service, laundry service and dry cleaning, meet-
      ing rooms, parking (fee). AE, D, DC, MC, V.*

$$$$ 🏨 **Westin Michigan Avenue.** Large and impersonal, the Westin buzzes
      with activity in the lobby, where enormous icicle chandeliers reveal its
      '60s origins: You expect Doris Day to bound down the staircase at any
      moment. The Michigan Avenue location is perfectly situated for shop-
      ping, especially in winter, as the major malls are steps from the door.
      For extra space request one of the Tower rooms, which have a sitting
      area and a TV and phone in the bathroom. ⊠ *909 N. Michigan Ave.,
      60611,* ☎ *312/943–7200 or 800/228–3000,* F𝖆X *312/943–9347. 713
      rooms, 27 suites. Restaurant, bar, in-room modem lines, minibars, no-
      smoking floor, room service, beauty salon, massage, sauna, exercise
      room, laundry service and dry cleaning, concierge, business services,
      meeting rooms, parking (fee). AE, D, DC, MC, V.*

$$$$ 🏨 **Westin River North.** Westin took over the management of the Hotel
      Nikko in 1997 and excised the Japanese influence. Rooms have stun-
      ning views of the Chicago River and nice extras such as a coffeemaker
      with Starbucks coffee. Skyline Rooms, which cost a bit more, are geared
      to business travelers. If you forget your workout gear, they'll lend some
      to you at the well-equipped fitness center. The location is convenient
      to the Loop, the Merchandise Mart, and the House of Blues. ⊠ *320
      N. Dearborn St., 60610,* ☎ *312/744–1900 or 800/937–8461,* F𝖆X
      *312/527–2650. 400 rooms, 22 suites. Restaurant, lobby lounge, in-
      room modem lines, minibars, no-smoking rooms, room service, mas-
      sage, sauna, exercise room, laundry service and dry cleaning, concierge,
      business services, meeting rooms, parking (fee). AE, D, DC, MC, V.*

$$$$ ☷ **Whitehall Hotel.** Upon entering the charming lobby of the sole Chicago member of Preferred Hotels & Resorts, one is transported back to a simpler time. A top-notch hotel since 1984, the Whitehall offers travelers the most precious commodities: peace, quiet, and friendly, attentive service. Features such as video games, modem hookups, and voice mail bring modern touches to the intimate, old-world-style rooms, many featuring four-poster beds. ✉ *105 E. Delaware Pl., 60611,* ☎ *312/944–6300 or 800/948–4255,* FAX *312/944–8552. 213 rooms, 8 suites. Restaurant, bar, outdoor café, in-room modem lines, in-room safes, minibars, no-smoking floor, room service, exercise room, laundry service and dry cleaning, concierge, concierge floor, meeting rooms, parking (fee). AE, D, DC, MC, V.*

$$$–$$$$ ☷ **Ambassador West.** Faded tapestries, carved wood columns, and crystal chandeliers convey a sense of the 1924 origins of this boutique hotel. The furnishings are what you would expect in an aspiring European-style hotel. Room size varies greatly, and regular rooms don't bring much in the way of amenities, though you do get free coffee in the lobby, the use of a small fitness room, and a newspaper. The neighboring Omni Ambassador East, still joined to its former sister by an underground passageway, maintains a more glamorous profile. ✉ *1300 N. State Pkwy., 60610,* ☎ *312/787–3700 or 800/300–9378,* FAX *312/640–2967. 160 rooms, 60 suites. Restaurant, lobby lounge, minibars, no-smoking floor, room service, barber shop, beauty salon, exercise room, laundry service and dry cleaning, concierge, concierge floor, meeting rooms, parking (fee). AE, D, DC, MC, V.*

$$$–$$$$ ☷ **Courtyard by Marriott Chicago Downtown.** Business travelers get exactly what they want here: soothing, large rooms with desks; well-lighted work areas; and voice mail. The location is a few blocks north of the Chicago River, making it convenient to the Loop. Shaw's Crab House and Tucci Milan are good nearby dining options, and it's a short walk to the House of Blues. If you're really beat, there's always the Pizza Hut within the hotel. ✉ *30 E. Hubbard St., 60611,* ☎ *312/329–2500 or 800/321–2211,* FAX *312/329–0293. 299 rooms, 35 suites. Restaurant, bar, in-room modem lines, no-smoking floor, room service, indoor lap pool, hot tub, exercise room, coin laundry, laundry service and dry cleaning, meeting rooms, parking (fee). AE, D, DC, MC, V.*

$$$–$$$$ ☷ **Omni Ambassador East.** Tucked into the quiet residential Gold
★ Coast, this small 1920s hotel is a 10- to 15-minute cab ride from the Loop. The secluded setting makes it popular with movie stars and literary figures. The lobby has an old-world elegance, with crystal chandeliers, marble floors, and curving banisters. Hotel-wide renovations in 1998 included a face-lift to the infamous Pump Room (☞ Piano Bars *in* Chapter 5); new cherrywood furniture in the guest rooms; and the addition of a lobby lounge, exercise room, and business center. ✉ *1301 N. State Pkwy., 60610,* ☎ *312/787–7200 or 800/843–6664,* FAX *312/787–4760. 223 rooms, 52 suites. Restaurant, bar, lobby lounge, in-room modem lines, in-room safes, minibars, no-smoking floors, room service, barbershop, beauty salon, exercise room, laundry service and dry cleaning, concierge, business services, parking (fee). AE, D, DC, MC, V.*

$$$–$$$$ ☷ **Raphael Chicago.** Originally a dorm for nursing students, this 1920s
★ building on a wealthy residential side street near Water Tower Place retains its honest charm. The spacious, comfortable rooms have a quirky style, with chaise longues, sitting areas, and arched entries. Obliging service, terry-cloth robes, and attractive weekend packages are among the features that draw a loyal following. ✉ *201 E. Delaware Pl., 60611,* ☎ *312/943–5000 or 800/983–7870,* FAX *312/943–9483. 99 rooms, 73 suites. Restaurant, piano bar, in-room modem lines, in-room safes, minibars, no-smoking floors, room service, library, laundry service and dry cleaning, meeting rooms, parking (fee). AE, D, DC, MC, V.*

$$$–$$$$ 🏨 **Regal Knickerbocker Hotel.** This 1927 hotel is now up to speed with its Michigan Avenue competition. Rose moiré wallpaper lines the hallways, and exuberant floral bedspreads combine with gold- and cream-striped pillows for a rich European look. In keeping with its vintage heritage, bathrooms tend to be tiny, but closets are spacious. In the lobby there's a martini lounge serving 44 varieties. ⊠ *163 E. Walton Pl., 60611,* ☎ *312/751–8100 or 800/621–8140,* ℻ *312/751–9205. 290 rooms, 15 suites. Restaurant, bar, coffee bar, lobby lounge, outdoor café, in-room modem lines, minibars, no-smoking floor, room service, exercise room, laundry service and dry cleaning, concierge, concierge floor, business services, meeting rooms, parking (fee). AE, D, DC, MC, V.*

$$$–$$$$ 🏨 **Sheraton Chicago Hotel and Towers.** Built in 1992, the hotel appeals to business travelers with its handsomely modern appointments and its lighthouselike location on the river, which guarantees unobstructed views. Weekend rates drop dramatically in winter to lure leisure travelers. Although the hotel is quite vast, with the largest ballroom in the Midwest, you won't feel in danger of getting lost. ⊠ *301 E. North Water St., 60611,* ☎ *312/464–1000 or 800/233–4100,* ℻ *312/464–9140. 1,152 rooms, 52 suites. 2 restaurants, sports bar, lobby lounge, snack bar, in-room modem lines, minibars, no-smoking rooms, room service, indoor lap pool, massage, sauna, exercise room, laundry service and dry cleaning, concierge, concierge floor, business services. AE, D, DC, MC, V.*

$$$–$$$$ 🏨 **Summerfield Suites Hotel.** A small, intimate lobby paneled in cherrywood sets the tone for this traditional-looking all-suite hotel down the block from Neiman Marcus and the hub of Michigan Avenue shopping. Suites are equipped with microwaves, coffeemakers, refrigerators, VCRs, work desks, and pullout sofa beds. A rooftop pool keeps kids entertained in summer, and Gino's will deliver its famous deep-dish pizza to the rooms. The rate includes an extensive breakfast buffet. ⊠ *166 E. Superior St., 60611,* ☎ *312/787–6000 or 800/833–4353,* ℻ *312/787–4331. 120 suites. Restaurant, bar, snack bar, in-room modem lines, kitchenettes, no-smoking floor, in-room VCRs, pool, barbershop, exercise room, recreation room, coin laundry, laundry service and dry cleaning, meeting rooms, parking (fee). AE, D, DC, MC, V.*

$$$–$$$$ 🏨 **Tremont.** This small European-style hotel is genteelly tucked away on a side street just off North Michigan Avenue. Rooms are fitted with traditional Williamsburg-style decor and Baker furniture, with carefully mixed-and-matched florals, plaids, and stripes. Standard rooms can be quite cramped, with the desk placed in the narrow entry, so ask about size. Rooms come with a fax machine, CD player, VCR, three telephones, and Frette robes. ⊠ *100 E. Chestnut St., 60611,* ☎ *312/751–1900 or 800/621–8133,* ℻ *312/751–8691. 120 rooms, 9 suites. Restaurant, bar, in-room modem lines, minibars, no-smoking floor, room service, in-room VCRs, laundry service and dry cleaning, meeting rooms, parking (fee). AE, D, DC, MC, V.*

$$–$$$$ 🏨 **Claridge Hotel.** On a tree-lined street in the Gold Coast, this vintage hotel is peaceful, quiet, and genteel. Standard rooms with one queen bed are on the small side; deluxe rooms are twice the size and contain either a king or two queen beds, a sitting area, and a coffeemaker. In-room amenities aren't lavish, but Continental breakfast, Starbucks coffee in the lobby, and morning limousine service within a 2-mi radius are included. ⊠ *1244 N. Dearborn Pkwy., 60610,* ☎ *312/787–4980 or 800/245–1258,* ℻ *312/266–0978. 166 rooms, 1 suite. Restaurant, lobby bar, in-room modem lines, minibars, no-smoking floor, room service, laundry service and dry cleaning, meeting rooms, parking (fee). CP. AE, D, DC, MC, V.*

$$–$$$$ 🏨 **Days Inn Lake Shore Drive.** The lakefront location and fabulous views are the best things about this concrete high-rise. Rooms are pleasant

and sunny. Some nice extras, such as an outdoor pool on the seventh floor and Nintendo on the in-room TVs, make it popular with families, as does its proximity to the Children's Museum and the Ferris wheel at Navy Pier. For breakfast enjoy a bountiful buffet overlooking Lake Michigan. ⊠ *644 N. Lake Shore Dr., 60611,* ☎ *312/943–9200 or 800/ 541–3223,* FAX *312/255–4411. 569 rooms, 9 suites. Restaurant, lounge, in-room modem lines, in-room safes, no-smoking floors, room service, pool, exercise room, coin laundry, laundry service and dry cleaning, meeting rooms, parking (fee). CP. AE, D, DC, MC, V.*

\$\$–\$\$\$\$ ⊞ **Holiday Inn Chicago City Centre.** This standout Holiday Inn draws rave reviews from families for its outdoor pool, free access to the indoor pool and health club down the hall at McClurg Court, and well-tended rooms. It's close to the lakefront and a beach, the Children's Museum at Navy Pier, and Michigan Avenue. In winter weekend rates can drop to \$150 or less. Unless you have business at the Merchandise Mart, this location is preferable to the Holiday Inn Mart Plaza. ⊠ *300 E. Ohio St., 60611,* ☎ *312/787–3055 or 800/465–4329,* FAX *312/787–6238. 491 rooms, 9 suites. Restaurant, café-patisserie, sports bar, no-smoking floors, room service, outdoor pool, health club, coin laundry, laundry service and dry cleaning, concierge, meeting rooms, parking (fee). AE, D, DC, MC, V.*

\$\$–\$\$\$\$ ⊞ **Lenox Suites.** The lobby of this all-suite hotel evokes an English drawing room. Rooms resemble furnished corporate apartments, which is often what they are. The location is excellent, just a block from Michigan Avenue. Suites range in size and amenities: One-bedroom suites have spacious living rooms with sleeper sofas; all have kitchenettes. Juice and a muffin are delivered to your door every morning. ⊠ *616 N. Rush St., 60611,* ☎ *312/337–1000 or 800/445–3669,* FAX *312/337– 7217. 324 suites. Restaurant, bar, coffee shop, in-room modem lines, kitchenettes, minibars, no-smoking floors, room service, exercise room, coin laundry, laundry service and dry cleaning, concierge, meeting rooms, parking (fee). CP. AE, D, DC, MC, V.*

\$–\$\$\$\$ ⊞ **Comfort Inn of Lincoln Park.** The half-timbered Tudor exterior of this reasonably priced hotel is incongruously wedged into a busy area of Lincoln Park, a youthful neighborhood with plenty of nightlife; it's close to the lake and convenient to Wrigley Field. Unusual architectural features, such as wagon-wheel wood trim, add a quirky note to an otherwise clean, no-frills lodging. The three suites have hot tubs, and two have saunas. A complimentary Continental breakfast is served in a pleasant room off the Victorian-style lobby. ⊠ *601 W. Diversey Pkwy.,* ☎ *773/348–2810 or 800/228–5150,* FAX *773/348–1912. 71 rooms, 3 suites. In-room modem lines, no-smoking rooms, meeting room, parking (fee). CP. AE, D, DC, MC, V.*

\$\$\$ ⊞ **Best Western Inn of Chicago.** One block east of Michigan Avenue, this heavily trafficked 1927 hotel is usually a bargain for visitors who want to be near the Magnificent Mile: Weekend rates often hover around \$100. Rooms are basic and unremarkable but comfortable and clean. For a fee, guests can use the full health club across the street. ⊠ *162 E. Ohio St., 60611,* ☎ *312/787–3100 or 800/557–2378,* FAX *312/573–3136. 332 rooms, 26 suites. Restaurant, bar, no-smoking floor, room service, coin laundry, laundry service and dry cleaning, concierge, meeting rooms, parking (fee). AE, D, DC, MC, V.*

\$\$–\$\$\$ ⊞ **Belden-Stratford.** A magnificent '20s facade beckons guests to this
★ relatively untrafficked area near Lincoln Park. The Belden-Stratford is primarily an upscale apartment building, but management keeps some attractively priced studios and suites for overnights. A complimentary bottle of wine awaits guests in the 9-ft-ceiling rooms, which all have some form of kitchenette. Hand-painted clouds grace the ceiling of the elegant lobby, which houses two popular restaurants: Ambria and

Un Grand Café (for both, ☞ Lincoln Park and North *in* Chapter 3). ⊠ *2300 N. Lincoln Park W, 60614,* ☎ *773/281–2900 or 800/800– 8301,* FAX *773/880–2039. 25 studios and suites. 2 restaurants, deli, kitchenettes, beauty salon, exercise room, coin laundry, laundry service and dry cleaning, parking (fee). AE, D, MC, V.*

$$–$$$ ★ **River North Hotel.** Look for this ice warehouse turned Best Western in the heart of the thriving River North entertainment district. The undistinguished exterior and outdated Deco-inspired lobby are more than offset by clean, large, and reasonably priced guest rooms outfitted with pinstriped duvet covers, buffalo-plaid blankets, and black-and-white tiled bathrooms. Parking is free, a cost-saving rarity downtown. The sofa sleepers in the suites and the indoor pool make it a family favorite. ⊠ *125 W. Ohio St., 60610,* ☎ *312/467–0800 or 800/727–0800,* FAX *312/467–1665. 122 rooms, 26 suites. Bar, pizzeria, in-room modem lines, no-smoking floor, room service, indoor pool, sauna, exercise room, dry cleaning, meeting room, free parking. AE, D, DC, MC, V.*

$$–$$$ **Seneca.** Originally solely an apartment building, the Seneca is steadily increasing the number of rooms it rents out on a nightly basis. The majority are suites of varying sizes with either kitchenettes or full kitchens; even the smallest rooms have a refrigerator and a coffeemaker. The two restaurants and the popular deli in the building deliver. ⊠ *200 E. Chestnut St., 60611,* ☎ *312/787–8900 or 800/800–6261,* FAX *312/ 988–4438. 50 rooms, 75 suites. 2 restaurants, 2 bars, deli, in-room modem lines, kitchenettes, no-smoking floors, refrigerators, beauty salon, exercise room, coin laundry, laundry service and dry cleaning, meeting rooms, parking (fee). AE, D, DC, MC, V.*

$–$$$ **Margarita European Inn.** Just north of Chicago in the suburb of Evanston (two blocks from both the train and bus), the Margarita is a charming alternative to the more generic hotels close to Northwestern University. Rooms range in size from monklike cells to comfortable minisuites and are furnished with cheerful prints and antiques. Guests help themselves to a complimentary Continental breakfast in an antiques-filled parlor lined with a wall of arched windows. Downstairs, Va Pensiero serves some of the area's best northern Italian cooking at haute cuisine prices. ⊠ *1566 Oak Ave., Evanston 60201,* ☎ *847/ 869–2273,* FAX *847/869–2353. 45 rooms, 20 with bath. Restaurant, breakfast room, in-room modem lines, library, coin laundry, meeting rooms, parking (fee). CP. AE, D, MC, V.*

$–$$ ★ **City Suites Hotel.** You might want to come here just for the famed cinnamon buns from nearby Ann Sather (☞ Lincoln Park and North *in* Chapter 3), which are served as part of the free Continental breakfast and available via room service. Two-thirds of this affordable hotel consists of suites, which have a separate sitting room, a pull-out couch, and a refrigerator. The hotel is on a heavily trafficked street in the Lake View neighborhood, so if noise is a concern, request a room on the east side of the building. ⊠ *933 W. Belmont, 60657,* ☎ *773/404–3400 or 800/248–9108,* FAX *773/404–3405. 16 rooms, 29 suites. In-room modem lines, room service, coin laundry, parking (fee). CP. AE, D, DC, MC, V.*

$–$$ **HoJo Inn.** On a main boulevard in downtown Chicago, this classic L-shape, two-story motor lodge stands as a campy vestige of another era. The rooms are well maintained, the staff is pleasant, parking is free, and the location is just a short walk from such tourist favorites as Planet Hollywood and Michael Jordan's Restaurant. ⊠ *720 N. LaSalle St., 60610,* ☎ *312/664–8100 or 800/446–4656,* FAX *312/664–2356. 68 rooms, 3 suites. Coffee shop, no-smoking rooms, free parking. AE, D, DC, MC, V.*

$ **Cass Hotel.** Built in 1927, the Cass is a favorite bargain find of tourists and business travelers looking for cheap sleeps just a short walk from

Michigan Avenue shopping and River North nightlife. Rooms are clean, small, and functional, and the bathrooms show their age, but furnishings and fixtures are slowly being upgraded. Ask for one of the renovated rooms, which all have a refrigerator, a wet bar, and a dataport phone. The $1.99 breakfast in the lobby coffee shop is a steal. ⊠ *640 N. Wabash Ave., 60611, ☎ 312/787–4030 or 800/227–7850, FAX 312/787–8544. 175 rooms. Bar, coffee shop, coin laundry, parking (fee). AE, D, DC, MC, V.*

$ 🏨 **Chicago International Hostel.** European students flock to these well-maintained dormitory-style accommodations near Loyola University in Rogers Park. Dorm beds go for $13 a night, linens are provided, and a kitchen is available. One drawback—there's a curfew of midnight or 2 AM, depending on the day. The hostel is closed from 10 AM to 4 PM for cleaning. It's close to the Loyola stop on the Howard Street El line, making it easy to zip downtown. ⊠ *6318 N. Winthrop Ave., 60660, ☎ 773/262–1011, FAX 773/262–3673. 85 dorm beds; 6 private rooms, 2 with bath. Coin laundry, free parking. No credit cards.*

$ 🏨 **Days Inn Lincoln Park North.** This well-kept up Days Inn in the lively
★ Lincoln Park neighborhood is a real find. A complimentary breakfast is served off the lobby in a pleasant room with a pressed-tin ceiling and brass chandeliers. Cheery floral bedspreads and light furniture brighten up the basic rooms, although bathrooms are cramped and show their age. For about $15 extra a night, you can upgrade to a business suite. All guests have free use of a nearby health club. ⊠ *644 W. Diversey Pkwy., 60614, ☎ 773/525–7010 or 800/329–7466, FAX 773/525–6998. 130 rooms, 5 suites. In-room safes, no-smoking floor, coin laundry, meeting rooms, parking (fee). CP. AE, D, DC, MC, V.*

$ 🏨 **Park Brompton Inn.** A welcoming fire burns in the library-style
★ lobby of the Park Brompton, creating the atmosphere of an old English inn. Rooms are quaint and simple and suites have kitchenettes. The staff is helpful and the reasonable price includes Continental breakfast featuring Ann Sather's (☞ Lincoln Park and North *in* Chapter 3) cinnamon buns. The Lake View location puts you four blocks from Wrigley Field, close to the lakefront jogging path, restaurants, nightlife, and transportation downtown. ⊠ *528 W. Brompton Ave., 60657, ☎ 773/404–3499 or 800/727–5108, FAX 773/404–3495. 31 rooms, 22 suites. In-room modem lines, coin laundry, meeting room, parking (fee). CP. AE, D, DC, MC, V.*

$ 🏨 **Surf Hotel.** A bust of Louis XIV surveys the formal French lobby of this boutique hotel on a tree-lined street in the Lincoln Park neighborhood. The rooms are decorated with pleasant floral prints and Impressionist posters. The hotel, built in the 1920s, offers a good value in a lively neighborhood that's three blocks from the lake and a 10-minute walk to the Lincoln Park Zoo. Like the Park Brompton and City Suites Hotel, the Surf wins kudos for serving Ann Sather's (☞ Lincoln Park and North *in* Chapter 3) cinnamon buns as part of its complimentary Continental breakfast. ⊠ *555 W. Surf St., 60657, ☎ 773/528–8400 or 800/787–3108, FAX 773/528–8483. 51 rooms, 4 suites. In-room modem lines, coin laundry, parking (fee). CP. AE, D, DC, MC, V.*

O'Hare Airport

$$$$ 🏨 **Hotel Sofitel Chicago.** The murals in the lobby, fancy restaurant and more casual café serving true French gourmet food, and the upscale gift shop might have you wondering what continent you're on. Rooms are spacious and guests receive a rose and a bottle of Evian at turndown and a crispy baguette upon checkout. ⊠ *5550 N. River Rd., Rosemont 60018, ☎ 847/678–4488 or 800/233–5959, FAX 847/678–4244.*

300 rooms, 11 suites. 2 restaurants, bar, patisserie, in-room modem lines, minibars, no-smoking floors, room service, indoor pool, massage, sauna, exercise room, laundry service and dry cleaning, concierge, business services, meeting rooms, airport shuttle, parking (fee). AE, D, DC, MC, V.

$$$$ **Hyatt Regency O'Hare.** Connected to the Rosemont Convention Center by a skyway, this Hyatt is heavily geared toward the business traveler. The atrium lobby has all the personality of an office park, and none of the other public spaces—except the resortlike circular swimming pool—alters that impression. Rooms are spacious. ⊠ *9300 W. Bryn Mawr Ave., Rosemont 60018,* ☎ *847/696–1234 or 800/233– 1234,* FAX *847/698–0139. 1,099 rooms, 58 suites. 4 restaurants, sports bar, deli, in-room modem lines, no-smoking rooms, room service, indoor pool, massage, sauna, exercise room, laundry service and dry cleaning, concierge, concierge floor, business services, meeting rooms, airport shuttle. AE, D, DC, MC, V.*

$$$$ **Rosemont Suites Hotel O'Hare.** The public spaces of this handsome hotel directly across the street from the Rosemont Convention Center are decorated in the unmistakable style of Frank Lloyd Wright. Wright's design is also carried throughout the guest rooms. A full breakfast and evening cocktails are complimentary. ⊠ *5500 N. River Rd., Rosemont 60018,* ☎ *847/678–4000 or 888/476–7366,* FAX *847/928–7659. 296 suites. Restaurant, bar, breakfast room, in-room modem lines, kitchenettes, minibars, no-smoking floor, room service, indoor pool, hot tub, sauna, exercise room, video games, coin laundry, laundry service and dry cleaning, concierge, business services. BP. AE, D, DC, MC, V.*

$$–$$$$ **O'Hare Hilton.** The only hotel actually at the airport, the Hilton is
★   connected to the terminals and is within easy access of public transportation to the city. Several Sleep Tight rooms have all manner of relaxation aids, from CD players to sound machines. Day rates are available for travelers with short stopovers. The ample recreational facilities include extensive workout equipment, a pool, and a golf simulator. ⊠ *Box 66414, O'Hare International Airport, 60666,* ☎ *773/ 686–8000 or 800/445–8667,* FAX *773/601–2873. 840 rooms, 18 suites. 2 restaurants, bar, coffee shop, sports bar, in-room modem lines, minibars, no-smoking floor, room service, indoor lap pool, hot tub, massage, sauna, steam room, exercise room, video games, laundry service and dry cleaning, concierge, business services. AE, D, DC, MC, V.*

$ **Travelodge Chicago O'Hare.** The rooms in this two-story cinderblock motel are basic, but they're regularly redecorated, tidy, and incomparably cheap. ⊠ *3003 Mannheim Rd., Des Plaines 60018,* ☎ *847/296– 5541 or 800/578–7878,* FAX *847/803–1984. 94 rooms. In-room modem lines, no-smoking rooms, pool, laundry service and dry cleaning, meeting room, free parking. AE, D, DC, MC, V.*

5 Nightlife and the Arts

Chicago's nightlife scene reflects the city's verve and variety. Renowned companies such as the Lyric Opera and the Steppenwolf Theatre share the spotlight with late-night theater productions and alternative rock clubs, and the air sizzles with homegrown blues and jazz. This is the city that not so long ago gave birth to the sometimes raucous "poetry slam" at the Green Mill bar. It's also the place that decades ago first unleashed comedic talent through the Second City club.

NIGHTLIFE

Updated by
Eve Becker

Chicago's entertainment varies from loud and loose to sophisticated and sedate. *The Reader* and *New City* (distributed Thursday in bookstores, record stores, and other city establishments) are your best guides to the entertainment scene. These free weeklies have comprehensive, timely listings and reviews. The Friday *Chicago Tribune* and *Chicago Sun-Times* are also good sources of information. Shows usually begin at 9 PM; cover charges generally range from $3 to $15, depending on the day of the week; Friday and Saturday nights are the most expensive. Most bars stay open until 2 AM Friday night and 3 AM Saturday, except for larger dance bars, which are often open until 4 AM Friday night and 5 AM Saturday. Some bars are not open seven days a week, so call before you venture out.

Parking in North Side neighborhoods, particularly Lincoln Park and Lake View, can be extremely scarce on weekends. If you're visiting nightspots in these areas, consider taking cabs or public transportation. The list of blues and jazz clubs includes several South Side locations: Visitors to Chicago should be cautious about transportation here late at night because some of these neighborhoods can be unsafe. Drive your own car or take a previously reserved cab or limo, and avoid public transportation. Some clubs have guarded parking lots or can arrange cab service for visitors.

Bars

If you want to find the famous Chicago bar scene known as **Rush Street,** don't bother looking on Rush Street itself. Most of the nightlife is now on Division Street between Clark and State streets, after having been pushed north by office and apartment development. Among the better-known singles bars are **Butch McGuire's** (⊠ 20 W. Division St., ☎ 312/337–9080), the **Lodge** (⊠ 21 W. Division St., ☎ 312/642–4406), and **Original Mother's** (⊠ 26 W. Division St., ☎ 312/642–7251), featured in the motion picture *About Last Night.* On warm weekend nights the street has a carnival-like atmosphere. The crowd here consists mostly of out-of-towners on the make.

River East Plaza (⊠ 435 E. Illinois St.) is the center of a small nightlife area just north of the Loop and east of Michigan Avenue. You can find an atmosphere similar to that of Rush Street in such establishments as the **Baja Beach Club** (⊠ 401 E. Illinois St., ☎ 312/222–1993) and **Dick's Last Resort** (⊠ 435 E. Illinois St., ☎ 312/836–7870).

Those who want to try some more relaxed spots have many great choices, of which these are just a few.

Gingerman Tavern (⊠ 3740 N. Clark St., ☎ 773/549–2050), up the street from the Cubs' stadium in Wrigleyville, deftly manages to avoid being pigeonholed as a sports bar. Folks here take their beer and billiards seriously.

Green Door Tavern (⊠ 678 N. Orleans St., ☎ 312/664–5496) was originally a speakeasy during Prohibition. The building dates from 1872 and has housed a tavern since 1921. The bar and restaurant retain many of the old fixtures from those days, such as an old brass cash register and faded ads.

Holiday Club (⊠ 1471 N. Milwaukee Ave., ☎ 773/486–0686), a swinger's mecca, attracts goodfellas with its '50s decor and well-stocked CD jukebox with selections ranging from Dean Martin and Frank Sinatra to early punk. Down a pint of good beer (or even bad

BONUS MILES MAKE GREAT SOUVENIRS.

Earn Miles With Your MCI Card.

Take the MCI Card along on this trip and start earning miles for the next one. You'll earn frequent flyer miles on all your calls and save with the low rates you've come to expect from MCI. Before you know it, you'll be on your way to some other international destination.

Sign up for MCI by calling 1-800-FLY-FREE

Is this a great time, or what? :-)

Earn Frequent Flyer Miles.

MIDWEST EXPRESS AIRLINES

You've read the book. Now book the trip.

For all the best deals on flights, hotels, rental cars, and vacation packages, book them online at www.previewtravel.com. Then click on our Destination Guides featuring content from Fodor's and more. You'll find hotels, restaurants, attractions, and things to do around the globe. There are even interactive maps, videos, and weather forecasts. You'll have everything you need to make your vacation exactly what you want it to be. All it takes is a trip online.

Travel on Your Terms™
www.previewtravel.com
aol keyword: previewtravel

preview travel℠

beer in cans). On Sunday nights, the place turns into a bamboo lounge with Polynesian surf music.

John Barleycorn (✉ 658 W. Belden Ave., ☎ 773/348–8899), a historic pub with a long wooden bar, can get somewhat rowdy despite the classical music and the art slides shown on video screens. It has a popular summer beer garden, a good pub menu and selection of beers, and a separate darts area.

Liquid Kitty (✉ 1807 W. Division St., ☎ 773/489–2700), with its orange and red '70s pyschedelia theme, has red couches and red lamps and a leopard-print rug. It exudes hip intelligence and is favored by young artists, filmmakers, and writers. Attached is the **Celluloid Movie Bar,** which shows three films a night.

The **Map Room** (✉ 1949 N. Hoyne Ave., ☎ 773/252–7636) might help you find your way around Chicago, if not the world. The walls of this self-described "travelers' tavern" are decorated with maps and travel books. International night on Tuesday features cuisines of different countries.

Northside (✉ 1635 N. Damen Ave., ☎ 773/384–3555) was one of the first anchors of the now-teeming Wicker Park nightlife scene. Arty (and sometimes slightly yuppie) types come to drink, eat, shoot pool, and see and be seen.

Red Lion (✉ 2446 N. Lincoln Ave., ☎ 773/348–2695), a dark, authentic British pub, is decked out with London Metro maps and serves up fish-and-chips, Guinness, and hard cider. A bookie joint in the 1930s, it's said to be one of America's most haunted places.

Sheffield's (✉ 3258 N. Sheffield Ave., ☎ 773/281–4989) spans the seasons with a beer garden in summer and a roaring fireplace in winter. This laid-back neighborhood spot has billiards and more than 50 kinds of beer, including regional microbrews and a "bad beer of the month."

Ten56 (✉ 1056 N. Damen Ave., ☎ 773/227–4906), once a speakeasy in the '30s, now is a swanky cocktail spot to hang out, play pool, and sip martinis without excessive attitude or a cover charge.

Cafés

Cafés throughout the city accommodate those who wish to hang out without necessarily drinking alcohol. Most serve the full gamut of coffees and teas, as well as gooey desserts. Some have small menus of real food, too. This section has a few of the more offbeat ones.

Earwax (✉ 1564 N. Milwaukee Ave., ☎ 773/772–4019), part comfortable café and part record, book, and video store, tunes you in to the scene in hip Wicker Park. Choose coffee, sweets, or vegetarian meals.

Kopi, a Traveler's Cafe (✉ 5317 N. Clark St., ☎ 773/989–5674) is a study in opposites, offering healthy vegetarian options and decadent desserts. In the Andersonville neighborhood, a 20-minute cab ride from downtown, this café has a selection of travel books (for sale), artifacts from foreign lands, and artfully painted tables.

Third Coast Café (✉ 29 E. Delaware Pl., ☎ 312/664–7225; ✉ 1260 N. Dearborn St., ☎ 312/649–0730) presents a choice of atmospheres in two locations under separate ownership. The trendy Delaware Street café has indoor and outdoor seating and has attracted such celebrities as Madonna and Alec Baldwin; the cavernous one on Dearborn Street is open 24 hours.

Voltaire (⊠ 3231 N. Clark St., ☎ 773/528–3136), with exposed brick and a vegetarian menu in addition to the usual coffee and desserts, caters to artists and entertains everyone else. A space downstairs doubles as a theater.

Xoinx Tea Room (⊠ 2933 N. Lincoln Ave., ☎ 773/665–1336) takes tea seriously, with 45 kinds of loose tea served in individual teapots. Coffee addicts shouldn't worry—espresso drinks are also offered. On Friday nights, Chicago Filmmakers presents avant-garde films in the back gallery.

Comedy Clubs

Improvisation has long had a successful following in Chicago; stand-up comedy hasn't fared as well. Most comedy clubs have a cover charge ($5–$16); many have a two-drink minimum on top of that.

All Jokes Aside (⊠ 1000 S. Wabash Ave., ☎ 312/922–0577) is the only stand-up outpost in the South Loop, with special events such as amateur night and ladies' night.

Barrel of Laughs (⊠ 10345 S. Central Ave., Oak Lawn, ☎ 708/499–2969), on the city's far southwest side, spotlights local and national comics. Although it's a 30-minute drive from downtown, the club gets crowded, so come early—unless you reserve seats as part of a dinner package with the adjacent Senese's restaurant.

ComedySportz (⊠ 3209 N. Halsted St., ☎ 773/549–8080) specializes in "competitive improv," in which two teams vie for the favor of the audience.

Improv Olympic (⊠ 3541 N. Clark St., ☎ 773/880–0199) has shows with student and professional improvisation every night but Tuesday. Team members present long-form comedic improvisations, which last about 40 minutes and draw on audience suggestions.

Second City (⊠ 1616 N. Wells St., ☎ 312/337–3992), an institution since 1959, has spawned some of the hottest comedians around. In recent years the once bitingly funny, loony improvisation has given way to a less imaginative and more raunchy style. There are two stages, the Main and the second-floor ETC.

Zanies (⊠ 1548 N. Wells St., ☎ 312/337–4027) books outstanding national talent and is Chicago's best stand-up comedy spot.

Dance Clubs

Most clubs don't get crowded until late at night, and they remain open into the early morning hours. Cover charges range from $5 to $15.

Dennis Rodman's Illusions (⊠ 157 W. Ontario St., ☎ 312/587–7792) is tamer than what you'd expect from "the Worm." On the tourist corridor of Ontario Street, this supper club and nightclub attracts an older, suburban crowd. A cabaret show Fridays and Saturdays features Las Vegas–style dancers, magicians, and fire-eaters. Rodman's wedding dress, feathered boa, spangled *Tonight Show* jumpsuit, and other artifacts are on view in glass display cases.

Drink (⊠ 702 W. Fulton St., ☎ 312/733–7800) and eat at this trendy spot in the former meatpacking district. The driving dance music is good, loud, and fun. The decor ranges from a '70s psychedelic room with multicolored floor to a Moroccan room complete with hookahs to a VIP cigar lounge with velvet banquettes.

Excalibur (✉ 632 N. Dearborn St., ☎ 312/266–1944), in River North, is a superdisco with multiple dance floors and bars, a video games room, and a restaurant. Popular with the twentysomething set, it attracts a large suburban crowd on weekends.

Funky Buddha Lounge (✉ 728 W. Grand Ave., ☎ 312/666–1695), a hot spot for hipsters, has an intimate bar and dark dance floor, where patrons groove to house, funk, and hip-hop. Funky doesn't begin to describe this trendy spot, with long black banquettes, leopard-print pillows, red velvet drapes, a smell of incense, and a big metal Buddha guarding the front door.

Karma (✉ 318 W. Grand Ave., ☎ 312/321–1331) bouncers insist you have done something right in your previous life to make it past them. Once you're granted entrance, proceed through a candlelit underground lounge and up to the second-floor Temple dance room, where dancers are obscured by thick smoke from the fog machine, cigars, and cigarettes. The third floor has another dance floor, booths offering privacy, a few pool tables, and a VIP room with a 300-gallon fish tank.

Neo (✉ 2350 N. Clark St., ☎ 773/528–2622) has been eclipsed in grandeur by newer, larger clubs, but it's still a good spot for Gothic, industrial, and underground dance music.

Polly Esther's (✉ 213 W. Institute Pl., ☎ 312/664–0777) celebrates the '70s and '80s with its "Saturday Night Fever" dance floor and lava lamps upstairs, and Michael Jackson tunes in the '80s Culture Club area downstairs. Don't forget your bell-bottoms.

Red Dog (✉ 1958 W. North Ave., ☎ 773/278–1009) calls itself a "supreme funk parlor," an appellation that's not far from the truth. The dance floor gets crowded with bodies in the wee hours of the morning. Enter from the alley off Damen Avenue.

Spy Bar (✉ 646 N. Franklin St., ☎ 312/587–8779) pulls some smooth moves. Image is everything at this subterranean bar, which attracts the occasional celebrity. Conversationalists stick to the comfy lounge area with velvety drapes and soft sofas, while poseurs hit the dance floor for house or hip-hop.

Gay and Lesbian Bars

Chicago's gay bars appeal to mixed crowds and tastes. Most are on North Halsted Street from Belmont Avenue to Addison Street, an area called Boys Town. Bars generally stay open until 2 AM weekends, but a few keep the lights on until 5 AM Sunday mornings. The **Windy City Times** (☎ 312/397–0025) and **Gay Chicago** magazine (☎ 773/327–7271) list nightspots, events, and gay and lesbian resources; both are free.

Baton Show Lounge (✉ 436 N. Clark St., ☎ 312/644–5269), featuring female impersonators, has catered to curious out-of-towners for 30 years. Some of the regular performers, such as Chili Pepper and Mimi Marks, have become Chicago cult figures.

Berlin (✉ 954 W. Belmont Ave., ☎ 773/348–4975), a multicultural, pansexual dance club, features progressive electronic dance music and fun theme nights, such as Prince night, disco Wednesdays, and boys' night, with male dancers.

Big Chicks (✉ 5024 N. Sheridan Rd., ☎ 773/728–5511) sponsors several men's and women's sports teams, making it a favorite with alternative jocks. The great jukebox and the fun-loving staff are the payoff for the hike to get here.

Charlie's (⊠ 3726 N. Broadway, ☎ 773/871–8887), a country-and-western dance club, lets you dance nightly to achy-breaky tunes. It's mostly a boots-and-denim crowd on weekends.

Locals describe the **Closet** (⊠ 3325 N. Broadway, ☎ 773/477–8533) as a "friendly joint." Don't miss this small bar's infamous Bloody Sundays, for what are hailed as the best Bloody Marys in town. The crowd is mixed gay and lesbian.

Gentry (⊠ 440 N. State St., ☎ 312/836–0933), one of the few gay bars downtown, has an upscale piano bar where the staff wears tuxedos and a downstairs video bar that attracts a younger crowd.

Most of the city's gay bars attract a mixed crowd; but not **Girlbar** (⊠ 2625 N. Halsted St., ☎ 773/871–4210), which caters to lesbians (except Wednesday when it becomes Boybar). In the heart of Lincoln Park, the comfortable spot attracts a clean-cut, fun crowd. Downstairs is an intimate mirrored dance floor, while the upstairs has pool tables, a dartboard, and an outdoor deck.

Little Jim's (⊠ 3501 N. Halsted St., ☎ 773/871–6116) is a neighborhood bar with a good mix of regulars. Video screens show films of varying repute.

Roscoe's Tavern (⊠ 3356 N. Halsted St., ☎ 773/281–3355), a crowded, friendly, upscale bar, has great dance music, a poolroom, a fireplace, and an outside café in the summer.

Music

Blues

The blues traveled to Chicago during the 1930s with African-Americans who moved here from the Deep South. In the years following World War II, Chicago-style blues grew into its own musical form, flourishing during the 1950s, then fading during the 1960s with the advent of rock and roll. You can still find the South Side clubs where it all began, but since 1970 the blues has migrated to the North Side and attracted new devotees among largely white audiences. The **Chicago Blues Festival** (☎ 312/744–3370) each June testifies to the city's continuing affection for this music.

Blue Chicago (⊠ 536 N. Clark St., ☎ 312/661–0100; ⊠ 736 N. Clark St., ☎ 312/642–6261) has two bars within two blocks of each other. Both have good sound systems and attract a cosmopolitan audience that's a tad more diverse than some of the baseball-capped crowds in Lincoln Park. One cover gets you into both bars.

B.L.U.E.S. (⊠ 2519 N. Halsted St., ☎ 773/528–1012), narrow and intimate, draws the best of Chicago's musicians, including Son Seals, Otis Rush, Big Time Sarah, and Magic Slim. This Lincoln Park venue is often packed to its smoke-filled capacity.

B.L.U.E.S. Etcetera (⊠ 1124 W. Belmont Ave., ☎ 773/525–8989), a spacious and comfortable change from overcrowded spots, has less atmosphere than other blues bars but headlines the same big-name talent.

Buddy Guy's Legends (⊠ 754 S. Wabash Ave., ☎ 312/427–0333) serves up Louisiana-style barbecue along with the blues in a big club in the South Loop with good sound, good sight lines, and pool tables. Local blues legend and owner Buddy Guy often sits in.

Checkerboard Lounge (⊠ 423 E. 43rd St., ☎ 773/624–3240) is one of the great old South Side clubs. Although the neighborhood is rough, the music by name performers is usually worth the trip.

CHICAGO SINGS THE BLUES

"Come on baby, don't you want to go,
Back to the same old place, sweet home Chicago."

–Robert Johnson

THE SEARING, SOULFUL STRAINS of the blues are deeply woven into the fabric of Chicago's history. Blues originated in the Mississippi Delta, traveled with migrating blacks through Memphis, and settled in Chicago. Here, the country blues became charged by the tougher, louder life of the city. These urban, hard-edged electric blues are marked by a fiery style, driving rhythm, and dynamic sound.

The first stop for many arrivals was Maxwell Street, where blues musicians played in jam sessions in the open-air flea market. That legacy is fading fast, though. At the **New Maxwell Street Market** (⊠ Canal St. between Taylor and 16th Sts., ☎ 312/922–3100), recently relocated to a smaller space a half mile east of the original, you can sometimes find blues musicians playing Sundays 7 AM–3 PM in summer.

For a walk into history, stop by the **Blues Heaven Foundation,** which occupies the former home of the legendary Chess Records. The foundation, run by the widow and daughter of blues musician Willie Dixon, offers tours of the facility, which displays a few artifacts including the Chess recording studio, rehearsal room, and basement echo chamber where Chuck Berry once slept. ⊠ *2120 S. Michigan Ave.,* ☎ *312/808–1286.* ⊠ *$10.* ☉ *Mon.–Sat. noon–2 PM.*

Chicago is still active in recording the blues. Alligator Records has offices on Chicago's North Side. And Delmark Records is here too; owner Bob Koester also runs the **Jazz Record Mart** (⊠ 444 N. Wabash Ave., ☎ 312/222–

1467 or 800/684–3480), which claims to be the world's largest jazz and blues record shop.

In the '90s blues had a resurgence, reaching new audiences and new heights of commercialization with the opening of the **House of Blues** (☞ Nightlife for information on this and other blues clubs). A House of Blues Hotel was scheduled to open here in September 1998, carrying the blues theme even further.

Chicago is still the capital of the blues. The city's annual **Chicago Blues Festival** (☎ 312/744–3370), usually held the first weekend in June, draws some 650,000 fans to Grant Park near Chicago's lakefront for a free four-day festival featuring outdoor concerts on several stages.

Year-round, the passion pours forth from blues bars seven nights a week, with local artists like Son Seals, Lonnie Brooks, Koko Taylor, Eddy Clearwater, Otis Rush, and Pinetop Perkins.

Catch bluesman Buddy Guy at his club, **Buddy Guy's Legends.** Or swing by the **Checkerboard Lounge,** on a stretch of 47th Street the city renamed Muddy Waters Drive. Farther south, fill up at **Lee's Unleaded Blues** (⊠ 7401 S. South Chicago Ave., ☎ 773/493–3477). The two **Blue Chicago** clubs downtown often turn the spotlight on female vocalists. In Lincoln Park, **Kingston Mines** presents two bands on two stages, and the intimate **B.L.U.E.S.** pulses with rhythm. **Smoke Daddy** (⊠ 1804 W. Division St., ☎ 773/772–6656) serves Southern barbecue along with a hearty side dish of blues and jazz.

House of Blues (✉ 329 N. Dearborn St., ☎ 312/527–2583) uses its size and national fame to attract top performers in roots music, although you won't get much homegrown Chicago blues here. The decor is an elaborate cross between a blues bar and an ornate opera house.

Kingston Mines (✉ 2548 N. Halsted St., ☎ 773/477–4646), the North Side's oldest blues spot, continues to attract large numbers of blues lovers and cruising singles. The first group comes because of its top-notch, big-name continuous live weekend entertainment on two stages, the second because of its late closing.

Rosa's (✉ 3420 W. Armitage Ave., ☎ 773/342–0452) could well be Chicago's friendliest blues bar. Tony, the owner, came here from Italy out of love for the blues; his mother, Mama Rosa, is a fixture behind the bar in this diverse neighborhood.

Country

Cadillac Ranch (✉ 1175 W. Lake St., Bartlett, ☎ 630/830–7200), in the western suburbs, has line and couples' dancing, with live bands on the weekends and dance lessons Monday–Thursday.

Carol's Pub (✉ 4659 N. Clark St., ☎ 773/334–2402) showcased country before it was cool. The house band, South of Midnight, plays country and country-rock tunes you can dance to.

Lakeview Lounge (✉ 5110 N. Broadway, ☎ 773/769–0994) has a small dance floor and a house band on weekends.

Eclectic

Clubs in this category don't limit themselves to a single type of music. Call ahead to find out what's playing.

Beat Kitchen (✉ 2100 W. Belmont Ave., ☎ 773/281–4444) brings in the crowds because of its good sound system and local rock, jazz, country, and rockabilly acts. The second floor of this small club is decorated like an old apartment, with easy chairs and board games.

Elbo Room (✉ 2871 N. Lincoln Ave., ☎ 773/549–5549), a multilevel space in an elbow-shape corner building, has a basement rec-room feel. The bar plays host to a wide range of talented live bands seven days a week, with a strong dose of acid jazz, funk, and soul.

Fitzgerald's (✉ 6615 W. Roosevelt Rd., Berwyn, ☎ 708/788–2118), though a bit out of the way, draws crowds from all over the city and suburbs with its mix of folk, jazz, blues, zydeco, and rock. This early 1900s roadhouse has great sound and sight lines in addition to its wide range of roots music.

Mad Bar (✉ 1640 N. Damen Ave., ☎ 773/227–2277), a see-and-be-seen Bucktown joint, is often tightly packed with trendies. DJs play house music while bodies crowd the small dance floor. There's some seating in the back, though, for those who would rather observe.

Park West (✉ 322 W. Armitage Ave., ☎ 773/929–5959) usually favors glossily performed shows by national rock, pop, and jazz groups. The large hall, which retains a mid-'80s decor, has good sight lines and acoustics.

The Vic Theatre (✉ 3145 N. Sheffield Ave., ☎ 773/472–0366), a former movie palace, advertises "all ages" shows heavy on rock and alternative. Some nights are "brew and view"—movies with beer—when there's no live concert.

Folk and Ethnic

Abbey Pub (✉ 3420 W. Grace St., ☎ 773/478–4408) showcases Irish and Celtic music in a large concert hall with a separate busy, smoky pub. By day, the hall is used to show soccer and rugby games from the U.K. and Ireland.

Baby Doll Polka Club (✉ 6102 S. Central Ave., ☎ 773/582–9706) has some of the best polka dancing in the city, with live music Saturdays and Sundays. You'll see mostly regulars at the Baby Doll, a neighborhood institution near Midway Airport on the Southwest Side.

Fadó Irish Pub (✉ 100 W. Grand Ave., ☎ 312/836–0066) uses imported wood, stone, and glasswork to create five distinct areas from a 6th-century Gaelic pub to a public house in Dublin. Although it's a bit gimmicky, the result works with expertly drawn Guinness, a fine selection of Irish whiskeys, occasional live Irish music, and plenty of beer to go around.

Kitty O'Shea's (✉ 720 S. Michigan Ave., ☎ 312/922–4400), a handsome room in the Chicago Hilton and Towers, re-creates an Irish pub, complete with Irish music, food by Irish chefs, and, of course, Irish bartenders.

No Exit (✉ 6970 N. Glenwood Ave., ☎ 773/743–3355) has folk, jazz, poetry readings, theater, and comedy sketches in a comfortable coffeehouse setting reminiscent of the 1960s—not too surprising, since it opened in 1958. Backgammon, chess, and the Chinese board game Go help you kick back.

Old Town School of Folk Music (✉ 909 W. Armitage Ave., ☎ 773/525–7793), Chicago's first and oldest folk music school, has served as folk central in the city since 1957. A friendly spot (what else would you expect from a folk joint?), Old Town presents outstanding performances by top national and local acts in a large, bare concert hall filled with folding chairs.

Tania's (✉ 2659 N. Milwaukee Ave., ☎ 773/235–7120), a Cuban restaurant, becomes a showy nightclub on Friday and Saturday only, with salsa bands playing cha-cha, salsa, and merengue.

Wild Hare (✉ 3530 N. Clark St., ☎ 773/327–4273) is the place for infectious live reggae and world beat music, with a wide-open dance floor. Caribbean decor adds to the atmosphere.

Jazz

Jazz thrives all around town. For a recorded listing of upcoming live performances, call the **Jazz Institute Hot Line** (☎ 312/427–3300), which is updated twice a week.

Andy's (✉ 11 E. Hubbard St., ☎ 312/642–6805), a popular after-work watering hole with a substantial bar menu, has become one of Chicago's best spots for serious jazz. The jazz at noon weekdays is a boon for music lovers who aren't night owls.

Cotton Club (✉ 1710 S. Michigan Ave., ☎ 312/341–9787), at the far end of the South Loop, is a favorite of upscale young black professionals. The elegant room draws big crowds and good bands. There's an open mike every Monday.

Green Dolphin Street (✉ 2200 N. Ashland Ave., ☎ 773/395–0066) attracts top ensembles and smooth-voiced jazz divas to this large, open club for bossa, bebop, Latin, and world jazz.

Green Mill (✉ 4802 N. Broadway, ☎ 773/878–5552), a Chicago institution off the beaten track in untrendy Uptown, has been around for most of this century. Deep leather banquettes and ornate wood paneling line the walls, and a photo of Al Capone occupies a place of honor on the piano behind the bar. The entertainment ranges from good to outstanding. The Uptown Poetry Slam, a competitive poetry reading, takes center stage on Sunday.

Jazz Showcase (⊠ 59 W. Grand Ave., ☎ 312/670–2473), the second-oldest jazz club in the country, presents top national and international names in jazz. The snazzy space has soft yellow walls and black-and-white photos of performers.

Pops for Champagne (⊠ 2934 N. Sheffield Ave., ☎ 773/472–1000), despite the incongruous name, is a good spot for serious jazz fans. A champagne bar and a selection of tasty appetizers and desserts enhance the scene.

Rock

Chicago has an active rock scene with many local bands, some of which—including the Smashing Pumpkins—have won national acclaim.

Cubby Bear (⊠ 1059 W. Addison St., ☎ 773/327–1662), a large sports bar and music venue with an emphasis on rock and country-rock, lies across the street from Wrigley Field. During baseball season the Cubby Bear opens in the afternoon to give Cubs fans another place to drown their sorrows.

Double Door (⊠ 1572 N. Milwaukee Ave., ☎ 773/489–3160) welcomes national groups as well as up-and-coming local and alternative ones. In hip Wicker Park, the large bar is a good spot to see a small band.

Empty Bottle (⊠ 1035 N. Western Ave., ☎ 773/276–3600) may have toys and knickknacks around the bar, but when it comes to booking rock, punk, jazz, and rockabilly bands from the indie scene, it's a serious place with no pretensions.

Lounge Ax (⊠ 2438 N. Lincoln Ave., ☎ 773/525–6620) presents an eclectic blend of local and national alternative rock, folk, and country, with an emphasis on indie rock. This small space in the heart of Lincoln Park can be uncomfortable if it's crowded.

Metro (⊠ 3730 N. Clark St., ☎ 773/549–0203) presents progressive nationally known artists and the cream of the local crop. A former movie palace, it's an excellent place to see live bands. Downstairs is Smart Bar, a funky late-night dance club that starts hopping after 11.

Schubas Tavern (⊠ 3159 N. Southport Ave., ☎ 773/525–2508) favors rock bands with a strong folk or country edge. The wood-paneled back room has good seating and a laid-back atmosphere.

Piano Bars

Coq d'Or at the Drake Hotel (⊠ 140 E. Walton St., ☎ 312/787–2200) is where Chicago legend Buddy Charles holds court Tuesday–Saturday nights. The dark room, which has highly polished wood paneling in cherry tones, draws hotel guests as well as neighborhood regulars with its fine music and cocktails served in blown-glass goblets.

Pump Room (⊠ Omni Ambassador East Hotel, 1301 N. State Pkwy., ☎ 312/266–0360), a longtime celebrity hangout, calls out for dancing cheek to cheek, especially on weekends. Jackets are required.

Seasons Lounge (⊠ 120 E. Delaware Pl., ☎ 312/280–8800), in the Four Seasons Hotel, serves drinks or dessert to the sounds of jazz. A trio performs Saturday night at the lounge, which also has a martini menu and cigar bar.

Yvette Wintergarden (⊠ 311 S. Wacker Dr., ☎ 312/408–1242) has an ornate, intimate pavilion where cabaret singers perform.

Zebra Lounge (⊠ 1220 N. State St., ☎ 312/642–5140), small and funky, attracts a good crowd of regulars who come to sing along with the pianist or, on Tuesday, watch a magician perform.

Sports Bars

Gamekeepers (⊠ 345 W. Armitage Ave., ☎ 773/549–0400) is full of former frat boys. The beer is cheap when there's a drink special—and so is the conversation. With more than 30 TVs and complete satellite sports coverage, there's barely a game Gamekeepers doesn't get.

Hi-Tops Cafe (⊠ 3551 N. Sheffield Ave., ☎ 773/348–0009), within a ball's toss of Wrigley Field, may be the ultimate sports bar. Big-screen TVs, a lively crowd, and good bar food keep the Cubs fans coming. A laid-back martini bar upstairs provides a respite from the crowd.

North Beach Chicago (⊠ 1551 N. Sheffield Ave., ☎ 312/266–7842) has multiple large-screen TVs plus three sand-filled indoor volleyball courts, a full-size basketball court, a 9-hole miniature golf course, and four bowling lanes.

Sluggers (⊠ 3540 N. Clark St., ☎ 773/248–0055) is packed after Cubs games in the nearby stadium, and the players themselves make occasional appearances in summer. Check out the fast- and slow-pitch batting cages on the second floor, as well as the pool tables, air hockey tables, and indoor golf range.

THE ARTS

Chicago is a splendid city for the arts. The Shubert, Auditorium, Chicago, and Goodman theaters—Chicago bases for Broadway-scale shows—have been joined by more than 75 small, neighborhood-based theaters where young actors polish their skills. The Lyric Opera plays to houses that are always sold out; the Chicago Opera Theatre augments the Lyric's repertoire with a spring season of smaller works. Chicago Symphony subscriptions are also a sellout; the Ravinia Festival and the Grant Park Concerts pack people in. Music lovers hungry for more turn to smaller performing groups: Music of the Baroque, His Majestie's Clerkes, the Oriana Singers, and dozens more; and dance aficionados enjoy performances of outstanding companies.

For complete music and theater listings, check two free weeklies, *The Reader* and *New City,* both published Thursday; the Friday and Sunday editions of the *Chicago Tribune* and *Chicago Sun-Times*; and the monthly *Chicago* magazine.

Ticket prices vary wildly depending on whether you're seeing a high-profile group or venturing into more obscure territory. Chicago Symphony tickets range from $20 to $79, the Lyric Opera from $20 to $110 (if you can get them). Smaller choruses and orchestras charge from $10 to $25; watch the listings for free performances. Commercial theater ranges from $15 to $70; smaller experimental ensembles might charge $5, $10, or pay-what-you-can. Movie prices range from $8.25 for first-run houses to as low as $2 at some suburban second-run houses. Some commercial chains take credit cards.

Dance

Dance in Chicago often doesn't receive the recognition it should, but several talented companies perform regularly, with a wide range of styles.

The most popular dance performance spaces are the **Shubert Theatre** (✉ 22 W. Monroe St., ☎ 312/977–1700), the **Dance Center of Columbia College** (✉ 4730 N. Sheridan Rd., ☎ 773/989–3310), and the **Athenaeum Theatre** (✉ 2936 N. Southport Ave., ☎ 773/935–6860). The **Chicago Dance Coalition Information Hot Line** (☎ 312/419–8383) is a recording that lists upcoming dance performances.

The well-received **Spring Festival of Dance** runs March–May annually and showcases renowned international, national, and local companies. For information call the co-presenter, **Music and Dance Theater Chicago** (☎ 312/629–8696).

Ballet Chicago (☎ 312/251–8838), founded in 1988, is Chicago's own critically acclaimed resident classical ballet company.

Gus Giordano Jazz Dance Chicago (☎ 847/866–6779) is a jazz dance company based in suburban Evanston.

Hubbard Street Dance Chicago (☎ 312/663–0853), Chicago's most notable success story in dance, exudes a contemporary, jazzy vitality that has made it extremely popular.

Joffrey Ballet of Chicago (☎ 312/739–0120) enriched the city's ballet offerings when it moved from New York to Chicago in 1995, garnering acclaim for its energetic performances.

Muntu Dance Theatre of Chicago (☎ 773/602–1135) presents dynamic interpretations of contemporary and traditional African and African-American dance.

River North Dance Company (☎ 312/944–2888) has attracted attention with accessible works rich in Chicago's strong jazz dance traditions.

Film

Chicago supports an enticing variety of films, from first-run blockbusters to art and revival releases. For recorded movie previews and show times at area theaters, call **MoviePhone** (☎ 312/444–3456), a service that also allows you to purchase tickets over the phone for many cinemas.

For two weeks in October, the **Chicago International Film Festival** (☎ 312/332–3456) presents more than 100 films, including premieres of Hollywood films, international releases, documentaries, short subjects, animation, videos, and student films. Movie stars usually make an appearance at the opening events.

Many Near North cinemas show first-run Hollywood movies on multiple screens. **Water Tower Theater** (✉ 845 N. Michigan Ave., ☎ 312/649–5790) has four screens on the second level of the Water Tower Place mall and three on the mall's ground-level entrance off Chestnut Street. The two screens of the **900 North Michigan Cinemas** (☎ 312/787–1988) are conveniently located in the lower level of the 900 North Michigan Avenue shopping complex. The **600 North Michigan Cinemas** (☎ 312/255–9340), with an entrance at the corner of Rush and Ohio streets, has nine screens on three levels. **McClurg Court Cinemas** (✉ 330 E. Ohio St., ☎ 312/642–0723) has two small screens and one large theater with a great sound system, ideal for viewing action flicks.

Biograph Theatre (✉ 2433 N. Lincoln Ave., ☎ 773/348–4123) is a North Side first-run movie house of some historical interest; gangster John Dillinger was shot dead in front of it by FBI agents in 1934.

Brew and View (✉ 3145 N. Sheffield Ave., ☎ 312/618–8439) shows movies at the Vic Theatre when the hall is not in use for concerts. Expect recent releases, cult films, midnight shows, and a rowdy crowd, which comes for the cheap movies and beer specials.

Burnham Plaza (⌧ 826 S. Wabash Ave., ☎ 312/922–1090) is the most convenient first-run movie theater for those staying in the South Loop.

Celluloid Movie Bar (⌧ 1805 W. Division St., ☎ 312/707–8888), attached to the **Liquid Kitty** bar, has a small screening room with comfy padded movie chairs and bar stools. Three movies run each night—a mix of independent films, cult favorites, and second-run shows. There's a constant chatter, though, as patrons slip back and forth from the bar.

Esquire (⌧ 58 E. Oak St., ☎ 312/280–0101), an Art Deco landmark on the Gold Coast that shows first-run movies, has kept its facade but is divided into six modern theaters.

Facets Multimedia (⌧ 1517 W. Fullerton Ave., ☎ 773/281–4114) presents a variety of rare and exotic films in its cinema and video theater; call to find out whether a particular day's fare appeals to you, or rent an arts film from the well-stocked video store.

Film Center at the School of the Art Institute (⌧ 280 S. Columbus Dr., ☎ 312/443–3737) specializes in unusual current films and revivals of rare classics. The program here changes almost daily, and filmmakers sometimes give lectures at the Film Center.

Fine Arts Theatre (⌧ 418 S. Michigan Ave., ☎ 312/939–3700) devotes its four screens to independent, foreign, and avant-garde films.

Music Box Theatre (⌧ 3733 N. Southport Ave., ☎ 773/871–6604), a small and richly decorated 1920s movie palace, shows a mix of foreign flicks, classics, and outstanding recent films, emphasizing independent filmmakers. The theater organ is played during intermission at special events and as an accompaniment to silent films. If you love old theaters and old movies, don't miss a trip here.

Music

The Chicago Symphony is internationally renowned, and Chicago's Lyric Opera is one of the top three opera companies in America today. Season subscribers take virtually all the tickets to these performances, but subscribers who can't use their tickets sometimes return them to the box office. If you go to Orchestra Hall or the opera house a half hour before performance time, you may find someone with an extra ticket to sell. If you can't get tickets to these top draws, though, take heart: Chicago has a wealth of exciting performing groups.

Choral and Chamber Groups

Apollo Chorus of Chicago (☎ 630/960–2251), formed in 1872, is one of the country's oldest oratorio societies. Apollo performs Handel's *Messiah* every December and other choral classics throughout the year.

Chicago Baroque Ensemble (☎ 312/464–0600), a unique group of musicians, plays throughout the city on such period instruments as the harpsichord, viola da gamba, and baroque cello. The ensemble also has vocal soloists.

Chicago Children's Choir (⌧ Chicago Cultural Center, 78 E. Washington St., ☎ 312/849–8300) draws its members, ages 4 to 18, from a broad spectrum of racial, ethnic, and economic groups. Performances are given each year during the Christmas season and in early June; other concerts are scheduled periodically.

His Majestie's Clerkes (☎ 312/461–0723) takes its name from a Renaissance term for a professional chorister. The group performs mostly sacred and a cappella music in churches throughout the city. The season runs October–May.

Music of the Baroque (☎ 312/551–1414), one of the Midwest's leading music ensembles specializing in Baroque and early classical music, schedules eight programs a year from October through May. Performances are in beautiful Chicago neighborhood churches.

Oriana Singers (☎ 773/262–4558) is an outstanding a cappella sextet with an eclectic classical and jazz repertoire.

William Ferris Chorale (✉ 690 W. Belmont Ave., ☎ 773/325–2000), a distinguished choral ensemble, focuses on 20th-century music and gives concerts throughout the year.

Concert Halls

Mandel Hall (✉ 1131 E. 57th St., ☎ 773/702–7300), on the University of Chicago campus, schedules classical music, jazz, a folk festival, and opera performances.

The neo-Georgian **Orchestra Hall** (✉ 220 S. Michigan Ave., ☎ 312/294–3000), home of the world-famous Chicago Symphony Orchestra (CSO), is now part of the much larger new Symphony Center. In addition to more than 100 symphonic performances between late September and late May, the hall's schedule includes jazz, pop, chamber, and world music concerts, presented in association with the Ravinia Festival in north suburban Highland Park. Unfortunately, CSO subscription sales exhaust virtually all the available symphony tickets. You'll have better luck hearing the symphony during the summer if you make the trek to Ravinia Park. Sometimes it pays to stop by Orchestra Hall about an hour before a concert; there may be last-minute ticket returns at the box office. If you'd like to see the inside of Orchestra Hall, call to schedule a tour or buy a ticket to one of the recitals that are scheduled frequently, particularly on Sunday afternoon. The view is splendid from the balcony and the acoustics excellent.

Among the smaller halls in the Loop and Near North areas is **Curtiss Hall,** in the **Fine Arts Building** (✉ 410 S. Michigan Ave., ☎ 312/939–3380), a chamber music venue. **Fullerton Auditorium,** in the Art Institute of Chicago (✉ Michigan Ave. and Adams St., ☎ 312/443–3600), has occasional programming that includes some chamber ensembles in addition to lectures. The **Newberry Library** (✉ 60 W. Walton St., ☎ 312/943–9090) presents four concerts a year by the Newberry Consort, which performs music from the 13th to the 17th centuries, as well as a number of concerts related to events or exhibits at the library. The historic **Three Arts Club** (✉ 1300 N. Dearborn Pkwy., ☎ 312/944–6250) hosts periodic jazz performances as well as other concerts in a landmark 1912 building modeled after a Tuscan palazzo.

Opera and Light Opera

Chicago Opera Theatre (☎ 773/292–7578) stages innovative versions of traditional favorites, contemporary American pieces, and important lesser-known works, emphasizing theatrical as well as musical aspects of the shows. All performances are sung in English.

Light Opera Works (✉ Cahn Auditorium, Emerson St. and Sheridan Rd., Evanston, ☎ 847/869–6300) stages Gilbert and Sullivan operettas, as well as Viennese, French, and other light operettas and American musicals, June–December.

Lyric Opera of Chicago (✉ 20 N. Wacker Dr., ☎ 312/332–2244) almost always sells out its superb performances. Don't worry about understanding German or Italian; English translations are projected above the stage. The season at the Ardis Krainik Theater runs September–March.

Orchestras

Chicago Sinfonietta (☎ 312/857–1062) presents highly polished classical, romantic, and contemporary pieces exactly as they were written by the composer. The Sinfonietta performs about 15 times a year at various locations and is in residence at Dominican University in suburban River Forest.

Chicago Symphony Orchestra (✉ 220 S. Michigan Ave., ☎ 312/294–3000) performs at Orchestra Hall September–May, with music director Daniel Barenboim conducting. The historic hall underwent renovations in 1997, giving it additional lobby space, refurbished seating, a larger stage, and improved acoustics. The new Symphony Center complex contains an education center, a restaurant, and performance space.

In summer you can see and hear the Chicago Symphony at the **Ravinia Festival**, in Highland Park, a 25-mi train trip from Chicago. The park is lovely, and lawn seats are always available even when those in the Pavilion and the smaller Martin Theatre are sold out (a rarity). For Ravinia program, ticket, and travel information, call 847/266–5100.

Civic Orchestra of Chicago (✉ 220 S. Michigan Ave., ☎ 312/294–3000), the Chicago Symphony Orchestra's training orchestra, performs a repertoire similar to that of the parent organization and works with the same guest conductors. Performances are free, but advance tickets are required.

Grant Park Symphony Orchestra (☎ 312/742–7638), a program of the Chicago Park District, gives free concerts during the summer at the James C. Petrillo Music Shell, in Grant Park between Columbus and Lake Shore drives at Jackson Boulevard. Performances usually take place evenings Wednesday–Sunday.

Theater

Road-show productions of Broadway hits do come to Chicago, but the theater scene's true vigor springs from the multitude of small ensembles that have made a home here. They range from the critically acclaimed Steppenwolf and the Goodman Theatre, a pioneer of regional theater in the United States, to fringe groups that specialize in experimental work. Larger, more elaborate productions tend to be concentrated in the Loop, while theaters on the Near North Side present some offbeat productions as well as more popular fare.

The theater district in the Loop is currently undergoing a revival, and many grand old theaters have recently been redeveloped, including the Shubert and the Oriental; renovation of the old Harris and Selwyn theaters was in the planning stages at press time. With the completion of several new projects, Chicago will become one of the top three downtown theater markets in the country.

Many smaller companies perform in tiny or makeshift theaters, where admission prices are inexpensive to moderate. You can save money on seats at **Hot Tix** (☎ 312/977–1755), where unsold tickets are available, usually at half price (plus a service charge), on the day of performance; you won't know what's available until that day. You must buy the tickets in person, not over the phone; call for booth hours. The Hot Tix booths are at 108 N. State St., the historic Water Tower at 806 N. Michigan Ave., 1616 Sherman Ave., in suburban Evanston, and at Chicago-area Tower Records stores. Hot Tix also sells advance tickets. You can charge full-price tickets over the phone at **Ticketmaster** (☎ 312/559–1212 for rock concerts and general interest events; 312/902–1500 for the arts line).

Commercial Theater

Most of the houses listed here are hired by independent producers for commercial (and sometimes nonprofit) productions; they have no resident producer or company.

The **Athenaeum Theatre** (✉ 2936 N. Southport Ave., ☎ 773/935–6860) is home to a variety of provoking music, opera, dance, and drama performances, some brought in from around the world.

Auditorium Theatre (✉ 50 E. Congress Pkwy., ☎ 312/922–2110), a Louis Sullivan architectural masterpiece, has excellent acoustics and sight lines. You're likely to see touring productions of such Broadway hits as *Les Misérables* or *Phantom of the Opera.*

Briar Street Theatre (✉ 3133 N. Halsted St., ☎ 773/348–4000), a modest space in Lake View, often hosts local productions of hit Broadway plays.

Chicago Theatre (✉ 175 N. State St., ☎ 312/443–1130), a restored former movie palace and vaudeville house, presents family musicals, such as *Beauty and the Beast,* as well as concerts and special events.

Drury Lane Theatre (✉ 100 Drury La., Oakbrook Terrace, ☎ 630/530–0111) caters mostly to suburbanites with its dinner-theater format. Musicals and other Broadway imports are usually well produced.

The **Ford Center for the Performing Arts, Oriental Theatre** (✉ 24 W. Randolph St., ☎ 312/855–9400), which was recently restored to its original 1920s splendor, presents musical theater and features an intimate auditorium and spacious lobbies.

Ivanhoe Theater (✉ 750 W. Wellington Ave., ☎ 773/975–7171) mounts musicals and other Broadway shows; some long-running standards have been *Hell Cab* and *Late Night Catechism.*

Mayfair Theatre (✉ Blackstone Hotel, 636 S. Michigan Ave., ☎ 312/786–9120) has been performing the audience-participation mystery *Shear Madness* since 1982.

Royal George Theatre Center (✉ 1641 N. Halsted St., ☎ 312/988–9000) has one large, gracious theater with good sight lines, plus a smaller studio theater and a cabaret space.

Shubert Theatre (✉ 22 W. Monroe St., ☎ 312/977–1700), built in 1906, is a grand, building in the Loop's rejuvenated theater district.

Theatre Building (✉ 1225 W. Belmont Ave., ☎ 773/327–5252), a rehabbed warehouse, provides a permanent home for small companies of varying professionalism.

Performing Groups

Chicago's reputation as a theatrical powerhouse was born from its small not-for-profit theater companies that produce everything from Shakespeare to Sondheim. The groups listed do consistently interesting work, and a few have gained national attention. Some, such as Steppenwolf and Lookingglass, are ensemble troupes; others, notably the Goodman, the Court, and Victory Gardens, are production companies that use different casts for each show. Be open-minded when you're choosing a show; even a group you've never heard of may be harboring one or two underpaid geniuses. *The Reader* carries complete theater listings and reviews of the more avant-garde shows.

Bailiwick Arts Center (✉ 1229 W. Belmont Ave., ☎ 773/883–1090) presents new and classical material. Its Pride Performance series, held every summer, features plays by gays and lesbians.

Court Theatre (✉ 5535 S. Ellis Ave., ☎ 773/753–4472), on the University of Chicago campus, revives classic plays, often presenting two plays in rotating repertory.

Goodman Theatre (✉ 200 S. Columbus Dr., ☎ 312/443–3800), one of the oldest and best theaters in Chicago, is known for its polished performances of classic and contemporary works starring well-known actors. The company's space behind the Art Institute also includes the Studio Theater, where new works and one-act plays are staged. In the fall of 2000, the Goodman plans to take over two historic theater buildings in the heart of the Loop.

Lookingglass Theatre Company (☎ 773/477–9257) creates a unique, acrobatic style of performance utilizing theater, dance, music, and circus arts. This ensemble produces physically—and artistically—daring works.

Neo-Futurists (✉ 5153 N. Ashland Ave., ☎ 773/275–5255) perform their long-running late-night cult hit *Too Much Light Makes the Baby Go Blind* in a space above a funeral home. The piece is a series of 30 ever-changing two-minute plays whose order is chosen by the audience. In keeping with the spirit of randomness, the admission price is set by the roll of a die, plus $4.

Organic Touchstone Company (✉ 2851 N. Halsted St., ☎ 773/404–4700) specializes in Midwest premieres of plays that have recently been successful in New York, London, and Los Angeles.

Pegasus Players (✉ 1145 W. Wilson Ave., ☎ 773/878–9761) tackles interesting and difficult works, usually producing at least one Stephen Sondheim musical each season. The spacious theater is at the city's Truman College.

Shakespeare Repertory (✉ 1016 N. Dearborn Pkwy., ☎ 312/642–2273) devotes its considerable talents to keeping the Bard's flame alive in the Chicago area. In the fall of 1999, the company plans to move into a new facility on Navy Pier, with an English-style garden.

Steppenwolf Theatre Company (✉ 1650 N. Halsted St., ☎ 312/335–1650), with a national reputation, brings a dark, brooding, Method-acting style to its consistently successful productions. Illustrious alumni include John Malkovich, Gary Sinise, Joan Allen, and Laurie Metcalf.

Theatre School, DePaul University (✉ 60 E. Balbo Dr., ☎ 312/922–1999), with performances in the grand and ornate Merle Reskin Theatre, produces a series of plays for adult audiences as well as Chicago Playworks for Families and Young Audiences.

Victory Gardens (✉ 2257 N. Lincoln Ave., ☎ 773/871–3000), known for its workshops and Chicago premieres, stages works solely by local playwrights.

6 Outdoor Activities and Sports

Many of Chicago's outdoor pleasures are linked to the Lake Michigan shoreline, which hugs the east side of the city. In warm weather miles of beaches and paths beckon joggers, bikers, swimmers, sailors, and anyone who welcomes awesome city views along with exercise. Spectators can join Chicago's passionate fans for the classic experience of cheering the Cubs at Wrigley Field, the Sox, the Bears, or—if you're lucky—Michael Jordan and the beloved Bulls.

SOME THINK CHICAGO IS CALLED THE WINDY CITY largely because of its braggadocio. One thing natives can definitely boast about is the city's sports life. Chicago claims such sports legends as Michael Jordan and the NBA champion Bulls, as well as the perennially losing but beloved Cubs. In this town sports enthusiasts are often athletes, too, particularly if they like to play at the beach. Lake Michigan creates a summer haven for joggers, volleyball enthusiasts, swimmers, windsurfers, and sailors. However, to enjoy the outdoors, visit between May and October. The winter months are brutal, with cold gusts coming off the lake—the real reason Chicago is called the Windy City.

Updated by Stuart Courtney

Beaches

Chicago has about 20 mi of lakefront, most of it sand or rock beach. Beaches are open to the public daily from 9 AM to 9:30 PM, Memorial Day–Labor Day, and many beaches have changing facilities. The **Chicago Park District** (☎ 312/747–0832) provides lifeguard protection during daylight hours throughout the swimming season. The water is too cold for swimming at other times of the year.

Along the lakefront you'll see plenty of broken-rock breakwaters with signs that warn NO SWIMMING OR DIVING. Although natives frequently ignore these signs, you should heed them: The boulders below the water are slippery with seaweed and may hide sharp, rusty scraps of metal, and the water beyond is very deep. It can be dangerous even if you know the territory.

All references to North and South in beach listings refer to how far north or south of the Loop each beach is. In other words, 1600–2400 North means the beach begins 16 blocks north of the Loop (or Madison Street, which is the 100 block) and extends for eight blocks.

North Avenue Beach (⊠ 1600–2400 North) is heavily used; the crowd tends to be more family oriented than at Oak Street Beach. There are bathrooms, changing facilities, and showers. The south end of this beach has plenty of lively volleyball action in summer and fall.

Oak Street Beach (⊠ 600–1600 North) probably rates as Chicago's most popular, particularly in the 1000 North block, where the shoreline curves. You can expect it to be mobbed with trendy singles and people-watchers on any warm day in summer. There are bathrooms, but for official changing facilities you'll have to make the walk to the North Avenue Beach bathhouse, which is 1600 North. The concrete breakwater that makes up the southern part of Oak Street Beach is a busy promenade on hot summer nights. You can walk along the water all the way to Grand Avenue (about ¾ mi from Oak Street), where you'll find both Navy Pier and Olive Park.

South Shore Country Club Beach (⊠ 7100 South), one of the newest and nicest beaches, stands out for being quite pretty and not over-crowded. There are bathrooms, changing facilities, and showers. Enter through the South Shore Country Club grounds at 71st Street and South Shore Drive; you may see the police training their horses in the entry area.

The best of the other Chicago beaches (all of which have changing facilities) on Lake Shore Drive are as follows:

Foster Beach (⊠ 5200 North)

Jackson Beach, Central (⊠ 5700–5900 South)

Leone/Loyola Beach (⊠ 6700–7800 North)

Montrose Beach (⊠ 4400 North)

Osterman Beach (⊠ 5800 North)

31st Street Beach (⊠ 3100 South)

12th Street Beach (⊠ 1200 South at 900 E., south of Adler Planetarium)

Participant Sports and Fitness

Bicycling

There are many scenic routes along the lake, downtown, and in greater Chicago. For information contact the **Chicagoland Bicycle Federation** (⊠ 417 S. Dearborn St., ☎ 312/427–3325).

Chicago's **lakefront bicycle path** extends about 20 mi, with awesome views of the lake and the skyline. The panorama of the harbor, created with landfill a number of years ago when Lake Shore Drive's notorious S-curve between Monroe Street and Wacker Drive was straightened, is lovely. Be careful: A few blocks to the north, Grand Avenue is one of a few places along the route where the path crosses a city street (two others are parallel to Lake Shore Drive in the downtown area).

In Lincoln Park, you can rent a bike for the day or by the hour from the **Bike Stop** (⊠ 1034 W. Belmont Ave., ☎ 773/868–6800) and **On the Route** (⊠ 3167 N. Lincoln Ave., ☎ 773/477–5066).

Bike Chicago (☎ 312/944–2337 or 800/915–2453)—with locations at Oak Street Beach, Lincoln Park Zoo, Buckingham Fountain, and Navy Pier—will deliver a bike to your hotel. It runs a free two-hour lakefront tour daily, weather permitting.

Boating

The lakefront harbors are packed with boats, but if you're not familiar with Great Lakes sailing, it's best to leave the navigating to an experienced skipper. Sailboat lessons and rentals are available from the **Chicago Sailing Club** (⊠ Belmont Harbor, ☎ 773/871–7245) or **Sailboats Inc.** (⊠ Monroe Harbor, ☎ 800/826–7010). For a more placid water outing, try the paddleboats at **Lincoln Park Lagoon** (⊠ 2021 N. Stockton Dr., ☎ 312/742–2038), just north of Farm in the Zoo.

Fishing

Plenty of folks stand ready to charter boats if you're interested in fishing for coho or chinook salmon, trout, or perch. Call the **Chicago Sportfishing Association** (⊠ Burnham Harbor, ☎ 312/922–1100). If you want to skip the boat and do your fishing from the shore, **Henry's Sport and Bait,** near Burnham Harbor and McCormick Place (⊠ 3130 S. Canal, ☎ 312/225–8538), and **Park Bait** (⊠ Montrose Harbor, ☎ 312/271–2838) will set you up with a rod and reel and tell you where they're bitin'.

Golf

The **Chicago Park District** (☎ 312/245–0909) maintains six golf courses—five with 9 holes and one (Jackson Park) with 18—as well as two driving ranges, one in Jackson Park and one at Lake Shore Drive and Diversey Avenue (where there are heated stalls and an 18-hole miniature golf course). The Jackson Park facility is a couple of blocks east of Stony Island Avenue at 63rd Street.

Chicago Family Golf Centers (⊠ 221 N. Columbus Dr., ☎ 312/616–1234), in the heart of the business and hotel district, is a 9-hole, par-

3 course with lots of angled greens. The course, open year-round, costs $12 for 9 holes Monday–Thursday and $15 for 9 holes Friday–Sunday. For 18 holes, it's $18 Monday–Thursday and $22 Friday–Sunday.

Suburban Chicago has more than 125 public golf courses with greens fees ranging from $10 to nearly $100. Most accept reservations up to a week in advance; some require a credit card deposit. The following are a few of the more highly rated ones. **Cantigny** (✉ 27 W. 270 Mack Rd., Wheaton, ☎ 630/668–8463) has mature trees on each of the 27 holes. **Cog Hill Golf and Country Club** (✉ 12294 Archer Ave., Lemont, ☎ 630/257–5872), with four 18-hole courses, hosts the PGA tour's Western Open in early July. **Kemper Lakes** (✉ Old McHenry Rd., Long Grove, ☎ 847/320–3450) is one of the region's most expensive courses ($115 with mandatory cart rental included) and is the only local public course to have hosted a major PGA championship. **Village Links of Glen Ellyn** (✉ 485 Winchell Way, Glen Ellyn, ☎ 630/469–8180) has 27 holes and a driving range.

Health Clubs

Some Chicago health clubs have agreements with hotels that give guests access to their facilities; check with your hotel. One of the finest is the **Athletic Club Illinois Center** (✉ 211 N. Stetson Ave., ☎ 312/616–9000). For a daily rate of $18, hotel guests may use an eight-lane lap pool, a full-court gym, an indoor running track, weight training, and a seven-story indoor rock-climbing wall. At the downtown location of the **Lakeshore Athletic Club** (✉ 441 N. Wabash Ave., ☎ 312/644–4880), area hotel guests pay a daily rate of $15 (not including court time) to use a quarter-mile track, free and fixed weights, aerobic equipment, and a swimming pool. **Hoops the Gym** (✉ 1380 Randolph St., ☎ 312/850–4667) offers open basketball from 11:30 AM to 1:30 PM every Monday, Wednesday, and Friday for a $15 fee. The **Chicago Fitness Center** (✉ 3131 N. Lincoln Ave., ☎ 773/549–8181) has free and fixed weights and aerobic equipment for $7 a day. For a daily rate of $15, you can pump some serious iron at **River North Fitness** (✉ 820 N. Orleans St., ☎ 312/664–6537) or the **World Gym and Fitness Center** (✉ 100 S. Wacker Dr., ☎ 312/357–9753 downtown; ✉ Lincoln Park at 909 W. Montrose Ave., ☎ 773/348–1212).

Ice-Skating

In winter you can ice-skate at the **Daley Bicentennial Plaza** (✉ Randolph St. and Lake Shore Dr., ☎ 312/294–4790). A small fee is charged ($2 for adults, $1 for children 14 and under, no charge for senior citizens 65 and over), and skate rentals are available; the great views of the lake and the Loop are free.

There is free ice-skating (charge for rentals) in winter at **Skate on State** (☎ 312/744–3315), on State Street between Washington and Randolph streets. Skating lessons are free on Saturday morning 9–11.

In-Line Skating

In-line skating is a popular lakefront pastime. You can rent blades from **Londo Mondo** (✉ 1100 N. Dearborn St., ☎ 312/751–2794), **Windward Sports** (✉ 3317 N. Clark St., ☎ 773/472–6868), or **Bike Chicago** (☞ Bicycling, *above*). There's also a rental stand during peak times (roughly Memorial Day–Labor Day, and later if the weather's nice) near the North Avenue beach house, though hours there are unpredictable. On the lakefront path keep to the right and watch your back for bicyclists. Skating is also allowed on Daley Bicentennial Plaza. Wrist guards, helmets, and knee pads are a good idea wherever you skate.

Jogging

The 20-mi lakefront path accommodates joggers, bicyclists, and skaters, so you'll need to be attentive while you admire the views. You can pick up the path at Oak Street Beach (across from the Drake Hotel), at Grand Avenue underneath Lake Shore Drive, or by going through Grant Park on Monroe Street or Jackson Boulevard until you reach the lakefront.

On the lakefront path joggers should stay north of McCormick Place; muggers sometimes lurk in the comparatively empty stretch between the convention center and Hyde Park. Loop streets are a little spooky after dark and too crowded during the day for useful running. In the Near North joggers will want to stay east of Orleans Street.

Various groups also hold organized races. Call the **Chicago-Area Runners Association** (☎ 312/666–9836) for schedules.

Swimming

Lake Michigan provides wonderful swimming between Memorial Day and Labor Day, particularly toward the end of the summer, when the lake has warmed up (☞ Beaches, *above*). Indoor swimming facilities also are available (☞ Health Clubs, *above*).

Tennis

The Chicago Park District maintains hundreds of outdoor tennis courts, most of them free. The facility at the **Daley Bicentennial Plaza** (⊠ Randolph St. at Lake Shore Dr., ☎ 312/294–4790) is the closest to downtown and Near North hotels; the 12 lighted courts cost $5 an hour and must be reserved a day in advance beginning at 10 AM.

Spectator Sports

Chicago's determinedly loyal sports fans turn out regularly year after year to watch what have not been the winningest teams in professional sports (with the exception, of late, of the Chicago Bulls). The Cubs won two division championships in the 1980s, and the White Sox won one most recently in 1993, but it's been a while since either has captured a league title. And as baseball fans know, the city's beloved Cubs last won a World Series in 1908, the Sox in 1917.

Auto Racing

At press time, **Sportsman's Park** (⊠ 3301 S. Laramie Ave., Cicero, ☎ 708/652–2812), a 15,000-seat horse racing track, was being converted into a 67,000-seat dual-purpose facility that also will host auto racing, including a major Indy car race planned for Labor Day weekend.

Baseball

The **Chicago Cubs** (National League) play at **Wrigley Field** (⊠ 1060 W. Addison St., ☎ 773/404–2827); the baseball season begins the last week in March and ends the first weekend in October. From downtown the classic, ivy-covered ballpark is reached by the Howard Street El; take the B Train to Addison Street. Wrigley Field has had lights since 1988, when it became the last major-league ballpark in the nation to be lighted for night games. But the Cubs still play most of their home games during the day, and the bleachers are a great place to listen to Chicagoans taunt the visiting outfielders. The grandstand has a more sedate atmosphere but still plenty of local flavor. Most games start at 1:20 PM, but phone for exact starting times.

The **Chicago White Sox** (American League) play from April to October at **Comiskey Park** (⊠ 333 W. 35th St., ☎ 773/924–1000), a high-tech stadium built in 1991 to replace the old one. Games usually start at 7 PM. Take the A or B Dan Ryan El to 35th Street.

Basketball

The **Chicago Bulls** play at the new **United Center** (✉ 1901 W. Madison St., ☎ 312/455–4000); the National Basketball Association regular season extends from November through April, and games usually start at 7:30 PM. Single tickets have long been scarce—the Bulls have sold out every game for the last several seasons—but can be obtained for a price from any of a number of local ticket brokers listed in the phone book. Avoid leaving the game early or wandering around this neighborhood at night.

Football

The **Chicago Bears** play at **Soldier Field** (✉ 425 E. McFetridge Dr., ☎ 847/295–6600) from August (preseason) through December. Although subscription sales generally account for all tickets, you can purchase single-game seats from local ticket brokers listed in the phone book. To reach Soldier Field, take the Jeffrey Express Bus 6 to Roosevelt Road and Lake Shore Drive and follow the crowd. The stadium is just south of the Field Museum of Natural History.

The **Northwestern Wildcats** have enjoyed a college football resurgence; the long-downtrodden 'Cats earned berths in the 1996 Rose Bowl and the 1997 Citrus Bowl. Northwestern plays on Saturday afternoon in the fall at **Ryan Field** (✉ 1501 Central St., Evanston, ☎ 847/491–2287), and tickets are almost always available.

Hockey

The **Chicago Blackhawks,** of the National Hockey League, play games before their exuberant fans at the **United Center** (✉ 1901 W. Madison St., ☎ 312/455–7000) from October to April. Games usually start at 7:30 PM. It's best not to leave the game early or wander around the neighborhood at night.

The **Chicago Wolves** of the International Hockey League offer a high-quality and more affordable alternative to the Blackhawks; the Wolves play at the **Rosemont Horizon** (✉ 10550 Lunt Ave., Rosemont, ☎ 847/390–0404), with most games starting at 7 PM.

Horse Racing

The **Hawthorne Race Course** (✉ 3501 S. Laramie Ave., Stickney, ☎ 708/780–3700), just beyond the Chicago city limits, offers Thoroughbred and harness racing, as does neighboring **Sportsman's Park** (✉ 3301 S. Laramie Ave., Cicero, ☎ 708/652–2812). **Maywood Park** (✉ 8600 W. North Ave., Maywood, ☎ 708/343–4800) and **Balmoral Park** (✉ 26435 S. Dixie Hwy., Crete, ☎ 708/672–7544) offer harness racing and Thoroughbred simulcasts.

Soccer

The **Chicago Fire,** the city's latest entry on the professional soccer scene, plays the world's most popular sport March–September at **Soldier Field** (✉ 425 E. McFetridge Dr., ☎ 888/657–3473). The 1999 season will be the Fire's second of Major League Soccer competition.

7 Shopping

From grand old Marshall Field's on State Street to glittering stores along the Magnificent Mile, the Second City delivers plenty of first-class shopping. Look for discount jewelry and watches in the Loop, designer boutiques on Oak Street, and funky antiques on Lincoln Avenue. Character still counts in Chicago, too, and all around town are specialty shops offering personal service and goods that convey the city's uniqueness—whether you're looking for Frank Lloyd Wright reproductions or blues recordings.

A POTENT CONCENTRATION of famous retailers around Michigan Avenue and neighborhoods bursting with unique shops combine to make Chicago a shopper's nirvana. The one-of-a-kind experience on Michigan Avenue lures 250 charter busloads of avid shoppers per week during Christmas season. Where else can you find Neiman Marcus, Marshall Field's, Saks Fifth Avenue, Lord & Taylor, and Barneys New York within walking distance of each other? Shoppers averse to paying retail, however, won't have to venture far to unearth bargains on everything from fine jewelry to business attire. The city is also home to singular stores renowned for their specialty, whether books on architecture, Prairie-style furniture, cowboy boots, or cookie jars.

To help you plan your shopping, the following pages survey Chicago's more popular shopping areas and list some specialty stores that sell certain kinds of goods. If you have no concrete goals, simply choose a major shopping district and browse to your heart's content. A shopping expedition can help you get a feeling for a particular city neighborhood, whether it's on or off the beaten path.

Be forewarned that an 8.75% state and county sales tax is added to all purchases except groceries and prescription drugs. Neighborhood shops on the North Side (including Bucktown), especially those catering to a young crowd, tend to open late—around 11 or noon. Most stores, particularly those on North Michigan Avenue and the North Side, are open on Sunday, although this varies by type of business; where applicable, more information is provided at the beginning of each area or category.

Three maps accompany this chapter: Downtown Shopping, Near North Shopping, and Lincoln Park Shopping. Most of the stores and malls mentioned appear on these maps; however, some shops and districts away from the city's three main shopping areas are not on the maps. All can be easily reached via car, taxi, or public transportation.

Blitz Tours

Antiques

Chicago tempts furniture buyers with a wide range of antiques, collectibles, and architectural artifacts at prices that generally beat those on either coast. Many shops are clustered in malls or neighborhoods. For a rundown on dealers, buy a copy of **Taylor's Guide to Antique Shops in Illinois and Southern Wisconsin,** which is available in some bookstores and many antiques shops (to order, call ☎ 847/392–8438). Many of the antiques districts also publish free pamphlets that list dealers in the neighborhood; look for them in the shops.

Assuming your interest runs more toward 20th-century collectibles than Biedermeier, take a No. 11 Lincoln Avenue bus or a taxi to the **Chicago Antique Centre** (⊠ 3045 N. Lincoln Ave.) to browse through the wares of its 30 dealers. From there, it's a short walk to the **Lincoln Antique Mall** (⊠ 3141 N. Lincoln Ave.), which is a treasure trove for everything from kitchenwares to furniture, mostly post-1920. Keep your eyes open for other antiques and vintage clothing shops along this stretch. Take a taxi over to the Belmont Avenue antiques area: Start with the **Belmont Antique Mall** (⊠ 2039 W. Belmont) and **Phil's Factory Antique Mall** (⊠ 2040 W. Belmont), where you may have to dig a bit harder for your finds but you'll be rewarded with lower prices than in other areas of the city. Head west to hit **Danger City** (⊠ 2129 W. Belmont), which stocks great barware and other reminders of swank living from the '50s, '60s, and '70s. If you're up for more, continue west to the **Belmont Antique Mall West** (✉ 2229 W. Belmont). Take a taxi to the **Wrigleyville Antique Mall** (✉ 6130 N. Broadway), where the displays of Heywood-Wakefield furniture, vintage jewelry, and kitchen collectibles rarely fail to entice. From there, it's an easy walk to Belmont Avenue to take the Howard or Ravenswood El downtown. To catch the maximum number of open dealers, it's best to tackle this route after brunch on a weekend or on a Thursday or Friday.

Art

The contemporary art scene is thriving in Chicago, particularly in the **River North** area. More than 60 galleries are clustered within a one-block radius of the intersection of Superior and Franklin streets; most are open Tuesday through Saturday. A few renowned galleries are on Michigan Avenue, some above street level. Emerging artists call **Wicker Park** and **Bucktown** home; gallery hours there tend to fluctuate. For more information on exhibits and specific dealers, pick up a free copy of *Chicago Gallery News,* available at visitor information centers and galleries. Openings are scheduled on Friday evenings and don't require an invitation. The first Friday after Labor Day is the biggest night of the year, marking the opening of the season.

To get an overview of the city's vibrant art scene, start with the classics on Michigan Avenue. **R. S. Johnson Fine Art** (✉ 645 N. Michigan Ave.) carries both old masters and 20th-century works worthy of many museums. The **Richard Gray Gallery** (✉ John Hancock Center, 25th floor, 875 N. Michigan) represents modern masters. From there, take a taxi to the intersection of Superior and Franklin streets in River North. Pick up a free copy of *Chicago Gallery News* at any gallery to steer you to exhibits of particular interest. Otherwise, wander around the neighboring blocks, where more than 60 galleries reside. **Douglas Dawson** (✉ 222 W. Huron St.) always has a captivating display of art and artifacts from other cultures. **Portia Gallery** (✉ 207 W. Superior St.) showcases glowing examples of contemporary glass. Photography buffs won't want to miss the **Catherine Edelman Gallery** (✉ 300 W. Superior St.). If you're a collector of art glass, stop by **Fly-by-Nite Gallery** (✉ 714 N. Wells St.) to admire early 20th-century work.

Discount Jewelry and Watches

Chicago is a regional powerhouse in the wholesale jewelry business, and the blocks surrounding the intersection of Wabash Avenue and Madison Street in the Loop are designated as Jewelers Row. Five high-rises cater to the wholesale trade, but many showrooms sell to the public at prices 25%–50% below retail. The **Jeweler's Center at the Mallers Building** (✉ 5 S. Wabash Ave.) publishes a directory of its tenants and welcomes the public on the first 13 floors of its Art Deco building. There's even a deli on the third floor. The following are a few well-regarded jewelers in the district: **Harold Burland & Son** (✉ 5 S. Wabash Ave.), **Irving Cohn Jewelers** (✉ 5 S. Wabash Ave.), **Marshall Pierce & Co.** (✉ 29 E. Madison St.). Wholesale jewelers operate from 10 to 5 weekdays. Some are open until 1 PM on Saturdays; call to check hours.

The Magnificent Mile

A visit to Chicago wouldn't be complete without a tour of the world-class stores on North Michigan Avenue; several stores rate as must-see attractions, either for their design, merchandise, or sheer fun. Start on the east side of the avenue at the Chicago River and continue up to Oak Street. The don't-miss stops include **NikeTown** (669 N.), **Neiman Marcus** (737 N.), **Water Tower Place** (835 N.), and **Gucci** (900 N.). Turn left on Oak Street, where you'll want to check out the shoes at **Stephane Kélian** (121 E.), the designer clothing at **Ultimo** (114 E.), the home accoutrements and fashion accessories at **Elements** (102 E.), the menswear at **Sulka** (55 E.), the minimalist styles at **Jil Sander** (48 E.), and the cosmetics department and Chelsea Passage gift area at **Barneys New York** (25 E.). Take a left on Rush Street for a look at **Urban Outfitters** (935 N. Rush St.), and another left on Walton to pick up some chic French basics at **agnès b.** (46 E. Walton St.) and to pop into new home furnishings stores such as **Ligne Roset** (56 E. Walton St.) and **The Morson Collection** (100 E. Walton St.). Just before reaching Michigan Avenue, you can duck into **Bloomingdale's** and the other stores inside the **900 N. Michigan Shops.**

Bucktown and Wicker Park

Once artists and musicians claimed this run-down area near the intersection of North, Damen, and Milwaukee avenues, the trendy coffeehouses, nightclubs, and restaurants followed. The shopping has only recently caught up with the neighborhood. Clothing boutiques, art galleries, alternative music stores and antiques shops all have an individualistic point of view. The neighborhood is very youth-oriented and still gritty, so it's not for everyone. Many stores don't open until at least 11 AM, some shops are closed on Monday and Tuesday, and hours can be erratic. Spend a late afternoon shopping before settling in for dinner at one of the neighborhood's popular restaurants. To get here from downtown on the El, take the Blue line toward O'Hare and exit at Damen Avenue.

Antiques and Collectibles

abn (✉ 1472 N. Milwaukee Ave., ☎ 773/276–2525) stands for the identical initials of the two sisters who own the shop. There's a feeling that you've stepped into a bygone era, with an emphasis on quirky items that manage to be both industrial and rustic. The selection may range from typewriter keys to Adirondack chairs. A smattering of new merchandise made by artists adds to the eclectic mix. It's closed Monday and Tuesday.

Green Acres (✉ 1464 N. Milwaukee Ave., ☎ 773/292–1998) entices shoppers with its well-priced, well-chosen selection of Victorian, Empire, and Federal furniture.

Modern Times (✉ 1538 N. Milwaukee Ave., ☎ 773/772–8871) celebrates the home furnishings of this century, particularly the 1940s, '50s, and '60s.

Clothing
WOMEN'S

Pentimento (✉ 1629 N. Milwaukee Ave., ☎ 773/227–0576) takes a romantic view of clothing, hats, and accessories and represents many local designers.

Phoebe 45 (✉ 1643 N. Damen Ave., ☎ 773/862–4523) stocks the latest trends from a cadre of up-and-coming designers in a funky salon setting.

Gifts

Eclectic Junction for Art (✉ 1630 N. Damen Ave., ☎ 773/342–7865) showcases functional art from drawer pulls to toilet seats that expresses an irrepressible joie de vivre.

Clybourn Corridor

Once a run-down industrial area, the Clybourn Corridor now bustles with chain superstores, strip shopping centers, and small boutiques. Most shops are on Clybourn Avenue between North Avenue (1600 N.)

and Fullerton Avenue (2400 N.). Because this area is so spread out, it's best explored by car.

Kitchenware, Tabletops, and Home Furnishings

Crate & Barrel (⊠ 850 W. North Ave., ☎ 312/573–9800) opened a three-floor megastore for both housewares and furniture in 1998.

Ethnic Enclaves

Chicago is famed for its ethnic neighborhoods, which give visitors the chance to shop the globe without actually leaving the city. **Chinatown** has a dozen or so shops along four blocks of Wentworth Avenue south of Cermak Road. The Far Eastern imports range from jade to ginseng root to junk. In the **North Side Lincoln Square neighborhood,** a stretch of Lincoln Avenue between Leland and Lawrence avenues, are German delis and stores that sell imported toys and European-made health and beauty products. Many non-U.S. visitors make the trek to a cluster of dingy but well-stocked electronics stores in an **Indian neighborhood** on the city's far North Side (⊠ Devon Ave. between Western and Washtenaw Aves.) to buy electronic appliances that run on 220-volt currency. Because the United States has no value-added tax—as of yet—it's often cheaper for international visitors to buy here than at home. The same stretch of Devon Avenue is a great source for spectacularly rich sari fabrics. For more information about this area, *see* the Devon Avenue Close-Up *in* Chapter 2.

Lake View

Lake View is a diverse neighborhood just north of Lincoln Park, where the most famous draw is Wrigley Field, the home of the Cubs. The diversity of the area has spawned a number of worthwhile shopping strips. **Clark Street** between Diversey Avenue (2800 N.) and Addison Street (3600 N.) has myriad clothing boutiques and specialty stores. Farther north on **Halsted Street** between Belmont Avenue (3200 N.) and Addison Street (3600 N.) are more gift shops and boutiques—several with a gay orientation—as well as a smattering of vintage clothing and antiques stores. In West Lake View, distinctive boutiques have sprung up on **Southport Avenue** between Belmont Avenue (3200 N.) and Grace St. (3800 N.). **Broadway** between Diversey Avenue and Addison Street also claims its share of intriguing shops. The **Century Mall,** in a former movie palace at Clark Street, Broadway, and Diversey Parkway, houses a variety of stores catering to a young and trendy crowd. To reach this neighborhood from downtown, take Clark Street Bus 22 at Dearborn Street or Broadway Bus 36 at State Street heading north. Or, take the Howard or Ravenswood El north to the Belmont stop from downtown, which will drop you into the heart of Lake View.

Antiques and Collectibles

BELMONT AVENUE

Fans of Art Deco, kitchen collectibles, and bar memorabilia can poke into the shops and malls lining Belmont Avenue starting a bit west of Ashland Avenue (1600 W.) and running to Western Avenue (2400 W.). You may have to scrounge around more to unearth treasures in these stores, but you'll be rewarded with some of the lowest prices in the city. The shops are usually open weekends but may be closed on one or more weekdays. Call before making a special trip.

Danger City (⊠ 2129 W. Belmont Ave., ☎ 773/871–1420) can be counted on for fun and funky remnants of the mid-20th century. The **Good Old Days** (⊠ 2138 W. Belmont Ave., ☎ 773/472–8837) carries a wide selection of vintage radios along with bar and sports memorabilia. **Father Time Antiques** (✉ 2108 W. Belmont Ave., ☎ 773/880–5599) specializes in fully restored vintage timepieces. Chicago's unpredictable weather and the erratic hours of many antiques stores make the Belmont malls particularly attractive. **Belmont Antique Mall** (✉ 2039 W. Belmont Ave., ☎ 773/549–9270) begs to be browsed. The stalls in its rambling rooms represent about 40 dealers and contain an entertaining selection of furniture and housewares from the Civil War era to the 1950s. **Belmont Antique Mall West** (✉ 2229 W. Belmont Ave., ☎ 773/871–3915) houses the wares of 20 dealers and sells patio and garden furnishings as well as collectibles better suited to the indoors. Both antiques malls are open 11–6 seven days a week.

Wrigleyville Antique Mall (✉ 6130 N. Broadway, ☎ 773/868–0285) showcases 55 dealers on two levels, with an emphasis on 20th-century collectibles and furnishings. Heywood-Wakefield furniture, '50s dinette sets, costume jewelry, kitchenwares, and Czech pottery are charmingly displayed for maximum effect.

LINCOLN AVENUE

A 1½-mi stretch of Lincoln Avenue, is noted for its funky antiques, collectibles, and vintage clothing. The shops start around the intersection of Lincoln Avenue and Diversey Parkway (2800 N.) and continue until Irving Park Road (4000 N.). A car or Lincoln Avenue Bus 11 is the best way to navigate this area. To pick up the bus from downtown, take the Howard (Red line) or Ravenswood (Brown line) El to the Fullerton stop, and after exiting the El station, walk one-half block east to the intersection of Fullerton and Lincoln. Most of these shops are open weekends but may be closed early in the week.

The **Chicago Antique Centre** (✉ 3045 N. Lincoln Ave., ☎ 773/929–0200) has 30 dealers.

Jazz'e Junque (✉ 3831 N. Lincoln Ave., ☎ 773/472–1500) stocks 1,500 cookie jars, both new and vintage, and other kitchen collectibles.

Lincoln Antique Mall (✉ 3141 N. Lincoln Ave., ☎ 773/244–1440) is filled with dozens of dealers carrying trendy treasures, mostly post-1920.

Books

The Stars Our Destination (✉ 1021 W. Belmont Ave., ☎ 773/871–2722) attracts science fiction, horror, and fantasy book fans. It's also a source for periodicals, videos, and related merchandise. In the back are shelves of used books.

Clothing
WOMEN'S

Hubba-Hubba (✉ 3338 N. Clark St., ☎ 773/477–1414) splits its mix between well-chosen vintage clothing and new clothing with a retro flavor. Jewelry and accessories convey the same period mood.

VINTAGE

Flashy Trash (✉ 3524 N. Halsted St., ☎ 773/327–6900) fills its store with men's and women's vintage clothing and accessories in beautiful condition. The prices attract prom goers as well as more mature buyers. The front is stocked with new clothes on the supertrendy side.

Silver Moon (✉ 3337 N. Halsted St., ☎ 773/883–0222) showcases fine vintage clothing and accessories for men and women. Vintage wedding gowns are a specialty.

Kitchenware, Tabletop, and Home Furnishings

P.O.S.H. (✉ 3729 N. Southport Ave., ☎ 773/529–7674) piles never-used, vintage hotel and restaurant china in such charming displays that you'll find it all hard to resist. There's also an impressive selection of silver gravy boats, creamers, and flatware that bear the marks of ocean liners and private clubs.

Music

Reckless Records (⊠ 3157 N. Broadway, ☎ 773/404–5080) ranks as one of the city's leading alternative and secondhand record stores.

Special Stops

Aiko's Art Materials (⊠ 3347 N. Clark St., ☎ 773/404–5600) attracts the creatively inclined for its hundreds of stenciled, marbled, textured, and tie-dyed papers—most from Japan. It's closed Sunday and Monday.

Sporting Goods

Windward Sports (⊠ 3317 N. Clark St., ☎ 773/472–6868) specializes in equipment and clothing for skateboarding, in-line skating, snowboarding, and windsurfing and serves as a central gathering place for the young and trendy devotees of these sports. Check out the skateboarding ramp in the basement. It's closed Tuesdays.

Lincoln Park

The upscale residential neighborhood of Lincoln Park entices with its mix of distinctive boutiques, where each store has a highly personal point of view. **Armitage Avenue** between Halsted Street (800 W.) and Kenmore Avenue (1050 W.) is one of the city's best shopping areas for browsing through boutiques filled with clothing, tablewares, jewelry, and gifts. There are also worthwhile stops on Halsted and on Webster Avenue. The area is easily reached by taking the Ravenswood El to the Armitage stop.

Books

Barnes & Noble has two large stores (⊠ 659 W. Diversey, ☎ 773/871–9004; ⊠ 1441 W. Webster Ave., ☎ 773/871–3610) in Lincoln Park and ten other stores throughout the Chicago area.

Clothing

WOMEN'S

Art Effect (⊠ 651 W. Armitage Ave., ☎ 312/664–0997) can be counted on for relaxed clothing with a creative spin and well-designed accessories and tabletop accents. Several local designers are represented.

Cynthia Rowley (⊠ 808 W. Armitage Ave., ☎ 773/528–6160), a Chicago-area native, stocks her Lincoln Park store with the exuberant, well-priced dresses and separates that have made her so popular. The store also carries her shoes. Rowley decorated the hip Hotel Allegro Chicago (☞ Chapter 4), which opened in 1998.

Jane Hamill (⊠ 1115 W. Armitage Ave., ☎ 773/665–1102) sells her own interpretations of the season's top silhouettes at reasonable prices. This is a great source for sophisticated bridesmaid's dresses.

Zone (⊠ 2150 N. Seminary St., ☎ 773/472–4007), the tiniest of shops tucked just off of Webster, features original designs by local Pamela Vanderelinde. She favors simple silhouettes that make use of unusual fabrics, contrast linings, and vintage buttons. Expect to spend $500 on a suit. It's closed Monday and Tuesday.

Kitchenware, Tabletop, and Home Furnishings

Motif (⊠ 1101 W. Webster Ave., ☎ 312/880–9900) delights the senses with its up-to-the-minute selection of tabletop accessories, accent lights, candles, jewelry, and baby clothes. The style is slightly whimsical but avoids cute. It's closed Monday and Tuesday.

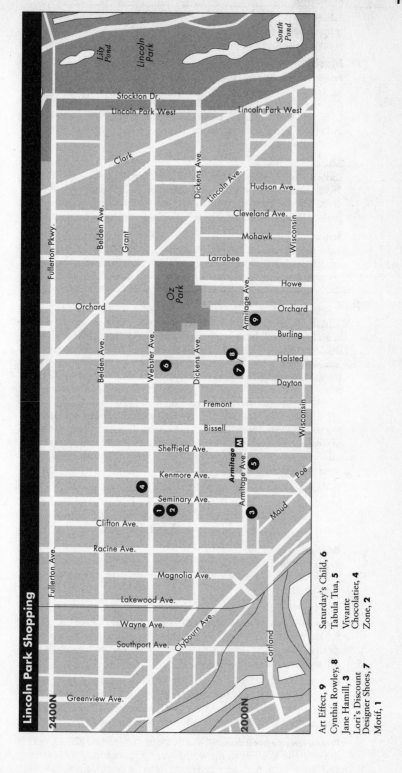

Lincoln Park Shopping

2400N

2000N

Art Effect, **9**
Cynthia Rowley, **8**
Jane Hamill, **3**
Lori's Discount
Designer Shoes, **7**
Motif, **1**

Saturday's Child, **6**
Tabula Tua, **5**
Vivante
Chocolatier, **4**
Zone, **2**

Tabula Tua (✉ 1015 W. Armitage Ave., ☎ 773/525–3500) stays away from standard formal china. Instead, the emphasis is on colorful, contemporary dishes and tabletop accessories.

Music
Tower Records/Videos/Books (✉ 2301 N. Clark St., ☎ 773/477–5994; ✉ 214 S. Wabash Ave., ☎ 312/987–9044), with 150,000 music titles, is a surefire way to torpedo a vacation budget. The selection of Latin and world music is particularly strong. The North Clark store, in Lincoln Park, is the nicer than the one in the Loop and stays open until midnight.

Shoes
Lori's Discount Designer Shoes (✉ 824 W. Armitage Ave., ☎ 773/281–5655), a self-service store in a popular Lincoln Park shopping area, undercuts department-store prices with its women's designer shoes from Joan & David and others. The selection of bridal footwear is excellent.

Toys
Saturday's Child (✉ 2146 N. Halsted St., ☎ 773/525–8697) feels like an old-fashioned toy store, but one that emphasizes educational and creative toys.

The Loop

This area—named for the elevated train track that encircles it—is the heart of Chicago's business and financial district. Two of the city's major department stores, Marshall Field's and Carson Pirie Scott, anchor State Street, which is striving to regain the stature it had in the days when it was immortalized as "State Street, that great street." After being closed to automobile traffic since 1979, the key shopping stretch was reopened to vehicles in late 1996 and spruced up with 1920s-style lampposts and granite planters. New stores, including a major branch of Old Navy, are starting to move in. LaSalle Street, with its proximity to the Board of Trade, has several fine men's clothiers. Not all Loop stores maintain street-level visibility: Several gems are tucked away on upper floors of office buildings.

Department stores and major chains are generally open on Sunday. Smaller stores are likely to be closed on Sunday and keep limited Saturday hours. Loop workers tend to start their day early, so many stores keep pace by opening by 8:30 and closing at 5 or 6.

Books
Super Crown (✉ 105 S. Wabash Ave, ☎ 312/782–7667) aggressively discounts best-sellers and offers a broad selection of current fiction and nonfiction.

SPECIALTY

Afrocentric Bookstore (✉ Chicago Music Mart at DePaul Centre, 333 S. State St., ☎ 312/939–1956) carries a full range of books—from novels to religious titles—with a black orientation. The store regularly hosts prominent authors for signings.

Powell's (✉ 828 S. Wabash Ave., ☎ 312/341–0748; ✉ 2850 N. Lincoln Ave., ☎ 773/248–1444; ✉ 1501 E. 57th St., ☎ 773/955–7780) carries used books and remainders with an intellectual bent. Marxism, the occult, and philosophy all have their own section.

Prairie Avenue Bookshop (✉ 418 S. Wabash Ave., ☎ 312/922–8311) draws architecture buffs the world over for its nearly 7,000 new, rare, and out-of-print titles on architecture, interior design, and urban planning. Massive conference tables in the Prairie-style interior give browsers room to spread out.

Downtown Shopping

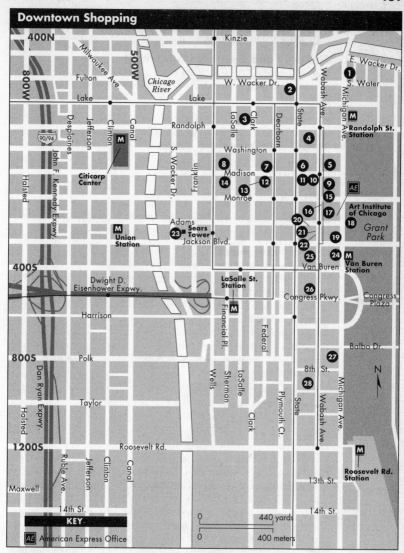

Savvy Traveller (⊠ 310 S. Michigan Ave., ☎ 312/913–9800) stocks an impressive selection of travel books, maps, luggage, and videos, along with gadgets that can improve the quality of life on the road.

Cameras and Electronic Equipment

Central Camera (⊠ 230 S. Wabash Ave., ☎ 312/427–5580) is stocked to the rafters with cameras and darkroom equipment at competitive prices. The century-old store is a Loop institution.

Wolf Camera & Video ⊠ 66 E. Madison St., ☎ 312/346–2288; ⊠ 42 S. Clark St., ☎ 312/759–8030; ⊠ 100 W. Randolph St., ☎ 312/269–9984; ⊠ 145 S. Wabash Ave., ☎ 312/857–2313; and other locations) has an array of popular film and cameras and high-quality one-hour film processing.

Clothing

MEN'S

Syd Jerome (⊠ 2 N. LaSalle St., ☎ 312/346–0333) caters to Board of Trade types who prefer a more outspoken, European style.

Department Stores

Carson Pirie Scott (⊠ 1 S. State St., ☎ 312/641–7000), a longtime Chicago emporium, looks a bit tired, but renovations have improved the main floor. It carries a full range of clothing, housewares, accessories, and cosmetics, with an emphasis on moderately priced goods. Sports fans will find a strong selection of Chicago Bulls merchandise on the Wabash Avenue side of the main floor. The building, the work of famed Chicago architect Louis Sullivan, is worth visiting just to see the iron scrollwork on the northwest door at the corner of State and Madison streets.

Marshall Field's (⊠ 111 N. State St., ☎ 312/781–1000; ⊠ Water Tower Place, 835 N. Michigan Ave., ☎ 312/335–7700) in the Loop stands as a glorious reminder of how grand department stores used to be. Founder Marshall Field's motto was "Give the lady what she wants!" and for many years both ladies and gentlemen have been able to find everything from furs to personalized stationery on one of the store's nine levels. The basement level, called Down Under, contains a series of small boutiques that sell kitchenwares, luggage, books, gourmet food, wine, and Field's famous Frango mints, which many consider to be Chicago's greatest edible souvenirs. Make sure to see the Tiffany Dome—designed in 1907 by Louis Comfort Tiffany—visible from the fifth floor near women's lingerie. The glossy Water Tower (☞ Near North Shopping map) branch also stocks a fine selection of merchandise but lacks the old-world atmosphere.

Discount Jewelry and Watches

Harold Burland & Son (⊠ 5 S. Wabash Ave., ☎ 312/332–5176), a diamond specialist, makes educating shoppers about stones part of the selling process.

Irving Cohn Jewelers (⊠ 5 S. Wabash Ave., ☎ 312/236–3021) is the retail name for the wholesaler M. Y. Finkelman Co. The store carries gems of all kinds in classic settings, along with Italian gold, Breitling watches, and Mont Blanc pens.

Marshall Pierce & Co. (⊠ 29 E. Madison St., ☎ 312/372–2415) substantially discounts top-of-the-line watches, such as Audemars Piguet, Ebel, Movado, and Rado.

Factory Outlets and Off-Price Stores

Filene's Basement (✉ 1 N. State St., ☎ 312/553–1055; ✉ 830 N. Michigan Ave., ☎ 312/482–8918) can pay off for patient shoppers willing to flip through racks of clothing for a great find or two. The State Street branch probably has the best merchandise outside the Boston original. Women can do well at either the State Street or Michigan Avenue (☞ Near North Shopping map) location, but men will find a superior selection of designer names at State Street. Watch newspaper ads midweek for special shipments and such events as the bridal gown sale.

Gifts

Gallery 37 Store (✉ 1 W. Wacker Dr. (entrance on State St.), ☎ 312/251–0370) carries the work of student artists in the nonprofit Gallery 37 programs, and proceeds are pumped back into the organization. Selection varies greatly but may include everything from hand-painted bird baths to small ceramics, all at affordable prices. At press time, the store was scheduled to move to 70 E. Randolph St. in the fall of 1999, but call ahead to be certain.

Illinois Artisans Shop (✉ James R. Thompson Center, 100 W. Randolph St., ☎ 312/814–5321) culls the best work of craftspeople from around the state and sells their jewelry, ceramics, glass, and African-American dolls at very reasonable prices. It's closed on weekends.

Music

Carl Fischer (✉ 312 S. Wabash Ave., ☎ 312/427–6652; ✉ 333 S. State St., lower level, ☎ 312/427–6652 ext. 240), a venerable institution, carries the largest selection of piano, vocal, choral, and band sheet music in Chicago at its main store on Wabash Avenue.

Chicago Music Mart (✉ 333 S. State St., ☎ 312/362–6700) contains nearly a dozen stores devoted to all things musical—instruments, CDs, sheet music, and music-theme gifts and souvenirs. Stop by at lunchtime to rest your feet and hear a free concert.

Shoes

Altman's Men's Shoes and Boots (✉ 120 W. Monroe St., ☎ 312/332–0667) is usually packed with men trying on everything from Timberland and Tony Lama boots to Allen-Edmonds and Alden oxfords, all at a decent discount. Don't be deceived by the store's minuscule size—the stockrooms hold more than 10,000 pairs of men's shoes in sizes from 5 to 19 and in widths from AAAA to EEE.

Souvenirs

Accent Chicago (✉ Sears Tower, 233 S. Wacker Dr., ☎ 312/993–0499; ✉ Chicago Hilton & Towers, 720 S. Michigan Ave., ☎ 312/360–0115; ✉ 333 S. State St., ☎ 312/922–0242) is stocked with the requisite souvenirs and Chicago memorabilia.

Art Institute of Chicago's Museum Shop (✉ 111 S. Michigan Ave., at Adams St., ☎ 312/443–3535; ✉ 900 N. Michigan Ave., ☎ 312/482–8275) showcases museum reproductions in the form of jewelry, posters, and books, along with striking tabletop accents, decorative accessories, and toys.

Special Stops

Iwan Ries & Co. (✉ 19 S. Wabash Ave., 2nd floor, ☎ 312/372–1306) did not jump on the cigar bandwagon; the family-owned store has been around since 1857. Cigar smokers are welcome to light up in the smoking area, which also displays antique pipes. Almost 100 brands of cigars are in stock; so are 10,000 or so pipes, deluxe Elie Bleu humidors, and all manner of smoking accessories.

Michigan Avenue and Vicinity

Chicago's most glamorous shopping district stretches along Michigan Avenue from the Chicago River (400 N.) to Oak Street (1000 N.). Some of the most exclusive names in retailing line the street, and even such familiar mall stores as **Banana Republic** (✉ 744 N.)and the **Gap** (✉ 679 N.) make an extra effort on their Magnificent Mile branches.

The block of Oak Street between Michigan Avenue and Rush Street is Chicago's answer to Rodeo Drive and Worth Avenue. Here you'll find a slew of boutiques devoted to upscale clothing as well as fine jewelry, luxury linens, and stylish home accessories. "Chicago's Magnificent Mile Area Guide," a free brochure available at hotels and tourist information centers, includes maps indicating many of the key stores on Michigan Avenue and Oak Street.

Art Galleries

R. S. Johnson Fine Art (✉ 645 N. Michigan Ave., 2nd floor, entrance on Erie St., ☎ 312/943–1661) gives lessons in art education to connoisseurs as well as casual browsers. The family-run gallery sells old masters along with art by Pablo Picasso, Edgar Degas, and Fernand Léger to museums and private collectors.

Richard Gray Gallery (✉ John Hancock Center, 875 N. Michigan Ave., Suite 2503, ☎ 312/642–8877) doesn't offer much for the merely curious, but serious collectors flock here for fine modern masters.

Books

Borders (✉ 830 N. Michigan Ave., ☎ 312/573–0564) is a prominent bookstore on the Mag Mile that sells music, coffee, and snacks as well as discounted best-sellers.

SPECIALTY

Europa Books (✉ 832 N. State St., ☎ 312/335–9677) is the place to come for foreign-language books, newspapers, and magazines. This well-stocked bookstore carries French, Spanish, German, and Italian titles and is known for its selection of Latin-American literature.

Rand McNally Map & Travel Store (✉ 444 N. Michigan Ave., ☎ 312/ 321–1751) stocks a broad, if predictable, selection of travel books, maps, and travel accessories.

Cameras and Electronic Equipment

Sony Gallery (✉ 663 N. Michigan Ave., ☎ 312/943–3334) doesn't offer any deals but does provide plenty of high-tech diversion—visitors can sample the latest in electronics.

Wolf Camera & Video (✉ 750 N. Rush St., ☎ 312/943–5531) has an array of popular film and cameras and high-quality one-hour film processing.

Clothing

MEN'S

Bigsby & Kruthers (✉ 605 N. Michigan Ave., ☎ 312/397–0430; ✉ 1750 N. Clark St., ☎ 312/440–1750; ✉ 10 S. LaSalle St., ☎ 312/236– 6633; ✉ 835 N. Michigan Ave., ☎ 312/944–6955) wants men to like shopping for clothes—hence the cigar-smoking room at its 605 North Michigan flagship store. The focus is on business and casual clothing for well-to-do men who prefer an understated look. The flagship also carries a selection of women's attire.

Paul Stuart (✉ John Hancock Center, 875 N. Michigan Ave., ☎ 312/ 640–2650) sells top-quality traditional men's clothing for the boardroom and the golf course, and some women's clothing.

Near North Shopping

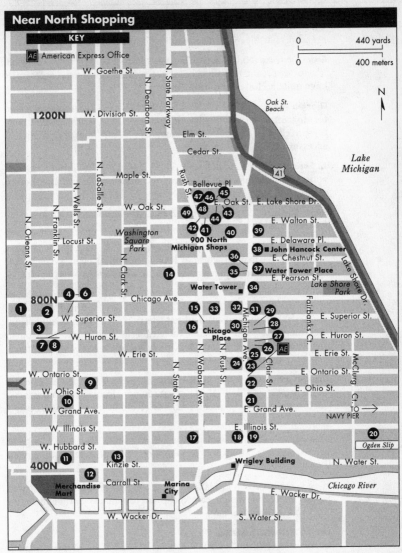

Abraham Lincoln Book Shop, **1**

Accent Chicago, **37**

agnès b., **41**

Antiquarians Building, **2**

Antiques Centre at Kinzie Square, **11**

Avventura, **37**

Barneys New York, **48**

Belvedere, **49**

Biba Bis, **16**

Bigsby & Kruthers, **22, 37**

Bloomingdale's, **40**

Borders, **35**

Carl Hammer Gallery, **4**

Catherine Edelman Gallery, **2**

Chiasso, **37**

Chiaroscuro, **30**

Chicago Place, **30**

Chicago Architecture Foundation, **38**

City of Chicago Store, **34**

Cole-Haan, **29**

Crate & Barrel, **24**

Douglas Dawson, **8**

Enzo, **28**

Europa Books, **14**

F.A.O. Schwarz, **35**

Filene's Basement, **36**

Fly-By-Nite Gallery, **6**

Gianni Versace, **43**

Giorgio Armani, **44**

G.R. N'Namdi Gallery, **7**

Gucci, **40**

Hammacher Schlemmer, **19**

Hino & Malee, **46**

Jazz Record Mart, **17**

Jil Sander, **47**

John Hancock Center, **38**

June Blaker, **4**

L'Appetito, **15, 38**

Lord & Taylor, **37**

Mark Shale, **39**

Marshall Field's, **37**

Michael FitzSimmons Decorative Arts, **3**

Michael Jordan Golf, **37**

Neiman Marcus, **31**

900 N. Michigan Shops, **40**

The North Face, **38**

North Pier, **20**

NikeTown, **27**

Paul Stuart, **38**

Polo/Ralph Lauren, **32**

Portia Gallery, **5**

R.S. Johnson Fine Art, **23**

Rand McNally Map & Travel Store, **18**

Richard Gray Gallery, **38**

Saks Fifth Avenue, **30**

Salvatore Ferragamo, **25**

Sawbridge Studios, **13**

Sony Gallery, **26**

Sotheby's Midwest, **10**

Sportmart, **9**

Timberland, **21**

Ultimo, **45**

Urban Outfitters, **42**

Water Tower Place, **37**

Wolf Camera & Video, **33**

MEN'S AND WOMEN'S

agnès b. (⊠ 46 E. Walton St., ☎ 312/642–7483) is a prime source of French basics for men and women who treasure their own style.

Gianni Versace (⊠ 101 E. Oak St., ☎ 312/337–1111) isn't for the timid. It's not surprising that these bold, overtly sexy clothes and accessories have quite a Hollywood following.

Giorgio Armani (⊠ 113 E. Oak St., ☎ 312/751–2224) makes a case for discreet luxury in this boutique devoted to the Italian designer's top-priced label (a cut above the department store line) of clothing and accessories.

Jil Sander (⊠ 48 E. Oak St., ☎ 312/335–0006) has captured the devotion of the fashion flock for her innovative styling and attention to quality tailoring. Prices are at the upper end of the designer range.

Mark Shale (⊠ 919 N. Michigan Ave., ☎ 312/440–0720) has three floors of conservative yet stylish attire geared to the corporate world.

Polo/Ralph Lauren (⊠ 750 N. Michigan Ave., ☎ 312/280–1655) pays homage to the genteel world of Ralph Lauren for men, women, children and the home, in a new 30,000-square-ft setting—his largest U.S. store.

Ultimo (⊠ 114 E. Oak St., ☎ 312/787–0906) has earned an international reputation for its well-edited selection of designer clothing from such names as John Galliano, Richard Tyler, and Zoran for women and Ermenegildo Zegna for men. Oprah Winfrey is just one of the store's many high-profile customers.

Urban Outfitters (⊠ 935 N. Rush St., ☎ 312/640–1919; ⊠ 2352 N. Clark St., ☎ 773/549–1711) carries funky clothing and accessories for the terminally hip, along with a selection of home accessories.

WOMEN'S

Biba Bis (⊠ 724 N. Wabash Ave., ☎ 312/988–9560) offers a good price-to-quality ratio for its contemporary private-label clothing with a fashion edge.

Hino & Malee (⊠ 50 E. Oak St., ☎ 312/664–7475) is a locally based husband-and-wife design team known for top-quality clothing with distinctive asymmetrical cuts.

Department Stores

Barneys New York (⊠ 25 E. Oak St., ☎ 312/587–1700) is a smaller, watered-down version of the Manhattan store known for austere men's and women's designer fashions. It's heavy on private-label merchandise, although Donna Karan and edgy European designers are represented. A full **Vera Wang** salon caters to brides and their wedding parties. An expansion in 1998 increased the size of the cosmetics department, the Chelsea Passage gift area, and the baby offerings, making it feel a bit more like the New York store.

Bloomingdale's (⊠ 900 N. Michigan Ave., ☎ 312/440–4460), built in a clean, airy style that is part Prairie School and part postmodern (and quite unlike its New York City sibling), gives you plenty of elbow room to sift through its selection of designer labels and check out its trendy housewares.

Lord & Taylor (⊠ Water Tower Place, 835 N. Michigan Ave., ☎ 312/787–7400) carries moderate to upscale clothing for men and women, plus shoes and accessories, frequently at sale prices.

Neiman Marcus (⊠ 737 N. Michigan Ave., ☎ 312/642–5900) may have high prices, but they're matched by the taste level at this first-class branch of the Dallas-based store. The selection of designer clothing and accessories for men and women is outstanding, and the gourmet food area on the top floor carries hard-to-find delicacies, fine chocolates, and impeccable hostess gifts.

Nordstrom (⊠ Oakbrook Center, Oak Brook, ☎ 630/571–2121; ⊠ Woodfield Mall, Schaumburg, ☎ 847/605–2121; ⊠ Old Orchard Mall, Skokie, ☎ 847/677–2121) doesn't plan to open a downtown branch until 2000, but the Seattle-based store's extraordinary service has quickly made it a local favorite.

Saks Fifth Avenue (⊠ 700 N. Michigan Ave., ☎ 312/944–6500), a smaller, less-crowded cousin of the original New York store, doesn't scrimp on its selection of designer clothes for men and women.

Food

L'Appetito (⊠ John Hancock Center, 875 N. Michigan Ave., lower level, ☎ 312/337–0691; ⊠ 30 E. Huron St., ☎ 312/787–9881) is the place to go for Italian specialty foods as well as pastries, gelato, and delicious *panini*.

Gifts

Chiasso (⊠ Water Tower Place, 835 N. Michigan Ave., ☎ 312/280–1249) focuses on high-style contemporary accessories for the home and office, with plenty that appeals to men.

Chiaroscuro (⊠ Chicago Place, 700 N. Michigan Ave., ☎ 312/988–9253) represents artists who create whimsical jewelry, home accessories, and furniture.

Hammacher Schlemmer (⊠ Tribune Tower, 445 N. Michigan Ave., ☎ 312/527–9100) beckons with upscale gadgets and unusual gifts—it even has an area where shoppers can try out some of the toys.

Kitchenware, Tabletops, and Home Furnishings

Belvedere (⊠ 948 N. Rush St., ☎ 312/664–4200) delightfully mixes the old and the new in porcelain, silver, crystal, and linens. Even if you can't afford the lofty prices, stop by to admire the table settings—and glean a few ideas.

Crate & Barrel (⊠ 646 N. Michigan Ave., ☎ 312/787–5900; ⊠ 850 W. North Ave., ☎ 312/573–9800) has its perpetually crowded flagship store on Michigan Avenue. The exterior is indeed shaped like a crate alongside a barrel. Inside are two floors of stylish and affordable cookware, glassware, and home accessories—plus two floors of pricey but tempting furniture. A second store similar in scope to the flagship opened at North and Clybourn to cater to locals who didn't want to battle Michigan Avenue congestion.

Malls

Aside from dozens of designer shops, Michigan Avenue has three vertical malls. **Water Tower Place** (⊠ 835 N.) is the most popular—shoppers spend more than $300 million a year here—and contains branches of **Marshall Field's** and **Lord & Taylor,** as well as seven floors of specialty stores. Many are standard mall stores, but there are quite a few more unusual shops, including **Michael Jordan Golf, Alfred Dunhill, Jacadi** children's wear, and **Rizzoli;** the Ritz-Carlton Hotel sits atop the entire complex. The slightly ritzier **900 North Michigan Shops** houses the Chicago branch of **Bloomingdale's,** along with dozens of smaller boutiques and specialty stores, such as **Gucci, J. Crew, Cashmere Cashmere,** and **Oilily.** The 900 building has a Four Seasons Hotel on top. The restaurants and movie theaters in both malls are a good option for entertainment during inclement weather. A third mall,

Chicago Place (✉ 700 N.), has **Saks Fifth Avenue,** the sleek furniture store **Room & Board,** and several boutiques carrying distinctive art for the table and home, including **Chiaroscuro, Tutti Italia,** and the **Real Nancy Drew.** You get all that and an airy food court with a fabulous view on the top floor.

Music

Jazz Record Mart (✉ 444 N. Wabash Ave., ☎ 312/222–1467) bills itself as the world's largest jazz record store. Its vast, in-depth selection of jazz and blues and knowledgeable sales staff make the store a must for music lovers. Stock includes used jazz vinyl records and a good representation of world music. Sometimes you can catch a live performance here on a Saturday afternoon.

Shoes

Michigan Avenue and Oak Street have many fine shoe stores at street level and in the malls.

Avventura (✉ Water Tower Place, 835 N. Michigan Ave., ☎ 312/337–3700) rates as a favorite stop for professional basketball players in need of European-style footwear. This men's shoe shop keeps sizes up to 16 in stock.

Cole-Haan (✉ 673 N. Michigan Ave., ☎ 312/642–8995) is renowned for its timeless, high-quality footwear for men and women.

Enzo (✉ 701 N. Michigan Ave., ☎ 312/642–4135) stocks the season's trends for women at reasonable prices.

Gucci (✉ 900 N. Michigan Ave., ☎ 312/664–5504) stays a step ahead of the fashion pack with its cutting-edge footwear and accessories, all at prices that aren't for the faint of heart.

Salvatore Ferragamo (✉ 645 N. Michigan Ave., ☎ 312/397–0464) proves that it offers a lot more than pumps with grosgrain bows. In recent seasons, the Italian company has aggressively updated its luxury-priced footwear, leather goods, and clothing for men and women.

Timberland (✉ 545 N. Michigan Ave., ☎ 312/494–0171) puts its best foot forward in this showcase store, a frequent stop for Europeans seeking U.S. prices on rugged footwear for men and women.

Souvenirs

Accent Chicago (✉ Water Tower Place, 835 N. Michigan Ave., ☎ 312/944–1354) is stocked with the requisite souvenirs and Chicago memorabilia.

Chicago Architecture Foundation (✉ 224 S. Michigan Ave., ☎ 312/922–3432; ✉ John Hancock Center, 875 N. Michigan Ave., ☎ 312/751–1380) displays stylish reminders of the Windy City and its architecture in the form of books, posters, T-shirts, toys, and ties.

City of Chicago Store (✉ Chicago Waterworks Visitor Information Center, 163 E. Pearson St., ☎ 312/742–8811) carries unusual souvenirs of the city—anything from a street sign to a brick from the old Comiskey Park. It's also a good source for guidebooks, posters, and T-shirts.

Sporting Goods

Michael Jordan Golf (✉ Water Tower Place, 835 N. Michigan Ave., ☎ 312/944–4545) sells golf apparel and equipment with a Jordan logo and shows videos of His Airness in action. The best sellers are sets of orange golf balls painted to look like basketballs bearing Number 23. If you miss this stop, there's an outpost at O'Hare Airport, in Terminal 1.

NikeTown (✉ 669 N. Michigan Ave., ☎ 312/642–6363) ranks as one of Chicago's top tourist attractions. Many visitors—including professional athletes—spend more than an hour here, taking in the sports memorabilia, road testing a pair of sneakers on the mini–basketball court, watching the inspirational videos, or staring at the fish behind the aquatic footwear display. Merchandise showcases the latest styles in athletic clothing and footwear for men, women, and children.

The **North Face** (✉ John Hancock Center, 875 N. Michigan Ave., ☎ 312/337–7200) can inspire even the most seasoned couch potato with its upscale outdoor sports equipment, clothing, and accessories.

Toys
F.A.O. Schwarz (✉ 840 N. Michigan Ave., ☎ 312/587–5000) is a fantasy toy emporium that's only a tad smaller than the chain's New York flagship.

Navy Pier

Extending more than a half mile onto Lake Michigan from 600 East Grand Avenue, Navy Pier treats visitors to spectacular views of the skyline (☞ Near North *in* Chapter 2). Stores and carts gear their merchandise to families and visitors and don't merit a special trip. But if you're out there, check out Illinois Market Place for souvenirs. Many stores are open late into the evening, especially in summer.

Souvenirs
Illinois Market Place (✉ Navy Pier, 700 E. Grand Ave., ☎ 312/832–0010), a joint venture between the city and state, showcases the products and artists of Illinois. The shop has gift merchandise from many museums, including items related to Abraham Lincoln, Frank Lloyd Wright, and Route 66.

North Pier

This development on the water (☞ Chapter 2), at 435 E. Illinois Street, attracts summer boating parties that dock at the slip. Virtual reality games and food make it an entertaining complex in which to stroll around, particularly for families and teenagers. Merchandise in the hodgepodge of shops tends to be touristy.

River North

Contained by the Chicago River on the south and west, Clark Street on the east, and Oak Street on the north, River North is home to art galleries, high-end antiques shops, home furnishings stores, and clothing boutiques. All have a distinctive style that fits in with this artsy area. It's also become a wildly popular entertainment district; you'll find theme restaurants such as Planet Hollywood, Michael Jordan's Restaurant, and Rainforest Café, all of which peddle logo merchandise as aggressively as burgers.

Antiques and Collectibles
For fine, high-end antiques, head to River North around the Merchandise Mart (☞ *below*). The **Antiques Centre at Kinzie Square** (✉ 220 W. Kinzie St., ☎ 312/464–1946) represents 18 dealers in fine furniture, porcelain, jewelry, and art. Near the Antiques Centre at Kinzie Square, the **Antiquarians Building** (✉ 159 W. Kinzie St., ☎ 312/527–0533) displays the wares of more than 20 dealers in Asian and European antiques, with some examples of modernism and Art Deco for good measure. From Kinzie Street wander north on Wells Street and explore the side streets around Huron and Superior streets for other shops. Look

for the free River North Antiques Dealers Association brochure to guide you. The dealers in this area tend to be closed on weekends.

Fly-By-Nite Gallery (✉ 714 N. Wells St., ☎ 312/664–8136) chooses decorative and functional art objects from 1890 to 1930 with a curatorial eye. It's particularly noted for European art glass and pottery.

Michael FitzSimmons Decorative Arts (✉ 311 W. Superior St., ☎ 312/787–0496) has a homelike environment for the eponymous owner's renowned collection of furniture and artifacts from the American Arts and Crafts movement. On display are works by Frank Lloyd Wright, Louis Sullivan, and Gustav Stickley, along with some quality reproductions.

Art Galleries
See the Art Blitz Tour at the beginning of this chapter.

Carl Hammer Gallery (✉ 200 W. Superior St., ☎ 312/266–8512) focuses on outsider and self-taught artists, such as Lee Godie and Mr. Imagination.

Catherine Edelman Gallery (✉ 300 W. Superior St., ☎ 312/266–2350) specializes in contemporary photography.

Douglas Dawson (✉ 222 W. Huron St., ☎ 312/751–1961) brings the spirit of ancient peoples to life with art, textiles, furniture, and urns from Africa, China, and Tibet.

G. R. N'Namdi Gallery (✉ 230 W. Huron St., ☎ 312/587–8262) represents contemporary painters and sculptors, with an emphasis on black and Latin American artists.

Portia Gallery (✉ 207 W. Superior St., ☎ 312/932–9500) draws collectors of contemporary art glass.

Auctions
Sotheby's Midwest (✉ 215 W. Ohio St., ☎ 312/670–0010), like its New York City counterpart, hosts civilized bidding four or five days a month. Call for a recording of upcoming auctions.

Books
Abraham Lincoln Book Shop (✉ 357 W. Chicago Ave., ☎ 312/944–3085) is a used-book store that draws Civil War buffs from all over. It specializes in Lincolniana, historical documents, and Civil War books.

Clothing
MEN'S AND WOMEN'S
June Blaker (✉ 200 W. Superior St., entrance on Wells St., ☎ 312/751–9220) has developed a loyal following, especially among gallery district types, for her avant-garde Japanese labels such as Comme des Garçons and Yohji Yamamoto.

Kitchenware, Tabletops, and Home Furnishings
Sawbridge Studios (✉ 406 N. Clark St., ☎ 312/828–0055) displays custom handcrafted furniture by about 20 U.S. artisans. Specialties include Frank Lloyd Wright reproductions and Shaker furniture. It's also a source for high-quality crafts.

Merchandise Mart
This massive marketplace between Wells and North Orleans streets just north of the Chicago River is notable for its Art Deco design but not for its shopping. Although much of the building is reserved for the design trade, the first two floors have been turned into retail. Stores are predominantly run-of-the-mill mall fare. Unlike the Michigan Avenue

malls, it is usually closed on Sunday, and stores keep relatively short Saturday hours.

Sporting Goods

Sportmart (✉ 620 N. LaSalle, ☎ 312/337–6151; ✉ 3134 N. Clark St., ☎ 773/871–8500; ✉ 6420 W. Fullerton, ☎ 773/804–0044) stocks more than 60,000 items for athletes and spectators at competitive prices, including plenty of team merchandise. Take a minute to compare handprints with famous athletes (all with a local connection) on the exterior and first floor of the LaSalle Street flagship.

Worth a Special Trip

Antiques and Collectibles

Salvage One (✉ 1524 S. Sangamon St., entrance on 16th St., ☎ 312/733–0098) draws home remodelers and restaurant designers from around the country to its 100,000-square-ft warehouse chock-full of stained lead glass, garden ornaments, fireplace mantles, hutches, bars, and other architectural artifacts. It's about 2 mi southwest of the Loop in an isolated area on the edge of the Pilsen neighborhood, so drive or take a taxi.

Apothecary

Merz Apothecary (✉ 4716 N. Lincoln Ave., ☎ 773/989–0900) conveys an old-world air with its homeopathic and herbal remedies. This store, in the Lincoln Square neighborhood about 6½ mi northwest of the Loop, also carries hard-to-find European toiletries. From downtown, take the Ravenswood El (Brown Line) north to the Western Avenue stop, and walk one block east to Lincoln. The shop is closed Sunday.

Books

Women & Children First (✉ 5233 N. Clark St., ☎ 773/769–9299) carries books for and about women. This feminist bookstore in the Andersonville neighborhood 6½ mi north of the Loop stocks fiction and nonfiction, periodicals, journals, and small-press publications. The children's section has a great selection of books, all politically correct. From downtown, take the Howard El (Red line) north to Addison, walk one-half block west to Clark Street, and transfer to a northbound No. 22 bus.

Cameras and Electronic Equipment

Helix Camera & Video (✉ 310 S. Racine Ave., ☎ 312/421–6000; ✉ 70 W. Madison St., ☎ 312/444–9373; ✉ 233 N. Michigan Ave., ☎ 312/565–5901) draws professional photographers to its eight-story warehouse on Racine Avenue just west of Greektown (1½ mi west of the Loop) to buy or rent camera and darkroom paraphernalia. A good selection of used equipment is available. Underwater photography is a specialty. Take a taxi or drive to the Racine Avenue location; the others are centrally located in the Loop.

Factory Outlets and Off-Price Stores

Gap Factory Outlet (✉ 2778 N. Milwaukee Ave., ☎ 773/252–0594) is worth a detour to the Logan Square neighborhood to net substantial savings on overruns and seconds on men's, women's, and children's clothing from the Gap, Banana Republic, and Old Navy. From downtown, it's a 3-mi ride northwest on the O'Hare El (Blue line) to the Logan Square stop.

Mark Shale Outlet (✉ 2593 N. Elston Ave., ☎ 773/772–9600) lowers the prices on unsold men's and women's clothing from Mark Shale stores by 30% to 70%. In a strip shopping center about 2¼ mi northwest of the Loop, this store stocks corporate and weekend clothing from the likes of Polo and Joseph Abboud. A car is necessary to navigate this area, which is just west of the Clybourn Corridor and full of strip shopping centers.

Western Wear

Alcala's Western Wear (⊠ 1733 W. Chicago Ave., ☎ 312/226–0152) stocks more than 10,000 pairs of cowboy boots—many in exotic skins—for men, women, and children. Located in Ukrainian Village about 2½ mi west of Michigan Avenue, it's a bit out of the way, but the amazing array of Stetson hats and rodeo gear makes this a must-see for cowboys, caballeros, and country-and-western dancers. It's best to drive or take a taxi to this area.

8 Side Trips

In Chicago's western suburbs, gracious villages that date from the 1800s mingle with more modest developments from the postwar housing boom. An essential stop is Oak Park, one of the most interesting neighborhoods of residential architecture in the United States. Brookfield has one of the country's foremost zoos. Farther west in DuPage County are a string of pleasant destinations, including Old Naper Settlement, the best living history museum in the Chicago area, and Cantigny, a lavish estate.

THE CHICAGO SUBURBS showcase some outstanding examples of American architecture as well as some appealing natural, historic, and human-made attractions. Frank Lloyd Wright lived in Oak Park, just west of the city, and had a great influence not only in that town but in many villages that hug Chicago's border. The homes, parks, and gardens north of the city—built by wealthy midwestern industrialists—are beautiful and can be a pleasant escape on a hot summer day or in the fall.

Updated by
Joanne Cleaver

Many of the varied sights on these side trips, which are all less than two hours from downtown, are popular destinations for area residents. Each trip has its pleasures, but visitors to a city like Chicago, already with so much to do within its borders, will most likely decide to go on a day trip only because of a special interest. Architecture and literary buffs may choose the North Shore or Oak Park, while fans of botanical gardens may head to the Chicago Botanic Garden in Glencoe. If you enjoy zoos, the Brookfield Zoo is a must-see; music lovers may plan an evening at the Ravinia Festival. Families will want to visit Blackberry Historical Farm or the Kohl Children's Museum. Most of the trips require a car—but there is train or bus service to individual sights that are worthwhile by themselves.

The eateries listed are either some of the best in the area or the most convenient for the destinations. For price-category information, *see* the dining chart *in* Chapter 3. Because side trips to the Chicago suburbs don't take more than an hour or two from downtown, no hotels are suggested.

THE WESTERN SUBURBS

In Chicago's western suburbs, gracious villages that date from the 1800s mingle with more modest developments from the postwar housing boom. An essential stop is Oak Park, one of the most interesting neighborhoods of residential architecture in the United States. Brookfield has one of the country's foremost zoos. Farther west in DuPage County are a string of pleasant destinations, including Old Naper Settlement, the best living history museum in the Chicago area, and Cantigny, the lavish estate of Chicago *Tribune* publisher Robert McCormick (a turn-of-the-century Chicago mogul), now a complex of public museums and gardens.

Numbers in the margin correspond to numbers on the Northeastern Illinois map.

Oak Park

★ ❶   *10 mi west of downtown Chicago.*

Founded in the 1850s just west of the city border, Oak Park is not only one of Chicago's oldest suburbs but also a living museum of American architectural trends and philosophies. It has the world's largest collection of buildings from the Prairie School, an architectural style created by resident Frank Lloyd Wright to reflect the expanses of the Great Plains. Here, among familiar clapboard and Colonial-style houses, are 25 houses designed or renovated by Wright and many others designed by architects who followed his views. Constructed from materials indigenous to the region, Prairie School houses hug the earth with their emphatic horizontal lines; inside, open spaces flow into each other rather than being divided into individual rooms (☞ "The Builders of Chicago" *in* Chapter 9).

Ernest Hemingway once called Oak Park—his birthplace and childhood home, from 1899 to 1917—a town of "broad lawns and narrow minds." The ethnic and political leanings of this village have diversified quite a bit since Hemingway played on its streets, due in part to the past decade's influx of young professionals fleeing the city with their children in search of safer streets, better public schools, and easy access to the Loop.

To get to the heart of Oak Park, take the Eisenhower Expressway (I–290) west to Harlem Avenue and exit to the left. Turn right at the top of the ramp, head north on Harlem Avenue to Chicago Avenue, turn right, and proceed to Forest Avenue. You can also take the Green Line of the El to the last stop, the Harlem Street exit, or the Chicago & North Western train to the Oak Park stop at Marion Street. Either way you'll get off at the south end of downtown Oak Park, just six blocks from the historic district. To get to the Frank Lloyd Wright Home and Studio from the El, take a left from the station exit to Harlem Street and a right onto Chicago Avenue. It's about a 25-minute walk.

The **Oak Park Visitors Center** sells tickets for area attractions, offers maps and guidance and has a gift shop. ⊠ *158 N. Forest Ave.,* ☏ *708/ 848–1500 or 888/625–7275.* ⊙ *Daily 10–5.*

A visit to the **Frank Lloyd Wright Home and Studio** provides a unique look into the architect's developing ideas over time as he remodeled this house. In 1889 the 22-year-old Wright began building his home, financed by a $5,000 loan from his then-employer and mentor, Louis Sullivan. The home combines elements of the 19th-century Shingle style with subtle innovations that stamp its originality. Over the next 20 years Wright expanded his business as well as his modest cottage, establishing his own firm in 1894 and adding a studio to his house in 1898.

In 1909 Wright spread his innovative designs across the United States and abroad (at this time he also left his wife and six children for the wife of a client). He sold his home and studio in 1925; they were subsequently turned into apartments that eventually fell into disrepair. In 1974 a group of local citizens calling itself the Frank Lloyd Wright Home and Studio Foundation, together with the National Trust for Historic Preservation, embarked on a 13-year, $2.2 million restoration that returned the building to its 1909 appearance.

Wright's home, made of brick and dark shingles, is filled with natural wood furnishings and earth-tone spaces. The architect's determination to create an integrated environment prompted him to design the furniture as well—though his apparent lack of regard for comfort is often the subject of commentary by visitors. In the lead windows are colored-glass art designs, and several rooms have skylights or other indirect lighting. A spacious barrel-vault playroom on the second floor is built to a child's scale. The adjacent studio is made up of four spaces—an office, a large reception room, an octagonal library, and an octagonal drafting room that uses a chain harness system rather than traditional beams to support its balcony, roof, and walls. Well-informed guides take small groups on tours throughout the day, pointing out various artifacts from the family's life and telling amusing stories of the rambunctious Wright clan.

The **Ginkgo Tree Bookshop** at the home and studio carries architecture-related books and gifts and has tour information (children under age 6 are not allowed on tours). Pick up a map (or on weekends, a guided tour) to guide you to other examples of Wright's work that are within easy walking or driving distance. Tour reservations are required for groups of 10 or more. ⊠ *951 Chicago Ave.,* ☏ *708/848–1976.* ⊟ *$8.*

🕐 *Tour weekdays at 11, 1, and 3 and continuously on weekends 11–3:30.*

You can stroll around Oak Park and look at a number of **Frank Lloyd Wright houses** and other spectacular examples of early 20th-century architecture. All are privately owned, so you'll have to be content with what you can view from the outside. Take a look at 1019, 1027, and 1031 Chicago Avenue—all typical Victorians that predate the Wright home. Turn left on Marion Street and then left again on Superior Street to reach 1030 Superior Street. Continue down Superior Street and turn right onto Forest Avenue, which is lined with textbook examples of late-19th- and early 20th-century architecture. Don't miss the **Moore–Dugal Home** (✉ 333 N. Forest Ave.), an 1895 Tudor design that Cindy Crawford and Richard Gere considered buying. Another Wright-designed house is at 6 Elizabeth Court. Along the way you'll be able to compare and contrast then-revolutionary Wright homes cheek by jowl with overdecorated Victorians, blowsy Queen Annes, and upright Tudors.

One of Wright's early public buildings and one of the great religious buildings of the century is **Unity Temple,** built for a Unitarian congregation in 1906 and still in use as a house of worship. The stark concrete building consists of two spaces, a sanctuary and a parish house, connected by the low-ceiling main entrance. The cubical sanctuary, stucco with wood trim, is lighted by high windows of stained glass. It conveys a sense of calm and balance that also invokes the spiritual. Wright would no doubt be delighted to find his original furniture still in use here. ✉ *875 W. Lake St.,* ☎ *708/383–8873.* 🎧 *Audiocassette tour $3, guided tour $5.* 🕐 *Daily 1–4; tour, weekends at 1, 2, and 3; call for longer summer hrs.*

Hemingway fans can look at **Ernest Hemingway's boyhood home** (✉ 600 N. Kenilworth Ave.). This unassuming gray stucco house is privately owned and not open to the public.

Part of the literary legacy of Oak Park is the **Ernest Hemingway Birthplace,** which has furnished period rooms, videos, and photographic displays about the writer's early life. ✉ *339 N. Oak Park Ave.,* ☎ *708/ 848–2222.* 🎧 *$4; joint ticket with Hemingway Museum $6.* 🕐 *Wed., Fri., and Sun. 1–5, Sat. 10–5.*

At the small **Ernest Hemingway Museum,** run by the same foundation that maintains the birthplace, exhibits and videos focus on the author's first 20 years in Oak Park and their impact on his later work. The subjects of special exhibits range from movies made from Hemingway's books to his war experiences. ✉ *200 N. Oak Park Ave.,* ☎ *708/848– 2222.* 🎧 *$4; joint ticket with Hemingway Birthplace $6.* 🕐 *Fri. and Sun. 1–5, Sat. 10–5.*

Oak Park Avenue runs parallel to Harlem Avenue and perpendicular to Chicago Avenue. If you're coming from the Frank Lloyd Wright Home and Studio, take a right on Chicago Avenue and another right onto Oak Park Avenue; Hemingway's birthplace will be on your right and the museum will be across the street on your left. If you continue south on Oak Park Avenue, cross Lake Street and turn right, Unity Temple will be on your left. The Oak Park El station is a five-minute walk south of Unity Temple.

Dining

$$–$$$$ ✕ **Philander's.** This hotel dining room feels like a classy tavern and serves a wide selection of reliable seafood, pastas, and vegetarian dishes. One of Oak Park's few fine-dining spots, Philander's usually

has a crowd. ⊠ *Carleton Hotel, 1120 Pleasant St.,* ☎ *708/848–4250. AE, D, DC, MC, V. Closed Sun. No lunch.*

$ ✕ **Khyber Pass.** The clubby interior of this Indian restaurant in downtown Oak Park belies a reasonably priced menu of imaginative curries and stews, not to mention a fragrant nan (Indian flat bread). ⊠ *1031 Lake St.,* ☎ *708/445–9032. Reservations not accepted. AE, MC, V.*

$ ✕ **Original Pancake House.** Indulge in a Chicago tradition by ordering a German pancake served with powdered sugar and a wedge of lemon along with a cup of excellent coffee. ⊠ *954 Lake St.,* ☎ *708/ 524–0955. No credit cards. No dinner.*

$ ✕ **Peterson's Old-Fashioned Ice Cream Parlor.** As its name implies, this place has ice cream sodas, malts, and sundaes that'll make you nostalgic for the good old soda-fountain days. Light meals are also available. ⊠ *1100 Chicago Ave.,* ☎ *708/386–6130. No credit cards.*

Brookfield

The zoo is 3½ mi southwest of Oak Park (take Harlem Ave. south 2 mi, turn west on Cermak Rd. 1 mi, then south on 1st Ave. to zoo entrance), 15 mi southwest of downtown Chicago.

The spacious zoo within its borders is what draws most people to this suburban town. To get here from Oak Park, take I–290 west to 1st Avenue; go south and turn right on 31st Street.

★ ☾ ❷ The naturalistic settings of the 200-acre **Brookfield Zoo** aim to give visitors the sense of being in the wild (though you'll have to pretend not to see the hordes of schoolchildren and strollers that regularly migrate through the zoo). It's easy to spend most of a day here studying the more than 2,000 animals. The popular **Tropic World** exhibit, simulating a tropical rain forest, comprises the world's largest indoor zoo of mixed species: Monkeys, otters, birds, and other rain-forest fauna cavort in a carefully constructed setting of rocks, trees, shrubs, pools, and waterfalls. Thunderstorms occur at random intervals, although visitors on the raised walkway are sheltered from the rain.

In the **Aquatic Bird House** visitors can test their "flying strength" by "flapping their wings" on a machine that simultaneously measures wing action and speed and decides what kind of bird they would be, based on how they flap. A 5-acre **Habitat Africa** has a water hole and rock formations characteristic of the African savannah. Here visitors can see such tiny animals as klipspringer antelope, which are only 22 inches tall, and rock hyraxes, which resemble prairie dogs. The **Swamp** is about as realistic as you would want an exhibit on swamps to be, with a springy floor, push-button alligator bellows, and open habitats with low-flying birds vividly demonstrating the complex ecosystems of both southern and Illinois wetlands. Like many of the zoo's other exhibits, it has a touch table where visitors can handle artifacts such as turtle shells and animals skins. At the **Living Coast,** visitors venture into a totally dry underwater environment with sharks, rays, jellyfish, and turtles swimming through huge glassed-in passageways. Numerous interactive exhibits introduce visitors to the daily lives of penguins, turtles, shore critters, and even anchovies. Back at ground level, the daily dolphin shows, a highlight of the zoo, are a favorite even among jaded adults—the show area accommodates 2,000 spectators. Seals and sea lions inhabit a rocky seascape exhibit that simulates a Pacific Northwest environment, and there's a splendid underwater viewing gallery.

From late spring through early fall the "motorized safari" tram will carry you around the grounds for $2.50; in winter the free, heated *Snow-*

Northeastern Illinois

ball Express does the job. You can also rent strollers and wheelchairs. The **Children's Zoo** requires a separate fee to access the petting farm, excellent animal shows, and the Big Barn with its daily milking demonstrations. ⊠ *8400 W. 31st St.,* ☎ *708/485–0263 or 312/242–2630.* ⚏ *Zoo $6 Apr.–Sept., Mon., Wed., and Fri.–Sun.; $4 Tues. and Thurs.; free Oct.–Mar. Tues. and Thurs. Children's zoo $1 Mar.–Oct., free Nov.–Feb. Dolphin show $2; parking $4.* ⊙ *Daily 9:30–5:30.*

Lisle

10 mi west of Brookfield, 25 mi southwest of downtown Chicago.

The old farm town of Lisle is being gentrified as the suburbs and new corporate centers sprawl west. Its main public attraction, the Morton Arboretum, was once in the countryside; now major roads surround it. To get to Lisle from Brookfield or downtown Chicago, take I–290 west to I–88 (the East-West Tollway), going west. At Route 53 exit and go north a half mile.

★ ❸ Established by salt magnate Joy Morton in 1922, the **Morton Arboretum** has 1,500 serene acres of plants, woodlands, and outdoor gardens. In spring the flowering trees are spectacular. A love of trees ran in the Morton family: Joy's father, J. Sterling Morton, originated Arbor Day.

Unlike other arboretums, this one allows cars to drive through some of its grounds. Still, you'll see more by walking along the 13 mi of trails. Most take only 15–30 minutes to complete; some are designed around themes, such as conifers or plants from around the world.

Plan your tour with the assistance of the free map, which will help you decide among such options as "Northeast Asia" and "Azaleas and Rhododendrons." Ten visitor stations with interactive exhibits help you understand the unique characteristics of the surrounding flora. Also on the grounds are a restaurant, coffee shop, library, and gift shop. Tours and special programs are scheduled most Sunday afternoons. ⊠ *Rte. 53,* ☎ *630/719–2400.* ⚏ *$6 per car, walk-ins free.* ⊙ *Daily 7–7.*

Wheaton

5 mi northwest of Lisle, 30 mi west of downtown Chicago.

Several dozen religious publishers and organizations are based in Wheaton, the county seat of suburban DuPage County; evangelical Wheaton College is here, too. Many visitors, however, come to see the magnificent grounds and museum of Cantigny. You can take I–90 west to I–88; exit at Winfield Road and head north 3 mi.

❹ Colonel Robert McCormick, legendary editor and publisher of the *Chicago Tribune* from 1925 to 1955, willed his 500-acre estate, **Cantigny,** to Wheaton as a public park. Splendid formal gardens, a restored 1870s mansion, and a tank park make it one of the key attractions in this old town. The estate is named after the village of Cantigny, France, which McCormick helped capture in World War I as a member of the U.S. Army's First Division. The **First Division Museum** is devoted to the history of this infantry division from 1917 to Desert Storm. In the **tank park** you'll see tanks from World War II, the Korean War, and the Vietnam War. Children are encouraged to play on the tanks, which are surrounded by soft wood chips. The first and second floors of the 35-room plantation-style mansion are open to the public and are furnished with antiques and artwork collected by Colonel McCormick's two wives. An entertaining introductory video is shown periodically in the home's own art deco–style theater. Well-informed guides help provide a glimpse into the "Upstairs, Downstairs" lifestyle of mid-20th-century gentry: They'll even show you the dumbwaiters that delivered course after course from the basement kitchen to the formal dining room. On the grounds is a beautiful wooded picnic area. Cantigny hosts a parade of special events throughout the year, including regionally known art shows and family festivals. Call ahead for details. ⊠ *1 S. 151 Winfield Rd.,* ☎ *630/668–5161.* ☞ *Free, parking $5.* ☉ *Park daily 9–6, mansion Tues.–Sun. 10–3:15, museum Tues.–Sun. 10–4; Memorial Day–Labor Day, sites open 1 hr later.*

☾ Just 4 mi northeast of Cantigny, the **Wheaton Park District Community Center** makes a fun summertime stop. At the excellent **DuPage Children's Museum,** a carpentry shop with real hand drills, hammers, and saws is perpetually popular with children who have edifice complexes. Kids can stand at waist-high water tables, splashing simulated dams and channels, and arrange their own multistory marble raceways from wooden tubes and chutes. Outside is the municipally owned **Rice Water Park,** a huge complex with several multistory water slides, children's play areas, and a sand volleyball pit. ⊠ *1777 S. Blanchard Rd. DuPage Museum:* ☎ *630/260–9960 or 630/690–4880.* ☞ *$13.* ☉ *Mid-June–late Aug., Mon.–Sat. 11–9, Sun. noon–9. Rice Water Park:* ☎ *630/260–9960 or 630/690–4880.* ☞ *$13.* ☉ *Mid-June–late Aug., Mon.–Sat. 11–9, Sun. noon–9.*

Naperville

❺ *3 mi south of Cantigny, 25 mi southwest of the Loop.*

Though the far-western suburb of Naperville is often cited as a prime example of suburban sprawl (with some good reason), its prairie-village heritage is still happily intact. Winding its way through Naperville is the sluggish, shallow DuPage River. Two miles of landscaped, park-studded river walks line its banks, with the most scenic stretch at the city's downtown. You can string together an agreeable outing from **Naper Settlement** (the Chicago area's only living history museum worth mentioning), lunch or afternoon tea in downtown Naperville, and a leisurely stroll along the river walk. From I–88 exit south on Naperville Road. Proceed south, passing through the city's lovely historic residential district and downtown Naperville, and follow signs to Naper Settlement.

When Chicago was incorporated in 1837, Naperville was already six years old. One of its original families prospered, built a huge Italianate mansion (the Martin-Mitchell House), and early in the century willed the house and several hundred acres to the city. The local historic society began buying historically significant houses in the area, moving them to the grounds of Naper Settlement, and restoring and furnishing them. The impressive result is a bricks-and-sticks time line of the evolution of a 19th-century prairie town. Unlike many other living history museums, Naper Settlement is relatively compact and can be visited in a single afternoon. Many of its buildings have hands-on activities and demonstrations.

Start at the **Pre-Emption House Visitor Center,** modeled after an inn and tavern that was at the epicenter of the town's growth in the 1830s and 1840s. Must-sees on the grounds include the 1864 **American Gothic chapel,** with its board-and-battens exterior and pre-Raphaelite–style stained glass. The **Martin-Mitchell House** is a rare, nearly untouched celebration of Victorian excess, right down to the original light fixtures, mourning wreaths of braided human hair, and massive mahogany furniture. The Greek Revival **Murray House,** represents the typical (read: cramped) life of a first-generation prairie lawyer. Children particularly enjoy the re-created log-picket **Fort Payne** and the rough-hewn, one-room **Paw Paw house**, where they can climb a ladder and peek into the sleeping loft. Naper Settlement regularly stages special events and weekend-long historical reenactments. Call ahead for details. ⊠ *523 S. Webster St.,* ☎ *630/420–6010.* 🖾 *$6.* ⊙ *Apr.–Oct., Tues.–Sat. 10–4, Sun. 1–4; Nov.–Mar., holidays and special programs only (call for details).*

Just a mile north of Naper Settlement, **downtown Naperville** is a charming two- by four-block area bordered to the west by the DuPage River. Stroll along the river walk, stopping to enjoy its many shrubbery-shaded nooks, playgrounds, and even a covered bridge. Shoppers will enjoy the specialty clothing stores, home accessories shops, and reasonably priced antiques stores.

Dining

$$–$$$ ✕ **La Sorella di Francesca.** Innovative twists on pasta and riffs on Italian and contemporary sauces earn this trattoria a loyal following. ⊠ *18 W. Jefferson St.,* ☎ *630/961–2706. MC, V.*

$ ✕ **Jefferson Hill Tea Room.** Walking into this Victorian mansion–cum–shopping arcade is like stepping into the pastel-sweet interior of a wedding cake. All manner of feminine accoutrements, from stationery to decorative dolls, are arranged in little alcoves. The tearoom is regionally famous for its delicate salads and commensurately rich desserts. ⊠ *43 E. Jefferson Ave.,* ☎ *630/420–8521. MC, V.*

Aurora

❻ *8 mi west of Naperville via I–88, 33 mi southwest of downtown Chicago.*

Though Aurora's downtown has little to offer in the way of charm, a few nearby sights make a trip here worthwhile, especially if you're coming from Naperville. Within the downtown area is the **Paramount Arts Center** (⊠ 23 E. Galena Blvd., ☎ 630/896–6666), which hosts large-scale concerts and plays in its meticulously restored 1920s theater. From Naperville, take I–88 west for about 6 mi. Exit south on Farnsworth Avenue and turn west (right) at New York Street.

Three blocks north of downtown Aurora is Walter Payton's **Roundhouse,** which alone merits a trip. The former football great, along with some investors, bought a decaying railroad repair station and transformed it into a huge steak house ($$–$$$) and on-site microbrewery. Inside the complex, the one-room **Payton Museum** displays a 5-ft-high replica of Payton on a Wheaties box, among other Super Bowl memorabilia. If you'd rather meet the man in person, stick around the restaurant, where he regularly meets and greets guests. The doughnut-shape building has an entirely enclosed plaza with a golf-putting green, gardens, and outdoor dining. From Chicago you can take the train from the North Western station straight to the Roundhouse and back again to the Loop without setting foot outside—an appealing option in winter. ⊠ *205 N. Broadway,* ☎ *630/264–2739.* ⊙ *Daily noon–midnight.* 🖾 *Free.*

↺ Three miles west of the Roundhouse on Galena Boulevard is **Blackberry Historical Farm-Village,** where pioneer life is re-created in a prairie-town streetscape with a replica log cabin and an 1840s farmhouse. At the center of the complex is a small lake; a miniature train circles its gentle shoreline. There are also pony rides and a carousel. Sheep-shearing days, quilting bees, and other special events are held throughout the summer. ⊠ *Galena Blvd. and Barnes Rd.,* ☎ *630/892–1550.* 🖾 *$7.* ⊙ *Late Apr.–Labor Day, daily 10–4:30.*

OFF THE
BEATEN PATH

FERMI NATIONAL ACCELERATOR LABORATORY – On Aurora's northeast border, about 12 mi northeast of Blackberry Historical Farm-Village, visitors can observe both the minuscule and the mammoth. The underground Tevatron atomic collider is full of self-guided exhibits on subatomic particles, nuclear reactions, and the history of atomic power in the United States. If you find these subjects inscrutable, stay above ground to watch buffalo roaming the prairie. From I–88 take the Route 59 exit north to Batavia Road and head west (left) about 2 mi. ⊠ ¼ mi west of intersection of Batavia Rd. and Rte. 59, ☎ 630/840–3351. ☎ Free. ⊙ Daily 6 AM–8 PM.

Western Suburbs A to Z

Arriving and Departing

BY CAR

This side trip is best done by car, and all towns are within 5 to 15 mi of each other. The main arteries serving the western suburbs are the Eisenhower Expressway (I–290), which goes west from the Loop and turns into I–88 at the border of DuPage County; the Tri-State Tollway (I–94/294), which semicircles the region from north to south; and I–355, which connects I–290 with I–55, the road from Chicago to St. Louis.

BY TRAIN

You can take **Metra** commuter trains (☎ 312/322–6777 or 312/836–7000) to individual attractions. The **Metra Union Pacific West Line** departs from the station at Citicorp Center (⊠ 165 N. Canal St.) and stops in Oak Park and Wheaton. The **Metra Burlington Northern Line** (☎ 312/836–7000) departs from Union Station (⊠ 210 S. Canal St.) and stops at Brookfield, Lisle, Naperville, and Aurora.

Contacts and Resources

GUIDED TOURS

The **Chicago Architecture Foundation** (☞ Visitor Information, *below*) has tours of Oak Park and occasional tours of other suburbs. The **Oak Park Visitors Center** (☞ Visitor Information, *below*) has self-guided tours of Oak Park and adjacent River Forest, as well as information on guided tours.

VISITOR INFORMATION

The **Chicago Office of Tourism** (⊠ 78 E. Washington St., ☎ 312/744–2400 or 800/406–6418) has some information on major attractions in the western suburbs, as does the **Illinois Bureau of Tourism** (⊠ 100 W. Randolph St., ☎ 312/814–4732 or 800/226–6632). Also check with the **Chicago Architecture Foundation** (☎ 312/922–8687).

The **Oak Park Visitors Center** (⊠ 158 N. Forest Ave., ☎ 708/848–1500) has useful detailed maps, tour information, and tickets for tours of other historic buildings in the River Forest–Oak Park area, including those by Prairie School architects E. E. Roberts and George Maher.

SHERIDAN ROAD AND THE NORTH SHORE

All along the shore of Lake Michigan north of Chicago you'll find well-to-do old towns with gracious houses on lots ever larger and more heavily wooded the farther you travel north. The most southern of these towns is Evanston, which sits on the northern border of Chicago and is home to the lakefront campus of Northwestern University. Hollywood films have helped make the North Shore synonymous with the upper middle class through such hit films as *Home Alone* (filmed in Winnetka), *Ordinary People* (Lake Forest), and *Risky Business* (Glencoe).

The drive up Sheridan Road, in most spots a stone's throw from the lakefront, is pleasant in itself, even if you don't stop. It's particularly scenic in spring, when the trees flower profusely, and in the fall, when their foliage is downright gaudy. Although Sheridan Road goes all the way to the Wisconsin border, it twists and turns and occasionally disappears. Don't lose hope; just look for small signs indicating where it went. When in doubt, keep heading north and stay near the lake. You can make a pleasant loop by heading north on Sheridan Road from Evanston to Lake Forest, then returning via Green Bay Road. You'll pass through the self-consciously tasteful downtowns of Highland Park, Winnetka, Kenilworth, and Wilmette on your way back to Evanston.

Evanston

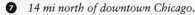 *14 mi north of downtown Chicago.*

First settled in 1826, Evanston is the home of five institutions of higher learning, among them Northwestern University. The student population and the diversity of its residents have given the town a distinct identity: Here Birkenstocks never went out of style. Well-preserved or meticulously restored Victorians, Prairie houses, hip-roof bungalows, and turreted Queen Anne–style houses create a kaleidoscope of architectural styles on elm-arched streets, making the area delightful for walking any time of year. Throughout the warm months Evanston's lakefront parks are the stage for diverse special events, from highbrow art fairs to nearly rowdy ethnic music festivals. Even when things are quiet, the sandy beaches, sailboat launches, and playgrounds that dot the city's Lake Michigan shore give this area a lasting appeal. Frances Willard, who started the Women's Christian Temperance Union, lived in Evanston, and the town is still the WCTU headquarters—though these days the town is by no means dry.

The **Evanston Historical Society** occupies the châteaulike former home of Nobel Peace Prize winner Charles Gates Dawes, U.S. vice president under Calvin Coolidge. The 28-room mansion, built in 1894, has been restored to its 1920s appearance and has spectacular 20-ft vaulted ceilings, stained-glass windows, Renaissance-style paneling, and period furniture, much of it original to the Dawes family and evocative of Dawes's diplomatic travels. The historical society also maintains a small but well-preserved costume collection and research facilities. ⊠ *225 Greenwood St.*, ☎ *847/475–3410.* ☜ *$5.* ☉ *Wed.–Sun. 1–5.*

Founded in 1855, **Northwestern University** has an attractive campus that stretches along the lakefront for 1 mi starting two blocks north of the Dawes House. Some 7,400 undergraduates and 4,300 graduate students attend Northwestern, which also has professional schools in Chicago. The university's schools of business, journalism, law, and medicine are nationally known, and its school of speech has trained many actors, including Charlton Heston and Ann-Margret, among others. Its football team is a perennial underdog in the Big Ten Midwestern Conference, in which Northwestern is the only private school; however, the team did go to the Rose Bowl in 1996, which accounts for the many purple "N" flags that adorn houses and cars in the area.

There is no public access road running north–south through the school. You can park on either end of the campus and walk to the interior or to the peninsula, where winding paths loop around the lagoon (a panoramic view of the Loop skyline will tempt you to linger). To the west is the heart of the old campus, with shady groves of mature trees and the idyllic Deering Meadow.

The **visitor center,** in a Tudor Revival mansion at the corner of Sheridan Road and Clark Street, has a map of the campus. The undergraduate admissions office gives complete campus tours (☞ Guided Tours *in* Sheridan Road and the North Shore A to Z, *below*).

The **Mary and Leigh Block Gallery,** a Northwestern-owned fine-arts museum, hosts a variety of traveling exhibits: European Impressionist and American Realist paintings, photography, decorative arts, and modern sculpture. The adjacent sculpture garden has large-scale sculptures by Henry Moore, Joan Miró, and Arnoldo Pomodoro. ⊠ *1967 S. Campus Dr.,* ☎ *847/491–4000.* ☜ *Free.* ☉ *June–Aug., Tues.–Sun. noon–5; Sept.–May, Thurs.–Sun. noon–8.*

The irregularly shaped white building on campus is the **Pick-Staiger Concert Hall** (⊠ 1977 S. Campus Dr., ☎ 847/491–5441; 847/467–7425 for performance schedules), with a 1,003-seat auditorium that regularly presents performances by internationally known artists as well as Northwestern faculty and students. The hall is acclaimed for its acoustics.

The **Shakespeare Garden** (⊠ Sheridan Rd. between Garrett Pl. and Haven St.) provides a tranquil campus refuge. Set back from the street and enclosed by 6-ft hedges, it is planted with 70 flowers, herbs, and trees mentioned in Shakespeare's plays. Park on the side streets west of Sheridan Road.

Grosse Point Lighthouse was built in 1873 to help guide ships into the port of Chicago. Although Lake Michigan looks placid most of the time, it has enough fog, violent storms, and sandbars to make navigation treacherous. The lighthouse was decommissioned in 1935, but the Evanston Historical Society (☞ *above*) has restored it and leads guided tours of the interior several months of the year. The surrounding park is open year-round and has a nature center and a community arts center. ⊠ *2601 Sheridan Rd.,* ☎ *847/328–6961.* ☉ *Lighthouse tour June–Sept., weekend afternoons (call for schedule).* ☜ *Free.*

Dining

Evanston has many ethnic restaurants and a handful of elegant establishments such as Trio (☞ Worth a Special Trip *in* Chapter 3).

$–$$$ ✕ **Davis Street Fishmarket.** In a casual storefront setting you can sample the closest approximation of New England clam chowder that the Midwest can muster, plus daily specials of succulent grilled fillets and imaginative sandwiches and seafood salads. It's two blocks west of Sheridan Road on the eastern edge of downtown Evanston. ⊠ *501 Davis St.,* ☎ *847/869–3474. AE, MC, V.*

$–$$$ ✕ **The Roxy Cafe.** Academics come here for imaginative salads and pasta dishes. For dessert try caramel apple pizza, made with a sweet-roll crust. ⊠ *626 Church St.,* ☎ *847/864–6540. AE, MC, V.*

$–$$ ✕ **Noyes Street Café.** Drop in at this low-key café, three blocks west of the Northwestern campus, for oversize salads, Greek specialties, and several cups of coffee. ⊠ *828 Noyes St.,* ☎ *847/475–8683. MC, V.*

Wilmette

❽ *4 mi north of Evanston (from Sheridan Rd., turn west on Central St. in Evanston and continue to Green Bay Rd.; turn north and continue ½ mi to Central/Green Bay intersection), 18 mi north of downtown Chicago.*

In this affluent village along the North Shore you'll find one of the area's most popular destinations, the Baha'i House of Worship, as well as many delightful, verdant streets.

Even if you aren't traveling with children, consider dropping in at the ☺ **Kohl Children's Museum.** Its exhibit on Marc Chagall is a masterpiece, blending the historical context of his life with brilliantly simple demonstrations of his use of light, simplified form, paint, and glass in various works. On the first floor there's a child-size grocery store, a kid's version of King David's temple, a re-created ancient sailing ship, and an excellent educational toy store. ⊠ *165 Green Bay Rd.,* ☎ *847/256–6056.* ☜ *$3.* ☉ *Tues.–Sat. 10–4, Sun. noon–4.*

Rising near the lake, the **Baha'i House of Worship** is an intriguing nine-sided building that incorporates architectural styles and symbols from many of the world's religions. The temple is the U.S. center of the Baha'i faith, which celebrates the unity of all religions. With its delicate lacelike details and massive dome, the Louis Bourgeois design emphasizes the 19th-century Persian origins of the Baha'i religion. As symmetrical and harmonious as the 191-ft-tall building are the formal gardens that surround it. The visitor center has exhibits explaining the Baha'i faith; here you can also ask for a guide to show you around. ⊠ *100 Linden Ave., Wilmette,* ☎ *847/853–2300.* ☜ *Free.* ☉ *May–Sept., daily 10–10; Oct.–Apr., daily 10–5.*

Gilson Park, the jewel of Wilmette's lakefront, is an eighth of a mile north of the Baha'i House of Worship along Sheridan Road. Its public beach is good for swimming and rarely crowded. Bordering the east side of the park is a row of impressive houses that give you a glimpse of the wealth of this area.

Dining

$–$$$ ✗ **Betise.** Though it's in a shopping center (the Plaza del Lago, just west of Sheridan Road in northern Wilmette), Betise serves surprisingly tasty Italian dishes, most of them based on tomatoes, potatoes, fish, and roasted chicken. Cobblestone floors and off-white walls add to the Riviera atmosphere. ⊠ *1515 Sheridan Rd.,* ☎ *847/853–1711. AE, D, DC, MC, V.*

$ ✗ **Walker Bros. Original Pancake House.** This popular, traditional breakfast-all-day spot has fluffy omelets, several varieties of pancakes (try the apple), and fresh-ground coffee served with whipping cream. ⊠ *153 Green Bay Rd.,* ☎ *847/251–6000. D, MC, V.*

Highland Park

❾ *7 mi north of Wilmette, 26 mi north of downtown Chicago.*

The attractive homes of Highland Park are a year-round pleasure, but in warm weather the town hosts one of Chicago's top musical events. If you enjoy music under the stars, the outdoor concerts at **Ravinia Park** are a stellar treat. The Ravinia Festival (☞ The Arts *in* Chapter 5) is the summer home of the Chicago Symphony Orchestra, and the festival also showcases superb jazz, chamber music, pop, and dance performances. You can pack a picnic and blanket and sit on the lawn for about the cost of a movie (seats are also available in the pavilion for a significantly higher price). There are also restaurants and snack bars on the park grounds. Concerts usually start at 8; plan to arrive at the park no later than 6:30 to allow time for parking, hiking from the parking lot to the lawn, and getting settled. ⊠ *Green Bay and Lake Cook Rds.,* ☎ *847/266–5100.*

A successful early example of the Prairie style, the **Willits House,** at 1445 Sheridan Road, was built by Frank Lloyd Wright in 1902. Outside, the house shows the influence of Japanese architecture in its overhanging eaves. The cruciform plan of the interior is built around a large central fireplace—a technique that Wright and other Prairie School architects used frequently. The house is now privately owned.

Highwood

⑩ *2 mi north of Highland Park, 28 mi north of downtown Chicago.*

A working-class ethnic community, Highwood is an anomaly on the North Shore. The village was incorporated in 1887, and its fortunes have been entwined with those of the adjacent army post, Fort Sheridan, which was opened in the same year to maintain an army presence near Chicago in the wake of the labor unrest surrounding the Haymarket Riot. During its early days Highwood was the only place nearby where soldiers could get a drink because most of the North Shore suburbs were dry. A large Italian population has given rise to a number of excellent dining spots, including generations-old Italian restaurants and other diverse ethnic eateries.

NEED A BREAK?   Many of Highwood's restaurants are open only for dinner, but you can grab a bite throughout the day at **Virginia's Restaurant** (⊠ 415 Sheridan Rd., ☎ 847/433–1555). For Italian-style picnic fare, try **Bacio Foods** (⊠ 424 Sheridan Rd., ☎ 847/432–1090).

En Route   Between Highwood to the south and Lake Forest to the north are the distinctive yellow buildings of **Fort Sheridan,** designed by the noted Chicago firm of Holabird and Roche and constructed from 1888 to 1891. Though the fort is currently being subdivided to make way for a military cemetery and houses (the world-class golf course will remain untouched), it's worth driving by to glimpse a period community frozen in time.

Dining

$$–$$$ ✕ **Froggy's French Cafe.** This comfortable bistro is known for sumptuous six-course prix fixe dinners and lunches, excellent cassoulet and other hearty dishes, and a huge wine list. Expect a wait at peak hours. ⊠ *306 N. Green Bay Rd.,* ☎ *847/433–7080. D, DC, MC, V. Closed Sun.*

Lake Forest

⑪ *4 mi north of Highwood, 32 mi north of downtown Chicago.*

By the 1870s this village was acknowledged as the toniest and most exclusive of the city's suburbs. The town plan created winding roads that follow the course of the ravines near the lake, taking you past the beautifully landscaped campuses of Lake Forest and Barat colleges, as well as many sumptuous mansions set far back on heavily wooded lots. One of the nation's oldest planned shopping centers, **Market Square,** built in 1916, still thrives, with intriguing shops and boutiques selling high-price, one-of-a-kind clothes, home accessories, and knickknacks. To reach Market Square, veer west off Sheridan Road on Deerpath Road to the quaint Lake Forest business district and the Square.

NEED A BREAK?   Within Market Square, **Lake Forest Food & Wine Specialties** (⊠ 672 Western Ave., ☎ 847/234–0620) is the perfect place to buy picnic supplies or to stop for a quick midday snack.

Glencoe

7 mi southwest of Lake Forest (take Deerpath Rd. west to Green Bay Rd., turn right to go south), 24 mi from downtown Chicago.

★ ⑫ The 15 gardens of the **Chicago Botanic Garden** cover 300 acres and provide a feast for the senses. Among the different environments are a rose garden, a three-island Japanese garden, an Illinois prairie, a waterfall garden, a sensory garden for people with visual impairments, an aquatic garden, a learning garden, and a 3½-acre fruit-and-vegetable garden whose yields are donated to area soup kitchens. The garden's three big biodomes showcase a desert, a rain forest, and a formal topiary garden year-round, and 10 greenhouses are full of flowers all winter long. Special events and shows are scheduled most weekends, many sponsored by local plant societies; standouts are the spring daffodil show, the Japan Festival in May, an August bonsai show, and a winter orchid show. To get here from Lake Forest, turn right off Green Bay Road onto Lake Cook Road and follow it to Glencoe's northwest corner. To reach the Botanic Garden from elsewhere, exit I–94 at Lake Cook Road heading east and proceed ¼ mi to the entrance. ⊠ *Lake Cook Rd. and Rte. 41,* ☎ *847/835–5440.* ⬚ *$5 per car, tram tour $3.50.* ☉ *Daily 8 AM–sunset; tours every ½ hr weekdays 10:30–3:30 and weekends 10:30–4:30.*

Sheridan Road and the North Shore A to Z

Arriving and Departing

BY CAR

This side trip is designed as a drive, although you can take a commuter train to individual attractions (☞ *below*). The route follows Sheridan Road along the lakeshore, then turns west at Lake Forest to connect with Green Bay Road heading south. The other major artery serving the North Shore is the Edens Expressway (I–94).

BY TRAIN

The **Metra** Union Pacific North line (☎ 312/322–6777 or 312/836–7000) departs from the station at Citicorp Center (⊠ 165 N. Canal St.) and stops in Evanston (Davis Street), Wilmette, Glencoe, Ravinia Park (special trains on concert nights), Highland Park, Highwood, Fort Sheridan, Lake Forest, Waukegan, and Zion.

The **Chicago Transit Authority's** Howard (Red) line (☎ 312/836–7000) and an extension will take you as far as Wilmette, with multiple stops in Evanston. Board it northbound along State Street in the Loop or at Chicago Avenue and State Street in the Near North area. Change at Howard for the Evanston (Purple line) shuttle. To reach the Northwestern campus, get off at Foster Avenue and walk east to Sheridan Road. The Howard line is not recommended after dark.

Contacts and Resources

GUIDED TOURS

The **Chicago Architectural Foundation** (☎ 312/922–8687) has occasional walking, bicycle, and bus tours of parts of the North Shore. The **Office of Undergraduate Admissions** at Northwestern University (⊠ 1801 Hinman Ave., ☎ 847/491–7271) organizes tours of the campus October–April, daily at 2, with additional tours Saturday at 12:30.

VISITOR INFORMATION

Call the **Illinois Bureau of Tourism** (⊠ 100 W. Randolph St., ☎ 312/814–4732 or 800/226–6632) or the **Lake County Illinois Convention and Visitors Bureau** (☎ 847/662–2700).

9 Portraits of Chicago

The Builders of Chicago

Books and Videos

THE BUILDERS OF CHICAGO

ITY DWELLERS DEVASTATED by the aftermath of the Great Chicago Fire of 1871 couldn't have known that the leveled landscape before them would soon set the stage for the birth of a modern architecture that would influence the entire world.

Because Chicago had been built mainly of wood, it was wiped out by the fire. The lone, yellow stone Water Tower of 1869 loomed eerily near the intersection of North Michigan and Chicago avenues. Today, its fake battlements, crenellations, and turrets recall Disneyland rather than a real part of a vibrant and serious city. It serves now as a tourist information center, and even amid the amazingly varied architecture of central Chicago, it appears to be an anachronism.

In the years following the fire, many remarkable future builders flocked to the city that sprawled for miles along the western shore of Lake Michigan and inland along the branches of the Chicago River. Creative and brilliant minds such as engineer William LeBaron Jenny and MIT- and Paris-trained future architect-philosopher Louis Sullivan were joined by ingenious architects and engineers from diverse parts of America and Europe: Dankmar Adler (from Denmark), William Holabird (from New York), John Wellborn Root (from Georgia), Frank Lloyd Wright (from Wisconsin), Henry Hobson Richardson (from Louisiana via Boston and Paris), Daniel H. Burnham (from New York), and Martin Roche (from Ireland), among others. These pioneering men created the foundations of modern architecture and construction during the 1880s and 1890s in Chicago.

It's difficult to figure out precisely who did what, as they worked for and with one another, living in each other's pockets, shifting partnerships, arguing the meaning of what they did as well as how best to do it. Jenney and Adler were essentially engineers uninterested in decoration; with the exception of Richardson's Romanesque motifs, Sullivan's amazing ornament, and Wright's spatial and ornamental forms, these builders did not have distinct, easily discernible styles. It becomes an academic exercise to try to identify their individual efforts.

Philosophically, the Chicago architects sought to express the soul of American civilization, an architecture pragmatic, honest, healthy, and unashamed of wealth and commerce. Sullivan, a philosopher, a romantic, and a prolific writer (his most famous book on architecture, *Kindergarten Chats*, is a Socratic dialogue), originated and propagated the ideas that "form follows function" and "a building is an act." Sullivan believed that in order to create an architecture of human satisfaction, social purpose and structure had to be integrated.

The skyscraper was born here. The "curtain wall," a largely glass exterior surface that does not act as a "wall" supporting the building but is supported on the floors from within, originated here. Modern metal-frame, multistory construction was created here. The Chicago Window—a popular window design used in buildings all over America (until air-conditioning made it obsolete) consisting of a large fixed-glass panel in the center, with a narrow operable sash on each side—was developed here. In light of the fire that inspired the building boom, Chicago builders also discovered how to fireproof the metal structures that supported their buildings, which would otherwise melt in fires and bring total collapse: They covered the iron columns and beams with terra-cotta tiles that insulated the structural metal from heat.

The Chicago School's greatest clients were wealthy businessmen and their wives. The same lack of inhibition that led Mrs. Potter Palmer and Mrs. Havemeyer to snap up Impressionist paintings that had been rejected by French academic opinion (and today are the core of the Art Institute collection) led sausage magnates to hire young, inventive local talent to build their mansions and countinghouses. Chicagoans may have been naive, but history has vindicated their taste.

Although they started building in the 1870s, nothing of note remains from before 1885. The oldest important structure is Richardson's massive granite Italian Romanesque–inspired Glessner House, with its decorative interiors derived from the innovative English Arts and Crafts movement. The only Richardson building left in Chicago, the Glessner House is considered by some his highest creation; Wright was influenced by its flowing interior space. The building is at 1800 South Prairie Avenue in the Prairie Avenue Historic District.

Downtown, Richardson designed a wholesale building for Marshall Field that was later demolished. An addition to the Field store in the same architectural vocabulary, done by Burnham in 1893 and now part of the Marshall Field block, stands at the corner of Wabash and Washington streets. Burnham completed the block in 1902–1907 but in the airy, open, metal-frame Chicago Window style.

In 1883 Jenney invented the first "skyscraper construction" building, in which a metal structural skeleton supports an exterior wall on metal shelves (the metal frame or skeleton, a sort of three-dimensional boxlike grid, is still used today). His earliest surviving metal-skeleton structure, the Second Leiter Building of 1891, stands at the southeast corner of State and Van Buren streets in the Loop. The granite-face facade is extremely light and open, suggesting the metal frame behind. The building looks so modern that it comes as a shock to realize it is more than a century old.

At 209 South LaSalle Street, the Rookery Building of 1886, a highly decorated, structurally transitional building by Burnham and Root, employs masonry-bearing walls (brick, terra-cotta, and stone) on the two major street facades and lots of iron structure (both cast-iron columns and wrought-iron beams) elsewhere. Here the decoration emphasizes the structural elements—pointing out, for example, the floor lines. Specially shaped bricks are used to create edges at the window openings and to make pilasters. This freestanding square "doughnut" was unusual at the time. A magnificent iron-and-glass skylight covers the lower two stories of the interior courtyard, which was renovated

in 1905 by Frank Lloyd Wright, who designed light fixtures and other decorative additions.

The nearby Marquette Building of 1894, at 140 South Dearborn Street, by Holabird and Roche, seems to be a prototype for the modern office building, with its skeleton metal frame covered by decorative terra-cotta and its open, cellular facade with Chicago Windows. The marble lobby rotunda, a veritable hymn to local history, has Tiffany mosaic portraits of famous Native American leaders and Père Marquette.

The most advanced structure from this period, one in which the exterior wall surface is freed of all performance of support, is Burnham's Reliance Building of 1895, at 36 North State Street. Here the proportion of glass to solid is very high, and the solid members are immensely slender for the era. The white terra-cotta cladding brightens the street. Most critics consider the Reliance the masterpiece of the Chicago School's office buildings.

TO APPRECIATE FULLY the giant leap taken by the architects of the Reliance, look at Burnham and Root's Monadnock Building of 1889–92, at 53 West Jackson Boulevard. Its 16 stories are supported by conventional load-bearing walls, which are 6 ft thick at the base! Although it is elegant in its stark simplicity, its ponderousness contrasts sharply with the delicate structure and appearance of the Reliance Building. The Monadnock Building may have been the swan song of conventional building structure in Chicago, yet its very verticality expressed the aspirations of the city.

The impetus toward verticality was an essential feature of Chicago commercial architecture. Verticality seemed to embody commercial possibility, as in "The sky's the limit!" Even the essential horizontality of the 12-story, block-long Carson Pirie Scott store is offset by the rounded corner tower at the main entrance.

Jenney's Manhattan Building of 1890, at 431 South Dearborn Street, with its variously shaped bay windows, was the first tall building (16 stories) to use metal-skeleton structure throughout; it is admired more for its structure than for its appearance. Both it and the equally tall Monadnock would never have come into being without Elisha Otis's invention of the elevator, which was already in use in New York City in buildings of 9 or 10 stories.

The Chicago School created new decorative forms to apply to their powerful structures, and they derived them largely from American vegetation rather than from classical motifs. The apogee of this lush ornament was probably reached by Sullivan in his Carson Pirie Scott and Company store of 1899–1904, at State and Madison streets. The cast-iron swirls of rich vegetation and geometry surround the ground-floor show windows and the entrance, and they grow to the second story as well, with the architect's initials, LHS, worked into the design. (A decorative cornice that was originally at the top was removed.) The facade of the intermediate floors is extremely simple, with wide Chicago Windows surrounded by a thin line of delicate ornament; narrow vertical and horizontal bands, all of white terracotta, cover the iron structure behind.

Terra-cotta plaques of complex and original decoration cover the horizontal spandrel beams (the beams that cover the outer edges of the floors, between the vertical columns of the facades) of many buildings of this era, including the Reliance and the Marquette. Even modest residential and commercial structures in Chicago began to use decorative terra-cotta, which became a typical local construction motif through the 1930s.

Adler and Sullivan's Auditorium Building of 1887–89 was a daring megastructure sheathed in massive granite, and its style derives from Romanesque forms. Here the shades of stone color and the rough and polished finishes provide contrasts. Built for profit as a civic center at South Michigan Avenue and Congress Street, facing Lake Michigan, the Auditorium Building incorporated a theater, a hotel, and an office building; complex engineering solutions allowed it to carry heavy and widely varying loads. Adler, the engineer, devised a hydraulic stage lift and an early air-conditioning system for the magnificent theater. Sullivan freely decorated the interiors with his distinctive flowing ornamental shapes.

In the spirit of democracy and populism, Adler wanted the Auditorium to be a "people's theater," one with lots of cheap seats and few boxes. It is still in use today

as the Auditorium Theater, and Adler's belief in the common man was upheld when thousands of ordinary Chicagoans subscribed to the restoration fund in 1968. The rest of the building is now Roosevelt University.

FRANK LLOYD WRIGHT, who had worked for a year on the Auditorium Building in Adler and Sullivan's office, remained in their employ and in 1892 designed a house for them in a wealthy area of the Near North Side of town. The Charnley House, 1365 North Astor Street, built of long, thin, yellowish Roman brick and stone, has a projecting central balcony and shows a glimmer of Wright's extraordinary later freedom with volumes and spaces. The Charnley House, with its exquisite interior woodwork and the exterior frieze under the roof, has now been completely restored. Soon after the Charnley House project, Wright left Adler and Sullivan to work on his own.

Wright's ability to break apart and recompose space and volume, even asymmetrically, was given full range in the many houses he built in and around Chicago. What became typical of American domestic "open plan" interiors (as opposed to an arrangement of closed, boxlike rooms) derived from Wright's creation, but they could never have been practical without the American development of central heating, which eliminated the need for a fire in each room.

Wright was the founder of what became known as the Prairie School, whose work consisted largely of residences rather than buildings intended for commerce. Its principal characteristic of horizontality was evocative of the breadth of the prairies and contrasted with the lofty vertical shafts of the business towers. Like his teacher Sullivan, Wright also delighted in original decorative motifs of geometric and vegetable design.

The opening of the Lake Street El railway west to the new suburb of Oak Park presented Wright with an enormous opportunity to build. In 1889 he went to live there at 951 Chicago Avenue, where he created a studio and a home over the next 22 years. Dozens of houses in Oak Park, of wood, stucco, brick, and stone, with beautiful lead- and stained-glass windows and carved woodwork, were designed or renovated by him. He became almost obsessively involved with his houses, wanting to design and control the placement of furniture and returning even after his clients had moved in. For Wright a house was a living thing, both in its relationship to the land and in its evolution through use.

Yet Wright's masterpiece in Oak Park is not a house but the Unitarian Unity Temple of 1906, at Kenilworth Avenue and Lake Street, a short walk from the Oak Park Avenue El stop. Strict budget limitations forced him to build it of the daring and generally abhorred material poured concrete, with only the simplest details of applied wood stripping. Nevertheless, Wright's serene creation of volume and light endures to this day. It is lighted by high windows from above and has operable colored-glass skylights inserted into the "coffers" of the Roman-style "egg-crate" ceiling, intended for ventilation as well as light. His window and skylight design echoes the designs applied to the walls, the door grilles, the hinges, the light fixtures; everything is integrated visually, no detail having been too small to consider.

Unity Temple was built on what became known as an H plan, which consisted of two functionally separate blocks connected by an entry hall. The Unity Temple plan has influenced the planning of public buildings to the present day. Restored to its original interior greens and ochers, Unity Temple is well worth a pilgrimage to Oak Park.

The most famous of all Wright's houses is on the South Side of Chicago. The Robie House of 1909 is now on the University of Chicago campus, at 5757 South Woodlawn Avenue. Its great horizontal overhanging rooflines are echoed by the long limestone sills that cap its low brick walls. Wright designed everything for the house, including the furniture. Because of a resurgence of interest in Wright's career, his stock has soared: A single lamp from the Robie House recently sold at auction for $750,000.

Complex political reasons caused Eastern architects to take the lead in planning the World's Columbian Exposition of 1893 at Midway Park in South Chicago. These architects brought the influence of the international Beaux Arts style to Chicago. A furious Louis Sullivan prophesied that "the damage wrought to this country by the Chicago World's Fair will last half a century." He wasn't entirely wrong in his prediction—the classicist style vied sharply over the next decades with the native creations of the Chicago and Prairie schools, all the while incorporating their technical advances. But the city fathers succumbed to the "culture over commerce" point of view, so most of the museums and public buildings constructed before World War II in Chicago were built in classical Greek or Renaissance style.

MANY OF THESE public buildings are fine works in their own right, but they do not contribute to the development of 20th-century architecture. The most notable of them, the Public Library of 1897, at 78 East Washington Street, by Shepley, Rutan and Coolidge, has gorgeous interiors of white and green marble and glass; it now serves as the Chicago Cultural Center.

In 1922 an important international competition offered a prize of $100,000 for the design of a Tribune Building that would dominate the Chicago River just north of the Loop. Numerous modernist plans were submitted, including one by Walter Gropius, of the Bauhaus in Dessau, Germany, the world's leading modern design center. Raymond Hood's Gothic design—some called it Woolworth Gothic—was chosen. The graceful and picturesque silhouette of the Tribune Tower was for many years the symbol of Chicago until general construction resumed following World War II. More important, the Tribune Building moved the center of gravity of downtown Chicago north and east, prompting construction of the Michigan Avenue Bridge and opening the Near North Side to commercial development along Michigan Avenue.

One architect dominated the postwar Chicago school, influencing modern architecture around the world: Ludwig Mies van der Rohe. The son of a stonemason, Mies was director of the Bauhaus from 1930 until Nazi pressure made him leave in 1937. On a trip to the United States he met John Holabird, son of William, who invited him to head the School of Architecture at the Armour Institute, later the Illinois Institute of Technology. Mies accepted—and redesigned the entire campus as part of the deal. Over the next 20 years he created a School of Architecture that disseminated his thinking into architecture offices everywhere.

WHATEVER MIES OWED to Frank Lloyd Wright, such as Mies's own open-plan houses, his philosophy was very much in the tradition of Chicago, and the roots of Bauhaus architecture can be traced to the Chicago School. Mies's attitudes were profoundly pragmatic, based on solid building techniques, technology, and an appreciation of the nature of the materials used. He created a philosophy, a set of ethical values based on a purist approach; his great aphorisms were "Less is more" and "God is in the details." He eschewed applied ornament, however, and in that sense he was nothing like Wright. All Mies "decoration" is generated by fine-tuned structural detail. His buildings are sober, sometimes somber, highly orderly, and serene; their aesthetic is based on the almost religious expression of structure.

The campus of IIT was built between 1942 and 1958 along South State Street between 31st and 35th streets. Mies used few materials in the two dozen buildings he planned here: light cream-color brick, black steel, and glass. Quadrangles are only suggested; space is never rigidly defined. There is a direct line of descent from Crown Hall (1956), made of black steel and clear glass, with its long-span roof trusses exposed above the level of the roof, to the great convention center of 1970, on South Lake Shore Drive at 23rd Street: McCormick Place, by C. F. Murphy, with its great, exposed, black-steel, space-frame roof and its glass walls.

Age requirements forced Mies to retire from IIT in 1958, but his office went on to do major projects in downtown Chicago, along Lake Shore Drive, and elsewhere. He had impressed the world in 1952 with his black-steel and clear-glass twin apartment towers, set at right angles to one another, almost kissing at the corner, at 860–880 North Lake Shore Drive. Later he added another, darker pair just to the north, at 900–910.

In 1968 Heinrich and Schipporeit, inspired by the 860 building and by Mies's Berlin drawings of 1921 for a free-form glass skyscraper, built Lake Point Tower.

This dark bronze metal-and-glass trefoil shaft, near Navy Pier at East Grand Avenue, is a graceful and dramatic component of the Chicago skyline. It is one of the few Chicago buildings, along with Bertram Goldberg's Marina City of 1964—twin round concrete towers on the river between State and Dearborn streets—to break with strict rectilinear geometry.

Downtown, Mies's Federal Center is a group of black buildings around a plaza, set off by a bright red steel Alexander Calder stabile sculpture, on Dearborn Street between Jackson Boulevard and Adams Street. The Dirksen Building, with its courthouse, on the east side of Dearborn, was built in 1964; the Kluczynski office building at the south side of the plaza and the single-story Post Office to the west were added through 1975. The north side of the large Federal Plaza is enclosed by the Marquette Building of 1894, integrating the past with the present. The last office building designed by Mies, the IBM Building of 1971, is a dark presence north of the river, between Wabash and State streets.

Perhaps the most important spin-off of Miesian thinking was the young firm of Skidmore, Owings & Merrill (SOM), which blossomed after the war. Their gem of the postwar period was the Inland Steel Building of 1957, at 30 West Monroe Street, in the Loop. The bright stainless-steel and pale green glass structure, only 18 stories high, with exposed columns on the long facade and a clear span in the short dimension, has uninterrupted interior floor space. It is considered a classic.

SOM became the largest architecture firm in America, with offices in all major cities. In Chicago the firm built, among other works, the immensely tall, tapering brown Hancock Tower of 1965–70, with its innovative exterior crisscross wind-bracing, and the even taller Sears Tower (1970–75), with two of its nine shafts reaching to 1,450 ft, now the second-tallest structure in the world. SOM may have achieved the epitome of the vertical commercial thrust of the Chicago School.

Meanwhile, Mies's Federal Plaza started a Chicago tradition, that of the outdoor plaza with a focus of monumental art. These plazas are real, usable, and used; they are large-scale city gathering places, and they shape the architectural and spatial character of downtown Chicago.

A STRING OF PLAZAS, featuring sculptures by Picasso and Dubuffet and mosaic murals by Chagall, leads one up Dearborn and Clark streets to the Chicago River. The south-bank quays, one level down from the street, are a series of imaginatively landscaped gardens. Here one can contemplate the ever-changing light on the river and the 19th-century riveted-iron drawbridges, which prefigure Calder's work. Other monumental outdoor sculpture downtown include Joan Miró's *Chicago* and Claes Oldenburg's *Batcolumn*.

A Jean Dubuffet sculpture stands before the James R. Thompson Center (formerly the State of Illinois Building) of 1985, at the corner of Randolph and Clark streets. Here there are really two plazas: one outdoors, the other inside the stepped-back, mirrored-glass and pink-paneled irregular doughnut of a building. This wild fantasy is the work of Helmut Jahn, a German who came to Chicago in the 1960s to study at IIT. His colorful, lighthearted, mirrored Chicago buildings provide a definite counterpoint to the somber Mies buildings of the 1950s and 1960s, and they appear everywhere, influencing the design and choice of materials of the architecture of the 1980s.

Jahn's first important contribution to the Chicago scene was a sensitive addition to the Board of Trade in 1980. The Board of Trade was housed in an architectural landmark at 141 West Jackson Boulevard, at the foot of LaSalle Street, a jewel of Art Deco design by the old Chicago firm of Holabird and Root in 1930. Murphy/Jahn's glittering addition echoed numerous features of the original structure. Both parts of the building have sumptuous interior atrium spaces. Marble, nickel, and glass motifs from the earlier edifice are evoked and reinterpreted—but not copied—in the high-tech addition. Within the new atrium, framed by highly polished chromium-plated trusses and turquoise panels, hangs a large Art Deco painting rescued from the older building during renovation. This complex captures the spirit of Chicago architecture: Devoted to commerce, it embraces the present without denying the past.

Next came Jahn's sleek, curving Xerox Center (1980) of white metal and reflective glass, at Monroe and Dearborn streets; it's now known simply as 55 West Monroe. Mirrored glass, introduced by Jahn, has become one of the favorite materials in Chicago commercial buildings. It acts as a foil to the dark Miesian buildings, especially along the river, where it seems to take on a watery quality on an overcast day. The elegant but playful high-tech United Airlines Terminal 1 (1987) at O'Hare Airport has been praised as a soaring technological celebration of travel, in the same splendid tradition as the 19th-century European iron-and-glass railroad stations that Jenney had studied.

Today, two disparate threads of architectural creation are weaving the modern tissue of Chicago, providing aesthetic tension and dynamism, just like the period following the World's Columbian Exposition of 1893. Chicago is a city with a sense of continuity, where the traditions of design are strong. Money and technology have long provided a firm support for free and original intellectual thought, with a strong populist local bias.

Chicagoans may talk of having a second-city mentality, but it seems certain through the history of architecture development in this city that they have a strong, enduring sense of self; perhaps being "second" has freed them to be themselves.

—Barbara Shortt

A practicing architect and an architectural historian, Barbara Shortt writes frequently on architecture and travel.

BOOKS AND VIDEOS

Books

Chicago has been celebrated and vilified in fiction and nonfiction, as well as on film. For the flavor of the city a century ago, pick up a copy of Theodore Dreiser's *Sister Carrie,* the story of a country innocent who falls from grace in Chicago. Upton Sinclair's portrayal in *The Jungle* of the meatpacking industry's squalor and employee exploitation raised a public outcry. *The Pit,* Frank Norris's muckraking 1903 novel, captures the frenzy (yes, even then) of futures speculation on the Board of Trade.

More recently, native Chicagoan Saul Bellow has set many novels in the city, most notably *Humboldt's Gift* and *The Adventures of Augie March.* Richard Wright's explosive *Native Son* and James T. Farrell's *Studs Lonigan* depict racial clashes in Chicago from the black and white sides, respectively. The works of longtime resident Nelson Algren—*The Man with the Golden Arm, A Walk on the Wild Side,* and *Chicago: City on the Make*—show the city at its grittiest, as does playwright David Mamet's *American Buffalo.* On a lighter but still revealing note, two series of detective novels use a current-day Chicago backdrop: Sara Paretsky's excellent V. I. Warshawski novels (the 1991 movie *V. I. Warshawski* starred Kathleen Turner) and the Monsignor Ryan mysteries of Andrew Greeley. Greeley has set other novels in Chicago as well, including *Lord of the Dance.*

Chicago was once the quintessential newspaper town; the play *The Front Page,* by Ben Hecht and Charles MacArthur, is set here. Local reporters have penned some excellent chronicles, including *Fabulous Chicago,* by Emmett Dedmon; and *Boss,* a portrait of the late mayor Richard J. Daley, by Mike Royko. Lois Wille's *Forever Open, Clear and Free* is a superb history of the fight to save Chicago's lakefront parks. Books by Studs Terkel, a great chronicler of Chicago, include *Division Street: America* and *Chicago.* Jack Schnedler's *Chicago* (Compass American Guides) provides a fine overview of the city as well as practical information.

Architecture buffs can choose from a number of excellent guidebooks. Ira J. Bach, former Director of City Development, is the author of *A Guide to Chicago's Public Sculpture.* James Cornelius has revised *Chicago on Foot,* by Ira J. Bach and Susan Wolfson; the book contains dozens of walking tours that concentrate on architecture. Franz Schulze and Kevin Harrington edited the fourth edition of *Chicago's Famous Buildings,* a pocket guide to the city's most important landmarks and notable buildings. The *A.I.A. Guide to Chicago,* edited by Alice Sinkevitch, is an exhaustive source of information about local architecture. Finally, David Lowe's *Lost Chicago,* published in 1975, is a fascinating and heartbreaking history of vanished buildings.

Videos

Chicago has been the setting for films about everything from gangsters to restless suburbanites. Classic early gangster flicks include *Little Caesar* (1930), with Edward G. Robinson, and *Scarface* (1932), starring Paul Muni and George Raft. *Carrie* is the 1952 adaptation of Dreiser's novel about a country girl who loses her innocence in the city; Laurence Olivier and Jennifer Jones are the stars. Lorraine Hansberry's drama about a black Chicago family, *A Raisin in the Sun,* became a film with Sidney Poitier in 1961.

As Elwood and Jake, respectively, Dan Aykroyd and the late John Belushi brought wild energy and cool music to the screen in *The Blues Brothers* (1980). *Ordinary People,* the Oscar-winning 1980 film, starred Mary Tyler Moore in a drama about an affluent and agonized North Shore family. John Hughes directed 1986's *Ferris Bueller's Day Off,* in which Matthew Broderick and a couple of his high school friends play hooky and tour Chicago for a day, taking in everything from the Board of Trade and a Cubs game to a parade in the Loop; the film has wonderful scenes of the city. In *About Last Night* (1986), which is based on the David Mamet play *Sexual Perversity in Chicago,* Demi Moore and Rob Lowe go through realistic modern dating games with the help (and hindrance) of hilarious friends played by Elizabeth Perkins and Jim Belushi. Brian De Palma's *The Untouchables* (1987) stars Kevin Costner as Eliot Ness and Robert De Niro as Al Capone in a gangster tale with a 1920s Chicago background. Steve James's *Hoop Dreams* (1994), a documentary, is a powerful look at a couple of inner-city teens who dream that basketball will be their ticket out. *My Best Friend's Wedding* (1997) is a romantic comedy starring Julia Roberts, who tries to break up the wedding of Dermot Mulroney and Cameron Diaz.

INDEX

NOTES

NOTES

NOTES

NOTES

Looking for a different kind of vacation?

Fodor's makes it easy with a full line of guidebooks to suit a variety of interests—from sports and adventure to romance to family fun.

At bookstores everywhere.
www.fodors.com

Fodor's Travel Publications

Available at bookstores everywhere. For descriptions of all our titles and a key to Fodor's guidebook series, visit http://www.fodors.com/books/

Gold Guides

U.S.

Alaska

Arizona

Boston

California

Cape Cod, Martha's Vineyard, Nantucket

The Carolinas & Georgia

Chicago

Colorado

Florida

Hawai'i

Las Vegas, Reno, Tahoe

Los Angeles

Maine, Vermont, New Hampshire

Maui & Lāna'i

Miami & the Keys

New England

New Orleans

New York City

Oregon

Pacific North Coast

Philadelphia & the Pennsylvania Dutch Country

The Rockies

San Diego

San Francisco

Santa Fe, Taos, Albuquerque

Seattle & Vancouver

The South

U.S. & British Virgin Islands

USA

Virginia & Maryland

Washington, D.C.

Foreign

Australia

Austria

The Bahamas

Belize & Guatemala

Bermuda

Canada

Cancún, Cozumel, Yucatán Peninsula

Caribbean

China

Costa Rica

Cuba

The Czech Republic & Slovakia

Denmark

Eastern & Central Europe

Europe

Florence, Tuscany & Umbria

France

Germany

Great Britain

Greece

Hong Kong

India

Ireland

Israel

Italy

Japan

London

Madrid & Barcelona

Mexico

Montréal & Québec City

Moscow, St. Petersburg, Kiev

The Netherlands, Belgium & Luxembourg

New Zealand

Norway

Nova Scotia, New Brunswick, Prince Edward Island

Paris

Portugal

Provence & the Riviera

Scandinavia

Scotland

Singapore

South Africa

South America

Southeast Asia

Spain

Sweden

Switzerland

Thailand

Toronto

Turkey

Vienna & the Danube Valley

Vietnam

Special-Interest Guides

Adventures to Imagine

Alaska Ports of Call

Ballpark Vacations

The Best Cruises

Caribbean Ports of Call

The Complete Guide to America's National Parks

Europe Ports of Call

Family Adventures

Fodor's Gay Guide to the USA

Fodor's How to Pack

Great American Learning Vacations

Great American Sports & Adventure Vacations

Great American Vacations

Great American Vacations for Travelers with Disabilities

Halliday's New Orleans Food Explorer

Healthy Escapes

Kodak Guide to Shooting Great Travel Pictures

National Parks and Seashores of the East

National Parks of the West

Nights to Imagine

Orlando Like a Pro

Rock & Roll Traveler Great Britain and Ireland

Rock & Roll Traveler USA

Sunday in San Francisco

Walt Disney World for Adults

Weekends in New York

Wendy Perrin's Secrets Every Smart Traveler Should Know

Worlds to Imagine

Fodor's Special Series

Fodor's Best Bed & Breakfasts
America
California
The Mid-Atlantic
New England
The Pacific Northwest
The South
The Southwest
The Upper Great Lakes

Compass American Guides
Alaska
Arizona
Boston
Chicago
Coastal California
Colorado
Florida
Hawai'i
Hollywood
Idaho
Las Vegas
Maine
Manhattan
Minnesota
Montana
New Mexico
New Orleans
Oregon
Pacific Northwest
San Francisco
Santa Fe
South Carolina
South Dakota
Southwest
Texas
Underwater Wonders of the National Parks
Utah
Virginia
Washington
Wine Country
Wisconsin
Wyoming

Citypacks
Amsterdam
Atlanta
Berlin
Boston
Chicago
Florence
Hong Kong
London
Los Angeles
Miami
Montréal
New York City
Paris

Prague
Rome
San Francisco
Sydney
Tokyo
Toronto
Venice
Washington, D.C.

Exploring Guides
Australia
Boston & New England
Britain
California
Canada
Caribbean
China
Costa Rica
Cuba
Egypt
Florence & Tuscany
Florida
France
Germany
Greek Islands
Hawai'i
India
Ireland
Israel
Italy
Japan
London
Mexico
Moscow & St. Petersburg
New York City
Paris
Portugal
Prague
Provence
Rome
San Francisco
Scotland
Singapore & Malaysia
South Africa
Spain
Thailand
Turkey
Venice
Vietnam

Flashmaps
Boston
New York
San Francisco
Washington, D.C.

Fodor's Cityguides
Boston
New York
San Francisco

Fodor's Gay Guides
Amsterdam
Los Angeles & Southern California
New York City
Pacific Northwest
San Francisco and the Bay Area
South Florida
USA

Karen Brown Guides
Austria
California
England B&Bs
England, Wales & Scotland
France B&Bs
France Inns
Germany
Ireland
Italy B&Bs
Italy Inns
Portugal
Spain
Switzerland

Pocket Guides
Acapulco
Aruba
Atlanta
Barbados
Beijing
Berlin
Budapest
Dublin
Honolulu
Jamaica
London
Mexico City
New York City
Paris
Prague
Puerto Rico
Rome
San Francisco
Savannah & Charleston
Shanghai
Sydney
Washington, D.C.

Languages for Travelers (Cassette & Phrasebook)
French
German
Italian
Spanish

Mobil Travel Guides
America's Best Hotels & Restaurants
Arizona

California and the West
Florida
Great Lakes
Major Cities
Mid-Atlantic
Northeast
Northwest and Great Plains
Southeast
Southern California
Southwest and South Central

Rivages Guides
Bed and Breakfasts of Character and Charm in France
Hotels and Country Inns of Character and Charm in France
Hotels and Country Inns of Character and Charm in Italy
Hotels of Character and Charm in Paris
Hotels of Character and Charm in Portugal
Hotels of Character and Charm in Spain
Wines & Vineyards of Character and Charm in France

Short Escapes
Britain
France
Near New York City
New England

Fodor's Sports
Golf Digest's Places to Play (USA)
Golf Digest's Places to Play in the Southeast
Golf Digest's Places to Play in the Southwest
Skiing USA
USA Today The Complete Four Sport Stadium Guide

Fodor's upCLOSE Guides
California
Europe
France
Great Britain
Ireland
Italy
London
Los Angeles
Mexico
New York City
Paris
San Francisco

WHEREVER YOU TRAVEL, *H*ELP IS NEVER FAR AWAY.

From planning your trip to providing travel assistance along the way, American Express® Travel Service Offices are always there to help you do more.

Chicago

American Express Travel Service
2338 North Clark Street
773/477-4000

American Express Travel Service
625 North Michigan Avenue
312/435-2570

American Express Travel Service
122 South Michigan Avenue
312/435-2595

do more AMERICAN EXPRESS

Travel

www.americanexpress.com/travel

**American Express Travel Service Offices
are located throughout the United States.
For the office nearest you, call 1-800-AXP-3429.**